PASS:

Essential Real Estate Exam Study Guide

Second Edition

KALIMAH J. JENKINS, Esq., MBA

Kalimah J. Jenkins, Esq., MBA

PASS: Essential Real Estate Exam Study Guide Copyright © 2024

Table of Contents

Use of this Study Guide:

Thank you for your purchase. It is imperative that you utilize the study guide in the manner intended to get the best results. As a person who has taken many standardized tests, preparation for the specific test you are taking is most important. This guide was written to provide you with a road map so that you can pass your real estate exam on the first try. Everything contained within it covers topics tested on both the PearsonVue or PSI administered exams. Topics include Property Ownership, Title Transfer, Land Use Regulations, Contracts, Valuation, Agency, Disclosures, Real Estate Practice, and more.

Each Chapter is specifically written for you to obtain a true understanding of the topic, starting with a comprehensive outline. Because you have already gone through pre-license, you should use this outline to ensure that you fully understand the topic before moving onto the exercises. The next section contains the essential real estate vocabulary. Vocabulary is your lifeline. You must have a good handle on it prior to moving on. A thorough knowledge of the vocabulary will get you through 30-40% of the exam because it allows you to positively answer a question or definitively eliminate answers. Each section thereafter intends to test you on what you've learned. The recall multiple choice and fill-in exercises only test your vocabulary knowledge. The matching exercises test vocabulary and the application of those concepts. The analysis fill-in and multiple choice exercises tests whether you can apply your vocabulary to the concepts. Vocabulary and application are both necessary components for passing any state exam.

Your goal is to score at least a 90% on all recall tests and at least an 80% on all application tests to be comfortable enough to ensure success.

A word about the math: I have included a math section with several math questions, answers, and step-by-step solutions. Teaching an entire math course is beyond the purview of this study guide. I did include a math formula sheet that should prove helpful and a link to my math only course: https://www.kjmethod.com/pricing-plans if you feel that you need greater assistance.

Again, thank you for your purchase. I wish you well on your journey to licensure.

Kalimah J. Jenkins, Esq., MBA
Founder, KJMETHOD

Chapter 1: Contracts

Section 1: *Outline*

I. <u>**Contracts** – One or more legally competent parties mutually agree, of their own free will, to do or refrain from doing some lawful act supported by a legal consideration</u>

   A. **Four Essential Elements:**

      1. **Valid Contract** *(CALL)*

         a. *C*onsideration – exchange of something of value between the parties
         b. *A*ssent – mutual agreement on essential elements (Mutual Assent) and entered into freely (Genuine Assent)
         c. *L*egal Capacity – capacity to contract
         d. *L*egal Purpose – cannot be for an illegal purpose

      All elements MUST be present for a valid contract

      2. **Written or Oral** – contracts do not necessarily have to be in writing to be **valid** but certain contracts **MUST** be in writing to be **enforceable** under the **Statute of Frauds**. A verbal contract may still be performed but it could not be resolved in court if there is no required writing
      3. **Void Contract** – Any one of the contract essential elements is missing
      4. **Voidable** – One where all the essential elements are present but one or more of the elements may be removed only at the option of a party who has acted under a "disability". Unless the contract is rescinded, it remains valid

   B. **Basic Contract Types:**

      1. **Express or Implied** – **Express contract** occurs when the parties communicate their intentions to each other in writing or verbally. **Implied contract** is created by the parties' actions
      2. **Enforceable or Unenforceable** – **Enforceable** contracts can be enforced in a court of law (Statute of Frauds). **Unenforceable** contracts can still be performed by the parties but cannot be enforced by a court of law
      3. **Executory and Executed** – **Executory** contract is one in which one or both parties still have obligations under the contract. **Executed contract** is one in which all obligations under the contract have been completed
      4. **Bilateral or Unilateral** – **Bilateral contract** is one in which both sides of the contract make promises and incur obligations. **Unilateral contract** is one in which only one side of the contract makes a promise and is obligated to perform

   C. **Essential Elements of a Contact (VOID if one is Missing)**

      1. **Consideration** – anything of value to induce someone to enter into a contract. The amount doesn't matter if the exchange is something of value in the eyes of the parties
      2. **Mutual Assent** – a **meeting of the minds** on all essential elements of the contract. The **offeror (buyer)** makes an offer to the **offeree (seller)**. The seller can accept the offer as written, reject it, or make a **counteroffer.**

Until both parties agree to the exact same thing, there can be no contract. Even then, there is still no binding contract until there is notification of acceptance by receipt (**actual communication**) or when sent (**constructive communication**). **Mutual Mistake** leaves the contract **VOID**

3. **Genuine Assent** – all parties must enter into the contract freely (**ALL VOIDABLE**)

    a. **Innocent Misrepresentation** – misstatement of facts made without any intention to deceive another person, an honest mistake. Must be of material value and relied upon

    b. **Negligent Misrepresentation** – also known as Constructive Fraud is similar to innocent misrepresentation except the person committing it had the ability to discover the fact and the duty to do so

    c. **Fraud:**

        1. **Actual Fraud** – deliberate act and malicious misrepresentation of a material fact, made with the intent of inducing a party to take an action he/she might not have otherwise taken

        2. **Negative Fraud** – concealment of important facts and failure to disclose vital information

        3. **Puffing** – is not fraud but a reasonable statement that someone would know is untrue

    d. **Duress and Menace** – anyone forced to sign (**duress**) or who has been coerced into signing by threat of force (**menace**) has a right to rescind

    e. **Undue influence** – influenced into signing a contract by another person due to a relationship of trust and confidence that existed between them

4. **Legal Capacity (Capacity to Contract)**

    a. **Minors** – a contract signed by a minor is **voidable** at the minor's option until the minor reaches majority and a reasonable time after

    b. **Mentally Incompetent** – when a person who has been declared to be mentally incompetent signs a contract it is **void**, however if the person signing the contract was declared mentally incompetent after the contract was signed and wants to make a claim that they were impaired at signing the contract is **voidable**

    c. **Intoxicated** – contract signed by a person intoxicated – **voidable**

    d. **Power of Attorney** – a **principal** authorizing an **agent** to act on his/her behalf, also known as an attorney-in-fact – **valid**

    e. **Corporation** –corporate board of directors authorizes certain officers to bind the corporation in contract matters – **valid**

    f. **Court Appointees** - administrators, trustees and guardians appointed by the court can sign contracts of another – **valid**

5. **Lawful purpose** – All contracts must be lawful

6. **In Writing, as required by law** – Statute of Frauds requires certain contracts to be in writing and signed in order to be enforceable. It applies to enforcement of contracts, not to their validity. It includes:

    a. All contracts for the sale of an interest in real estate property

    b. All contracts that cannot be performed in one year

    c. All contracts for the sale of personal property valued over $500

D. The Discharge of Contractual Obligations

1. **Performance** – **executory contracts** become executed upon performance. Most often, at the closing

2. **Supervening illegality** – a change in the law makes the formerly legal contract now impossible or illegal to perform

3. **Mutual Agreement and Mutual Rescission** – parties to a contract may discharge their obligations by mutually agreeing to cancel the contract

4. **Assignment of contract** – an assignment is the transfer of all of one's rights and obligations under a contract to another party. All contracts are assignable unless specifically prohibited. The **assignor** remains ultimately liable and the **assignee** becomes primarily liable

5. **Novation** – the process of discharging obligations under a contract by substituting a new contract for an existing once or by substituting a new party for an old one. Liability no longer exists for the novating party. Requires consent

6. **Destruction of the Property** – a contract might be discharged if the property is destroyed or substantially damaged before the transaction is complete. Must look to the terms of the contract

7. **Operation of Law (Voidable contracts)** – a party may unilaterally rescind a contract if the party was induced by fraud or misrepresentation, was coerced against their free will, or lacked the legal capacity to enter into a contract

E. Remedies for Breach of Contract

1. **Contractual Remedies** – often parties to a contract will agree to certain non-judicial remedies in case of default:

   a. **Mediation** – an independent 3rd party works with the disputing parties to help them resolve their differences, but the parties are not bound by the decision

   b. **Arbitration** – a disinterested party will hear both sides and decide how it will be resolved. The parties are bound by this decision

   c. **Liquidated Damages** – the contract specifies in advance, the cost to the breaching party. Earnest money is often a liquidated damage

2. **Remedies by law**

   a. **Damages** – if the loss suffered can be expressed in terms of money, the innocent party may sue the defaulting party for money damages caused by the default

   b. **Specific Performance** – the innocent party asks the court to require the defaulting party to perform as promised. No amount of damages will compensate

   c. **Rescission** – canceling of a contract and returning the parties to their original positions

      1. **Unilateral Rescission** – if the injured party decides to rescind, the other party is notified and any payments that have been received must be returned

      2. **Mutual Rescission** – Both parties to return to their original positions

F. Real Estate Contracts

1. **Listing Contracts** – the listing agreement serves as the broker's contract of employment. The seller is the principal and authorizes the broker as the agent to find a ready, willing, and able purchaser to meet the seller's terms

2. **Purchase and Sale Contracts** – the seller is committed to sell and the purchaser is committed to buy the property for the stated price and obligations

3. **Options Contracts** – a unilateral contract in which a property owner (**optionor**) agrees to give a prospective buyer or lessee (**optionee**) the right to buy or lease the property for a certain price and within a certain time limit

4. **Leases** – the **lessor**, conveys to the **lessee**, an exclusive right of possession and control for a specified time and for consideration called rent

5. **Property Management Agreement** – **the principal owner** authorizes **the agent broker** to carry out certain responsibilities contingent upon managing property

6. **Affiliation Agreement or Employment Contact** – the agency agreement between the **broker** as **principal** and the **salesperson** as **agent** to join a brokerage firm

7. **Land Contract** - also called **installment sale contract** or **contract for deed** is a seller financing arrangement for a home purchase. The seller retains legal title, and the buyer has equitable title for the duration of the loan. Title is passed to the buyer upon full payment

G. Closing the Transaction – the closing of a real estate transaction is the procedure of finalizing the contract. The deed is delivered to the buyer in exchange for the agreed upon purchase price. In some states, the closing is handled by an escrow agent, who performs the necessary duties according to an **escrow agreement.** In some states, closings are handled by **attorneys**

H. Other Contract Issues

1. **Statute of Limitations** – the time an injured party has the right to seek a legal remedy. Unless the legal steps are taken within the legal time, the party is barred from acting
2. **Parol Evidence Rule** – written agreements always take precedence over oral agreements. Once the contract is reduced to writing, all oral agreements are null and void
3. **Time is of the essence** – All time limits in the contract must be strictly adhered to. The non-adhering party is in breach
4. **Earnest Money** – An amount given by the offeror to ensure his performance. Never required on a contract and is not consideration for the contract
5. **Laches** – The failure to bring a cause of action in a reasonable period of time could result in the inability to bring it later

Section 2: *Vocabulary*

Actual Communication: Oral or written communication that becomes effective upon receipt

Actual Fraud: An intentional misrepresentation of a material fact

Addendum: An attachment to a contract that provides additional material or an explanation of the original terms

Assignment: Transferring of all of one's rights and obligations under a contract to another person, but with a retention of secondary liability under the contract

Bilateral Contract: A contract where both sides of the contract have made promises and are obligated to perform

Breach of contract: The failure to perform the obligations under a contract without legal excuse, resulting in damages to the non-breaching party

Commingling: Illegally mixing trust funds with personal funds

Consideration: An exchange of promises where each party gives up something of value in return for something of value

Contingency: When a contract is dependent upon the successful completion of some prior act or condition

Contract: A legally binding agreement between two or more parties that defines the rights and obligations between them

Counteroffer: An offeree's response to an offer that is different from the original offer

Constructive Communication: Communication that is effective when it is sent, rather than when it is received

Damages: A sum of money the law grants to a non-breaching party

Duress: Forcing another to enter into a contract by physical force

Earnest Money: An amount offered by a buyer to ensure performance

Enforceable Contract: A contract for which the law can provide a legal remedy

Executed Contract: A contract that has been completely performed by both parties

Executory Contract: A contract that has not been fully performed by either or both parties

Express Contract: A contract in which the terms of the agreement are fully and explicitly stated orally, or in writing

Genuine Assent: The act was completed with free will

Implied Contract: A contract formed by the parties' conduct, rather than expressly

Innocent Misrepresentation: An unintentional, but material misrepresentation made by a person in the transaction, and it's relied upon by the person hearing it

Laches: Delay or negligence in asserting one's legal rights

Land Contract: An installment agreement where a seller finances property for a buyer but retains legal title until all payments are made

Liquidated Damages: An amount agreed to when entering the contract that will represent the cost to the breaching party

Mutual Assent: When a buyer and seller, through the process of offer and acceptance, reach a meeting of the minds

Mutual Mistake: Both parties to a contract have an incorrect belief about a material fact

Negative Fraud: An intentional misrepresentation by failing to disclose or concealing vital information

Negligent Misrepresentation: An unintentional, but material misrepresentation by someone who had the duty to discover the correct facts and it's relied upon by the person hearing it

Novation: The substitution, by agreement, of a new contract for an old one or a new obligation for an old one, with the rights under the old one being terminated

Option Contract: A unilateral contract where one party is given an opportunity (optionee) to do or not do something for a specified price within a specified time period

Parol Evidence Rule: Oral agreements will have no effect once an agreement is put in writing

Rescission: To cancel the contract and to restore the parties to their original positions as if the contract never happened

Specific Performance: A legal action seeking to compel a party to carry out the agreed contract terms

Statute of Frauds: A law requiring that certain contracts be in writing to be enforceable

Statute of Limitations: A law that restricts the period of time within which an action may be brought to court

Survival Clause: Allows certain contractual provisions to survive the closing

Supervening Illegality: A change in the law makes the contract, which was legal at the time of entering, now illegal or impossible to perform

Time is of the essence: A phrase in a contract that requires the performance of a certain act within a stated time period

Undue Influence: When a party uses a position of trust or confidence to induce another to enter into a contract

Unilateral Contract: A contract where only one side of the contract has made a promise and has an obligation to perform

Valid Contract: A contract that contains all essential and elements: Consideration, Assent, Legal Purpose, Legal Capacity

Void Contract: A contract that never existed because an essential element was missing

Voidable Contract: A contract that may be legally voided or enforced by the party holding the right to rescind

Waste: Harmful or destructive use of real property by one who is in the rightful possession of it

Section 3: *Recall Multiple Choice*

1. **An unintentional, but material misrepresentation made by someone who had the ability and duty to discover the correct facts and that statement is relied upon by the person hearing it**
   - A. Negligent Misrepresentation
   - B. Undue Influence
   - C. Puffing
   - D. Arbitration

2. **An offeree's response to an offer that is different from the original offer**
   - A. Novation
   - B. Counteroffer
   - C. Contingency
   - D. Consideration

3. **Deliberate and intentional misrepresentation by failing to disclose or concealing vital information**
   - A. Executory Contract
   - B. Constructive Fraud
   - C. Negative Fraud
   - D. Actual Fraud

4. **When a buyer and seller, through the process of offer and acceptance, reach a meeting of the minds**
   - A. Bilateral Contract
   - B. Mutual Assent
   - C. Consideration
   - D. Earnest Money

5. **A contract for which the law can provide a legal remedy**
   - A. Valid Contract
   - B. Executory Contract
   - C. Enforceable Contract
   - D. Express Contract

6. **A phrase in a contract that requires the performance of a certain act within a stated period of time**
   - A. Breach of contract
   - B. Statute of limitations
   - C. Time is of the essence
   - D. Specific performance

7. **An unintentional, but material misrepresentation made by a person in the transaction and the statement is relied upon by the person hearing it**
   - A. Mutual Mistake
   - B. Duress
   - C. Undue Influence
   - D. Innocent Misrepresentation

8. **Transferring of all of one's rights and obligations under a contract to another person, but with a retention of secondary liability under the contract**
   - A. Consideration
   - B. Novation
   - C. Rescission
   - D. Assignment

9. **A contract formed by the parties' conduct; cannot be created in this manner if the parties expressed otherwise**
    A. Unilateral Contract
    B. Express Contract
    C. Executed Contract
    D. Implied Contract

10. **A contract where both sides to the contract have made promises and are obligated to perform**
    A. Implied Contract
    B. Express Contract
    C. Bilateral Contract
    D. Executory Contract

11. **Communication that is effective when it is sent, rather than when it is received**
    A. Pre-contractual Liability
    B. Constructive Communication
    C. Actual Communication
    D. Doctrine Of Prior Appropriation

12. **A term that makes the contract dependent upon the successful completion of some prior act or condition**
    A. Contingency
    B. Consideration
    C. Novation
    D. Assignment

13. **A contract where only one side of the contract has made a promise and has an obligation to perform**
    A. Unilateral Contract
    B. Implied Contract
    C. Executory Contract
    D. Express Contract

14. **Illegally mixing trust funds with personal funds**
    A. Commingling
    B. Consideration
    C. Novation
    D. Counteroffer

15. **An amount agreed to when entering the contract that will represent the cost to the breaching party**
    A. Voidable Contract
    B. Liquidated Damages
    C. Rescission
    D. Consideration

16. **A law that requires certain contracts to be in writing in order to be enforceable**
    A. Statute of Frauds
    B. Contract
    C. Parol Evidence Rule
    D. Statute of Limitations

17. **Oral or written communication that becomes effective upon receipt of the communication**
    A. Actual Communication
    B. Mutual Mistake
    C. Executed Contract
    D. Constructive Communication

18. **A change in the law that makes the contract, which was legal at the time of entering, now illegal or impossible to perform**
    A. Executory Contract
    B. Revocation
    C. Supervening Illegality
    D. Statute Of Frauds

19. **Both parties to a contract have an incorrect belief about a material fact resulting in no Mutual Assent**
    A. Undue Influence
    B. Mutual Assent
    C. Mutual Mistake
    D. Earnest Money

20. **A contract provision which allows certain contractual provisions to survive the closing**
    A. Extension Clause
    B. Bilateral Contract
    C. Defeasance Clause
    D. Survival Clause

21. **Deliberate and intentional misrepresentation of a material fact**
    A. Mutual Mistake
    B. Actual Fraud
    C. Negligent Misrepresentation
    D. Negative Fraud

22. **Delay or negligence in asserting one's legal rights**
    A. Duress
    B. Damages
    C. Novation
    D. Laches

23. **A contract that has been completely performed by both parties**
    A. Express Contract
    B. Unilateral Contract
    C. Executed Contract
    D. Valid Contract

24. **The substitution, by agreement, of a new contract for an old one or a new obligation for an old one, with the rights under the old one being terminated**
    A. Assignment
    B. Novation
    C. Guardian
    D. Rescission

25. **Harmful or destructive use of real property by one who is in rightful possession of it**
    A. Waste
    B. Rescission
    C. Laches
    D. Abuse

26. **The failure to perform the obligations under a contract without legal excuse, resulting in damages to the non-breaching party**
    A. Bilateral contract
    B. Rescission
    C. Statute of frauds
    D. Breach of contract

27. **A legally binding agreement between two or more parties that defines the rights and obligations between them when accompanied by consideration, assent, legal capacity, and legal purpose**
    A. Contingency
    B. Contract
    C. Consideration
    D. Novation

28. **A contract that contains all essential and mandatory elements:**
    A. Express Contract
    B. Valid Contract
    C. Executed Contract
    D. Implied Contract

29. **A legal action seeking to compel a party to carry out the agreed contract terms of the contract**
    A. Liquidated Damages
    B. Damages
    C. Specific Performance
    D. Option Contract

30. **A law that restricts the period of time within which an action may be brought to court**
    A. Statute of Frauds
    B. Time is of the essence
    C. Statute of Limitations
    D. Parol Evidence Rule

31. **When a party uses a position of trust or confidence to induce another to enter into a contract**
    A. Mutual Mistake
    B. Duress
    C. Innocent Misrepresentation
    D. Undue Influence

32. **A unilateral contract where one party is given an opportunity (optionee) to do or not do something for a specified price within a specified time period**
    A. Unilateral Contract
    B. Land Contract
    C. Express Contract
    D. Option Contract

33. **An attachment to a contract that provides additional material or an explanation of the original terms**
    A. Addendum
    B. Contingency
    C. Novation
    D. Counteroffer

34. **Forcing another to enter into a contract by physical force**
    A. Innocent Misrepresentation
    B. Undue Influence
    C. Duress
    D. Menace

35. **A contract that has not been fully performed by either or both parties**
    A. Implied Contract
    B. Executory Contract
    C. Express Contract
    D. Unilateral Contract

36. **An exchange of promises where each party gives up anything of any value in return for anything of any value**
    A. Counteroffer
    B. Consideration
    C. Contingency
    D. Mutual Assent

37. **The act was completed with free will, not under duress, or undue influence**
    A. Mutual Assent
    B. Genuine Assent
    C. Mutual Mistake
    D. Earnest Money

38. **A contract that was never a contract because one of the essential elements is missing**
    A. Void Contract
    B. Enforceable Contract
    C. Unilateral Contract
    D. Implied Contract

39. **Oral agreements will have no effect once an agreement is put in writing**
    A. Parol Evidence Rule
    B. Statute Of Frauds
    C. Statute Of Limitations
    D. Unilateral Contract

40. **A contract in which the terms of the agreement are fully and explicitly stated in orally, or in writing**
    A. Express Contract
    B. Implied Contract
    C. Executed Contract
    D. Unilateral Contract

41. **A sum of money the law grants to a non-breaching party**
    A. Consideration
    B. Arbitration
    C. Damages
    D. Rescission

42. **An amount of money deposited by a buyer when making an offer to ensure the buyer's performance**
    A. Express Contract
    B. Earnest Money
    C. Mutual Mistake
    D. Consideration

43. **A contract that may be legally voided by the party holding the right to rescind or he can choose to enforce it**
    A. Unilateral Contract
    B. Option Contract
    C. Voidable Contract
    D. Implied Contract

44. **A real estate installment agreement where a seller finances property for a buyer by retains legal title until all payments are made**
    A. Express Contract
    B. Option Contract
    C. Enforceable Contract
    D. Land Contract

45. **To cancel the contract and to restore the parties to their original positions as if the contract never happened**
    A. Novation
    B. Void Contract
    C. Rescission
    D. Damages

Section 4: *Recall Fill-In*

1. Communication that is effective when it is sent, rather than when it is received

   _____

2. To cancel the contract and to restore the parties to their original positions as if the contract never happened

   _____

3. A unilateral contract where one party is given an opportunity to do or not do something for a specified price within a specified time-period

   _____

4. An amount of money deposited by a buyer when making an offer to ensure the buyer's performance

   _____

5. Oral or written communication that becomes effective upon receipt of the communication

   _____

6. A change in the law that makes the contract, which was legal at the time of entering, now illegal or impossible to perform

   _____

7. Both parties to a contract have an incorrect belief about a material fact resulting in no Mutual Assent

   _____

8. The failure to perform the obligations under a contract without legal excuse, resulting in damages to the non-breaching party

   _____

9. Forcing another to enter into a contract by physical force

   _____

10. The act was completed with free will, not under duress, or undue influence

    _____

11. A law that restricts the period of time within which an action may be brought to court

    _____

12. A legally binding agreement between two or more parties that defines the rights and obligations between them when accompanied by consideration, assent, legal capacity, and legal purpose

    _____

13. A term that makes the contract dependent upon the successful completion of some prior act or condition

14. When a party uses a position of trust or confidence to induce another to enter into a contract

15. When a buyer and seller, through the process of offer and acceptance, reach a meeting of the minds

16. A contract that has been completely performed by both parties

17. An amount agreed to when entering the contract that will represent the cost to the breaching party

18. A contract for which the law can provide a legal remedy

19. A law that requires certain contracts to be in writing in order to be enforceable

20. A contract that was never a contract because one of the essential elements is missing

21. A contract provision which allows certain contractual provisions to survive the closing

22. A contract formed by the parties' conduct; cannot be created in this manner if the parties expressed otherwise

23. A contract that has not been fully performed by either or both parties

24. A contract in which the terms of the agreement are fully and explicitly stated in orally, or in writing

25. Oral agreements will have no effect once an agreement is put in writing

26. A phrase in a contract that requires the performance of a certain act within a stated period of time

27. A contract where both sides to the contract have made promises and are obligated to perform

_____

28. A contract where only one side of the contract has made a promise and has an obligation to perform

_____

29. A sum of money the law grants to a non-breaching party

_____

30. A real estate installment agreement where a seller finances property for a buyer by retains legal title until all payments are made

_____

31. An unintentional, but material misrepresentation made by a person in the transaction and the statement is relied upon by the person hearing it

_____

32. Harmful or destructive use of real property by one who is in rightful possession of it

_____

33. An unintentional, but material misrepresentation made by someone who had the ability and duty to discover the correct facts and that statement is relied upon by the person hearing it

_____

34. A legal action seeking to compel a party to carry out the agreed contract terms of the contract

_____

35. A contract that may be legally voided by the party holding the right to rescind or he can choose to enforce it

_____

36. An exchange of promises where each party gives up anything of any value in return for anything of any value

_____

37. Delay or negligence in asserting one's legal rights

_____

38. Illegally mixing trust funds with personal funds

_____

39. Transferring of all of one's rights and obligations under a contract to another person, but with a retention of secondary liability under the contract

_____

40. An offeree's response to an offer that is different from the original offer

41. The substitution, by agreement, of a new contract for an old one or a new obligation for an old one, with the rights under the old one being terminated

42. Deliberate and intentional misrepresentation by failing to disclose or concealing vital information

43. An attachment to a contract that provides additional material or an explanation of the original terms

44. A contract that contains all essential and mandatory elements:

45. Deliberate and intentional misrepresentation of a material fact

Section 5: *Matching*

A   Addendum

1 _____ A contract that may be legally voided by the party holding the right to rescind or he can choose to enforce it

B   Waste

2 _____ A contract where only one side of the contract has made a promise and has an obligation to perform.

C   Statute of Limitations

3 _____ A law that restricts the period of time within which an action may be brought to court

D   Breach of contract

4 _____ A legal action seeking to compel a party to carry out the agreed contract terms of the contract

E   Undue Influence

5 _____ An agreement where a seller finances property for a buyer but retains legal title until all payments are made

F   Land Contract

6 _____ An amount agreed to when entering the contract that will represent the cost to the breaching party

G   Voidable Contract

7 _____ An attachment to a contract that provides additional material or an explanation of the original terms

H   Mutual Mistake

8 _____ Both parties to a contract have an incorrect belief about a material fact resulting in no Mutual Assent

I   Negative Fraud

9 _____ Communication that is effective when it is sent, rather than when it is received

J   Liquidated Damages

10 _____ Delay or negligence in asserting one's legal rights.

K   Laches

11 _____ Deliberate and intentional misrepresentation by failing to disclose or concealing vital information.

L   Constructive Communication

12 _____ Harmful or destructive use of real property by one who is in rightful possession of it

M   Specific Performance

13 _____ The failure to perform the obligations under a contract, resulting in damages to the non-breaching party

N   Unilateral Contract

14 _____ When a party uses a position of trust or confidence to induce another to enter into a contract

O   Novation

15 _____ Substituting a new contract for an old one or a new obligation for an old one

A	Option Contract	1	_____	A contract for which the law can provide a legal remedy.
B	Survival Clause	2	_____	A contract provision which allows certain contractual provisions to survive the closing.
C	Actual Communication	3	_____	A unilateral contract where one party is given an opportunity to do something for a specified price within a specified time period.
D	Supervening Illegality	4	_____	A sum of money the law grants to a non-breaching party.
E	Rescission	5	_____	An amount of money deposited by a buyer when making an offer to ensure the buyer's performance.
F	Parol Evidence	6	_____	An offeree's response to an offer that is different from the original offer.
G	Contract Elements	7	_____	Consideration, Assent - Mutual and Genuine, Legal Purpose, Legal Capacity.
H	Genuine Assent	8	_____	Oral agreements will have no effect once an agreement is put in writing.
I	Counteroffer	9	_____	Oral or written communication that becomes effective upon receipt of the communication.
J	Commingling	10	_____	The act was completed with free will, not under duress, or undue influence.
K	Enforceable Contract	11	_____	To cancel the contract and to restore the parties to their original positions as if the contract never happened.
L	Damages	12	_____	A change in the law that makes the contract, which was legal at the time of entering, now illegal or impossible to perform.
M	Earnest Money	13	_____	A contract formed by the parties' conduct; cannot be created in this manner if the parties expressed otherwise.
N	Contract	14	_____	A legally binding agreement between two or more parties supported by consideration, assent, legal capacity, and legal purpose.
O	Implied Contract	15	_____	Illegally mixing trust funds with personal funds.

A	Contingency	1 _____	A term that makes the contract dependent upon the successful completion of some prior act or condition
B	Negligent Misrepresentation	2 _____	A contract in which the terms of the agreement are fully and explicitly stated in orally, or in writing.
C	Time is of the essence	3 _____	A contract that has been completely performed by both parties
D	Bilateral Contract	4 _____	A contract that has not been fully performed by either or both parties
E	Innocent Misrepresentation	5 _____	A contract that was never a contract because one of the essential elements is missing
F	Assignment	6 _____	A contract where both sides to the contract have made promises and are obligated to perform.
G	Consideration	7 _____	A law that requires certain contracts to be in writing in order to be enforceable
H	Express Contract	8 _____	A phrase in a contract that requires the performance of a certain act within a stated period of time
I	Statute of Frauds	9 _____	An exchange of promises where each party gives up anything of any value in return for anything of any value
J	Executory Contract	10 _____	An unintentional, but material misrepresentation made by a person in the transaction
K	Duress	11 _____	An unintentional, but material misrepresentation made by someone who had the duty
L	Actual Fraud	12 _____	Deliberate and intentional misrepresentation of a material fact
M	Executed Contract	13 _____	Forcing another to enter into a contract by physical force
N	Mutual Assent	14 _____	Transferring of all of one's rights and obligations under a contract by keeping secondary liability under the contract
O	Void Contract	15 _____	When a buyer and seller, through the process of offer and acceptance, reach a meeting of the minds.

Section 6: *Analysis Fill-In*

1. John agrees to give Sue an option on his home. What makes an option a Unilateral Contract?

2. What are the elements of a Valid Contract?

3. What is the difference between Actual and Constructive Communication?

4. What is the difference between Actual and Negative Fraud?

5. What is the purpose of an addendum in a contract?

6. John agrees to sell his home to Sue who agrees to purchase it for $500,000? What makes it a bilateral contract?

7. What would be an example of a Breach of Contract?

8. What would be an example of commingling?

9. What does Consideration mean?

10. What is an example of a Contingency?

11. When would a counteroffer occur?

12. What is an example of Duress?

13. What is the Purpose of Earnest Money?

14. What is an Enforceable Contract?

_____

15. What is the difference between Enforceability and Validity?

_____

16. Give an example of when a contract is executory:

_____

17. When is a contract executed?

_____

18. Give an example of an Express Contract?

_____

19. What does Genuine Assent mean?

_____

20. When would an Implied Contract be created?

_____

21. A seller finances property for a purchaser but keeps the legal title. What type of contract is this?

_____

22. That lawsuit had to be brought within 5 years. After 5 years, you cannot bring it. Which law is this?

_____

23. What is the Statue of Frauds?

_____

24. The condemnation prevented us from completing the contract. What would the condemnation be called?

_____

25. If you want any contractual obligations to continue after closing, you will need to include what in the contract?

_____

26. Whomever doesn't close by this date is in breach. This contract must have had:

_____

27. What does a void contract mean?

_____

28. What does it mean to have a Voidable Contract?

_____

29. Name three voidable contract situations:

_____

30. Is Earnest Money Required in a purchase and sale agreement?

_____

31. A person is Intoxicated. What type of contract does he have?

_____

32. Offer and Acceptance is also known as what contractual element:

_____

33. An already adjudged mentally incompetent person entered into a contract. He has what type of contract?

_____

34. Both the buyer and seller are mistaken about address of the house, the contract is:

_____

35. What is the difference between Innocent vs Negligent Misrepresentation?

_____

36. If a Grandson encourages his grandma to sign a bad contract, what type of contract would she have?

_____

37. What would be an example of Parol Evidence?

_____

38. What would be an example of Waste?

_____

39. Mary waits 4 years to sue when she could've sued in the first year. The court may say you waited too long to sue due to:

_____

40. John transfers all of his rights and obligations under a contract to Jim. What is it called?

_____

41. Who has primary liability in an assignment? Who has secondary liability?

_____

42. If John wants to transfer his contract rights without liability, he should request a:

_____

43. It will cost you $5,000 if you breach the contract, the $5,000 is called:

_____

44. Give two examples of when someone will have a Unilateral right to rescind:

_____

45. Sarah sues Mary because she wants her to complete the contract. She sues for:

_____

46. The buyer has what type of title in a land contract:

_____

47. Name 4 ways to terminate a contract:

_____

48. What is another name for a Land Contract?

_____

Section 7: *Analysis Multiple Choice*

1. **If there is a breach of contract for the sale of real property, an option available to the non-defaulting party is:**
   A. Rescission
   B. Reversion
   C. Suit for specific performance
   D. Suit for punitive damages

2. **Bill, a minor buyer, and Sally, as seller, orally agree that Bill will purchase Sally's home for $325,000. Prior to the closing, Bill decides that he has changed his mind and refuses to answer any of Sally's calls. The probable outcome is?**
   A. Bill will have to complete the purchase because there was a valid contract
   B. Bill will not have to complete the purchase because the contract is unenforceable
   C. Bill will not have to complete the purchase because the contract was invalid
   D. Bill will not have to complete the purchase because the contract was voidable

3. **An owner has been asked to grant a 60-day option to purchase a property. When should the purchase price be decided?**
   A. Upon creation and signing of the option to purchase
   B. When the buyer decides to exercise his option
   C. At any time during the 60-day option period
   D. Within the last 10 business days of the 60-day option period

4. **An option contract obligates:**
   A. The optionor to sell if the optionee exercises the option
   B. The optionee to buy before the end of the option time period
   C. The optionor to sell before the end of the option time period or return the option money
   D. No one

5. **An adult buyer who is illiterate signs a contract to purchase property from a seller. The buyer understands the nature of the contract because the terms were explained orally. Is the contract binding?**
   A. Yes, because all adults are considered legally competent
   B. Yes, because the buyer understands the terms of the contract
   C. No, because the buyer is illiterate and, therefore, legally incompetent
   D. No, because a conservator must sign for the buyer

6. **A tenant who wishes to transfer all their rights and interests in a lease uses which of the following?**
   A. An assignment but only if the landlord approves it
   B. An assignment if not prohibited by the lease
   C. An assumption and the tenant becomes secondarily liable
   D. A sublease

7. **A licensee is representing prospective buyers. The licensee orally informed the buyers that the developer would be paving the streets in front of a house in a rural subdivision. The licensee had not verified this but assumed that it was true because the developer had done the paving in similar subdivisions. The buyers relied on the licensee's statement in deciding to buy the house. If the written contract did not spell out the paving responsibilities, who can be held accountable for damages?**
   A. The developer because it is a developer's responsibility to pave streets up to existing arteries
   B. The licensee because his unverified statement was negligent misrepresentation
   C. The licensee because his unverified statement was intentional misrepresentation
   D. No one because no written promise of street-paving was made by either the licensee or the developer

8. A listing licensee is preparing an offer for a buyer. The property is listed for $205,000. The buyers want to offer $200,000 and require that the new free-standing stove and refrigerator remain with the property. The licensee prepares the offer, the buyers sign it, and the licensee presents the offer to the seller. The seller accepts the price and will leave the stove but will not leave the refrigerator. The licensee removes the part about the refrigerator staying, and the seller and his wife initial, sign, and date the document. Which of the following is true about this situation?
    A. The offer has been signed and accepted by all parties and is now considered a contract
    B. Neither the seller, nor his licensee, has a right to make any changes to the original offer
    C. The original offer is now terminated, and a counteroffer has been created
    D. If the buyers refuse to give up the refrigerator, the seller can accept their original offer

9. Zola is an agent representing a seller on a property. Given the very hot real estate market, multiple offers are received on the property on the first day. Zola should:
    A. Present only the first offer to the seller and let the seller accept or reject it before presenting the next one
    B. Present the offers to the seller in the order in which they were received allowing the seller to accept or reject each one before presenting the next one
    C. Present the highest offer first and allow her to accept or reject it before moving to the next
    D. Present all offers to the seller giving advice as to each one before the seller accepts or rejects any

10. Which of the following scenarios would most likely result in a suit for constructive fraud?
    A. A buyer lies about the ability to obtain a loan large enough to purchase the house
    B. The broker mistakenly tells the buyer that the house is 4,000 square feet
    C. The seller intentionally tells the buyer that he fixed the air conditioner when he didn't
    D. The broker conceals from the buyer that the basement leaks during bad rainstorms

11. What would be inserted into a contract if the seller agrees to have a tree cut down for the buyer, but it cannot be done until two months after the closing?
    A. Executed Contract Clause
    B. Survival Clause
    C. Contingency Clause
    D. Addendum

12. What is the key difference between an agreement to mediate or arbitrate?
    A. Mediation is ordered by the court, but Arbitration is not
    B. Arbitration is ordered by the court, but Mediation is not
    C. With Arbitration are parties are not bound, with Mediation they are bound
    D. With Arbitration the parties are bound, with Mediation they are not

13. What is the difference between a valid and an enforceable contract?
    A. There is no difference, and both are required to have a contract
    B. Valid contract means all elements are present, but enforceable means you can go to court
    C. Valid means that you can go to court with the contract; enforceable means it comports with the statue of frauds
    D. Valid means it didn't have to be in writing; enforceable means it had to be in writing

14. Very often a real estate contract states that if a purchaser breaches, the seller can retain the earnest money. This would be an example of:
    A. Negotiated Terms
    B. Liquidated Damages
    C. Specific Performance
    D. Damages

15. **Vanessa was hit by a car in 2015. She wanted to sue but failed to do so until 2022 where we learned that all car accident lawsuits must be brought within 6 years. Vanessa sues anyway and the court refuses to hear her claim on the basis of:**
    A. Violation of Statue of Frauds
    B. Violation of Doctrine of Laches
    C. Violation of Statue of Limitations
    D. Violation of Operation of Law

16. **The Statute of Frauds indicates that certain contracts be in writing to be enforceable. Which contracts?**
    A. All real estate contracts and all leases
    B. All real estate contracts and some leases
    C. Some real estate contracts and some leases
    D. Some real estate contracts and all leases

17. **The buyer and seller agree to a purchase price of $450,000 but during the time of the contract, the purchase price is reduced to $425,000 because the inspection revealed many issues. The new price is done by:**
    A. Amendment to the contract
    B. Addendum to the contract
    C. Exhibit to the contract
    D. Additional signatures on the main contract

18. **Ayers gave an option on her property for 90 days to Benitez and received $100 for it. Twenty days later, Benitez assigned his option to Columbus for $500. Before expiration of the option, Ayers decides that she no longer wants to sell the property. Which is correct?**
    A. The option is void because options cannot be assigned
    B. Columbus can compel Ayers to sell to him if he exercises the option before its expiration
    C. The option is not binding on Ayers because $100 is not sufficient consideration for an option
    D. Ayers can refuse to sell because Benitez is not entitled to make more money on the option than he paid

19. **Most contracts that assert that genuine assent was missing are:**
    A. Valid
    B. Voidable
    C. Void
    D. Unenforceable

20. **Mary is a seller and has signed an exclusive right to sell listing agreement with Todd, as broker. Mary is seeking an offer of $400,000 and wants to close the sale in 30 days. Todd brings a buyer who offers $390,000 and will close in 30 days. Mary agrees to that price, but at the closing, she fails to pay Todd. Todd sues. Will he win?**
    A. No, because he didn't bring a ready willing and able buyer to meet the terms
    B. No, because although he brought a buyer, it was for less than Mary was asking
    C. Yes, unless Mary can prove that Todd wasn't responsible for bringing the buyer
    D. Yes, since Mary entered into the contract even though it was for less than asking price

21. **Mary attempts to purchase Janice's home, but the bank will not loan Mary the money. Mary and Janice enter into an agreement where Mary will pay Janice $1,200 per month for the home for a period of 20 years, but for that period, Mary will just have possession and equitable title in the property. This arrangement is called:**
    A. Land Contract
    B. Contract for Deed
    C. Installment Sale Agreement
    D. All of the above

22. **Maggie and Don enter into a contract where Don, as seller, inserts the clause next to the closing date: December 14, 2022 "time is of the essence". Both parties' sign. What does the addition of this clause mean?**
    A. That Don is agreeing that he will close by December 14, 2022
    B. That all parties must meet each contract deadlines by December 14, 2022
    C. That whoever fails to close on December 14, 2022, is in breach
    D. That the parties should shoot for closing around December 14, 2022

23. **Julius makes an offer to purchase a home from Peter. The parties negotiate for some time, and they plan to put in all into writing on Friday. However, Peter dies on Thursday. What is the effect of Peter's death?**
    A. Peter's death will have no effect because they already negotiated the terms
    B. Peter's death will terminate the negotiations, meaning that there is no contract
    C. The promises made can be enforced by Peter's heirs
    D. The contract is not enforceable because it wasn't put in writing

24. **Julius and Drew were about to enter into a contract. Drew threatened Julius by stating that he would beat him up if he didn't sign the contract by 5:00 pm. Julius wasn't sure about the terms of the contract but was afraid of Drew. He decided to sign in order to avoid any further threats. Julius' contract is:**
    A. Void due to the threats made
    B. Voidable due to the threats made
    C. Valid, but Julius may be able to get out of it later
    D. Unenforceable since it wasn't in writing

25. **Jovan is about to purchase a home from Nate. During the contract, the county informs Nate that it will be taking part of his property to build the playground for the adjacent school they are also building, but at a price well below the amount that Jovan is purchasing the property for. Jovan notes that he no longer must purchase the property because he doesn't want to be near a school. Nate sues Jovan for specific performance. The most probable result:**
    A. Jovan will be successful because the taking is a supervening illegality
    B. Jovan will be successful because he wasn't informed of the school build prior to entering into the contract
    C. Nate because the county is not taking the entire property so Jovan will have to complete the purchase
    D. Nate if he can prove that the school is far enough away that it won't affect Jovan

26. **Which of the following best describes a contract?**
    A. An offer and acceptance between competent parties to do a specific legal act
    B. A written agreement between competent parties to abstain from doing a specific act
    C. An offer and acceptance between competent parties to do or not do a specific legal act for consideration
    D. A mutual agreement between two or more parties

27. **A written agreement wherein one person agrees to purchase, and another person agrees to sell real property is called a/an**
    A. Agency Agreement
    B. Assessment
    C. Fiduciary obligation
    D. Real Estate Contract

28. **John, an adult, entered into a contract with Paul, who is 16 years old. When John learned that Paul was a minor, he decided to terminate the contract. Which statement is true?**
    A. Contracts with minors are automatically void
    B. Contracts with minors are voidable at the option of the adult
    C. The contract is valid and binding on both parties
    D. The contract is valid and binding only on John

29. **A potential buyer speaks to a seller about the purchase of his home. The two agree on a price and a closing date and the seller also agrees to leave the above ground swimming pool. The contract is:**
    A. Implied
    B. Unenforceable
    C. Void
    D. Voidable

30. **When a seller makes a counteroffer, which of the following statements is NOT true?**
    A. It is a partial acceptance of the original offer
    B. The original offeror becomes the offeror in the counteroffer
    C. It is rejection of an earlier offer
    D. It may be withdrawn at any time prior to acceptance

31. **One party to the contract has the right to change his mind and not perform as agreed. This right:**
    A. Can be a condition of the contract itself
    B. Can be created by statute
    C. May require the payment of monetary damages
    D. Could be any of the above

32. **A contract for the sale of real estate that does not state the consideration and provides no basis on which consideration could be determined is considered:**
    A. Enforceable
    B. Voidable
    C. Executory
    D. Void

33. **Which of the following is essential for a contract for the sale of real property to be upheld by a court?**
    A. Written form
    B. Earnest money deposit
    C. Removal of all liens and encumbrances
    D. All of the above

34. **Which of the following is subject to the Statute of Frauds?**
    A. Six - month lease for an apartment
    B. Tenancy at will
    C. Two year - lease for real property
    D. Month to month rental

35. **A broker finds a buyer who is willing to enter into an option on a $200,000 property for 90 days. The potential buyer pays $1,000 for the option right which is acceptable to the property owner. Which of the following is TRUE?**
    A. The sale commission is earned only if the sale is closed
    B. The sales commission is earned only if the option is exercised
    C. The $1,000 must be credited to the sales price
    D. The commission is earned upon mutual signing of the option agreement

36. **A seller has rejected offers of $152,000 and $151,000. Another offer is presented from a cooperating broker who is representing a buyer. This offer is $150,000. Which action by the listing broker is MOST appropriate?**
    A. Present the offer
    B. Refuse to present the offer because it is a waste of time
    C. Present the offer and tell the seller that he could attempt to negotiate a higher price
    D. Increase the offer price from the buyer

37. An implied contract would arise from the:
   A. Spoken words of the parties
   B. Written words of the parties
   C. Actions of the parties
   D. Written or spoken words of the parties

38. A buyer and seller entered into a purchase and sale agreement on a property. At the time of the parties signing the contract, the:
   A. Seller retained legal title and the buyer had an equitable interest in the property
   B. Seller had equitable title and the buyer had legal title
   C. Legal title remained with the seller and the buyer received equitable title
   D. The buyer and seller held joint legal title until closing

39. An option is an example of
   A. Unilateral contract
   B. Bilateral contract
   C. Executed contract
   D. Voidable contract

40. A real estate sales agreement contains the language "time is of the essence". Such language in a contract most nearly means:
   A. The parties must perform within reasonable periods of time
   B. The time limits stipulated in the contract must be faithfully followed
   C. Any time limits in the contract are merely suggestions
   D. If the time limits are not met, the parties shall have 7 days to perform

41. Which of the following is NOT required for a real estate sales contract to be valid and enforceable?
   A. Consideration
   B. Performance
   C. In writing
   D. Offer and acceptance

42. Which of the following is TRUE concerning conflicting wording in a contract?
   A. Preprinted controls typewritten which controls handwritten
   B. Typewritten controls preprinted which controls handwritten
   C. Handwritten controls preprinted which controls typewritten
   D. Handwritten controls typewritten which controls preprinted

43. For a person to have contractual capacity, that person must:
   A. Be literate
   B. Be able to read
   C. Be able to write
   D. Mentally competent

44. With the payment of $2,000, Jim has acquired the right to purchase a property from Alice for $5,000 an acre sometime in the next 6 months. This most likely is:
   A. An option agreement
   B. A Right of first refusal
   C. A Sales Contract
   D. A lease with option to buy

45. **A sales contract contains special stipulations**
    A. To make it legal
    B. To express conditions specific to the sale
    C. To satisfy statute of frauds
    D. To satisfy RESPA

46. **In accordance with the statute of frauds, which of the following could be verbal and still valid and enforceable?**
    A. A purchase and sales contract
    B. A 6-month lease
    C. An option agreement
    D. A mortgage

47. **Bob leases an apartment from Bill. Three or four nights a week, neighbors have loud parties, and it is impossible for Bob to sleep. Bob has complained to Bill multiple times, but Bill is either incapable or unwilling to remedy the problem. Bob notifies Bill that he is leaving with no further obligation to pay rent. Bob is claiming:**
    A. Equitable redemption
    B. Statutory redemption
    C. Actual eviction
    D. Constructive eviction

48. **Able is leasing a property from Baker to use as an automobile repair facility. The property is 200' wide and 300' deep. The city has condemned 15' across the front of the property to use as a turn lane in a road widening project. Able claims that the condemnation terminates the lease. Is Able probably correct in this assertion?**
    A. Yes, because condemnation terminates a lease
    B. Yes, because Able will have lost access to the property
    C. No because condemnation never terminates a lease
    D. No because the property taken was not substantial

49. **What is the purpose of earnest money in a real estate sales contract?**
    A. To provide valuable consideration as required by law
    B. To prove the buyer has the cash to close
    C. To prove the seller's faithfulness in the negotiations
    D. To provide some assurance that the buyer will close the transaction

50. **A broker lists a home for $80,000. The broker brings an offer to the seller for $78,000 which is rejected by the seller. The broker obtains another offer for $80,000. Before she can discuss the offer with the seller, however, the offeror withdraws the offer by having her agent call the broker at the seller's home. There is:**
    A. An Implied Contract
    B. A Unilateral Contract
    C. No Contract
    D. An Executory Contract

Chapter 1 Answers

1. A	6. C	11. B	16. A	21. B	26. D	31. D	36. B	41. C
2. B	7. D	12. A	17. A	22. D	27. B	32. D	37. B	42. B
3. C	8. D	13. A	18. C	23. C	28. B	33. A	38. A	43. C
4. B	9. D	14. A	19. C	24. B	29. C	34. C	39. A	44. D
5. C	10. C	15. B	20. D	25. A	30. C	35. B	40. A	45. C

1. Constructive Communication	16. Executed Contract	31. Innocent Misrepresentation
2. Rescission	17. Liquidated Damages	32. Waste
3. Option Contract	18. Enforceable Contract	33. Negligent Misrepresentation
4. Earnest Money	19. Statute for Frauds	34. Specific Performance
5. Actual Communication	20. Void	35. Voidable Contract
6. Supervening Illegality	21. Survival Clause	36. Consideration
7. Mutual Mistake	22. Implied Contract	37. Laches
8. Breach of Contract	23. Executory Contract	38. Commingling
9. Duress	24. Express Contract	39. Assignment
10. Genuine Assent	25. Parol Evidence Rule	40. Counteroffer
11. Statute of Limitations	26. Time is of the Essence	41. Novation
12. Contract	27. Bilateral Contract	42. Negative Fraud
13. Contingency	28. Unilateral Contract	43. Addendum
14. Undue Influence	29. Damages	44. Valid Contract
15. Mutual Assent	30. Land Contract	45. Actual Fraud

Exercise 1

1. G	3. C	5. F	7. A	9. L	11. I	13. D	15. O
2. N	4. M	6. J	8. H	10. K	12. B	14. E	

Exercise 2

1. K	3. A	5. M	7. G	9. C	11. E	13. O	15. J
2. B	4. L	6. I	8. F	10. H	12. D	14. N	

Exercise 3

1. A	3. M	5. O	7. I	9. G	11. B	13. K	15. N
2. H	4. J	6. D	8. C	10. E	12. L	14. F	

1. Only John is obligated to perform. Sue doesn't have an obligation

2. Consideration, Assent – Mutual and Genuine, Legal Capacity, Legal Purpose

3. Actual – Good when received; Constructive – When Sent

4. Actual – Intentional Positive Act; Negative - Concealment

5. It clarifies some point in the original contract

6. Both John and Sue have obligations or are making promises

7. A person decides not to buy the home after all contingencies are met

8. A broker places his client's money into his personal account

9. A promise for a promise or an exchange of value between the parties

10. Financing, Due Diligence, Appraisal

11. Anytime there is a change to the original offer

12. Physical force to another to force them to sign a contract

13. To ensure the buyer's performance on a contract

14. A contract that can be heard in court and where the court can take action

15. Enforceability – Can the court hear the case? Validity – Are all elements present?

16. After the parties sign the contract, but prior to closing; obligations still exist

17. After the closing or when no further obligations exist

18. The parties intentionally entered into a contract; John and Sue wrote it down and signed it

19. The contract was entered into freely

20. The court must look at the parties' actions to determine if there was a contract

21. Land Contract

22. Statute of Limitations

23. Certain contracts must be in writing to be enforceable

24. Supervening Illegality

25. Survival Clause

26. Time is of the Essence Clause

27. At least one of the essential contract elements is missing

28. We thought all contract elements were present, but one can be removed by the person acting under a disability; He can rescind it

29. Minor, Intentional or Negligent Misrepresentation, Duress, Menace, Undue Influence, Fraud, Negative Fraud

30. No, it only shows the purchaser is serious

31. Voidable

32. Mutual Assent

33. Void

34. Void due to Mutual Mistake

35. Innocent is any party in the transaction; Negligent is a party with a duty

36. Voidable for Undue Influence

37. Two parties orally agree to certain things, but their later writing doesn't mention those items

38. A tenant allowing his children to write on the landlord's walls; A life estate holder damaging the property

39. Laches

40. Assignment

41. Assignee, Assignor

42. Novation

43. Liquidated Damages

44. Voidable Contract, Due Diligence, Financing, Appraisal, Lead Based Paint

45. Specific Performance

46. Equitable

47. Mutual Rescission, Supervening Illegality, Performance, Novation, Voidable Contracts

48. Contract for Deed, Installment Sale Agreement

SECTION 7 ANSWERS:

1. C. The non-defaulting party in a contract has several choices: He can sue for damages, sue for specific performance, or not sue at all. There is no rescission right when we have a breach of contract and punitive damages cannot be claimed in contract actions

2. B. Bill, even though a minor, will not have to complete the contract because it is unenforceable in court since it wasn't in writing. It is true that a minor holds a voidable contract that he can go through with or rescind. However, before we get to that point, we have to determine if it is even enforceable to begin with. Since it wasn't in writing as required by the statute of frauds, it is not. Their agreement can still be performed if the parties wish, but it cannot be enforced in court because it wasn't in writing

3. A. An option is a unilateral contract where the person could buy or not buy, but the price is set at the time of the signing of the option

4. A. The only person obligated under an option contract is the optionor and his only obligation comes if the optionee exercises the option within the stated time frame

5. B. Illiteracy doesn't equal incompetency under contract law. If the person is capable of understanding, he is not considered incompetent

6. B. A transfer of all rights under a contract is called an assignment. A sublease would be a transfer of some of the rights. Moreover, all contracts (lease is a type of contract) can be assigned unless prohibited by the contract

7. B. Because the licensee had a duty to find out the truth, it is considered negligent, not intentional misrepresentation

8. C. All offers must have mutual assent to be considered binding on that point. Until both parties agree to all items of the contract, there is no assent. An offer dies if not accepted as is and a counteroffer is created

9. D. All offers should be presented to the seller at one time, explaining each one to the seller, and then allowing the seller to reject or accept whichever she desires. The point is that she has all of the knowledge of all of the offers before making a decision

10. B. Constructive Fraud (aka Negligent misrepresentation) is when a person in the transaction who has a duty to give correct information mistakenly reveals incorrect information

11. B. Since at the closing, the contract goes from executory to executed, if we want some obligations to continue past the closing, a survival clause should be inserted into the contract

12. D. Both Arbitration and Mediation are contractual remedies that the parties agreed to when entering into a contract. However, only arbitration binds the parties to the decision. With mediation, if the parties don't agree with the decision, they can still sue in court thereafter

13. B. Validity and enforceability are different. Valid means that all contractual elements are present (CALL). Enforceable means it comports with a law that makes it able to be heard in court such as the Statute of Frauds (Enforceability)

14. B. That a seller can retain earnest money is a form of a liquidated damage - an amount that is determined ahead of time so that the breaching party knows the cost of the breach

15. C. Statute of Limitations prevents a court from hearing a case when a person waits too long to bring it under the time frame stated in the law

16. C. The statute of frauds states the certain real estate contracts and leases over 1 year must be in writing to be enforceable

17. A. Price changes are done by amendment to the contract. Amendments are meant to change the underlying contract where addenda are meant to clarify provisions of the underlying contract, but not change it

18. B. All option contracts are assignable unless prohibited. Since the option time was not expired, if Columbus exercises his right, Ayers will have to sell it to him.

19. B. Most items that come under genuine assent - fraud, duress, misrepresentation, undue influence will result in a voidable contract

20. D. Todd's only obligation was to bring a ready willing and able buyer. Although the amount was less than asking, once Mary signed the agreement, Todd fulfilled the obligation

21. D. All of the above. All three terms are used for this arrangement. Because Mary will pay Janice for a period of time and hold equitable title, we can assume that Janice will have legal title for the duration

22. C. Time is of the essence clauses mean that the time frame stated in the contract is strict. Whomever, in this case, doesn't close by December 14, 2022, is in breach of contract

23. B. There is no contract here at all. Peter's death will end all negotiations

24. B. Any contract entered into under duress or menace is considered voidable and may be enforced or canceled at the option of the holder

25. A. Jovan will be successful because the taking of the property, no matter how small, is a supervening illegality (makes performance of the contract as stated, illegal or impossible)

26. C. Valid Contracts have four elements – CALL – all are included in the C as a definition. It is more particular than all of the rest

27. D. Real Estate contract is when one person (seller) agrees to allow another person to purchase (buyer) his real property

28. D. The contract is valid or voidable but only at Paul's option. Therefore, the contract is only binding on John should Paul choose to enforce it

29. B. Because the contract was not in writing, it is unenforceable. It could still be valid, but the court will not hear the case if something goes wrong. If it was in writing it would have been valid and express, not implied

30. A. A counteroffer is never considered a partial acceptance. It is essentially a new offer and a rejection of the original offer

31. D. All answers are correct in that a party may be given the right to change his mind in all circumstances. It may cost him money to do so. Either way, a party is always free to not perform

32. D. Because consideration is an essential element of contract, if it is missing, the contract is void

33. A. Enforceability only goes to whether the contract was in writing

34. C. Statue of Frauds explains which contracts must be in writing to be enforceable. With respect to leases, only a lease over a year has to be in writing

35. B. An option does not force the purchaser to purchase. So, the commission is earned on an option at the point that the purchaser exercises it

36. C. The best answer here is the one that is more particularized. While A is correct, C is a better answer because it advises the seller that he also has additional options and doesn't have to accept the offer as presented

37. C. Implied = Action. Express is something that is intentional such as written and spoken words. When there are no words, we must look at the parties' actions to determine their intention

38. A. The purchaser here did not have title to the property YET. Thus, he had an equitable interest in the property. If this were a land contract, he'd have equitable title because he is an actual purchaser at the time of signing

39. A. Options are always unilateral since only one side is obligated

40. B. When time is of the essence is inserted into a contract, the time limits in the contract must be followed strictly. Whomever is unable to do so is in breach

41. B. A contract can be valid and enforceable as long as it has all essential elements and is in writing, but there is no requirement that it be actually performed

42. D. Handwritten is the latest thing to occur so that court will give it the most effect

43. D. Legal Capacity in a contract only goes to mental competence

44. A. An option agreement because it says Jim acquired the right. It doesn't state that he acquired the obligation

45. B. Special Stipulations are added to a contract to clarify points of the sale

46. B. The statute of frauds only requires certain contracts be in writing to be enforceable. A 6-month lease is one of them. It does require that deeds, purchase and sale contracts, leases over a year, and any contracts conveying an interest in real estate be in writing

47. D. Constructive eviction is the tenant's claim that the landlord is breaching a warranty. So, the tenant is claiming that it is "LIKE" you're evicting me

48. A. Yes, any form of condemnation (full or partial) terminates a contract

49. D. Earnest money is not required in a contract. It is simply to ensure that the purchaser will not breach their rights and obligations under the contract

50. C. Offers can be withdrawn at any time until acceptance and communication. Here, the offer was never accepted so there is no contract.

Chapter 2:
General Principles of Agency

Section 1: *Outline*

I. <u>**Agency**</u> – <u>The body of common law that determines when a principal (person who directs another)</u> <u>will be responsible for the agent's (person being directed) actions</u>

    A. **The Nature of Agency** - The **principal** authorizes another person or entity to act on their behalf. The **agent** acts on behalf of principal. When a principal hires an agent, the parties are in an agency **RELATIONSHIP**

        1. An agent owes absolute loyalty to the best interest of the principal

        2. The principal becomes accountable for the agent's words and actions as long as the agent was acting within the **SCOPE** (amount of authority) of the authority given by the principal

        3. The relationship between principal and agent is a **fiduciary** one – total trust and confidence from the agent to the principal, not from the principal to the agent

        4. The agency relationship is not created by the payment of a commission or the absence of a commission. Money has nothing to do with how it is created

        5. An agent can also engage with a **third party** – a person who the agent interacts with but is NOT in a relationship with

    B. **Types of Agents** (classified according to the amount of authority they are given)

        1. **Universal Agent** - authorized to perform **any** act the principal can perform

        2. **General Agent** – has the authority to bind the principal in the **ongoing** conduct of a particular **business**

            a. **Affiliation Agreement** – The agency agreement between the broker as principal and the salesperson as the agent

            b. **Property Management Agreement** – The agency agreement between the owner as principal and the broker as the agent

            c. **Community Association Management Agreement** – The agency agreement between the community association as principal and the broker as the agent

        3. **Special or Limited agent** – appointed for a **particular purpose** or for a particular occasion

            a. **Listing Agreement** – The agency agreement between the property owner as principal and the broker as the agent

            b. **Buyer Brokerage Agreement** – The agency agreement between the buyer as principal and the broker as the agent

Note: All Agency agreements between sellers, buyers, owners, and community managers are with the BROKER, not the SALESPERSON. The SALESPERSON is not considered the "AGENT" in any of those transactions. The BROKER is the "AGENT", and the SALESPERSON works for the BROKER

C. Creating an Agency Relationship

1. **Actual Agency** – An agency created when the parties to the agreement have entered into it intentionally, whether verbally or in writing
2. **Ostensible Agency** – An agency created when a third party relies on the principal's express or implied representation that another person is his/her agent, when no such agency ever existed between the principal and the other party
3. **Implied agency** – An agency created when an agent's word or actions cause another person, typically a buyer, to feel that agent is representing him, when that is not the agent's intention
4. **Power of attorney** (POA) – An agency created when one person authorizes another person to act on their behalf. A power of attorney document is used, and the person being authorized is also known as an **attorney-in-fact** (not necessarily a lawyer). All POAs expire at the death of the person giving it or the person receiving it

D. Scope of Authority

1. The amount of authority authorized by the principal should be clearly indicated to the agent
2. The principal is only responsible for the agent's actions if the agent was acting within the scope of the authority given unless the principal ratifies the acts of the agent. **Ratification** – an after the fact authorization of a previously unauthorized act
3. If the authorized authority is not clear, **implied authority** could arise if the act arises out of custom and common usage or if it makes sense to give that authority in that circumstance

E. Agent's Obligation to the Principal – (POLAND):

1. **Personal Performance** – The principal selected the agent based on the agent's expertise, so, the agent should be the one to perform the agreement
2. **Obedience** – An agent must obey the principal's instructions unless asked to do something unethical, illegal, or unreasonable
3. **Loyalty** – The agent must place the principal's interest above those of anyone else including those of the agent
4. **Accountability** – Agents must account for all monies and valuables, hold all of principal's funds in trust, never commingle or convert
5. **Notice** – The agent must keep the principal apprised of any matter that may affect the business at hand
6. **Due care and Diligence** – The agent must exercise the degree of care that a prudent agent would employ in a similar situation

F. Principal's Duties to the agent – (CRIP):

1. **Compensation** – the principal owes the broker compensation upon performance (bringing a ready, willing, and able buyer to meet the seller's terms)
2. **Reimbursement** – the principal should reimburse the agent for approved unrelated expenses, such as grass cutting
3. **Indemnification** – the principal is obligated to indemnify the agent against any loss suffered through no fault of the agent
4. **Performance** – a principal must give an agent a reasonable amount of cooperation and assistance

G. Termination of the Agency Agreement

1. **Performance** – The agreement no longer exists due to performance of the parties
2. **Expiration** – If the agreement has a time limit, it ends when time runs out
3. **Revocation** – The principal decides to end the agency, but he might be held accountable by the agent for services performed
4. **Renunciation** – The agent decides to end the agency, but she might be held accountable by the principal for breach of contract

5. **Abandonment** – The agreement is terminated by the principal if the agent makes no effort to perform
6. **Agreement** – Mutual agreement of the parties
7. **Death** – The agent (not the salesperson) or the principal dies
8. **Incapacity** – The agent (not the salesperson) or the principal declares bankruptcy or is judged legally incompetent
9. **Supervening Illegality** – A change in the law during the agency makes performance of the contract illegal
10. **Extinction** – Total destruction of the subject property

H. The Brokerage business

A. Types of Business

1. **Sole proprietorship** – Single owner runs the business and owner is personally liable for business loses
2. **Partnership** – An agreement must be filled. Each general partner is personally liable for the business loses. Limited partners' losses are limited to their investment
3. **Corporation** – Considered a separate person by law, it eliminates personal liability. It has perpetual existence, raises capital through stock offerings, and investors are called shareholders
4. **S Corporation** – A cross between a corporation and LLC. It has the pass-through tax benefits and offers shares (75 stockholders maximum)
5. **LLC** – Does not have perpetual existence. Personal liability limited and taxes passed through to members

B. The Broker's Responsibility – The salesperson owes the broker absolute loyalty. The broker in turn is responsible for all their actions within the scope of the authority given

1. **The Relationship between Broker and Salesperson**

   a. **Employee** – The broker has more control over the affiliates' activities; the broker will pay all worker's compensation, unemployment insurance and taxes
   b. **Independent contractor** – In business for themselves, they are only accountable to the broker for the results of the work performed; handles her own taxes and insurance
   c. **Compensation** – The employment contract specifies how the salesperson will be compensated. It is typically based on a percentage of sales but could be a 100% commission plan
   d. **Affiliation Agreement** – The employment contract must specify the amount of authority, how the agent will be paid when employed and when he leaves the employ
   d. **Agency Policy** – The broker is responsible for determining the company's policy regarding agency relationships and all policies must be included in a written manual

2. **The Listing** – is the broker's contract of employment with a seller authorizing the broker to find a buyer or tenant who is ready, willing, and able to meet the owner's terms

   a. **Open Listing** – An owner promises a commission to a broker who produces a ready willing and able buyer at the named price; Can be written or oral
   b. **Exclusive Agency listing** – Only one broker is authorized to market the property, but the owner reserves the right to sell it himself/herself with no obligation to pay commission
   c. **Exclusive right to sell listing** – Only one broker is authorized to market the property and is assured commission as long as the property sells during the listing period. These listings provide the maximum protection for the broker and is the most widely used
   d. **Net listing** – A seller has a certain sum in mind she wants to realize from the sale and authorizes the broker to market the property at any price and pocket the difference. This listing is illegal in most states

Multiple Listing Service - MLS is not a type listing but an organization of brokers who wish to share information and solicit the cooperation of other members in marketing their listing. There is an express or implied agreement to share commission earned by cooperating efforts

Terminating a Listing- A listing is a contract and can be terminated like all contracts: performance, mutual agreement breach and expiration

I. Right to a commission – In a listing agreement, the seller agrees to pay the broker a commission once the broker has performed according to the terms of the agreement. In case of breach of a non-exclusive or exclusive agency agreement, the broker must prove **procuring cause** – the broker who began an un-interrupted chain of events that eventually resulted in the sale

J. Types of Agency

1. **Buyer Agency (Selling agent)** – Brokerage agreement where the principal is the buyer, and the broker is the sales agent
2. **Seller Agency (Listing agent)** – Brokerage agreement where the principal is the seller, and the broker is the sales agent
3. **Sub-Agency** – Two different brokers, both of whom are representing the seller. In sub-agency the cooperating selling broker, although working with the buyer, is actually representing the seller because he becomes a sub-agent of the seller's broker
4. **Dual Agency** – Occurs when one license has both seller and buyer as clients in the same transaction. Risk is unavoidable since advice given to one client could represent disloyalty to the other; not illegal unless undisclosed
5. **Designated Agency** – Arises out of dual agency. To avoid the risk, the broker will designate another agent in the office to represent one of the parties from the dual agency
6. **The Transaction Broker** – A facilitator, with no agency relationship to either party in a transaction; works with third parties only

K. Third Parties

Agents can also engage with a **THIRD PARTIES** – a person who the agent interacts with but is NOT in a relationship with. We do not use the term **REPRESENTATION** when talking about third parties. We only work with third parties. It simply means that we do **LESS** for them

L. Agents' Obligations to Third Parties – (HADD)

1. **Honesty and integrity** – Agents must always provide factual information free from fraud and misrepresentation
2. **Accountability** – Agents must account for all monies and valuables, hold all monies in trust, never commingle or convert
3. **Due Care (Reasonable Skill and Care)** – The agent must exercise the degree of care that a prudent agent would employ in a similar situation
4. **Disclosure** – Truthful information regarding the property affecting the value or desirability must be also disclosed the third parties. **Latent defects** - those which are hidden and not readily apparent must be disclosed. **Patent defects** - those that are visible and can be easily discovered through an ordinary inspection (caveat emptor applies) and no disclosure is required

M. Working with a Third Party – An Agent is not an "AGENT" to a third party. There is no fiduciary duty and there is no loyalty. An agent can only perform ministerial acts for third parties **(Acts which don't require judgment or skill)**

Section 2: *Vocabulary*

Actual Agency: An agency agreement created intentionally

Affiliation Agreement: The employment contract between the sales agent and broker

Agency: The body of law that determines when a person principal is responsible for the agent's actions

Agent: One who is authorized and who agrees to act on behalf of another

Buyer's Agency: An agency where the agent represents the buyer in the transaction

Caveat Emptor: The buyer is responsible for finding the defects on his own

Co-Brokerage: A brokerage practice where licensees outside of the listing broker's agency assist in procuring a customer in exchange for a portion of the commission

Commission: The listing broker's compensation for finding a buyer who is ready, willing, and able to meet the seller's terms

Designated Agency: An agency that occurs when, as a result of dual agency, a second licensee is assigned by the broker to represent the buyer or seller in a transaction

Dual Agency: An agency that occurs when an agent in the brokerage represents both the buyer and the seller in the same transaction

Due Diligence Period: A period of time for the buyer to inspect the property to determine if the property meets the buyer's needs

Employee: A person who agrees to work for and be controlled by an employer

Exclusive Agency Listing: An agency arrangement where the principal exclusively hires one broker, but, at the same time, retains the right to sell the property on his own

Exclusive Right to Sell Listing: An agency agreement where the broker is given the exclusive right to market the seller's property and will receive a commission regardless of who sells the property during the listing period

Fiduciary: An agent holds a position of trust or confidence when in an agency relationship

General Agency: An agent is hired to conduct a broad range of day-to-day activities for the principal

Implied Agency: An agency created when an agent, by his actions, leads another to falsely believe that the agent is representing him

Implied Authority: Authority that is not expressed or written into the contract, but can be granted to the agent out of custom

Independent Contractor: One who works for an employer, but whose working conditions and methods are not controlled by the employer

Latent Defect: A defect which is either hidden or cannot be discovered by ordinary inspection

Listing Agent: A broker who represents the seller in the transaction

Listing Agreement: The agency agreement where a seller hires a broker to find a ready willing and able buyer to meet the seller's terms

Material Facts: Any fact that is relevant to the issue such that it would influence a decision, but cannot easily be discovered by a purchaser

Ministerial Acts: Acts that do not require any professional judgment or skill

Net Listing: A listing based on the net price the seller will receive at closing after all of seller's expenses have been paid

Open Listing: A unilateral, non-exclusive listing agreement where the seller agrees to pay a commission to any broker who brings the seller a ready, willing, and able buyer

Ostensible Agency: When one party relies on another party's statement that a third party is his agent when no such agency exists

Patent Defect: A visible, apparent defect that can be seen through an inspection of the property

Principal (Client): One who authorizes another person to act on his behalf

Power of Attorney (POA): Legal document in which one person appoints another person to act as his agent

Procuring Cause: An uninterrupted chain of events that eventually lead to the sale of the property

Purchase and Sale Agreement: A binding contract between a buyer and seller, where the seller agrees to sell, and the buyer agrees to buy for a certain price and certain terms

Ratification: An action by a principal approving a previously unauthorized act of an agent

Safety Clause: A listing agreement entitling the broker to a commission after the listing expires if the property is sold to one of the broker's prospects

Scope of Agency: The amount of authority given to the agent

Selling Agent: The broker who procures the buyer for a listed property

Special Agency: An agent is hired to perform acts which are limited in either time or scope

Sub-Agency: Two or more independent brokers represent the same principal, usually a seller

Transaction Agency: An agency where both the buyer and seller are unrepresented third parties

Third Party (Customer): A person with whom an agent interacts, but who is not in an agency relationship

Universal Agency: An agent is hired with complete authority to act for the principal in all situations

Section 3: *Recall Multiple Choice*

1. **A defect which is either hidden or cannot be discovered by ordinary inspection**
   A. Caveat Emptor
   B. Latent Defect
   C. Procuring Cause
   D. Material Facts

2. **Legal document in which one person appoints another person to act as an agent on his or her behalf**
   A. Cash on Delivery
   B. Power of Attorney
   C. Scope of agency
   D. Receipt versus Payment

3. **An agent holds a position of trust or confidence when in an agency relationship**
   A. Fiduciary
   B. Agency
   C. Agent
   D. Caveat Emptor

4. **A person who agrees to work for and be controlled by an employer**
   A. Agency
   B. Agent
   C. Employee
   D. Independent Contractor

5. **The listing broker's compensation for finding buyer who is ready, willing, and able to meet the seller's terms**
   A. Agency
   B. Affirmation
   C. Agent
   D. Commission

6. **One who authorizes another person to act on their behalf (agent)**
   A. Employee
   B. Implied agency
   C. Principal (Client)
   D. Agent

7. **The broker who procures the buyer for a listed property**
   A. Transaction Agency
   B. Procuring Cause
   C. Selling Agent
   D. Implied Agency

8. **An action by a principal approving a previously unauthorized act of an agent**
   A. Fiduciary
   B. Ratification
   C. Commission
   D. Implied Authority

9. **An agency arrangement where the principal exclusively hires one broker, but, at the same time, retains the right to sell the property on his own**
   A. Listing Agreement
   B. Exclusive Agency Listing
   C. Open Listing
   D. Exclusive Right To Sell Listing

10. **An agency that occurs when a brokerage represents both the buyer and the seller in the same transaction**
    A. General Agency
    B. Dual Agency
    C. Implied Agency
    D. Designated Agency

11. **A broker who represents the seller in the transaction**
    A. Buyer's Agency
    B. Transaction Agency
    C. Listing Agent
    D. Exclusive Agency Listing

12. **An agency where both the buyer and seller are unrepresented third parties**
    A. Transaction Agency
    B. Special Agency
    C. Listing Agent
    D. Dual Agency

13. **The agent represents and owes all loyalty to the buyer in a real estate transaction**
    A. Buyer's Agency
    B. Dual Agency
    C. Designated Agency
    D. Implied Agency

14. **A visible, apparent defect that can be seen through an inspection of the property**
    A. Affirmation
    B. Material
    C. Latent
    D. Patent

15. **A provision in a listing agreement that entitles the broker to a commission after the listing expires, provided the owner sells to one of the broker's prospects**
    A. Protection Clause
    B. Latent Defect
    C. Common Law
    D. Safety Clause

16. **A period of time for the buyer to inspect the property to determine if the property meets the buyer's needs**
    A. Due Diligence Fee
    B. Earnest Money
    C. Consideration
    D. Due Diligence Period

17. **An agent is hired to conduct a broad range of day-to-day activities for the principal**
    A. Special Agency
    B. General Agency
    C. Designated Agency
    D. Universal Agency

18. **The amount of authority given to the agent**
    A. Scope of Agency
    B. Universal Agency
    C. Power of Attorney
    D. Commission

19. **A listing based on the net price the seller will receive at closing after all of seller's expenses have been paid**
    A. Listing Agreement
    B. Exclusive Right To Sell Listing
    C. Exclusive Agency Listing
    D. Net Listing

20. **An agent is hired to perform acts which are limited in either time or scope**
    A. Universal Agency
    B. Dual Agency
    C. General Agency
    D. Special Agency

21. **A brokerage practice where agents and brokers outside of the listing broker's agency assist in procuring a customer in exchange for a portion of the commission**
    A. Co-Brokerage
    B. Reciprocity
    C. Cooperation
    D. Comity

22. **When one party leads a third party to believe that a second party is his agent, the courts will impose an agency**
    A. General Agency
    B. Universal Agency
    C. Ostensible Agency
    D. Implied Agency

23. **Authority that is not expressed or written into the contract, but can be granted to the agent out of custom**
    A. Implied Agency
    B. Ostensible Agency
    C. Implied Authority
    D. Universal Agency

24. **A fact that is relevant to the issue such that it would influence a decision, but cannot be easily discovered by a purchaser**
    A. Latent
    B. Patent
    C. Essential
    D. Material

25. **A person (third party) with whom an agent interacts, but there is no agency relationship**
    A. Employee
    B. Principal (Client)
    C. Third Party (Customer)
    D. Implied agency

26. **A unilateral, non-exclusive listing agreement where the seller agrees to pay a commission to any broker who brings the owner a ready, willing, and able buyer**
    A. Listing Agreement
    B. Exclusive Agency Listing
    C. Exclusive Right To Sell Listing
    D. Open Listing

27. **The body of law that determines when a person who sends another out (Principal) to act on his behalf (Agent) is responsible for the agent's actions**
    A. Agency
    B. Selling Agent
    C. Fiduciary
    D. Agent

28. **The employment contract between the sales agent and broker**
    A. Affiliation Agreement
    B. Functional Resume
    C. License Law
    D. Buyer Brokerage Agreement

29. **An agency agreement created intentionally**
    A. Ostensible Agency
    B. Actual Agency
    C. Implied Agency
    D. Buyer's Agency

30. **A person who is authorized and who agrees to act on behalf of another**
    A. Agency
    B. Agent
    C. Fiduciary
    D. Independent Contractor

31. **An uninterrupted chain of events that eventually lead to the sale of the property**
    A. Chain of Title
    B. Procuring Cause
    C. Scope of agency
    D. Chain of Sale

32. **Acts that do not require any professional judgment or skill**
    A. Universal Agency
    B. General Agency
    C. Special Agency
    D. Ministerial Acts

33. **An agency agreement where the broker is given the exclusive right to market the seller's property and will receive a commission regardless of who sells the property during the listing period**
    A. Exclusive Right to Sell Listing
    B. Exclusive Agency Listing
    C. Net Listing
    D. Open Listing

34. **A binding contract between a buyer and seller, where the seller agrees to sell and the buyer agrees to buy for a certain price and certain terms**
    A. Written, Unexpired Property Management Agreement
    B. Purchase and Sale Agreement
    C. Listing Agreement
    D. Property Management Agreement

35. **The buyer is responsible to find the defects on his own. Buyer Beware**
    A. Caveat Venditor
    B. Caveat Emptor
    C. Latent Defect
    D. Safety Clause

36. **The agency agreement between the seller and broker to find a ready willing and able buyer to meet the seller's terms**
    A. Open Listing
    B. Buyer Brokerage Agreement
    C. Listing Agreement
    D. Purchase And Sale Agreement

37. **An agency created when an agent, by his actions, leads another to believe that the agent is representing him**
    A. Ostensible Agency
    B. Actual Agency
    C. Implied Agency
    D. Universal Agency

38. **An agency that occurs when, as a result of dual agency, a licensee is assigned by the broker to represent the buyer or seller in a transaction**
    A. Designated Agency
    B. Implied Agency
    C. Buyer's Agency
    D. Dual Agency

39. **One who works for, and receives payment from, an employer but whose working conditions and methods are not controlled by the employer**
    A. Employee
    B. Independent Contractor
    C. Fiduciary
    D. Agent

40. **An agent is hired with complete authority to act for the principal in all situations**
    A. Universal Agency
    B. Dual Agency
    C. General Agency
    D. Special Agency

41. **Two or more independent brokers represent the same principal, usually a seller**
    A. Sub-Agency
    B. General Agency
    C. Implied Agency
    D. Dual Agency

Section 4: *Recall Fill-In*

1. Two or more independent brokers represent the same principal, usually a seller

   _____

2. An agency that occurs when, as a result of dual agency, a licensee is assigned by the broker to represent the buyer or seller in a transaction

   _____

3. A broker who represents the seller in the transaction

   _____

4. A visible, apparent defect that can be seen through an inspection of the property

   _____

5. One who authorizes another person to act on their behalf

   _____

6. The amount of authority given to the agent

   _____

7. The employment contract between the sales agent and broker

   _____

8. A provision in a listing agreement that entitles the broker to a commission after the listing expires, provided the owner sells to one of the broker's prospects

   _____

9. A person (third party) with whom an agent interacts, but there is no agency relationship

   _____

10. An agency arrangement where the principal exclusively hires one broker, but, at the same time, retains the right to sell the property on his own

    _____

11. Authority that is not expressed or written into the contract, but can be granted to the agent out of custom

    _____

12. Any fact that is relevant to the issue such that it would influence a decision, but cannot be easily discovered by a purchaser

    _____

13. Legal document in which one person appoints another person to act as an agent on his or her behalf

14. A unilateral, non-exclusive listing agreement where the seller agrees to pay a commission to any broker who brings the owner a ready, willing, and able buyer

15. A binding contract between a buyer and seller, where the seller agrees to sell and the buyer agrees to buy for a certain price and certain terms

16. The agent represents and owes all loyalty to the buyer in a real estate transaction

17. The body of law that determines when a person who sends another out (Principal) to act on his behalf (Agent) is responsible for the agent's actions

18. The agency agreement between the seller and broker to find a ready willing and able buyer to meet the seller's terms

19. An agency that occurs when a brokerage represents both the buyer and the seller in the same transaction

20. An agency where both the buyer and seller are unrepresented third parties

21. An agency agreement created intentionally

22. An agency agreement where the broker is given the exclusive right to market the seller's property and will receive a commission regardless of who sells the property during the listing period

23. An agent is hired to perform acts which are limited in either time or scope

24. A defect which is either hidden or cannot be discovered by ordinary inspection

25. A period of time for the buyer to inspect the property to determine if the property meets the buyer's needs

26. The broker who procures the buyer for a listed property

27. When one party leads a third party to believe that a second party is his agent, the courts will impose an agency

28. A listing based on the net price the seller will receive at closing after all of seller's expenses have been paid

29. Acts that do not require any professional judgment or skill

30. An uninterrupted chain of events that eventually lead to the sale of the property

31. An agent holds a position of trust or confidence when in an agency relationship

32. A brokerage practice where agents and brokers outside of the listing broker's agency assist in procuring a customer in exchange for a portion of the commission

33. The buyer is responsible to find the defects on his own. Buyer Beware

34. A person who agrees to work for and be controlled by an employer

35. An agent is hired with complete authority to act for the principal in all situations

36. An agent is hired to conduct a broad range of day-to-day activities for the principal

37. A person who is authorized and who agrees to act on behalf of another (Principal)

38. An action by a principal approving a previously unauthorized act of an agent

39. One who works for, and receives payment from, an employer but whose working conditions and methods are not controlled by the employer

_____

40. An agency created when an agent, by his actions, leads another to believe that the agent is representing him

_____

41. The listing broker's compensation for finding buyer who is ready, willing, and able to meet the seller's terms

_____

Section 5: *Matching*

A   Implied Authority   1 _____   An agency agreement created intentionally

B   Actual Agency   2 _____   Authority that is not expressed or written into the contract, but can be granted to the agent out of custom

C   Power of Attorney   3 _____   A listing agreement where the seller agrees to pay a commission to any broker who brings a ready, willing, and able buyer

D   Safety Clause   4 _____   A listing based on the net price the seller will receive at closing after all of seller's expenses have been paid.

E   Net Listing   5 _____   A period of time for the buyer to inspect the property to determine if the property meets the buyer's needs

F   Buyer's Agency   6 _____   A person (third party) with whom an agent interacts, but there is no agency relationship

G   Designated Agency   7 _____   A person who agrees to work for and be controlled by an employer

H   Open Listing   8 _____   A provision in a listing agreement that protects the broker after the listing expires

I   Exclusive Right to Sell   9 _____   An agency agreement where the broker is entitled to a commission if sold during the listing period.

J   Third Party (Customer)   10 _____   An agency that occurs when a licensee is assigned by the broker to represent the buyer or seller in a transaction

K   Commission   11 _____   Legal document in which one person appoints another person to act as an agent on his or her behalf

L   Employee   12 _____   The agent represents and owes all loyalty to the buyer in a real estate transaction.

M   Due Diligence Period   13 _____   The amount of authority given to the agent.

N   Scope of Agency   14 _____   The listing broker's compensation for finding buyer who is ready, willing, and able to meet the seller's terms

A	Fiduciary	1	_____	A broker outside of the listing broker's agency assists in bringing a buyer in exchange for a portion of the commission.
B	Co-op Brokerage	2	_____	Acts that do not require any professional judgment or skill
C	Principal (Client)	3	_____	An action by a principal approving a previously unauthorized act of an agent
D	Sub Agency	4	_____	An agent holds a position of trust or confidence when in an agency relationship
E	Special Agency	5	_____	An agent is hired to conduct a broad range of day-to-day activities for the principal
F	General Agency	6	_____	An agent is hired to perform acts which are limited in either time or scope
G	Caveat Emptor	7	_____	An uninterrupted chain of events that eventually lead to the sale of the property
H	Procuring Cause	8	_____	Any fact that is relevant to the issue such that it would influence a decision, but cannot be easily discovered by a purchaser
I	Ministerial Acts	9	_____	One who authorizes another person to act on their behalf
J	Agency	10	_____	The buyer is responsible to check for defects before a purchase is made.
K	Purchase and Sale	11	_____	The contract between buyer and seller, where the seller agrees to sell and the buyer agrees to buy for a certain terms.
L	Ratification	12	_____	The employment contract between the sales agent and broker
M	Material Facts	13	_____	The law that determines when a Principal is responsible for an Agent's actions
N	Affiliation Agreement	14	_____	Two or more independent brokers represent the same principal, usually a seller

A   Implied Agency   1 _____   A broker who represents the seller in the transaction

B   Listing Agent   2 _____   A defect which is either hidden or cannot be discovered by ordinary inspection

C   Selling Agent   3 _____   A person who is authorized and who agrees to act on behalf of another

D   Transaction Agency   4 _____   A visible, apparent defect that can be seen through an inspection of the property

E   Ostensible Agency   5 _____   An agency created when an agent, by his actions, leads another to believe that the agent is representing him

F   Independent Contractor   6 _____   An agency that occurs when a brokerage represents both the buyer and the seller in the same transaction

G   Listing Agreement   7 _____   An agency where both the buyer and seller are unrepresented third parties.

H   Exclusive Agency   8 _____   An agency where the principal exclusively hires one broker, but retains the right to sell the property on his own

I   Dual Agency   9 _____   An agent is hired with complete authority to act for the principal in all situations

J   Latent Defect   10 _____   One who works for an employer but who is not controlled by the employer

K   Universal Agency   11 _____   The agency agreement between the seller and broker to find a ready willing and able buyer to meet the seller's terms

L   Patent Defect   12 _____   The broker who procures the buyer for a listed property

M   Agent   13 _____   When one party leads a third party to believe that a second party is his agent, the courts will impose an agency

Section 6: *Analysis Fill-In*

1. Name three types of agents:

   _____

2. What is the definition of a Special Agent?

   _____

3. When dealing with the seller, the broker is what type of agent?

   _____

4. When dealing with your broker, the salesperson is what type of agent?

   _____

5. What must the agreement between you and your broker include?

   _____

6. What are three agent obligations to the principal?

   _____

7. Who is the fiduciary?

   _____

8. Don't show my house after 9 pm is an example of what agent duty to the principal?

   _____

9. What does ratification mean?

   _____

10. What is a three-party agency agreement that is created by the court?

    _____

11. Who does the sub-agent represent in a transaction?

    _____

12. A Principal who signs a listing agreement can also be known as:

    _____

13. Which defects must be disclosed to third parties?

    _____

14. Which party renunciates an agency agreement?

_____

15. Which party revokes an agency agreement?

_____

16. Provide an example of indemnification:

_____

17. Provide an example of accountability:

_____

18. Who are the parties in a purchase and sale agreement?

_____

19. Who are the parties in an affiliation agreement?

_____

20. Who are the parties in a listing agreement?

_____

21. Name two duties of the Principal to the Agent:

_____

22. What type of listing is a unilateral contract?

_____

23. The broker always gets paid in this type of listing agreement:

_____

24. If commission is denied, the broker must prove in court that:

_____

25. A transaction agent represents:

_____

26. The selling agent represents:

_____

27. A broker earns a commission when:

_____

28. A principal is responsible for only those agents' actions that:

_____

29. Dual agency requires that both seller and buyer:

_____

30. Name three ways to terminate an agency contract:

_____

31. Name two duties the Agent has to a Third Party (customer):

_____

Section 7: *Analysis Multiple Choice*

1. **Broker Bob is the listing agent in a transaction where Broker Smith is the selling agent. The brokers enter into a sub-agency agreement. The result of this transaction is that:**
   A. Broker Smith has a fiduciary duty to the buyer
   B. Broker Bob has a fiduciary duty to the buyer
   C. Both Broker Smith and Broker Bob have a fiduciary duty to the seller
   D. Both Broker Smith and Broker Bob have a fiduciary duty to the buyer

2. **Sal is the owner of a 25-unit property and decides to hire ABC Realty as it's manager. All tenants either have month to month or tenancy for years leases. On April 17th, Sal dies. The next rental payments are due on May 1st. Can ABC Realty continue to collect the rent?**
   A. Yes, because leases do not expire on death of the landlord
   B. No, because ABC Realty's agency terminated on Sal's death
   C. No, because all leases expire at the death of the landlord
   D. Yes, because 30 days have not passed since Sal's death, so the next lease payment is due

3. **Phillip is an agent on a listed property. His seller accepted an offer on the listing three weeks ago, but Phillip is concerned that the property will not close. So, he continually markets the property clearly indicating that the property is under contract but that back up offers are being accepted. Can Phillip's seller accept an offer on this property?**
   A. No, the property is already under contract, so he cannot accept any other offers
   B. No, the seller must wait for the purchaser to breach the contract by not purchasing
   C. Yes, if the new offer has a contingency placed in it that it can't be accepted until the other contract is extinguished
   D. Yes, offers should be presented and can be accepted at any time

4. **Your sister is a licensee and is working for ABC Realty Partners. You are a licensee with the same company. Your sister has a customer that puts an offer on a house that is listed by you. Your sister would be:**
   A. Working as a designated agent representing her customer
   B. Working as a dual agent representing both her customer and you
   C. Working as a sub agent representing you
   D. Working as an agent representing the seller

5. **Your sister asks you to help her sell her home. Which would be an act that might be illegal?**
   A. She lists with you and 2 other brokers
   B. She lists with you, but she puts her own for sale sign in the side yard
   C. She tells you that your commission will be anything over her loan payoff of $59,750
   D. She tells you she will not accept a contract from anyone over 65 years old

6. **Your broker authorizes you to sign contracts on his/her behalf. How is this authorization given to you?**
   A. The State Real Estate Commission issues this right under both the Agency and License Laws
   B. The employment or affiliation agreement you signed with your broker
   C. The Exclusive Right to Sell Listing Agreement
   D. By a separate Power of Attorney given to you by your broker

7. **You receive an earnest money check Monday at noon. When should the check be deposited with your broker?**
   A. No later than Tuesday at the close of business
   B. Unless all parties have agreed otherwise, as soon as possible
   C. As soon as the contract is accepted and binding
   D. Always by the weekend

8. **You have worked at Wonderful Realty for several years but have now decided to move across town to work at another company. How will you be compensated on any transactions that are in process but have not closed yet?**
   A. The local board of realtors that you are both members of will determine proper payment
   B. The Real Estate Commission determines how licensees are compensated when moving from one broker to another
   C. It will be negotiated between the two brokers
   D. It is determined based on the contract you signed when you joined Wonderful Realty

9. **You have an investor seller who wants you to list his property which needs many repairs. He tells you he's upside down in the property and therefore wants you to list the property for sale "as is". Should you list it?**
   A. Yes, it's perfectly ok as long as you list the property is listed in the MLS system with "AS IS" in bold letters
   B. Yes, fixer - uppers are often sought after by flippers
   C. Yes, but you should make sure all known defects are disclosed to the buyers
   D. No, "as is" sales are not allowed by the Real Estate Commission

10. **You go on a listing presentation and the homeowner tells you that he is in financial trouble and just needs to sell the property quickly. Can you take the listing?**
    A. Yes, as long as the listing reflects the market value of the property
    B. Yes, for any price the seller wishes, as long as you don't reveal that the seller is in financial trouble
    C. No, because the seller may be going into foreclosure
    D. No, it would be illegal for you to take such a listing

11. **You are showing property listed with another broker. The seller confides in you that her agent is doing a poor job and she wants to fire her. What should you tell the seller?**
    A. She should demand that her broker does a better job
    B. She can fire her agent, but she would be responsible for the commission
    C. She can file a complaint with the Real Estate Commission
    D. You can't say anything because you'd be violating license law

12. **You are doing an open house on your listing. One of the people looking at the house is interested in making an offer. To avoid dual agency, what should you do?**
    A. Refer the prospect to another company
    B. Refer the prospect to another agent within your company
    C. Tell the buyer that you can't answer her questions; she should come back with her own agent
    D. Treat the buyer as a third party/customer

13. **Which of the following would NOT be a job of the salesperson after contract but before closing?**
    A. Make sure the buyer is pre-qualified
    B. Assist in getting necessary estimates for repairs
    C. Follow up on contract contingencies
    D. Make sure all parties, including the closing attorney and lender, have a copy of the contract

14. **Which of the following would BEST describe a listing agreement?**
    A. An employment agreement between a real estate broker and the listing salesperson
    B. An employment agreement between a property owner and the real estate salesperson
    C. An employment agreement between a property owner and the listing broker
    D. The offer by the seller to sell the property at the listed price

15. **Which of the following is a requirement of an independent contractor relationship between a responsible broker and a licensee?**
    A. The licensee must enter into a written agreement with the responsible broker
    B. The licensee must not earn less than 65% of her annual income from real estate sales commissions
    C. The responsible broker must establish a daily work schedule
    D. The responsible broker must consider the licensee an employee for state and federal income tax purposes

16. **Which of the following is a characteristic of a limited partner's role in a limited partnership?**
    A. Reduced personal liability and no management decision making
    B. A fixed return on investments and a loss of income tax write-offs
    C. Official anonymity with certain tax exemptions and a loss of annual profits exceeding 20% of the investment
    D. Authority over larger decisions and active interest investment potential

17. **Which of the following instruments gives written authority to a listing licensee to sign a sales contract on an owner's behalf in the owner's absence?**
    A. Covenant of title
    B. A power of attorney
    C. A power of sale
    D. Conveyance

18. **What do special, general, and universal types of agencies have in common?**
    A. They originate with the principal
    B. They create ongoing work for the agent
    C. They empower the agent to sign all contracts for the principal
    D. They terminate upon the acceptance of an offer to purchase

19. **Under which of the following circumstances may a seller keep the earnest money deposit of a buyer?**
    A. If the buyer breaches the contract and there is a forfeiture clause
    B. If the buyer rescinds the contract and there is a forfeiture clause
    C. If the buyer cannot qualify for a mortgage and there is a mortgage contingency
    D. The seller is never entitled to the earnest money, it goes to the broker

20. **The real estate market in a property owner's area is deflated. During a listing period of 6 months, the owner lowered the price of her property a total of $20,000 before finally selling. Upset at taking such a loss on the property, the owner tells the licensee that she is going to lower the percent of commission on the property. Does the owner have a legal basis for this action?**
    A. Yes, the loss that the owner took on the property should rightfully be shared by the licensee through a lower commission rate
    B. Yes, since commission rates are negotiated, they can be changed at any time by the licensee or the seller
    C. No, once a commission rate has been negotiated and agreed upon in the listing contract, it cannot be changed unless both parties agree
    D. No, commission rates are set by the state real estate commission and cannot be changed

21. **The owner of an apartment building has just signed an agreement with a real estate firm. Has an agency been formed?**
    A. No, because an agency is formed only with a listing agreement between a seller and a real estate licensee
    B. No, because an agency with a licensee is formed only in situations of buying and selling, not managing, real estate
    C. Yes, because an agency is formed whenever one-party delegates to another the right to act on his behalf in certain business transactions
    D. Yes, because the agreement between a property owner and a property manager creates a universal agency

22. **On February 1, a licensee with ABC Realty takes a 3-month exclusive right-to-sell listing on a house. On March 1, the licensee moves out of state and inactivates his license. What happens to this listing?**
    A. It is automatically terminated
    B. It becomes an open listing contract
    C. It is voidable by the owner because the licensee is no longer active
    D. It remains a valid exclusive right-to-sell listing contract with ABC Realty

23. **Melissa is listing a property that has three roof leaks which are apparent through the upstairs bedroom ceiling. The seller wants top dollar for this property although Melissa believes that the seller should be asking for less due to the roof. Is Melissa allowed to list the property for the top dollar that the seller is asking?**
    A. No, it would be fraud for Melissa to go along with the seller in this situation
    B. Yes, as long as the roof leaks are disclosed to the purchaser
    C. Yes, and the roof leaks do not have to be disclosed to the purchaser
    D. No, houses must be listed for an amount that takes defects into account

24. **Mary signed a 4-month listing agreement, but after 42 days, she decides that she no longer wants to sell her property and informs the listing broker of her decision. When does the contract terminate?**
    A. On the last day of the four months
    B. On the day that Mary gives notice to the broker
    C. When the listing expires
    D. After the parties agree to a certain date

25. **Which of the following person is NOT usually an agent?**
    A. A broker employed by a seller
    B. A property manager employed by an owner to manage a property
    C. A broker employed by a buyer
    D. An employee of a multiple listing service

26. **A buyer and broker entered into a buyer agency agreement. The buyer's broker cooperated with another broker who was representing a seller. The buyers' broker would consider the seller to be a:**
    A. Client
    B. Principal
    C. Customer
    D. Agent

27. **A licensed real estate professional acting as an agent between two or more people in negotiating the sale, rental or purchase of a property is known as a(n):**
    A. A go between
    B. A broker
    C. A property manager
    D. An appraiser

28. **A builder has seven houses under construction and hires a real estate agent to find buyers for three of them. What type of agency relationship is most likely to have been established?**
    A. Dual agency
    B. Special agency
    C. Universal agency
    D. General agency

29. **When a seller signs an exclusive listing agreement with a broker, the real estate broker has become which of the following?**
    A. A general agent of the seller
    B. A dual agent of the seller
    C. A special agent of the seller
    D. A universal agent of the seller

30. **A salesperson of broker Callaway lists a condominium unit for sale. What position does the salesperson most probably hold in this transaction?**
    A. The salesperson has a personal relationship with the owner of the unit
    B. The salesperson acts on behalf of broker Callaway
    C. The salesperson acts on behalf of the condominium association
    D. The salesperson acts on behalf of themselves to sell the unit and claim a commission

31. **Which of the following would be considered dual agency?**
    A. A broker listing then sells the same piece of property
    B. Two brokers cooperating to sell the same piece of property
    C. A broker who is representing more than one principal at the same time
    D. A broker acting as an agent for both the buyer and the seller in the same transaction

32. **Can a broker represent both the buyer and the seller in the same transaction?**
    A. As long as the buyer and seller are both represented equally with no favoritism being shown by the broker
    B. As long as the broker is a sub-agent
    C. As long as both the buyer and seller have been informed and have given consent
    D. As long as commission is being paid by both the buyer and the seller

33. **As an exclusive agent of the buyer, a real estate broker:**
    A. Can guarantee that the property the buyer is considering an offer on will be able to be sold for at a profit later
    B. Can find a house listed in the MLS service that might fit the buyer's needs
    C. Can confide in the buyer how best to take title to the house because of the duty of POLAND
    D. Can change the terms of the offer on behalf of his buyer because of the Principal of Progression

34. **Broker Barnaby is assisting both the buyer and seller to fill out a sales contract but doesn't represent either party in this transaction. In what capacity is Broker Barnaby acting?**
    A. As a transactional broker
    B. As a dual broker
    C. As a traditional agency broker
    D. As a designated broker

35. **What type of agency is most often created when a property owner hires a broker to manage the owner's property?**
    A. A general agency
    B. A special agency
    C. A dual agency
    D. A universal agency

36. **Which of the following would BEST describe a buyer brokerage agreement?**
    A. An employment agreement between a real estate broker and the listing salesperson
    B. An employment agreement between a property owner and the real estate salesperson
    C. An employment agreement between a purchaser and the listing broker
    D. An employment agreement between a purchaser and real estate broker

37. **What type of listing agreement is it where only the listing broker AND/OR the seller can get paid?**
    A. Exclusive agency listing
    B. A net listing
    C. An exclusive right to sell listing
    D. An open listing

38. **When would a broker NOT be entitled to a commission under an Exclusive Agency listing?**
    A. The property is sold by another broker who found the listing in the MLS service
    B. The seller sells the property to their next - door neighbor
    C. The listing broker sells the property to an investor
    D. The listing broker sells the property to a customer of theirs

39. **A broker lists a home for a seller and finds a ready, willing, and able buyer during the original listing period. At closing the seller refused to pay the broker a commission. The broker sued for the commission and won, even though he couldn't prove procuring cause. What type of listing did the broker most likely have with the seller?**
    A. An open listing
    B. A net listing
    C. An Exclusive Right to Sell Listing
    D. An Exclusive Agency listing

40. **The type of listing agreement that allows for the payment of a commission to the broker even if the owner makes the sale without the help of the broker is called:**
    A. An Exclusive Agency listing
    B. An Exclusive Right to Sell listing
    C. A net listing
    D. An open listing

41. **What type of listing is prohibited in most states?**
    A. Listings that last for more than one year
    B. Listings without a safety clause
    C. Open Listings
    D. Net listings

42. **During your listing presentation, your client informs you that they want $175,000 for the house and anything above that you can keep for your commission. What type of listing would this be?**
    A. Gross listing
    B. Non - Exclusive listing
    C. Net listing
    D. Open listing

43. **Which listing agreement provides the least protection for the listing broker?**
    A. Open listing
    B. Exclusive Agency listing
    C. Exclusive Right to Sell Listing
    D. Net Listing

44. **A seller has listed their house with you for $350,000 which is $30,000 more than your CMA indicated the house is worth. After several weeks the house has not sold, and you lower the list price to $330,000 and immediately receive offers on the house. Your actions were:**
    A. Permitted because of your duties in the listing contract to find a ready, willing, and able buyer
    B. Permitted because of your duties of performance
    C. Prohibited because of the Principal of Substitution
    D. Prohibited because of your duties of Obedience

45. **You have an exclusive listing agreement with a seller. You bring the seller several offers, and the seller asks you the race and color of the buyer for each of the offers you unilaterally have in hand. You respectfully decline to answer. Have you violated your duties to your client?**
    A. Yes, you owe complete loyalty and notice to your client
    B. Yes, race and color are protected classes and the seller is making sure not to violate these
    C. No, the non - disclosure of race and color are not violations of your duties to your client
    D. No, as these are material facts which do not need to be disclosed

46. **You plan on advertising your client's local property in a national publication. Your client asks you not to advertise in that publication. The broker does as the client has instructed. Has the broker acted wisely?**
    A. No, advertising the property nationally would have brought a much higher price for your client which would have satisfied the economic principal of Highest and Best Use
    B. No, the advertising was being paid for by the broker and therefore the client was not burdened by the expense but would have benefited with the higher exposure
    C. Yes, as the client knows that the national publication would not have been seen by local buyers and therefore would have been a waste of money
    D. Yes, because the broker owes loyalty and obedience to the client

47. **A piece of residential property is listed by you with an Exclusive Right to Sell listing which will terminate in 6 months. During the listing period which of the following facts would you not have to disclose to potential buyers?**
    A. A new school is going to be built in 7 months across the street
    B. The seller is a moving to another state in 30 days
    C. A solid waste site which was closed and capped 5 years ago is ½ mile away
    D. A proposed highway that would have had a nearby exit to the property has been canceled

48. **Your seller has advised you that they are not willing to accept any offer under the asking price of $350,000. You receive 5 offers on the property, 3 of the offers are well below the asking price. What is your best course of action?**
    A. Present the offers that conform to your clients wishes
    B. Present just the highest offer and once your seller accepts it the others don't matter
    C. Present the acceptable offers and tell your clients the others didn't meet their requirements
    D. Present all offers

49. **Which of the following best defines the law of agency?**
    A. The rules and regulations that apply in all real estate transactions
    B. The principles that govern your conduct in business
    C. The rules of law that apply when a person acts on behalf of another
    D. The business of real estate brokerage

50. **A seller leads a buyer to believe that the seller's daughter is representing her in the sale of her home. The daughter tells the buyer that her mother will accept $300,000 for the home and the buyer goes and obtains a loan for that amount. In this case, the seller may be accused of creating:**
    A. Implied Agency
    B. Actual Agency
    C. Ostensible Agency
    D. Exclusive Agency

Chapter 2 Answers

1. B	6. C	11. C	16. D	21. A	26. D	31. B	36. C	41. A
2. B	7. C	12. A	17. B	22. C	27. A	32. D	37. C	
3. A	8. B	13. A	18. A	23. C	28. A	33. A	38. A	
4. C	9. B	14. D	19. D	24. D	29. B	34. B	39. B	
5. D	10. B	15. A	20. D	25. C	30. B	35. B	40. A	

1. Sub-agency
2. Designated Agency
3. Listing Agent
4. Patent Defect
5. Principal
6. Scope of Authority
7. Affiliation Agreement
8. Safety/Protection Clause
9. Customer (Third Party)
10. Exclusive Agency
11. Implied Agency
12. Material Fact
13. Power of Attorney
14. Open Listing
15. Purchase and Sale Agreement
16. Buyer's Agency
17. Agency
18. Listing Agreement
19. Dual Agency
20. Transaction Agent
21. Actual Agency
22. Exclusive Right to Sell
23. Special Agency
24. Latent Defect
25. Due Diligence
26. Selling Agent
27. Ostensible Agency
28. Net Listing
29. Ministerial Acts
30. Procuring Cause
31. Fiduciary
32. Co-Operative Agreement
33. Caveat Emptor
34. Employee
35. Universal Agent
36. General Agent
37. Agent
38. Ratification
39. Independent Contractor
40. Implied Agency
41. Commission

Exercise 1

1 B	3 H	5 M	7 L	9 I	11 C	13 N
2 A	4 E	6 J	8 D	10 G	12 F	14 K

Exercise 2

1. B	3. L	5. F	7. H	9. C	11. K	13. J
2. I	4. A	6. E	8. M	10. G	12. N	14. D

Exercise 3

1. B	3. M	5. A	7. D	9. K	11. G	13. E
2. J	4. L	6. I	8. H	10. F	12. C	

1. Universal, Special, General

2. An agent hired for a purpose that is limited time and scope

3. Special

4. General

5. The agent's specific duties and speak to compensation while there and when you depart

6. Personal Performance, Obedience, Loyalty, Accountability, Notice, Due Care

7. The Agent

8. Obedience

9. A principal authorizes an unauthorized act after the fact and agrees to be bound by it

10. Ostensible Agency

11. The Seller; all parties represent the seller

12. Seller

13. Latent defects (cannot be seen or discovered)

14. The Agent

15. The Principal

16. Principal lies about a repair and the agent is held responsible for the principal's lie

17. An agent can show where the earnest money is; an agent doesn't convert or commingle funds

18. Buyer and Seller

19. Broker and Sales Agent

20. Broker and Seller

21. Compensation, Reimbursement, Indemnification, Performance

22. Open Listing

23. Exclusive Right to Sell

24. He was the procuring cause of the sale

25. No One

26. The buyer

27. A ready, willing, and able buyer is brought to meet the seller's terms

28. Are within the scope of the agent's authority

29. Be informed of and knowingly consent to it

30. Death of the Principal or Agent, Supervening Illegality, Bankruptcy of Principal or Agent, Complete Destruction of the property, Mutual Agreement

31. Honesty, Accountability, Due Care, Disclosure of Latent Defects

SECTION 7 ANSWERS:

1. C. Sub-agency results in both brokers in the transaction representing the seller and no agent representing the purchaser. When Broker Smith brought the buyer, he became an agent of Broker Bob. Since he is Broker Bob's agent and Broker Bob represents the seller, Broker Smith also represents the seller

2. B. Even though leases do not expire on the death of the landlord, when the principal dies (Sal), the agency is automatically terminated. Thus, ABC Realty no longer has authority to collect the rent from the tenants

3. C. As long as the offer has a contingency in it indicating that it cannot be accepted until the first contract falls through, it can be accepted on that basis. But an offer cannot be outright accepted when there is another contract on the property

4. D. Your sister is an agent representing the seller. While your sister is working with the buyer, she doesn't represent the buyer. However, your sister's broker represents the seller, thereby making your sister an agent of the seller. She represents whomever her broker represents in a transaction

5. C. Net Listings are those where the seller is stating that he wants to clear a certain amount at closing, but that the broker can take any amount left over as commission. These are illegal in most states

6. B. The sales agent's (or any agent's) authority is given to him by the terms of the agency agreement. Here, the agency agreement is the affiliation agreement between agent and broker

7. B. All agents must turn earnest money over to the brokers as soon as possible unless all parties have agreed to another time

8. D. All agency contracts should address commission with the broker while in the employ and when the agent departs the brokerage

9. C. There is no problem listing property that needs repairs, but all latent defects must still be disclosed. No agent can use the term "as is" to get around the disclosure requirement

10. B. There is no problem with taking the listing in this situation but you would keep the information confidential. A seller can sell it for whatever price he chooses and foreclosure doesn't prevent sale

11. D. This is probably self-explanatory. When a person is represented by another broker, the other agent in the transaction must remain totally neutral and should not comment on the relationship

12. D. The person looking at the house is a third party/customer at the moment. You should continue treating them as such throughout the transaction. Dual agency can only occur when you have principals/clients on both sides

13. A. All pre qualifications (better would be a pre-approval) should be done prior to entering into the contract, not after

14. C. The listing agreement is the agency between the listing broker as agent and the seller as principal

15. A. All agents (independent contractors) must sign an agreement with the broker that states how the licensee will be compensated while in the employ, the scope of the authority, and how they will be compensated upon departure

16. A. A limited partner is not responsible for the day-to-day activities and as such, has limited liability

17. B. A power of attorney is the only document that would allow the agent to sign a listing contract on behalf of the owner. The listing agreement doesn't extend this authority

18. A. The principal is the person who creates the type of agent it wants. The scope of the authority (type of agent) is created by the principal

19. A. The only clear instance is if the buyer breaches the contract and the contract has language that says the seller can keep the earnest money. Rescission is not a breach. If the buyer cannot qualify, he gets the earnest money back, and the earnest money would go to the seller

20. C. No, the commission is negotiated during the listing period. There are times when a seller can ask for a renegotiation, but the agent doesn't have to accept the offer to renegotiate. Often, the seller gets less than asking but the commission is still based on whatever sales price the seller accepts

21. C. Yes, because an agency is formed whenever one-party delegates to another the right to act on his behalf in certain business transactions

22. D. The licensee is not the AGENT under the listing, the broker ABC Realty is. Therefore, the listing continues

23. C. The seller can list a property for whatever price the seller wishes as she is the principal and in this case, the agent is not obligated to disclosure the roof leaks because they are patent

24. B. The contract between Mary and the broker is one of agency. Mary is the principal and wishes to terminate her agreement. Mary is not forced to sell her home and there is no indication here that the broker performed. In such case, Mary's contract terminates on notice to the broker and she will not have any further obligation to the broker

25. D. In each situation, an agency is created and while technically, all employees are agents of the employer, in the context of this question, D would be the best answer

26. C. The buyer's broker is representing the buyer and thus, has no relationship with the seller. Therefore, the seller is a customer to him

27. B. The broker is essentially the facilitator of the sale

28. B. It doesn't matter how many houses the builder has; each agreement is a separate special agency that will end with the sale of that house

29. C. Because the agency is limited in both time and scope, the broker is a special agent of the seller

30. B. In most states, the salesperson works the transaction and has authority to speak with the seller because the salesperson's contract with the broker gives her that authority. But all contracts are the broker's

31. D. Whenever there is one agent or broker within the same agency representing both sides of a transaction (seller and buyer), a dual agency is created

32. C. The most important issue relating to dual agency is that the parties give their informed consent to it and understand the probable outcome of it. Dual agency is not illegal unless it is undisclosed

33. B. The broker can assist in finding a home, but must never exceed the authority given. Brokers/agents are also not allowed to make guarantees relating to profit or value of the home and definitely cannot give advice as to how to take title to the property

34. A. Because Broker Barnaby doesn't represent anyone in the transaction, he can only be a transactional broker

35. A. Property Managers can bind the owner in the day-to-day operations of the business and it is an ongoing relationship. Thus, it is a general agency

36. D. The agency created by a purchaser hiring a broker to find him a home that he is ready, willing and able to purchase

37. A. In an exclusive agency, the seller is only hiring one broker, but the seller is also retaining the right to sell the home herself. Essentially, the seller and broker are in competition to see who can sell the home first

38. B. In an exclusive agency, if the seller sells the property first, there is no obligation to pay the broker

39. C. Even though the broker couldn't prove procuring cause, he didn't have to as the broker would get paid anytime the property is sold during his listing period

40. B. An exclusive right to sell means the broker will get paid if the property is sold during the listing period. It doesn't matter who sells the property

41. D. Most states would prohibit net listings because the broker is a fiduciary and shouldn't benefit off of his client

42. C. A net listing is when a broker is allowed to keep the excess of the proceeds over the amount the seller wished to receive and is illegal in most states

43. A. An open listing does not provide any exclusivity to any one broker. So, it is essentially a free for all. Whomever sells the property first gets the commission

44. D. An agent can never lower the price of the listed property even if the property does sell without the permission of the seller

45. C. An agent has not violated his duties of obedience when the seller asks the agent to do something illegal. Discussion of the offeror's race would be a fair housing violation

46. D. The broker must be loyal and obedient to the client unless being asked to do something illegal

47. B. The agent would not have to disclose the seller's plans. However, the school, solid waste site, and proposed highway are all material facts that would require disclosure

48. D. An agent should present all offers to the seller in order for the seller to make the best decision. The agent has no authority to make the decision for the seller and must provide all offers. Note: In some states, the offer isn't presented under the obedience duty

49. C. Agency law determines when a principal would be responsible for his agent's actions

50. C. Ostensible agency is where one party (seller) leads another party (buyer) to believe that a third party (daughter) is representing her

Chapter 3: Practice of Real Estate

Section 1: *Outline*

Practice of Real Estate – A compilation of Federal law, Local Law, Police Power

A. Trust/escrow accounts

1. Purpose and definition of trust accounts, including monies held in trust accounts

The purpose of a trust account is to protect client's funds. In most states, brokers who handle funds on behalf of another must have a trust account. Because these are **NOT** the Broker's Funds, they are typically **NOT** subject to **ATTACHMENT.** State Law determines **TRUST ACCOUNT** specifics.

2. Responsibility for trust monies, including commingling/ conversion

The Broker has a **FIDUCIARY** responsibility to the **PRINCIPAL** to handle all **EARNEST MONEY** responsibly. The Broker is a **TRUSTEE** for the monies received during the transaction and they must go into a special **TRUST ACCOUNT.**
COMMINGLING – Mixing the **TRUST ACCOUNT** funds with **OPERATING ACCOUNT** funds or *CONVERSION* – **Converting** the funds for her **own use** are both **ILLEGAL** activities which can result in loss of license.

B. Federal fair housing laws and the ADA

Intended to eliminate discrimination in housing and as such, any violation can have serious implications. These laws only relate to residential property

The law created MINORITIES – classes of people who receive special protection, but who are not **MINORITIES** in the traditional sense, but based upon their inferior social, employment, wealth, and education status.

1. Protected classes

    a. Family – Only those families with children under the age of 18 are protected (final amendment).
    b. Race – No discrimination can ever occur based on race. It has no exemptions (initially).
    c. Sex – Male and Female Only; LGBTQ folks do not have any protection (first amendment).
    d. Handicap – Landlord must allow reasonable modifications to the property (final amendment).
    e. Color – rarely tested, just know it's a category (initially).
    f. Religion – No discrimination against any religion (initially).
    g. Nationality – rarely tested but recognizes people from certain countries (initially).

2. Prohibited conduct (red-lining, blockbusting, steering)

   a. Blockbusting – term used to describe a licensee soliciting business from prospects by stating that changes in their neighborhood, based on fair housing categories will diminish property value, increase crime and antisocial behavior

   b. Red-lining – a practice by lenders who refuse to make loans in certain areas

   c. Steering – limit a prospect's choice of neighborhoods based on any of the protected categories

   d. Less Favorable Treatment – treating minority customer or client less favorably than a non-minority customer or client.

   e. Discrimination – licensee refuses to show properties to a minority prospect or refuse to present an offer

   f. Improper Listing – a licensee takes a listing on a property knowing that the owner wishes to place restrictions on the parties to whom the property can be shown

   g. Advertising – indication of any preference or limitation based on protected category

3. Americans with Disabilities (ADA) – covers two primary areas

   Jobs – People with disabilities cannot be denied jobs that they may otherwise be able to do with reasonable modifications.

   Access – All new construction and remodeling of public buildings post July 1992 must be accessible to the handicap. There is a potential exception for remodeling that would cause significant hardship. ex. Grab bars, wide doors, entry ramps, parking, door access buttons

4. **Exemptions**

   While there are certain exemptions, discrimination based on race is *NEVER* tolerated. The Four Exemptions:

   1. A **single-family** homeowner:

      · **For sale by owner (No Broker is used).**
      · **No discriminatory advertising** can be used.
      · The owner is the **current** or **most recent resident.**
      · The owner does not have an interest in **more than three dwellings (investor).**

   2. **Mrs. Murphy's: Owner Occupied 1-4 family**

      · **For sale by owner (no broker is used).**
      · **No discriminatory advertising** can be used.

   3. **Private Clubs:**

      · Can discriminate in the sale or rental of housing as long as there is no discrimination in its membership.

   4. **Religious Organizations:**

      · Can discriminate in the sale or rental of housing as long as there is no discrimination in its membership.

      Other Exemptions:

      • Handicap is interpreted very broadly. Landlord must make reasonable accommodations for those with physical or mental disabilities even if it is AIDS, Cancer, Alcoholism, and Recovering addicts. It also requires exceptions to no parking or pet policy.
      • A landlord cannot discriminate against families with children under 18. This also includes putting them all in one building.
      • Senior Housing over 62 can discriminate against children and over 55 housing where 80% of residents are over 55.
      • Only Males/Females have protection. No LGBTQ rights

Equal Housing Opportunity – Display of the Equal Opportunity poster indicates and intent to comply with the law

C. Advertising and technology

1. Advertising practices

   a. Truth in advertising

   - All advertising must be done in a manner that is free from misrepresentation and fraud
   - **Puffing** (a statement of exaggeration that a reasonable person would know is untrue)
   - **Blind Ads** – Any advertisement that is missing necessary information (broker's name)

   b. Fair housing issues in advertising

   - A broker may not advertise in any manner showing a **preference for or limitation against** any **protected class.**
   - Brokers may use fair housing items, such as a church as a landmark to describe where a home is located

2. Use of technology

   a. Requirements for confidential information – Each state will have different laws, but overall, when using technology, brokers are to ensure that all client information remains confidential and can only be accessed by those with authority to do so.

   b) Do-Not-Call List – **Purpose:** Shield consumers from unwanted calls; realtors are considered telemarketers; they must follow the law set forth.

   - The law prohibits calls to numbers on the **DO NOT CALL LIST.**
   - Calls can only be made from **8:00 am – 9:00 pm.**
   - Once a number appears on the list, calls to that number must **cease in 31 days.**
   - Any consumer can request no further calls and the agent must comply

   ### Exceptions:

   - **Prior Business Relationship:** A telemarketer may call this number for 18 months from the last transaction
   - **Prior Inquiry:** A telemarketer may call this number for 3 months from the last inquiry.
   - **Granted Permission:** Calls can be made to those granting permission regardless of DO NOT CALL STATUS.

   CAN-SPAM Act of 2003 – Controlling mass emails. False or misleading header information is prohibited and must identity the person or business that sent it, a valid postal address must be included, subject line must be accurate, there must be a clear indication that the transmission is an advertisement or solicitation, must provide clear opt-out-provision and it must be removed within 10 days

D. Licensee and responsibilities

1. **Employee** – Broker Pays Your Taxes, Social Security, Insurance, Worker's Comp, receive a W-2, and the Broker has **CONTROL** over your movements.
2. **Independent Contractor** – Pay Your Own Taxes, Social Security, Insurance, Worker's Comp, receive a 1099, make your own hours, and you are only accountable to the broker for **RESULTS** of your work.
3. **Due diligence for real estate transactions**

   - Present **ALL** offers timely unless SPECIFICALLY told by your principal to NOT present it.
   - Never reveal client confidences unless it's against the law
   - Never fail to perform your due diligence
   - Always recommend that that your client contact the appropriate professionals

E. Antitrust laws

1. Antitrust laws and purpose

   - Enacted to protect the public from **anti-competitive behavior.**
   - The goal is to keep industries competitive for service and pricing.
   - Any monopolistic activity or one which endangers competition.
   - Look for activity **OUTSIDE OF THE BROKERAGE**, not within it
   - Results in **Significant penalties** for violation – jail, lost license, civil penalties of 10 years and $1,000,000 for **Individuals** and $100,000,000 for **Corporations**

2. Antitrust violations in real estate

   - Conspiring to fix commission rates
   - Dividing markets by exclusive territories
   - Conspiring to not to do business with a third company
   - Tie-In contracts: the sale of the first tied to the purchase of the second

Section 2: *Vocabulary*

Americans with Disabilities Act: Laws protecting a handicap person's access to employment and public buildings

Blind Ad: An ad that is missing certain essential elements

Blockbusting: Inducing homeowners to sell by telling them that certain "minorities" are moving into the area

Can Spam Act: A federal law that sets the rules for commercial email and text messaging

Commingling: Illegally mixing client funds with personal funds

Conversion: Utilizing client's funds for one's own

Discrimination: Refusing to work with a minority prospect

Do Not Call Registry: Registration of residential phone numbers to eliminate unsolicited phone calls

Federal Fair Housing Law: Prohibits discrimination in housing based on certain protected "minorities"

Improper listing: Taking a listing while knowing the owner wishes to place illegal restrictions on it

Less Favorable Treatment: Treating fair housing "minorities" different in the selling, buying, or leasing of real property

Minority: A protected class under the federal fair housing law

Puffing: An exaggerated statement that reasonable person would know is untrue

Redlining: Banks' refusal to make loans in certain geographic locations

Referral Fee: Money paid in exchange for leads when no service was performed

Steering: Limiting a prospective buyers' choice of neighborhoods based upon fair housing categories

Sherman Anti-Trust Law: Law designed to protect the public from activity endangering competition

Tie-in contracts: Requiring the sale of the first product or service be tied to a second product or service purchase

Trust Account: Account where client funds are kept separate from broker funds

Section 3: *Recall Multiple Choice*

1. **Registration of residential phone numbers to eliminate unsolicited phone calls**
   A. Consumer Protection List
   B. Limited Denial of Participation Registry
   C. Do Not Call Registry
   D. Can-spam Act

2. **Limiting a prospective buyers' choice of neighborhoods based upon fair housing categories**
   A. Redlining
   B. Steering
   C. Blockbusting
   D. Puffing

3. **When a broker utilizes client's funds for his own**
   A. Defamation
   B. Conversion
   C. Commingling
   D. Steering

4. **A federal law that sets the rules for commercial email and text messaging**
   A. Nothing
   B. Do Not Call Act
   C. Truth-in-mailing Act
   D. Can Spam Act

5. **Money paid in exchange for leads when no service was performed**
   A. Contingent Fee
   B. Referral Fee
   C. Referral Agent
   D. Non audit Fee

6. **Illegally mixing deposits collected from a client with personal funds**
   A. Commingling
   B. Conversion
   C. Redlining
   D. Blockbusting

7. **Refusing to work with a minority prospect**
   A. Segregation
   B. Intimidation
   C. Redlining
   D. Discrimination

8. **An ad that is missing certain essential elements**
   A. Display Ad
   B. Tax Certificate
   C. Ad Valorem Property Tax
   D. Blind Ad

9. **Prohibits discrimination in housing based on certain protected categories, called "minorities"**
   A. Americans With Disabilities Act
   B. 1844 Civil Rights Act
   C. Sherman Anti-Trust Act
   D. Federal Fair Housing Law

10. **Banks' refusal to make loans in certain geographic locations**
    A. Commingling
    B. Steering
    C. Blockbusting
    D. Redlining

11. **Taking a listing while knowing the owner wishes to place restrictions on it**
    A. Incentive zoning
    B. Cost basis
    C. Referral fee
    D. Improper listing

12. **An exaggerated statement that reasonable person would know is untrue**
    A. Steering
    B. Puffing
    C. Commingling
    D. Blockbusting

13. **Inducing homeowners to sell by telling them that certain "minorities" are moving into the area**
    A. Steering
    B. Commingling
    C. Redlining
    D. Blockbusting

14. **Treating a fair housing "minorities" different in the selling, buying, or leasing of real property**
    A. Less Favorable Treatment
    B. Tax Abatement
    C. Discrimination
    D. Board Of Arbitration

15. **Laws protecting a handicap person's access to employment and public buildings**
    A. Fair Labor Standards Act
    B. Americans with Disabilities Act
    C. Federal Fair Housing Law
    D. Fair Housing Act

16. **Law designed to protect the public from any activity endangering competition**
    A. Equal Credit Opportunity Act
    B. Sherman Anti-Trust Law
    C. Fair Credit Reporting Act
    D. Clayton Anti-Trust Act

17. **Requiring the sale of the first product or service be tied to a second purchase**
    A. Transfer tax
    B. Independent contractor
    C. Tie-in contracts
    D. Cost basis

18. Account where client funds are kept separate from broker funds
   A. Earnest Money
   B. General Account
   C. Cost Basis
   D. Trust Account

19. A protected class under the federal fair housing law
   A. Minors
   B. Majority
   C. Minority
   D. Redlining

Section 4: *Recall Fill-In*

1. An ad that is missing certain essential elements

_____

2. An exaggerated statement that reasonable person would know is untrue

_____

3. Requiring the sale of the first product or service be tied to a second purchase

_____

4. Refusing to work with a minority prospect

_____

5. Account where client funds are kept separate from broker funds

_____

6. Laws that prohibit discrimination in housing based on certain protected categories, called "minorities"

_____

7. Registration of residential phone numbers to eliminate unsolicited phone calls

_____

8. Laws protecting a handicap person's access to employment and public buildings

_____

9. Law designed to protect the public from activity endangering competition

_____

10. Inducing homeowners to sell by telling them that certain "minorities" are moving into the area

_____

11. Illegally mixing deposits collected from a client with personal funds

_____

12. Taking a listing while knowing the owner wishes to place restrictions on it

_____

13. Treating a fair housing "minorities" different in the selling, buying, or leasing of real property

_____

14. A protected class under the federal fair housing law

_____

15. A federal law that sets the rules for commercial email and text messaging

_____

16. Limiting a prospective buyers' choice of neighborhoods based upon fair housing categories

_____

17. Money paid in exchange for leads when no service was performed

_____

18. When a broker utilizes client's funds for his own

_____

19. Banks' refusal to make loans in certain geographic locations

_____

Section 5: *Matching*

A	Commingling	1	_____	A federal law that sets the rules for commercial email and text messaging
B	Minority	2	_____	Name used for those seeking to protect under Federal Fair Housing
C	Blockbusting	3	_____	There are 7 of these under the Federal Fair housing law
D	Puffing	4	_____	Account where client funds are kept separate from broker funds
E	Redlining	5	_____	An exaggerated statement that reasonable person would know is untrue
F	Independent Contractor	6	_____	Banks' refusal to make loans in certain geographic locations.
G	Conversion	7	_____	Illegally mixing deposits collected from a client with personal funds
H	Protected category	8	_____	Inducing homeowners to sell by telling them that certain "minorities" are moving into the area
I	Cam Spam Act	9	_____	Law designed to protect the public from activity endangering competition
J	Intimidation	10	_____	One who works for, receives payment from, but not controlled by the employer.
K	Trust Account	11	_____	Purposely frightening another person through threatening words, looks, or body language.
L	Sherman Antitrust Law	12	_____	When an utilizes client's funds for his own

A	Blind Ad	1	_____	An ad that is missing certain essential elements
B	Federal Fair Housing Law	2	_____	Laws protecting a handicap person's access to employment and public buildings
C	Discrimination	3	_____	Federal legislation intended to prohibit racial discrimination in the real estate.
D	Improper listing	4	_____	Limiting a prospective buyers' choice of neighborhoods based upon fair housing categories
E	Civil Rights Act of 1866	5	_____	Money paid in exchange for leads when no service was performed
F	Employee	6	_____	One who works for, receives compensation from, and is controlled by an employer.
G	Less Favorable Treatment	7	_____	Prohibits discrimination in housing based on certain protected categories, called "minorities"
H	Americans with Disabilities Act	8	_____	Refusing to work with a minority prospect
I	Referral Fee	9	_____	Registration of residential phone numbers to eliminate unsolicited phone calls
J	Tie-In Contract	10	_____	Requiring the sale of the first product or service be tied to a second purchase
K	Steering	11	_____	Taking a listing while knowing the owner wishes to place restrictions on it
L	Do Not Call Registry	12	_____	Treating a fair housing "minorities" different in the selling, buying, or leasing of real property.

Section 6: *Analysis Fill-In*

1. **Which Fair Housing Category prevents discrimination in all circumstances?**

_____

2. **Can a landlord charge a pet fee to a handicapped person who requires the animal?**

_____

3. **Can you ever refuse to show an African American family a property in a $500,000 neighborhood?**

_____

4. **Name 4 differences between an employee and independent contractor:**

_____

5. **What actions does Sherman Antitrust act make illegal?**

_____

6. **How long do you have to unsubscribe someone from an email list?**

_____

7. **What times of day are "do not call" registry calls permitted?**

_____

8. **How long do you have to call a prior contact under the do not call rules?**

_____

9. **Can you call a prior client who is listed on the do not call registry?**

_____

10. **When can an agent advertise a property in his own name?**

_____

11. **Give an example of puffing:**

_____

12. **Give an example of a Blind Ad:**

_____

13. **Name one situation where you can discriminate against a handicapped person:**

_____

14. Give an example of conversion of funds:

_____

15. What's the difference between a trust account and an operating account?

_____

16. What are the main categories covered by the ADA?

_____

17. Give an example of Blockbusting:

_____

18. Give an example of Steering:

_____

19. Name the 7 Fair Housing Categories

_____

20. There are Four Main Fair Housing Category Exemptions, Name Two:

_____

Section 7: *Analysis Multiple Choice*

1. **An African American family requests to see properties in only $500,000 neighborhoods, but you refuse to show them those neighborhoods because they are only pre-approved for $350,000. Have you committed a fair housing violation?**
   A. Yes, this is an example of steering and is not permitted under the fair housing law
   B. Yes, this is an example of blockbusting and is not permitted under the fair housing law
   C. No, this is totally permissible behavior on the part of the agent and no violation has occurred
   D. Yes, because the agent is obligated to show them properties in any neighborhood they wish

2. **Holly is building a new 5,600 square foot home which will be completed in two weeks. It will have a total of 8 bedrooms and 7 bathrooms, but only the 2 bedrooms on the main floor will be handicap accessible. There are 10 stairs to get to the main house and no ramp. Henry is a UPS driver who will make deliveries to the home. Henry sues Holly prior to completion of construction attempting to force her to install a ramp. What is the probable result?**
   A. Holly will have to install a ramp so that Henry can access the property
   B. Holly will not have to install a ramp since her home is not open to the public
   C. Holly will have to install a ramp since the property is being built after 1979
   D. Holly will not have to install a ramp due to laches

3. **A newly constructed apartment building for people 55 and over has opened. Prior to completion and taking applications, the developer made it clear that no children under the age of 18 would be allowed to reside there. Is this permissible?**
   A. Yes, as long as 80% of the occupants are 55 and older
   B. No, the exemption only applies to housing of persons 62 and older
   C. No, discrimination against children is never allowed
   D. Yes, because there was notice before taking applications

4. **Sally is the listing agent on a home. Mary, an agent, brings a prospective purchaser, John, who Mary is representing. John happens to notice that there are several African American children playing in the playground near the house. So, John asks Mary if she could tell him what the demographics are in the neighborhood. Mary is uncomfortable at this line of questioning, but she understands her role as a fiduciary to her principal. Mary's best reply would be:**
   A. The local school district would probably have that information
   B. That she can find out the information and provide it
   C. It doesn't matter because those children are from another neighborhood
   D. Any discussion of neighborhood demographics is against the law

5. **An agent has a new listing. In her ad to direct people to the home, she states that people should make a left on Midway Street. That's the corner where the Target sits on the left and Watkins Church sits on the right. Has the agent committed any fair housing violation?**
   A. Yes, because the agent didn't have to mention the church at all
   B. No, because the agent also included Target in her ad
   C. Yes, any mention of a church is a violation
   D. No, because the agent is only referring to the church for direction clarity, not preference

6. **A broker is holding funds for his seller in a trust account. During this period of time, a judgment is entered against the broker and the creditor is attempting to collect. The broker owes $37,000 and has $30,000 of it in his operating account. After seizing that account, the creditor goes after the trust account to get the balance of the funds. Will the creditor be able to attach that account?**
   A. Yes, but only for the $7,000 that it is owed
   B. No, trust accounts cannot be attached unless it was for the client's funds
   C. No, trust accounts can never be attached
   D. Yes, but only with notice to all parties involved

7. **Calls that are impacted by the Federal Do Not Call registry can be made between:**
   A. 9 AM and 8 PM
   B. 8 AM and 9 PM
   C. 8 AM and 9:30 PM
   D. 8:30 AM and 9:30 PM

8. **The Federal Do Not Call registry:**
   A. Applies to realtors only
   B. Applies to anyone making unsolicited calls to others
   C. Applies to most industries
   D. Applies to all calls made between 8 AM and 9 PM

9. **In which situation would a fair housing violation result?**
   A. A retirement home where at least 80% of the people are over 55 decide that they do not want to rent to children under 18
   B. A synagogue refuses to rent to a person of Muslim faith but does allow the Muslim to worship
   C. A homeowner who just moved out of her single-family home refuses to rent to an African American family
   D. An owner occupant of a duplex refuses to rent to a handicapped person

10. **Jovanni works for ABC Realty Partners, a real estate brokerage, in a right to work state, on a one-year contract, but it doesn't mention whether Jovanni is an employee or independent contractor. Jovanni's agreement with the brokerage indicates that on Fridays, Jovanni will be paid $500 in exchange for being in the office from 9-2 pm Monday - Friday. His duties essentially included answering the phones, filing, and dealing with people as they walk in. Jovanni is fully trained by ABC to perform these tasks. Jovanni will receive a 1099 at the end of the year, pay his own health insurance, and be responsible to pay his own worker's compensation and disability insurance. After 4 months on the job, ABC fires Jovanni and Jovanni sues ABC stating that he was an employee, not an independent contractor. ABC claims the opposite. Who is correct?**
    A. Jovanni, since he was an employee of ABC due to the amount of control
    B. ABC, since Jovanni was an independent contractor due to him paying his own expenses
    C. Jovanni, because he would've had to agree to be an employee of ABC
    D. ABC, since Jovanni agreed to be an independent contractor

11. **Modeste is a sales agent with RPM Venture Partners Real Estate, a licensed brokerage. Modeste is an independent contractor. As such, RPM cannot require:**
    A. That Modeste be in the office from 9 am - 12 noon Monday - Friday
    B. That Modeste read all rules and regulations as provided to him
    C. That Modeste not engage in the practice of steering
    D. That Modeste provide an ACH account for payment

12. **Mary is attempting to sell her single-family home without a broker. She has had on the market for 61 days. She is the most recent occupant. In her ad, she states that she doesn't want any people with children under the age of 18 because the neighbors on both sides are over 65 years of age. Is this permissible?**
    A. Yes, it is fine because she is not using a broker to sell the home
    B. Yes, because both neighbors are over the age of 62, so they get an exemption
    C. No, because discrimination is never allowed even by a for sale by owner
    D. No, because she used discriminatory advertising

13. **You need to contact a prior client who is on the Do Not Call Registry. Can you contact them?**
    A. Yes, as long as its prior to 9 PM and for up to 18 months since your last transaction with them
    B. Yes, as long as its prior to 9 PM and for up to 3 months since your last transaction with them
    C. No, because they are already on the Do Not Call Registry, you cannot call them
    D. Yes, if you have first received permission to call them and then you cannot call past 8 PM

14. **A broker advertises a property to have the most beautiful backyard that he has ever seen. The buyer purchases the property based on the broker's assertions. When the backyard of the month contest comes around, the buyer doesn't win. He sues the broker for false advertising. What is the result?**
    A. The purchaser should have checked out the other backyards before purchasing
    B. The "most beautiful backyard" is considered puffing
    C. The "most beautiful backyard" could reasonably be interpreted as being the most beautiful
    D. The broker engaged in false advertising

15. **A broker advertises a property as having the largest lot in the neighborhood. The purchaser purchases the land based upon the broker's assertions. Can the broker be accused of false advertising?**
    A. No, the purchaser should have found out the exact measurements of the lot
    B. No, because "largest lot" is considered puffing
    C. Yes, because "largest lot" couldn't reasonably be interpreted as being the largest
    D. Yes, because "largest lot" could reasonably be interpreted as being the largest lot

16. **The Federal Do Not Call Registry would allow an agent to call:**
    A. A former client only if not listed on the registry for up to 18 months
    B. A former client listed on the registry for up to 18 months
    C. A former contact only if not listed on the registry for up to 12 months
    D. A former contact only if not listed on the registry for up to 3 months

17. **Which scenario would be entitled to an exemption under the Federal Fair Housing Law?**
    A. Sally refuses to rent a room in her home to a lesbian female
    B. John refuses to rent an apartment in his 5-family dwelling to a family
    C. A single-family homeowner with a broker refuses to sell her property to a transgender person
    D. A private club refuses to rent a room to a woman but allows her membership into the club

18. **John is blind and wants to become an Uber driver. Uber refuses to hire him for that position due to his handicap. John sues. What is the probable result?**
    A. Uber will lose because discrimination against the handicap is not permitted
    B. Uber will lose unless it can find another position that John can do at Uber
    C. Uber will win since John is mentally impaired
    D. Uber will win because the ADA only requires reasonable accommodations

19. **Federal Fair Housing prohibits discrimination based on:**
    A. Race
    B. Sexual orientation
    C. Marital Status
    D. Age

20. **A mortgage broker contacts a bank on behalf of his client who is perfect by all banking standards. The bank, however, refuses to look at the client's credit profile, stating that the zip code where the property is located has a high percentage of crime and property values. Due to the increased risk, the bank policy is that it doesn't loan in that area. This is an example of:**
    A. Blockbusting, but it would be legal in this circumstance
    B. Redlining, and it is never legal
    C. Redlining, but it is legal here, due to the bank's increased risk
    D. Blockbusting and it is never legal

21. **A licensee plans to send out an e-mail offering his services. According to the CAN-SPAM Act, the licensee must**
    A. Include only the brokerage firm's name in the "Reply-To" line
    B. E-mail individuals who have given prior permission to be e-mailed
    C. Hire a company to market services
    D. Tell recipients how to opt out of receiving future e-mail

22. **Augusta National Golf Club has several rental units on its property for PGA golfers only. The charge for this housing is only $30 per night. Is this policy a violation of federal fair housing?**
    A. Yes, because once a price is charged, the exemption is lost
    B. Yes, because all housing must be open to everyone
    C. No, unless they are discriminating based on race
    D. No, since Golf Clubs always have an exemption

23. **Which of the following is NOT true about inducing sellers to sell in certain neighborhoods?**
    A. It only applies to race
    B. It applies to all protected classes
    C. It is activity normally engaged in by a sales agent
    D. It is also known as blockbusting

24. **John is the owner of a 4-family house where he lives upstairs. He rents out all other units. He places an ad in the local newspaper for one of the downstairs rentals. The ad is answered by a young, handicapped person. The person tells John that he would need a ramp installed in order to be able to move into the premises. The ramp is going to cost about $10,000. John decides that the ramp cost too much and decides not to rent to the person. Can John do this?**
    A. Yes, because John would have to bear the cost of the ramp
    B. Yes, because John doesn't have to rent to a handicapped person
    C. No, since John wouldn't have to bear the cost of the ramp, he must rent to the person
    D. No, because discrimination is never tolerated

25. **If Mary, a seller, wishes to sell her home that she currently lives in without advertising it and without the help of a broker, can she discriminate against others in that sale?**
    A. No, discrimination is never tolerated
    B. No, because she cannot sell the home without a broker
    C. Yes, as long as it's not based on race
    D. Yes, she gets an exception in all cases since she is not using a broker

26. **Nile is a real estate broker and he goes to take a listing on a home where the seller states that he would not sale the property to a person who is Muslim. Should Nile take the listing?**
    A. Yes, because Muslims are not a protected class
    B. No, because discrimination is never tolerated
    C. No, since a broker cannot be involved in such a transaction
    D. Yes, but just make sure to not show the home to Muslims

27. **A broker receives a car as an earnest money deposit from a purchaser. The broker should:**
    A. Refuse the car and request earnest money instead
    B. Accept the car, put it in trust, but ask the value of the car, and take the offer to his principal
    C. Tell the purchaser that the principal will not accept a car as a deposit
    D. Accept the car, but have it appraised before presenting it to his principal

28. **A broker collects escrow funds from a purchaser on behalf of a seller he is representing. The closing is to occur in 30 days. The broker decides to use the funds to purchase a bike for his son, but puts the money back into the escrow account in time for closing so that no one ever knows that the money was gone. Has the broker acted appropriately?**
    A. No, the broker converted funds and violated the license law
    B. No, the broker commingled funds and violated the license law
    C. No, the broker converted funds, but did not violate the license law
    D. No, the broker commingled funds, but did not violate the license law

29. **A broker decides to place all funds that he receives as payment for commission into his personal account rather than his business account. Has he committed any violation of the license law?**
    A. Yes, he is committing the act of commingling funds
    B. Yes, he is committing the act of conversion
    C. No, because conversion is not a violation of the license law
    D. No, because the license law is not concerned with these funds

30. **Which of the following best describes steering?**
    A. A licensee sells a property to a family with six children in a predominately older neighborhood
    B. A lending institution refuses to lend mortgage money within certain areas due to the ethnic make-up of the area
    C. Because of a prospect's national origin, an individual selling her own property advises the prospect that the property is sold when it is not
    D. A licensee shows prospects of a particular race properties only in areas populated by families of the same race

31. **A licensee was taking an upper income bracket listing from a seller. The seller told her that they had lived in the neighborhood a long time, had many friends there, and wanted to be selective about who bought their house. The licensee was to tell them the race and nationality of anyone making an offer. How should the licensee respond to this requirement?**
    A. She should refuse to do so by explaining she would not always know the people making the offer
    B. She should refuse to do so and explain that the seller's instruction could be a violation of federal law
    C. She could take the listing as it is legal as long as no discriminatory advertising is used
    D. She should agree to it because, as the agent of the seller, the licensee has the duty of obedience to the seller's instructions

32. **A church owns a retirement home and restricts the rental of the units to church members regardless of age, sex, race, color, or national origin. Is this policy a violation of federal fair housing laws?**
    A. Yes, because all discrimination on the basis of religion is illegal
    B. Yes, because only owners of single-family homes may discriminate on the basis of religion
    C. No, because nonprofit organizations are not subject to federal housing provisions
    D. No, because religious organizations may limit occupancy of dwelling units they own to persons of the same religions

33. **A seller is selling his only house. He will neither advertise the property nor use a broker's services. Can the seller legally refuse to sell the property to a member of a racial minority?**
    A. Yes, because the seller has not used the services of a real estate broker
    B. Yes, because the seller has not used racially discriminatory advertising or a broker's services
    C. No, because such discriminatory action is prohibited
    D. No, because the seller owns fewer than three houses

34. **Which could cause a broker to be in violation of the Sherman Anti-Trust Act?**
    A. Your broker keeps all of the earnest money deposits in a safe in his office
    B. Your broker encourages you to violate fair housing laws in order to sell more real estate
    C. Your broker meets with other brokers and sets commission rates for the area
    D. Your broker accepts money from attorneys for closing services referrals

35. **Is a Catholic who lists her house with you and refuses to sell her house to a French man because he doesn't speak English in violation of any law?**
    A. No, as long as she is an owner occupant and doesn't use any discriminatory advertising
    B. No, because no broker was used
    C. Yes, she is in violation of the Fair Housing Act
    D. Yes, she is in violation of the Truth in Selling Act

36. **Four brokers get together and decide to improve service they each need to concentrate on a separate part of the city and they agree to split the city into sections with each broker agreeing to do business in one section of the city, one gets the Northeast, one the Southeast, one the Northwest and one the Southwest section of the city. They do NOT agree to set commissions. Are they in violation of any law in doing this?**
    A. No, they did not fix commissions and are therefore not in violation of the Sherman Antitrust Act
    B. No, they have not violated the law because their actions will IMPROVE service
    C. Yes, they have violated the Sherman Antitrust Act because this action restricts competition
    D. Yes, they have violated Federal Fair Housing laws because their actions are the same as steering

37. **Mrs. Jones decides that she doesn't want to rent her 1–4-unit property to men. Is this permissible?**
    A. No, discrimination is never tolerated
    B. Yes, as long as she resides in the property also and does not use a broker
    C. Yes, because men are not in a protected class
    D. Yes, as long as the broker places the restriction in the adverting

38. **Agent Brown decides to only show properties to her African American clients, the Smiths, in an African American neighborhood. This is an example of:**
    A. Blockbusting
    B. Steering
    C. Redlining
    D. None of the above

39. **A landlord of a subdivision complex decides to place all families with children under 18 in buildings A, B, and C. Is this permissible?**
    A. Yes, as long as he doesn't deny them housing
    B. No, this would be a Federal Fair Housing violation
    C. Yes, because children under 18 are not a protected class
    D. No, because under the government's police power, this isn't permissible

Chapter 3 Answers

1. C	4. D	7. D	10. D	13. D	16. B	19. C
2. B	5. B	8. D	11. D	14. A	17. C	
3. B	6. A	9. D	12. B	15. B	18. D	

1. Blind Advertising
2. Puffing
3. Tie In Contract
4. Discrimination
5. Trust Account
6. Federal Fair Housing Law
7. Do Not Call Registry
8. Americans with Disabilities Act
9. Sherman Anti-Trust Law
10. Blockbusting
11. Commingling
12. Improper Listing
13. Less Favorable Treatment
14. Minority
15. Can Spam Act
16. Steering
17. Referral Fee
18. Conversion
19. Redlining

Exercise 1

1. I	3. H	5. D	7. A	9. L	11. J
2. B	4. K	6. E	8. C	10. F	12. G

Exercise 2

1. A	3. E	5. I	7. B	9. L	11. D
2. H	4. K	6. F	8. C	10. J	12. G

1. Race

2. No, even if the landlord charges others a pet fee

3. Yes, as long as the reason for not showing is not relating to their minority status

4. Employees – controlled to a greater extent, set hours, receive a W-2, timely paycheck, have disability and worker's comp paid by employer. Independent contractor – only responsible to employer for results, less control, 1099, pays own insurance, taxes, and expenses

5. Monopolistic or Anti-Competitive Behavior

6. 10 days

7. 8:00 AM to 9:00 PM

8. 3 months or until they ask you to stop

9. Yes, for up to 18 months from the last contact with them

10. Only when it is a for sale by owner and the broker gives written permission and has approved the ad

11. Best house in the neighborhood; Sunset every day of the year

12. Ad that is missing the broker's name

13. When you own a single-family home, don't use a broker, don't discriminatory advertise, are the most recent occupant OR when you own a 1-4 family and reside there, no discriminatory advertising and no broker

14. Broker uses the client's funds to buy himself a television for Christmas

15. A trust account is where funds of others is held in trust; An operating account is the account the broker uses for his personal funds

16. Access to Employment and Public Buildings

17. Knocking on Ms. Jones door telling her that her property value is going down due to the kids that just moved into the neighborhood

18. An agent decides to eliminate a certain neighborhood from the search because most people are of one religion

19. Family, Race, Sex, Handicap, Color, Religion, National Origin

20. There are Four Main Fair Housing Category Exemptions, Name One

Mrs. Murphy exemption – When you own a 1-4 family and reside there, no discriminatory advertising and no broker

Single-Family Homeowner – When you own a single-family home, don't use a broker, don't discriminatory advertise, are the most recent occupant

Private Clubs – Can discriminate in housing as long as it doesn't discriminate in membership

Religious Organizations – Can discriminate in housing as long as it doesn't discriminate in membership

Section 7 Answers:

1. C. No fair housing violation has been committed because the reason for not working with the African American family is that they aren't qualified, not that they are African American

2. B. The ADA only requires that the structure be open to the public to trigger the requirements. Had this been a library for example, the ADA would require access

3. A. Housing communities made up of people over the age of 55 can discriminate against children if over 80% of the residents are over 55

4. A. Mary's best reply would be to direct her client to the local school district for them to find the information themselves as discussion of this topic would be a fair housing violation. All discussions are not violative of the law, only those discussions relating to the fair housing categories. For example, if the discussion was about how many married couples were in the neighborhood, Mary could answer

5. D. Fair Housing prohibits the use of those categories in advertising when showing a preference or dislike for those categories

6. C. Trust accounts, always considered client's funds, are not subject to attachment

7. B. Calls can be made between the hours of 8 AM and 9 PM

8. C. The Do Not Call registry applies to most industries, but not all. For example, Political Calls and Surveys are excluded

9. C. Fair Housing provides an equal opportunity for all to buy or rent property of their choosing. There are some exceptions for which discrimination is allowed, but never based on race

10. A. Whether a person is an employee or independent contractor goes to the amount of control that the employer has. Here, because Jovanni was required to be in the office for a specified period of time and paid based on that time and tasks, he would be considered an employee regardless of what the parties have written

11. A. As Modeste is independent contractor, RPM cannot force Modeste to work certain hours, although it can force his to agree to abide by certain rules and regulations of the brokerage

12. D. Mary would not get an exemption in this situation because she used discrimination in her advertising

13. A. The law provides several exceptions as to when a person on the Do Not Call Registry can be contacted. Any prior client can be contacted for up to 18 months since the last transaction that you had with them. However, once the client asks that you do not contact them any longer, you must cease all calls

14. B. Puffing in advertising is totally permitted. It is a statement that a reasonable person would recognize as untrue, primarily an opinion

15. D. Largest lot (since it is making a clearly factual assertion) could reasonably be interpreted as true. So, the broker could be accused of false advertising

16. B. All former clients can be called for up to 18 months since the last transaction, whether listed on the registry. Same rule applies for former contacts, but only up to 3 months

17. D. The private club would have an exemption. No other situation comes under fair housing in that it doesn't protect the lesbian female, the 5-family dwelling would not be exempt, and the transgender person has no protection

18. D. The ADA only requires a company to make reasonable accommodations for a person applying for a position. It doesn't require that the person be put into a position that they cannot do due to their handicap

19. A. Race is the only protected category listed. To thwart confusion, age is not a protected category, but family is

20. B. Redlining and the bank's risk doesn't matter. The bank should only look at the client who is seeking the loan. If the property doesn't appraise at the set price, that is a different story. But a bank cannot have a blanket policy of not lending in certain areas

21. D. The question here asks what MUST be done: The law states that opting out is required

22. C. This would not be a fair housing violation unless it is discrimination based on race. All other discrimination against fair housing categories would be allowed as long as there is no discrimination in the membership

23. A. Blockbusting is the act of inducing sellers to sell because any of the protected minorities are moving into the neighborhood. It is not just limited to race

24. B. John would be claiming under Mrs. Murphy's exemption which states that as long as John is living in the property, doesn't use discriminatory advertising or a broker, he can discriminate

25. C. A single-family homeowner who is not using discriminatory advertising or a broker may discriminate against the protected classes as long as it's not based on race

26. C. While the seller would be able to discriminate under certain circumstances because a broker is involved, he cannot in this instance. If the broker took this listing, it would amount to an improper listing

27. B. The broker's duty here would be to accept the car, put it in trust, and indicate the value of the car on the offer. Earnest "money" can come in any form and just like money, the broker's first obligation is to accept whatever is given and take it to his principal

28. A. This is a classic conversion example. Conversion is when a trustee uses trust funds for his own purchase. Regardless of the money being put back timely, it still violated the license law. Commingling is the act of putting one's in an account where trust funds are held

29. D. The license law is only concerned with funds that the broker is holding in trust for another. These are broker funds and while it may be poor record keeping, it is not a license law violation

30. D. An act done by a licensee that limits the choices of a buyer based on a protected category

31. B. The licensee will explain to the seller his obligations under fair housing. If the seller insists, the licensee will not be allowed to take the listing

32. D. One exception to fair housing is that religious organizations can discriminate against fair housing categories as long as it doesn't discriminate in its membership

33. C. While there are many fair housing exemptions, no discrimination against racial minorities can be granted an exemption

34. C. Any attempt to limit competition or monopolize the market. Meeting with other brokers to set commission rates would be a violation because it limits choices of the consumer

35. C. The Fair Housing Law prevents discrimination in housing to certain protected categories. These include Family, Race, Sex, Handicap, Color, Religion and Nationality. Some discrimination against these categories is allowed, but never when a broker is involved

36. C. This activity would be a clear violation of the Sherman Antitrust Act because, even though they aren't setting commission, it directly limits competition on those areas. In other words, if a client is in the Southwest, he would only have the choice of one brokerage

37. B. Mrs. Murphy exception allows discrimination when the owner resides in one of the units as long as no discriminatory advertising is used, and no broker is involved

38. B. Steering occurs when an agent limits a clients' choice of neighborhood rather than choosing properties based on objective criteria

39. B. The fair housing law identified protected categories. Families with children cannot be discriminated against at all. Even though the landlord is allowing the families to live there, he is still discriminating against them

Chapter 4: Property Ownership

Section 1: *Outline*

I. <u>Property</u> – <u>consists of things **(real or personal)** and the rights of ownership **(bundle of rights)**</u>

  A. Types of property:

    1. Real – land and those things permanently attached to it; immovable; any **real property transfers upon sale;** ownership is transferred by **deed**

      a. Appurtenances – any right, interest, or improvement which automatically conveys with the ownership
      b. Attachments

        1. Tenements – things naturally, physically, or legally attached to the land by law
        2. Improvements – man made items that are attached to the land

    2. Personal – any property that is **not real**; also known as **chattels**; moveable things that **do not transfer on sale**; ownership is transferred by **bill of sale**

      Growing Things – Can be Real or Personal

        a. Fructus Naturales – natural growing things that require no cultivation. **REAL**
        b. Fructus Industrials or emblements – crops that are harvested each year. **PERSONAL**

  B. Land – a three-dimensional structure that includes the surface of the land, the subsurface to the center of the earth, and above the surface up to infinity. Each part may be sold or leased separately

    1. Rights of Real Property Ownership

      a. Water Rights

        1. Riparian Rights – properties that border a **river or stream** where the owner has the right to use the water for such things as swimming, boating, and fishing. Ownership extends to the **center of the river**
        2. Littoral Rights – properties that border navigable lakes or oceans. Ownership extends to the **high water or high tide mark**
        3. Percolating Water – Underground water that is not confined to a specific waterway. The level of the water is the **water table**
        4. Correlative Rights – a doctrine allowing owner only a reasonable share of water during times of short supply
        5. Prior Appropriation – a doctrine where use is secured by permit

      b. Mineral Rights – Rights to such things as coal oil and gas. Unless there is an express agreement stating otherwise, the law allows anyone who acquires mineral rights an **implied right to access** to extract the minerals

    1. **Right Of Lateral Support** – right of an adjacent landowner to have drilling done in a reasonable way to protect his property
    2. **Law of Capture** – for oil and gas, allows a well drilled on one property to extract from under an adjacent property. The first to extract is the owner

  c. **Air Rights** – May be sold or leased separate from the land itself. In the case of a Condo, each owner owns a block of air from inside wall to inside wall. This is called an **Air Lot**

2. **Property Changes**

  a. **Severance** – process by which an item of real property becomes personal property
  b. **Attachment** – process by which personal property becomes real property

  Fixtures – An item that was once personal property but was attached and is now considered to be real property. To determine if an item is indeed a fixture, we use (**MARIA**):

    1. **Modification** – When a building is modified to accept an article or when the article is modified to accept the building even if not attached to it; custom made
    2. **Attachment** – An item of personal property will be considered real property because it operates real property, ex. keys, garage door openers
    3. **Relationship to parties** – Business vs. Residential tenant

      a. **Trade fixtures** – property placed by a tenant for use in a business is considered **PERSONAL** until the lease expires. If a tenant fails to remove such property before lease expires, it will become the landlord's property by **accession**. Placement by a residential tenant is considered **REAL**

    4. **Intentions of Annexing party** – did the person intend for it to be a fixture? This rarely comes into consideration
    5. **Agreement** – The parties agree to allow removal

C. Land Characteristics

1. **Physical Characteristics**

  a. **Immobility** – Most distinctive; it cannot be moved
  b. **Non-Homogeneity** – No two parcels are exactly alike
  c. **Indestructibility** – It remains the same regardless of man-made or natural changes

2. **Economic Characteristics**

  a. **SITUS (Location Preference)** – sum of all factors affecting value
  b. **Improvements** – Value and Type of Improvements
  c. **Fixed Investment** – Economic usefulness or **economic life**
  d. **Scarcity** – Determined by the amount of land available; the less available, the higher the price

D. Description of Real Property

1. **Legal Description** – To identify the property in such a way that it cannot be mistaken with any other property in the world; Done by a surveyor

  Spot survey – identifies the boundaries and improvements on a parcel of property

  a. **Metes and Bounds** – Method of identifying a parcel by describing its boundaries. It must have a **point of beginning** and a **point of closure**. Metes (**distances and directions**) and Bounds (**landmarks and monuments**). **Monuments can be natural, or man made**
  b. **Rectangular Surveys (Govt Surveys)** – Based on **Principal Meridians (north and south)** and lines **Base Lines (east and west)**. This forms a grid with **Ranges, Townships** (6 miles per side or 36 sq miles) **and Sections** (1 mile per side or 1 sq mile or 640 acres). **Also,** there are 43,560 sq ft in an acre

  c. The Recorded Plat (Short-Form) Description – Recorded Plat provides convenience. A subdivision uses one large Metes and Bounds and only gives a short lot, block, district description to each home within the subdivision

 2. Vertical Land Description – **Datum** is a way to describe the **air rights** or the **subsurface rights**. It is a **base point** for **measuring height** and **depth**

 A sales contract or lease without a legal description is unenforceable

II. Property Rights – one's interest in the property

 A. Ownership – **Allodial system** – any individual who has the means can acquire rights of ownership. The assumption is that all property transfers come with the **bundle of rights (DUPE)** that go with private ownership. Any limitation or restriction on these rights are called **encumbrances.** The bundle of rights:

 1. Disposition – right to allow the owner to sell the land, give it away, or pass it to heirs

 2. Use or Control – right includes making profit from land, removing objects form it, building on it, framing on it, drilling, mining on it, leasing it, excluding others from it, granting an easement or license to others

 3. Possession – the right to occupy your property and to have **ingress** (go in) and **egress** (exit)

 4. Enjoyment – right that ensures against interference from others or nuisances from neighbors. The right to air, light, water, and lateral support

 B. Estates in Land – the quality, quantity, nature, and extent of the interest in the property. There must be a right to **possession**, whether current (possessory, ex. Tenant) or future (non-possessory, ex. Landlord)

 1. Freehold Estates – a possessory estate that will last an indefinite period

  a. Fee *(Inheritable)* Simple Absolute – owner possesses the **entire bundle of rights**. The most complete ownership one can have

  b. Conditional Fees – estate that does not represent complete rights of ownership because of conditions placed by the grantor

   1. Fee Simple Determinable – subject to certain conditions in the deed; Use of "for so long as"; **Automatic** reversion or remainder on breach

   2. Fee Simple on Condition Subsequent – subject to conditions in the deed; Use of "on the condition that"; No automatic reversion or remainder on breach, lawsuit is necessary

  c. Life Estate *(Non-Inheritable)* – Grant of the **full bundle of rights** for a person's lifetime; referred to as the **life tenant; ends on death**

   1. Ordinary Life Estate – created by deed, will, or trust. Interest ends when the life tenant dies

   2. Life Estate PurAutre Vie (Life of another) – the lifetime of an estate is measured by the life of an individual other than the person in possession of the premises

 2. Reverter Clauses – a clause in a deed that identifies what happens at the end of a lesser estate (Fee Simple Determinable, Fee Simple Condition Subsequent, and Life Estate, Tenancy)

  a. Remainder Estates – the estate creator designates a third party to receive it at the end of the estate

  b. Reversionary Estate – the estate creator designates himself or his heirs to receive it at the end of the estate

 3. Legal Life Estates – Created by law to protect a surviving spouse; amount is determined by state law

  a. Dower – wife's interest in any property her husband owns

  b. Curtesy – husband's interest in wife's estate

 4. Non-Freehold Estates – **Lessor** (landlord) conveys the exclusive right to possess and control the premises to a **Lessee** (tenant) for a specified time period in exchange for rent. Lessor has a **Leased Fee Estate**. Lessee has a **Leasehold Estate**

a. **Estate for Years** – a specific start and end date
b. **Estate from Period to Period** – with each payment, the time period is renewed
c. **Estate at Will** – a **temporary** arrangement in which the tenant can occupy the property for an **unspecified time period**
d. **Estate at Sufferance** – a tenant, who is legally renting, remains in possession after having been given notice to leave. Also known as a **holdover tenant**

C. <u>Encumbrances</u> – external limitation placed on the rights, title, or use of property which can diminish its value. Can be public or private

  1. **Public Encumbrances** – (PETE)

    a. **Police Power** – right of the government to enact laws regulating the safety, health, morals, and general well-being of the community. **No compensation**
    b. **Eminent Domain** – power to take private property for public use when **just compensation** has been paid
    c. **Taxation** – imposition of ad valorem or special assessment taxes
    d. **Escheat** – the right to take property where no heirs exist

  2. **Private Encumbrances (Affecting Title)**

Lien – a monetary claim a creditor has on the property of a debtor and the debtor's property is security for payment of the debt. Liens can be:

    a. **Voluntary** (with consent) or **Involuntary** (without consent)
    b. **Statutory** (act of legislature) or **Equitable** (out of justice or fair play)
    c. **Specific** (enforceable against the collateral) or **general** (after a judgment)

<u>Specific Lien Types</u>: **Enforceable against the collateral**

    1. **Property Tax** – **Ad valorem taxes** are assessed based on the value of property. **Special assessments** can be assessed to those receiving the benefit of the improvements
    2. **Mortgage** – Placed on the property when the bank loans money to a borrower
    3. **Mechanics** – Placed by those who "improved" another's property
    4. **Vendee's Liens** – a buyer's right to place a lien (record the contract) while the home is pending sale
    5. **Attachment Liens** – grants the court custody of a specific property to prevent the owner form transferring ownership while a suit is pending

<u>General Lien Types</u> – **Result of a Judgment** must locate the **debtor's real and personal property**

    1. **Judgment Lien** – arising out of a lawsuit
    2. **Federal and State Income Taxes**
    3. **Federal and State Inheritance Taxes** – against the decedent's estate
    4. **Decedents Debts** – all liens must be satisfied before property passes to the heirs

  3. **Private Encumbrances (Affecting Use)**

Easements – a written non-possessory, intangible right one person has to use another person's land in a specified manner or for a specified purpose

    1. **Easement Appurtenant** – **two properties, two owners, adjacent** to one another. The owner **granting** the easement is the **servient estate (burdened)** and gives access to the holder of the easement, the **dominant estate (benefits)**. **Runs with the land; aka Property Easements; irrevocable by the servient estate**
    2. **Easement in Gross** – **one** tract of land. It is a personal right to use the land of another and does not run with the land; **aka Personal Easements; irrevocable,** but **terminates** on **property sale** or at the **death** of the person who was given the easement; not inheritable or transferable

      a. **Commercial Easements in Gross** – granted to utility companies for access; freely inheritable and transferable

4. Other Private Encumbrances

Private Restrictions – limitations on the use of one's property in other to protect the rights of others. When private restrictions conflict with zoning laws, **the stricter will always prevail.** Private restrictions against public policy or the sale of property will not be enforced

1. **Covenants** – a promise made in a sales contract, lease or deed that specifies the property will or will not be used in a certain manner. The grantor or other parties can file an **injunction** to stop a prohibited use. If parties unduly delay in taking proper legal action, they could be prevented due to **laches**
2. **Conditions** – usually found in deeds, conditions differ from covenants because they **don't** usually **have** any **time limits** but they stray mark run with the land indefinitely
3. **Encroachments** – an improvement, building or other attachment that illegally extends beyond the boundaries of its owner's land onto adjoining land or airspace. Observable by a survey

D. Creation of Easements

a. **Grant** – owner grants a specific right to another person to the use grantor's land
b. **Reservation** – owner reserves an easement in the deed
c. **Implication** – created by operation of law
d. **Prescription** – acquired through use of another's property openly, continuously, without permission for a period prescribed by law
e. **Condemnation** – the government can acquire an easement over privately owned land
f. **Agreement** – parties may express their interest to create an easement in a written agreement
g. **Necessity** – when an owner sells land in such a way that deprives the buyer of reasonable access

E. Termination of easements

a. **Merger** – if both properties come under one ownership, easement no longer exists
b. **Release** – can be released in writing by the dominant estate to the servient estate
c. **Prescription** – when holder of the servient estate openly and continuously prevents the easement holder from using it for the statutory period of time
d. **Abandonment** – there must be a positive action that shows the holder of easement will no longer use it. Non-use is not necessarily abandonment
e. **Necessity** – if created by necessity, it will end when the necessity ends
f. **Expiration of Purpose** – if granted for a specific purpose, it ends when the purpose no longer exists

License – grants of personal permission to use the land of another **without creating an easement** for the user. It is usually a short-term privilege and is not transferable, inheritable. It is revocable at anytime

III. Ownership Types – Ways to take title to property

A. **The Concept of Ownership** – comprises of the **bundle of rights** (disposition, use or control, possession, enjoyment, aka **DUPE**)
B. **Types of Property Ownership**

1. **Sole Ownership** – an estate owned by **one person** or a **single legal entity**, is called **severalty** or **sole ownership**
2. **Concurrent Ownership** – when two or more people simultaneously own rights in the same piece of property; also known as **co-ownership.** In most co-ownership arrangements, a **partition suit** may be filed when the parties cannot agree on a method of dissolving the ownership

Most Tested Concurrent Ownership Topics:

a. **Tenancy in Common**

i. Most popular form of concurrent ownership because it imposes the fewest restrictions on the co-owners
ii. Each co-owner holds separate title to the property and has an **undivided interest** in the **entire property** regardless of how much each co-owner owns of the property **(POSSESSION)**

iii. Each co-owner can sell, mortgage, will or otherwise dispose of their share without the consent of the other owners

iv. Assumed type of tenancy if there is no other expressed indication of how the title will be held

v. Inheritable by the heirs of a deceased co-owner

vi. Ownership shares can be equal or unequal

b. **Joint Tenancy – In order to create, you must have PITT ("unities of title")**

i. Each co-owner holds an **undivided interest** in the **entire property (POSSESSION)**

ii. All Joint Tenants must have an equal interest in the property (**INTEREST**)

iii. All Joint Tenants must have acquired the title at the same time (**TIME**)

iv. There is only one title for the entire Joint Tenancy (**TITLE**)

v. Joint Tenancy has the right of survivorship (upon the death of a joint tenant, the surviving members of the Joint Tenancy take that person's share)

vi. Joint Tenancy can only be created through deed or express intent and not involuntarily by court action or statute

vii. Each co-owner can sell, mortgage, or dispose of their share without the consent of the other owners, but a Joint Tenant cannot **WILL** his share

c. **Tenancy by the Entirety** – Effectively, a Joint Tenancy for married couples, but there are some differences

i. Exclusively for married couples

ii. Neither spouse can sell, mortgage, or lease his/her interest without consent from the other

iii. Partition Suits are not allowed

iv. Not available in all states

v. Creditors cannot force the sale of half the property, without both signatures, to satisfy either spouse's personal or business debts

3. **Other Forms of Concurrent Ownership**

a. **Community Property** – applies only to married couples. It provides each spouse with ½ interest in any property acquired during the marriage **(marital property)** upon divorce. Property acquired before the marriage or gifts and inheritances are considered **separate property** and are not considered

b. **Tenancy in Partnership** – when two or more join forces for business purposes

1. **General Partnership** – Each partner is jointly and severally (together and individually) liable for the partnership obligations. The partners carry on the **management of the partnership** and can lose the partnership and their personal assets

2. **Limited Partnership** – Limited partners are essentially investors and have **no management involvement.** Their liability is limited to the investment put into the partnership

c. **Limited Liability Company (LLC)** – an entity formed to limit liability and to receive preferential tax treatment. The owners are called members and an LLC does not have eternal existence

d. **Trust** – Created when a property owner (**the trustor**) places the title to the property in the hands of someone else (**the trustee**) for a third-party **beneficiary.** It is created through a written instrument that may be a formal trust agreement, a will, or a deed

1. **Testamentary Trusts** – created by will to become effective after the owner's death

2. **Living Trusts** – created by agreement during the trustor's lifetime

3. **Land trust** – created by a trustor who will also be the beneficiary and who will retain control over management of the property

4. **Real Estate Investment Trusts (REIT)** –minimum of 100 investors in real estate intended to qualify for preferential income tax benefits

e. **Condominium Ownership** – allows multiple owners to hold a fee simple title to their individual unit. All owners are tenants in common with respect to the **common elements (playground, swimming pool)**. All owners must abide by **covenants, conditions, and restrictions (CC&Rs)** that govern how the common areas and units can be used

   1. **Master deed** – principle conveyance document used to create the condominium. It includes the legal description and thorough description of entire property

   2. **Declaration** – includes description of each unit, % of interest in the common elements that attach each unit, description of common areas and uses

   3. **Plat** – detailed site plan

   4. **By-laws** – establishes the framework for forming of a homeowners' association. Developer must turn over management to association when 80% off units are sold or after 3 years from date the declaration was recorded

f. **Timeshare** – also known as interval ownership; another application of condo ownership when a unit in a resort area is sold to multiple owners for a specific period

g. **Cooperative Ownership** – multiple unit building developed by a non-profit corporation. In exchange for the purchase of stock in the corporation, the co-op board grants an exclusive right to a unit for the life of the corporation by **proprietary lease**. The shareholder pays a monthly maintenance fee that covers a portion of the building's mortgage, taxes, and maintenance costs

Section 2: *Vocabulary*

Acre: A parcel of land that contains 43,560 square feet

Accession: Acquisition of title to real property

Allodial System: A system of land ownership which recognizes the right of individuals to own land independently of political superiors

Appurtenance: A right or privilege associated with the property and which always conveys with it

Bill of Sale: A document used to transfer ownership of personal property

Bundle of Rights: The corresponding rights that go with ownership of property

By-Laws: The internal rules and procedures to conduct homeowner's association affairs

Chattel: An item of personal property

Common Elements: Property which is concurrently owned as tenants in common with the other condominium unit owners

Community Property: Each person in a marriage is entitled to 1/2 of all marital property on divorce

Concurrent or Co-Ownership: Any form of ownership where more than one person or entity has an interest in the same property at the same time

Conditions: Limitations that generally go to use and are placed in the deed by the original grantor

Condominium Ownership: A form of concurrent ownership in which each occupant of a multiple unit building holds fee simple title to his individual unit

Conventional Life Estate: A freehold estate created by deed or will where the grantor limits the estate for the life of the grantee

Cooperative Ownership: A form of "ownership" where a purchaser of shares in a nonprofit corporation receives a proprietary lease on a specific apartment

Covenants: The promises that the parties make in a contract or lease agreement

Covenants, Conditions, and Restrictions (CC&Rs): Defines the use, requirements and restrictions of owners of a property

Datum: A legal description used when describing subsurface or air rights

Deed: The document used to transfer real property to another

Easement: A non-possessory interest in which one person has a right to use another's land in a specified manner or for a specific purpose

Easement Appurtenant: A right to use the land of another that runs with the land

Easement in Gross: A personal right granted to a specific person to use property of another

Encroachment: A permanent improvement, building, or other attachment that illegally onto neighboring land

Encumbrance: An external limitation to either the title, use, or rights in the property

Equitable Lien: A lien arising out fairness and justice

Escheat: A concept that allows the state to take over real property when no heirs exist or can be found

Estate in Land: The quality, quantity, nature, and extent of the interest that a person has in real property

Fixtures: An item that was once personal property, but that has been attached to and become part of the real property

Fee Simple Absolute: A freehold estate where the grantor places no restrictions or conditions on ownership

Fee Simple on Condition Subsequent: A freehold estate that can be held indefinitely "provided that" a certain condition is maintained

Fee Simple Determinable: A freehold estate where the grantor uses the language "so long as" when attaching a condition to the grant

Freehold Estate: An estate in land of indefinite duration

Fructus Industriales (Emblements): A form of personal property resulting from crops or cultivation of the land

Fructus Naturales: Growing things that are considered real property and require no annual cultivation

General Lien: The right of a creditor to have any of a debtor's property sold to satisfy a debt

Government Survey System: A legal description based upon a grid overlay of property broken down into principal meridians and base lines, townships, sections, and ranges

Immobility: The most distinctive physical characteristic of land

Improvements: Any artificial man-made attachment to the land

Injunction: A court order that forces to or limits a person from doing a particular thing

Joint Tenancy: A form of concurrent ownership that includes the right of survivorship

Land Trust: A two-party instrument where the trustor is also the beneficiary and retains control over the property

Legal Life Estate: A life estate established by state law, rather than created voluntarily by an owner

License: Revocable permission granted to enter another's land

Lien: An encumbrance in the form of a monetary claim that affects the title to property

Life Estate Pur Autre Vie: A freehold estate created by deed or will where the grantor measures the life tenant's estate by the life of a third party

Littoral Rights: A landowner's real property right in land when it borders a lake or ocean

Mechanic's Lien: A statutory lien, created to ensure payment for work performed and materials furnished in the improvement of property

Metes and Bounds: A legal land description that identifies the location by using a point of beginning, a point of closure and natural or artificial monuments

Mortgage Lien: A lien given to a lender to provide the security for a real estate loan

Partition Suit: An action to divide or sell property when co-tenants are unable to mutually agree on an acceptable plan of division or sale

Percolating Water: Underground water that is not confined to a specific waterway

Personal Property: Property that is movable or not classified as real property

Prescriptive Easement: An easement obtained by the open, continuous, and hostile use of the property belonging to someone else for a statutory period of time

Proprietary Lease: A lease issued by a cooperative to its shareholders

Real Estate: Real Property but without the bundle of rights

Real Property: Land, its attachments, and the corresponding bundle of rights

Recorded Plat (Short-Form): A legal description where a metes and bounds is created for one large parcel and all parcels within it only refer to the lot, block, and district number

Remainderman: A third party who has a future interest in property upon the termination of a lesser estate

Reversionary Interest: The remnant of an estate that the grantor or his heirs hold at the end of a lesser freehold estate

Right of Lateral Support: An adjacent landowner's right to not have his property damaged during mineral extraction

Right of Survivorship: A right which allows a deceased co-owner's interest in property to automatically pass to the surviving co-owners

Riparian Rights: An owner's rights in land when it borders a river or a stream

Section: A parcel of land used in a government survey that consists of one square mile or 640 Acres

Severalty Ownership: Ownership by one person or one legal entity

Severance: The act of changing real property into personal property

Situs: All of the factors that go into choosing a location

Specific lien: A lien affecting or attaching only to a certain, specific parcel of land

Tenants in Common: Ownership where each person owns a separate title to and has an undivided interest in property that passes to the heirs on death

Tenants by the Entirety: Co-ownership form that can only be used by married couples

Timeshare ownership: A form of condominium ownership where one property is divided among several owners who each have a specific period to use it

Township: A parcel of land used in a government survey that consists of 6 square miles on each side or 36 square miles

Trusts: A three-party arrangement where a trustor gives property to a trustee to hold for the benefit of a beneficiary

Section 3: *Recall Multiple Choice*

1. **A freehold estate where the grantor uses the language "so long as" when attaching a condition to the grant**
   A. Land Trust
   B. Legal Attachments
   C. Appurtenance
   D. Fee Simple Determinable

2. **A lease issued by a cooperative to its shareholders**
   A. Joint Venture
   B. Dower
   C. Prescriptive Easement
   D. Proprietary Lease

3. **A lien arising out fairness and justice**
   A. Trusts
   B. Proprietary Lease
   C. Equitable Lien
   D. Vendor's Lien

4. **A form of condominium ownership where one property is divided among several owners and each owner has a specific period of time in which to use the property**
   A. Real property
   B. Timeshare ownership
   C. Specific lien
   D. Undivided interest

5. **An item that was once personal property, but that has been attached to and become part of the real property**
   A. Tenement
   B. Fructus Naturales
   C. Trusts
   D. Fixtures

6. **The quality, quantity, nature, and extent of the interest that a person has in real property**
   A. Dower
   B. General lien
   C. Estate in land
   D. Lien

7. **An item of personal property**
   A. Chattel
   B. Severance
   C. Vendor's Lien
   D. Involuntary Lien

8. **A third party who has a future interest in property upon the termination of a lesser estate**
   A. Eminent Domain
   B. Easement
   C. Escheat
   D. Remainderman

9. **A legal description used primarily in subdivisions where a metes and bounds is created for the entire subdivision and all parcels within the subdivision only recite the lot, block, and district number**
   A. Allodial system
   B. Air rights
   C. Recorded plat (Short-Form)
   D. Metes and bounds

10. **Real Property itself but without legal rights and interests that go along with ownership**
    A. Littoral Rights
    B. Personal Property
    C. Real Estate
    D. Land Definition

11. **A system of land ownership which recognizes the right of individuals to own land independently of political superiors**
    A. Syndicates
    B. Allodial System
    C. Recorded Plat (Short-Form)
    D. Trustor

12. **A form of concurrent ownership that is accompanied by the right of survivorship**
    A. Joint Venture
    B. Dower
    C. Land Trust
    D. Joint Tenancy

13. **Property which is concurrently owned as tenants in common with the other condominium unit owners**
    A. Common Elements
    B. Trade Fixture
    C. Spot Survey
    D. Fixtures

14. **The remnant of an estate that the grantor or his heirs hold after granting a lesser freehold estate to another person**
    A. Reverter Clause
    B. Reversionary Interest
    C. Undivided Interest
    D. Riparian Rights

15. **A life estate established by state law, rather than created voluntarily by an owner**
    A. Land Trust
    B. Law Of Capture
    C. Life Tenant
    D. Legal Life Estate

16. **The most distinctive physical characteristic of land**
    A. Air Rights
    B. Covenants
    C. Attachment Lien
    D. Immobility

17. **Underground water that is not confined to a specific waterway**
    A. Percolating Water
    B. Party Wall
    C. Water Table
    D. Air Rights

18. **Limitations that generally go to use and are placed in the deed by the original grantor**
    A. Partition Suit
    B. Datum
    C. Condemnation Action
    D. Conditions

19. **Growing things which require no annual cultivation and are considered real property**
    A. Fixture Test
    B. Personal Property
    C. Legal Attachments
    D. Fructus Naturales

20. **A permanent improvement, building, or other attachment illegally extends beyond the boundaries onto neighboring land**
    A. License
    B. Benchmark
    C. Tenement
    D. Encroachment

21. **An action to divide or sell property when co-tenants are unable to mutually agree on an acceptable plan of division or sale**
    A. Specific Lien
    B. Partition Suit
    C. Trustee
    D. Party Wall

22. **A document that establishes the internal rules and procedures for conducting the affairs of the homeowner's association**
    A. Percolating Water
    B. Lis Pendens
    C. By-Laws
    D. Injunction

23. **A legal land description where the surveyor uses a point of beginning, a point of closure, natural or artificial monuments, distances, and compass directions**
    A. Metes and Bounds
    B. Mineral Rights
    C. Master Deed
    D. Law of Capture

24. **A two-party trust where the trustor, who is also the beneficiary, retains control over the property held by the trustee**
    A. Bundle Of Rights
    B. Escheat
    C. Voluntary Lien
    D. Land Trust

25. **A legal description based upon a grid overlay of principal meridians and base lines, townships, sections, and ranges**
    A. Metes And Bounds
    B. Allodial System
    C. Government Survey System
    D. Law Of Capture

26. **Ownership by one person or a single legal entity**
    A. Real Property
    B. Servient Estate
    C. Severalty Ownership
    D. General Partnership

27. **The promises that the parties make in a contract or lease agreement**
    A. Dower
    B. Covenants
    C. Deed
    D. Lien

28. **A parcel of land that contains 43,560 square feet**
    A. Acre
    B. Tenement
    C. Land Definition
    D. Littoral Rights

29. **A landowner's real property right in land when it borders a lake or ocean and extends to the high water mark or high tide mark**
    A. Littoral Rights
    B. Water Table
    C. Riparian Rights
    D. Law Of Capture

30. **Personal permission granted to enter one's land which can be revoked at any time**
    A. Lien
    B. Partition Suit
    C. License
    D. Limited Partnership

31. **A form of personal property resulting from crops or cultivation of the land**
    A. Easement in Gross
    B. Fructus Industrials (Emblements)
    C. Legal attachments
    D. Fee Simple on Condition Subsequent

32. **Land and the attachments to the land, with the corresponding bundle of rights**
    A. Real Property
    B. Specific Lien
    C. Estate In Land
    D. Homestead Protection

33. Legal description, measuring height or depth, used when describing subsurface or air rights
   A. Conditions
   B. Condemnation Action
   C. Datum
   D. Testamentary Trusts

34. The right of a creditor to have all of a debtor's property—both real and personal—sold to satisfy a debt
   A. Voluntary Lien
   B. Common Elements
   C. General Lien
   D. Eminent Domain

35. All of the factors that go into choosing a location
   A. Conditions
   B. Baselines
   C. Appurtenance
   D. Situs

36. A lien affecting or attaching only to a certain, specific parcel of land or piece of property
   A. Mechanic's lien
   B. Specific lien
   C. Deed
   D. Dower

37. An ownership in which the estate can be held indefinitely "provided that" a certain condition is maintained
   A. Fee Simple Determinable
   B. Life Tenant
   C. Fee Simple on Condition Subsequent
   D. Tenants in Common

38. A freehold estate created by deed or will where the grantor grants an estate to the life tenant, but measures the estate based on the life of a third party
   A. Life Tenant
   B. Land Trust
   C. Life Estate Pur Autre Vie
   D. Specific Lien

39. A right to use the land of another that runs with the land
   A. Easement Appurtenant
   B. General Lien
   C. Appurtenance
   D. Escheat

40. An estate in land of indefinite duration
   A. Personal Property
   B. Legal Description
   C. Dominant Estate
   D. Freehold Estate

41. A court order that forces or limits a person from doing a particular thing
   A. Deed
   B. Escheat
   C. Injunction
   D. Voluntary Lien

42. Co-ownership form that can only be used by married couples
   A. Tenants in Common
   B. Tenants by the Entirety
   C. Real Property
   D. Joint Venture

43. A statutory lien, created to ensure payment for work performed and materials furnished in the improvement of property
   A. Land Trust
   B. Encumbrance
   C. Mechanic's Lien
   D. Life Tenant

44. An external limitation to either the title, use, or right's in the property
   A. Specific Lien
   B. Dower
   C. Lien
   D. Encumbrance

45. An adjacent landowner's right to not have his property damaged during mineral extraction
   A. Right of Lateral Support
   B. Living Trust
   C. Law of Capture
   D. Termination of an Easement

46. Any artificial, man-made attachment to the land
   A. Covenants
   B. Conditions
   C. Tenement
   D. Improvements

47. Acquisition of title to real property
   A. Accession
   B. Involuntary Lien
   C. Possessory Estate
   D. Severance

48. A form of ownership where more than one person or entity has an interest in the same property at the same time
   A. Joint Venture
   B. Concurrent or Co-Ownership
   C. Right of Survivorship
   D. Voluntary Lien

49. A three party arrangement where a trustor gives property to a trustee to hold for the benefit of a third party - the beneficiary
   A. Joint Venture
   B. Specific Lien
   C. Trusts
   D. Fixtures

50. A personal right granted to a specific person to use property of another
   A. Easement in Gross
   B. Easement Appurtenant
   C. Community Property
   D. Voluntary Lien

51. A form of concurrent ownership in which each occupant of a multiple unit building holds fee simple title to his individual unit
   A. Township
   B. Condominium Ownership
   C. Real Property
   D. Joint Tenancy

52. The document used to transfer real property to another
   A. Covenants
   B. Chattel
   C. Deed
   D. Specific Lien

53. A document used to transfer ownership of personal property
   A. Legal Life Estate
   B. Bill of Sale
   C. Lien
   D. Specific Lien

54. A parcel of land used in a government survey that consists of one square mile or 640 Acres
   A. Section
   B. Condemnation Action
   C. Littoral Rights
   D. Homestead Protection

55. An encumbrance in the form of a monetary claim that affects the title to property
   A. Lien
   B. Deed
   C. Dower
   D. Chattel

56. A right or privilege associated with the property and which always conveys with it, 'Runs with the Land'
   A. Fee Simple Determinable
   B. Tenement
   C. Party Wall
   D. Appurtenance

57. The rights - possession, use/control, enjoyment, and disposition - that accompany property ownership
   A. Bundle of Rights
   B. Covenants
   C. Law of Capture
   D. Termination of an Easement

58. A form of "ownership" where in exchange for the purchase of shares, the shareholder receives a proprietary lease on a specific apartment and is obligated to pay a monthly maintenance fee
   A. Easement
   B. Land Trust
   C. Cooperative Ownership
   D. Township

59. A non-possessory interest in which one person has a right to use another's land in a specified manner or for a specific purpose
   A. Community Property
   B. Littoral Rights
   C. Easement
   D. Statutory Lien

60. A lien given to a lender by a borrower as security for a real estate loan
   A. Remainderman
   B. Deed
   C. Mortgage Lien
   D. Mechanic's Lien

61. A parcel of land used in a government survey that consists of 6 square miles on each side or 36 square miles
   A. Personal Property
   B. Township
   C. Cooperative Ownership
   D. Limited Partnership

62. An easement obtained by the open, continuous, and hostile use of the property belonging to someone else for a statutory period of time
   A. Prescriptive Easement
   B. Specific Lien
   C. Eminent Domain
   D. Tenement

63. A theory where each person is entitled to 1/2 of all marital property on divorce
   A. Community Property
   B. Government Survey System
   C. Land Trust
   D. Easement

64. An owner's rights in land when it borders a river or a stream and such rights extend to the center of the waterway
   A. Littoral Rights
   B. Riparian Rights
   C. Living Trust
   D. Conditions

65. Any property that is movable or not classified as real property
   A. Severance
   B. Personal Property
   C. Specific Lien
   D. Master Deed

66. **A concept that allows the state to take over real property when no heirs exist**
    A. Statutory Lien
    B. Law Of Capture
    C. Escheat
    D. Deed

67. **An estate where the grantor places no restrictions or conditions on ownership**
    A. Fee Simple Determinable
    B. Servient Estate
    C. Voluntary Lien
    D. Fee Simple Absolute

68. **A document defining the use, requirements and restrictions of owners of a property**
    A. Covenants, Conditions, and Restrictions (CC&Rs)
    B. Water rights
    C. Common elements
    D. Bill of sale

69. **The act of changing real property into personal property**
    A. Involuntary Lien
    B. Chattel
    C. Severance
    D. Personal Property

70. **Co ownership where each person owns a separate title to and has an undivided interest in the property that does not automatically pass to the survivor on death**
    A. Tenants in Common
    B. Community Property
    C. Voluntary Lien
    D. Eminent Domain

71. **A right which allows a deceased co-owner's interest in property to automatically pass to the surviving co-owners**
    A. Easement in Gross
    B. Right of Survivorship
    C. General Partnership
    D. Tenants in Common

72. **A freehold estate created by deed or will where the grantor limits the estate for the life of the grantee (life tenant)**
    A. Personal Property
    B. General Lien
    C. Joint Venture
    D. Conventional Life Estate

Section 4: *Recall Fill-In*

1. A landowner's real property right in land when it borders a lake or ocean and extends to the high water mark or high tide mark

_____

2. A legal description used primarily in subdivisions where a metes and bounds is created for the entire subdivision and all parcels within the subdivision only recite the lot, block, and district number

_____

3. An easement obtained by the open, continuous, and hostile use of the property belonging to someone else for a statutory period of time

_____

4. Real Property itself but without legal rights and interests that go along with ownership

_____

5. Limitations that generally go to use and are placed in the deed by the original grantor

_____

6. A form of personal property resulting from crops or cultivation of the land

_____

7. A lease issued by a cooperative to its shareholders

_____

8. A third party who has a future interest in property upon the termination of a lesser estate

_____

9. A life estate established by state law, rather than created voluntarily by an owner

_____

10. The act of changing real property into personal property

_____

11. The most distinctive physical characteristic of land

_____

12. Any artificial, man-made attachment to the land

_____

13. Underground water that is not confined to a specific waterway

_____

14. A freehold estate where the grantor uses the language "so long as" when attaching a condition to the grant

_____

15. A right which allows a deceased co-owner's interest in property to pass to the surviving co-owners

_____

16. A form of concurrent ownership that is accompanied by the right of survivorship

_____

17. A right or privilege associated with the property, and which always conveys with it, 'Runs with the Land'

_____

18. A lien given to a lender by a borrower as security for a real estate loan

_____

19. An external limitation to either the title, use, or right's in the property

_____

20. A legal description based upon a grid overlay of principal meridians and base lines, townships, sections, and ranges

_____

21. The document used to transfer real property to another

_____

22. A document defining the use, requirements and restrictions of owners of a property

_____

23. A personal right granted to a specific person to use property of another

_____

24. A court order that forces or limits a person from doing a particular thing

_____

25. A freehold estate created by deed or will where the grantor limits the estate for the life of the grantee (life tenant)

_____

26. Co ownership where each person owns a separate title to and has an undivided interest in the property that does not automatically pass to the survivor on death

_____

27. Acquisition of title to real property

_____

28. An ownership in which the estate can be held indefinitely "provided that" a certain condition is maintained

_____

29. A document used to transfer ownership of personal property

_____

30. An action to divide or sell property when co-tenants are unable to mutually agree on an acceptable plan of division or sale

_____

31. A parcel of land that contains 43,560 square feet

_____

32. Ownership by one person or a single legal entity

_____

33. Any property that is movable or not classified as real property

_____

34. A concept that allows the state to take over real property when no heirs exist

_____

35. An encumbrance in the form of a monetary claim that affects the title to property

_____

36. The promises that the parties make in a contract or lease agreement

_____

37. An estate in land of indefinite duration

_____

38. An owner's rights in land when it borders a river or a stream and such rights extend to the center of the waterway

_____

39. A lien arising out fairness and justice

_____

40. A parcel of land used in a government survey that consists of one square mile or 640 Acres

_____

41. The remnant of an estate that the grantor or his heirs hold after granting a lesser freehold estate to another person

_____

42. An adjacent landowner's right to not have his property damaged during mineral extraction

43. A two-party trust where the trustor, who is also the beneficiary, retains control over the property held by the trustee

44. A right to use the land of another that runs with the land

45. A form of ownership where more than one person or entity has an interest in the same property at the same time

46. Property which is concurrently owned as tenants in common with the other condominium unit owners

47. Personal permission granted to enter one's land which can be revoked at any time

48. Co-ownership form that can only be used by married couples

49. The right of a creditor to have all of a debtor's property—both real and personal—sold to satisfy a debt

50. A document that establishes the internal rules and procedures for conducting the affairs of the homeowner's association

51. A statutory lien, created to ensure payment for work performed and materials furnished in the improvement of property

52. A theory where each person is entitled to 1/2 of all marital property on divorce

53. A form of "ownership" where in exchange for the purchase of shares, the shareholder receives a proprietary lease on a specific apartment and is obligated to pay a monthly maintenance fee

54. Legal description, measuring height or depth, used when describing subsurface or air rights

55. Growing things which require no annual cultivation and are considered real property

---

56. A legal land description where the surveyor uses a point of beginning, a point of closure, natural or artificial monuments, distances, and compass directions

---

57. A system of land ownership which recognizes the right of individuals to own land independently of political superiors

---

58. A form of condominium ownership where one property is divided among several owners and each owner has a specific period of time in which to use the property

---

59. The rights - possession, use/control, enjoyment, and disposition - that accompany property ownership

---

60. An estate where the grantor places no restrictions or conditions on ownership

---

61. A parcel of land used in a government survey that consists of 6 square miles on each side or 36 square miles

---

62. An item that was once personal property, but that has been attached to and become part of the real property

---

63. A form of concurrent ownership in which each occupant of a multiple unit building holds fee simple title to his individual unit

---

64. A non-possessory interest in which one person has a right to use another's land in a specified manner or for a specific purpose

---

65. A lien affecting or attaching only to a certain, specific parcel of land or piece of property

---

66. All of the factors that go into choosing a location

---

67. The quality, quantity, nature, and extent of the interest that a person has in real property

---

68. A three party arrangement where a trustor gives property to a trustee to hold for the benefit of a third party - the beneficiary

_____

69. Another word for an item of personal property

_____

70. A freehold estate created by deed or will where the grantor grants an estate to the life tenant, but measures the estate based on the life of a third party

_____

71. A permanent improvement, building, or other attachment illegally extends beyond the boundaries onto neighboring land

_____

72. Land and the attachments to the land, with the corresponding bundle of rights

_____

Section 5: *Matching*

A	Legal Life Estate	1 _____	A Dead Person
B	Encroachment	2 _____	Benefits from the Easement
C	Dominant Estate	3 _____	Buyer records the purchase/sale contract
D	Attachment Lien	4 _____	Dower or Curtesy are good examples
E	Conditions	5 _____	Encumbrance placed pending a lawsuit
F	Easement Appurtenant	6 _____	Infringement on neighboring property
G	Covenants	7 _____	Lease starts on 1/20 and ends 1/31
H	Vendee's Lien	8 _____	Limitations in a deed
I	Estate for years	9 _____	Open, no permission, use for the statutory period
J	Escheat	10 _____	Promises in a contract
K	Prescriptive Easement	11 _____	This has both a Dominant Estate and Servient Estate
L	Decedent	12 _____	Unable to locate heirs, goes to the state

A	Equitable	1 _____	ATT can enter one's land
B	Ordinary Life Estate	2 _____	Disposition, Use, Possession, Enjoyment
C	Commercial Easement in Gross	3 _____	Estate created for one's life
D	Fee Simple Determinable	4 _____	Mechanic's Lien
E	Freehold	5 _____	Of indefinite duration
F	Bundle of Rights	6 _____	Out of Fairness and Justice
G	Contingent Remainder	7 _____	Personal permission to enter one's land
H	Eminent Domain	8 _____	Private Land, Public Use, Just Compensation
I	Specific, Statutory Lien	9 _____	Release, Merger, Expiration
J	License	10 _____	Remainder with a condition
K	Termination of Easements	11 _____	To Girls Scouts so long as, then to Boy Scouts

A	Appurtenance	1	_____	Business Personal Property
B	Legal Attachment	2	_____	Level where underground water is found
C	Chattels Real	3	_____	Changing Real Property into Personal Property
D	Emblements	4	_____	Describes Air Rights and Mineral Rights
E	Immobility	5	_____	Digging should not cause damage to adjacent landowner
F	Deed	6	_____	The most distinctive Physical Land Characteristic
G	Littoral Rights	7	_____	Fructus Industriales
H	Right of Lateral Support	8	_____	How to transfer Real Property
I	Correlative Rights	9	_____	Keys and Garage Door Opener
J	Water Table	10	_____	Legal Land Description
K	Situs	11	_____	Location Preference
L	Metes/Bounds	12	_____	Personal Property that Extends an Interest in Real Estate
M	Severance	13	_____	Real Property Rights adjacent to Lakes/Oceans
N	Trade Fixture	14	_____	Reasonable Use of Water when in short supply
O	Datum	15	_____	Runs with the Land

A	Joint Tenancy	1	_____	100 investors; preferred tax treatment
B	Corporation	2	_____	Avoids Probate, right of survivorship
C	Testamentary Trusts	3	_____	Building owned by a Non-Profit corporation
D	Plat	4	_____	Created by will and effective after death
E	Real Estate Investment Trust	5	_____	Detailed site plan for a condominium
F	Severalty	6	_____	Has perpetual existence
G	Timeshare	7	_____	How married couples can take title
H	General Partnership	8	_____	Also known as interval ownership
I	Unities of Title	9	_____	Marital property vs. Separate property
J	Land Trust	10	_____	Partners fully responsible; day-to-day management
K	A Cooperative	11	_____	Possession, Interest, Time, and Title
L	Tenants by the Entirety	12	_____	Property Owned by Government
M	Publicly Owned Real Estate	13	_____	Rules for how the HOA should perform
N	By Laws	14	_____	Sole Ownership
O	Community Property	15	_____	Trustor who is also the beneficiary

A   Declaration

B   Living Trust

C   Limited Liability Company

D   Proprietary Lease

E   Tenants in Common

F   Common Elements

G   Trusts

H   CC&R's

I   Limited Partnership

J   Partition Suit

K   Tenement

L   One Square Mile

M   Survey

N   43,560

O   Attachment

1 _____ Coop Unit; Personal Property Interest

2 _____ Description of each condo unit

3 _____ Lawsuit when the parties disagree

4 _____ Liability Limited to the investment

5 _____ Members, limited liability, preferred taxes

6 _____ Most often will involve 3 parties

7 _____ Playground, Swimming pool, Condo Owners

8 _____ Rules for the condominium owners

9 _____ Separate Titles, Undivided Interest

10 _____ Trust Effective during one's lifetime

11 _____ Section

12 _____ Shows Property Boundary Lines

13 _____ Things permanently attached to the land

14 _____ Changing Personal Property to Real Property

15 _____ Square Feet in an Acre

Section 6: *Analysis Fill-In*

1. What is meant by an Undivided interest in the whole?

_____

2. Name two differences between a limited and a general partnership:

_____

3. What test would you use to determine if an item is a fixture?

_____

4. What form of "ownership" uses a proprietary lease?

_____

5. What are common elements?

_____

6. In this arrangement, the trustor is also the beneficiary:

_____

7. Do joint tenants need consent of the others to sell or transfer their interest?

_____

8. In which form of ownership is a partition suit not allowed?

_____

9. What is most important factor when deciding on community property?

_____

10. Name two ways joint tenancy differs from tenants by the entirety:

_____

11. In what form of ownership, must the parties' interests be equal?

_____

12. Define right of survivorship:

_____

13. How many titles are there in a joint tenancy?

_____

14. What does severalty ownership mean?

_____

15. **What are the unities of title?**

_____

16. **When would you ask for an attachment lien?**

_____

17. **Two ways to terminate an easement:**

_____

18. **Two ways to create an easement:**

_____

19. **Name two ways a license and easement in gross differ:**

_____

20. **Give an example of an encroachment:**

_____

21. **Name two types of easements:**

_____

22. **Give one example of a general lien:**

_____

23. **Give two examples of a specific lien:**

_____

24. **Name the private encumbrances:**

_____

25. **Name the public encumbrances:**

_____

26. **Name one type of estate where there could be a reversionary interest:**

_____

27. **Name the Freehold estates:**

_____

28. **Estate in land definition:**

_____

29. What rights are contained in the bundle of rights?

_____

30. How many square feet are in an acre?

_____

31. What do we use to describe height or depth in a legal description?

_____

32. How do you find an encroachment?

_____

33. Name the economic characteristics of land:

_____

34. Name the physical characteristics of land:

_____

35. What is the most distinctive physical characteristic of land?

_____

36. Give an example of an appurtenance:

_____

37. What is a water table?

_____

38. How do you change real property to personal property?

_____

39. How do you change personal property to real property?

_____

40. What is the right of lateral support?

_____

41. What is a legal attachment?

_____

42. What term do we use for all factors that goes into choosing a location:

_____

Section 7: *Analysis Multiple Choice*

1. **Which of the following statements is TRUE?**
   A. Trade Fixtures installed by the landlord are still considered personal property
   B. When a tenant installs a stove in a premises, it is now real property
   C. A hood vent installed by Zaxby's in a rental premises is personal property after the lease expires
   D. Trade Fixtures installed after a landlord mortgages a property are considered personal property

2. **What do both Joint Tenancy and Tenants by the entirety have in common?**
   A. Deeds must be signed by all owners in order to convey an interest
   B. Deeds can be signed by one of the owners to convey an interest
   C. Neither allows partition suits
   D. The last survivor owns the property in severalty

3. **Syed owned an 80 acre parcel in a rural community. He sold 10 acres to Janice. Janice realized after the closing that she didn't have any access to the property. She contacted Syed and requested access through his property. He refused. Janice decided to take Syed to court and was granted access by the court even though she didn't have Syed's permission. The court granted:**
   A. An easement by prescription
   B. An easement by necessity
   C. An easement by court grant
   D. An easement by implication

4. **Real Property includes all of the following EXCEPT:**
   A. Appurtenances
   B. Emblements
   C. Tenements
   D. Attachments

5. **Mary is walking across the street in a downtown area and is hit by an automobile. Mary is severely injured and her attorney is concerned that the driver, a top executive, will begin to transfer his assets out of his name. Which of the following would not be appropriate at the beginning of the lawsuit under these circumstances?**
   A. Encumbrance
   B. Specific Lien
   C. General Lien
   D. Attachment Lien

6. **Malik goes to Florida with his family and decides to purchase a unit where he is deeded the right to use the property every year for one week during the summer season. Malik purchased a:**
   A. Condominium
   B. Timeshare
   C. Fee Simple Absolute
   D. Defeasible fee

7. **Life estate ownership includes all of the following except:**
   A. The right to mortgage the property
   B. The right to exclude others from the property
   C. The right to rent the property
   D. The right to sell the property

8. **Jon and June, a married couple, own their property as tenants by the entirety. Which of the following is FALSE?**
   A. There is one title of ownership while married
   B. Either party can seek to partition the property while married
   C. On divorce, they can remain owners of the property if they choose
   D. Neither party can sell the property without the others consent while married

9. **John hired Dale, a general contractor to complete an addition on his home. Dale hired 4 subcontractors to perform some of the work. John paid Dale the total amount of $100,000 at the end of the job. Five months later, one of the subcontractors placed a lien on John's home. Was this permissible?**
   A. Yes, even though John paid Dale, John should've gotten releases from all subcontractors
   B. No, because John paid Dale the full amount and Dale was responsible to pay the subcontractors
   C. No, because all mechanic's liens must be filed within 3 months of completion of the job
   D. No, because this type of lien should've been placed against John, not his home

10. **Harry and Jane own a condominium unit together in fee simple. When Jane dies, will Harry be able to take ownership of the unit in severalty?**
    A. Yes, because Harry is now the sole owner of the unit
    B. No, because it depends on what Jane's will states relating to the ownership
    C. Yes, if the parties owned the property as Joint Tenants
    D. No, because we'd have to wait and see whether Jane has heirs

11. **From the standpoint of the dominant estate, an easement is a(n) ____**
    A. Reversion
    B. Appurtenance
    C. Encumbrance
    D. Lien

12. **Five owners have a joint tenancy. One owner decides to sell the property to another person with the consent of the other joint tenants. The resulting interest is as follows:**
    A. Four joints tenants each owning 20% and a tenant in common owning 20%
    B. Five joint tenants because the interest cannot be sold without the consent of the other joint tenants
    C. All tenants in common, but the ownership amounts cannot be determined
    D. Four joint tenants each owning 25% in the joint tenancy and a tenant in common owning 25%

13. **Denzel is going to sell his home. He has no intent to leave his freestanding 100" big screen TV that he has customized to fit into a cabinet in his home. When showings begin, Denzel's agent explains that the TV will not be left to all who come to see the home and also includes it in the listing. When Denzel accepts an offer on the property, there is no mention of the TV. Since all were informed, prior to the closing, Denzel removes the TV and is sued by the purchaser. Was Denzel allowed to move the TV?**
    A. Yes, because it was freestanding and not attached
    B. Yes, because the agent informed everyone and included it in the listing
    C. Yes, if the parties now agree to amend the contract to allow him to take it
    D. Yes, because he never intended to leave it

14. **A Moe's Southwest Grill franchise owner requested that the landlord install a vent hood in the leased premises because Moe's needed to use it to sauté its vegetables. At the end of the lease, can Moe's remove the hood?**
    A. Yes, because all Trade Fixtures are personal property
    B. No, because even though a vent hood can be a trade fixture, it is not in this case
    C. Yes, as long as Moe's removes it prior to the end of the lease
    D. No, because any times use in a business must be left for the landlord

15. **A cooperative owner is moving out of the area and wishes to divest himself of the cooperative. In order to do so, he must:**
    A. Sell his shares, but doesn't need Board Approval to do so
    B. Sell his unit, but does need Board Approval to do so
    C. Sell his unit, but doesn't need Board Approval to do so
    D. Sell his shares, but does need Board Approval to do so

16. **With regard to priority of rights, which is true?**
    A. All liens have priority based upon the recordation date
    B. All federal income tax liens have priority regardless of when filed
    C. Special assessment liens always have priority
    D. Mortgage liens always have priority

17. **Why would a person file an attachment lien?**
    A. To prevent the conveyance of the property that is under contract
    B. To force a person to follow the deed restrictions
    C. To ensure that the vendor gets payment for labor and materials
    D. To prevent the conveyance of the property pending a lawsuit

18. **Which of the following two items are not classified as real property?**
    A. A shrub planted into the ground and a real estate contract
    B. Built in dishwasher and a throw rug
    C. Emblements and Trade Fixtures
    D. Fixtures and emblements

19. **Which of the following is the best description of a fee simple absolute estate?**
    A. A non-inheritable estate that extends for the period of a person's life
    B. An inheritable estate without conditions
    C. Interest in a property for which a party to the transaction has paid a fee
    D. Interest in a property that is supported by consideration

20. **Which of the following is not an encumbrance that affects property specifically?**
    A. Mechanic's Liens
    B. Deed restrictions
    C. Judgments
    D. Encroachments

21. **Which of the following is a purpose of a staked survey?**
    A. Estimating the value of a property
    B. Determining assessed value
    C. Locating property boundaries
    D. Evaluating marketability of title

22. **Which of the following is a characteristic of a limited partner's role in a limited partnership?**
    A. Reduced personal liability and no management decision making
    B. A fixed return on investments and a loss of income tax write-offs
    C. Official anonymity with certain tax exemptions and a loss of annual profits exceeding 20% of the investment
    D. Authority over larger decisions and active interest investment potential

23. **Which of the following easements must be created by written document?**
    A. Reservation
    B. Prescription
    C. Necessity
    D. Implication

24. Three people leased a waterfront bungalow. The lease began on June 15, 2010, and continued through July 31, 2010. They had:
    A. A tenancy at will
    B. A joint tenancy
    C. A tenancy for years
    D. A tenancy in common

25. There were several liens recorded on a particular home. The liens were a special assessment lien, a federal income tax lien, a first mortgage lien recorded before any of the liens. In what order will the liens be paid?
    A. First mortgage, federal income tax lien, special assessment lien
    B. First mortgage, special assessment lien, federal income tax lien
    C. Federal income tax lien, First mortgage, special assessment lien
    D. Special assessment lien, First mortgage, federal income tax lien

26. Ten Years ago, Mrs. Jones told her neighbor, Mr. Smith, that he can use her driveway anytime he wishes. He has been using it since then. When Mrs. Jones went to sell her property, the new purchaser refused to let Mr. Smith use the driveway. Can the purchaser do this?
    A. Yes, because Mrs. Jones granted Mr. Smith a license that terminated upon sale
    B. Yes, because easements in gross terminate upon sale of the property
    C. No, because Mr. Smith's right runs with the land
    D. No, because after the continued use, Mr. Smith has an easement by prescription

27. Mary decides to purchase an above ground swimming pool. She builds a custom deck around the pool. A year later, she decides to sell her home and wants to take the above ground pool with her. Will she be able to do so?
    A. No, the above ground swimming pool is now likely considered a fixture
    B. No, because above ground swimming pools are considered real property and must remain with the premises
    C. Yes, because above ground swimming pools are considered personal property and can be taken upon sale
    D. Yes, she can take it with her because there was no indication that she intended to leave it there

28. John, Jill, and Jane own property as joint tenants. Jane decides to sell her portion to Jim, but did not get consent from John or Jill. The result of this transfer:
    A. John, Jill, and Jim are now joint tenants and each own 33 1/3% of the property
    B. John, Jill, and Jane are still the owners of the property 33 1/3% because Jane needs consent to transfer her portion
    C. John Jill, and Jim are now joint tenants but John and Jill own 75% and Jim owns 25%
    D. John, Jill, and Jim own 33 1/3% each, but only John and Jill are joint tenants

29. John owns a property on a non-navigable stream. What kind of right does he have in the stream and where does his property line end?
    A. Riparian right to the high tide mark
    B. Littoral right to the high-water mark
    C. Riparian right to the high-water mark
    D. Riparian right to the center of the stream

30. A seller builds a deck and cuts a hole in it and sits the hot tub in the hole. The buyer is the seller's brother. The hot tub would most likely be considered:
    A. Personal Property given the way the hot tub was attached to the deck
    B. Real Property given that the deck was modified to receive the hot tub
    C. Personal Property because seller's intention was to keep the hot tub
    D. Real Property because the seller and buyer are related

Chapter 4 Answers

1. D	9. C	17. A	25. C	33. C	41. C	49. C	57. A	65. B
2. D	10. C	18. D	26. C	34. C	42. B	50. A	58. C	66. C
3. C	11. B	19. D	27. B	35. D	43. C	51. B	59. C	67. D
4. B	12. D	20. D	28. A	36. B	44. D	52. C	60. C	68. A
5. D	13. A	21. B	29. A	37. C	45. A	53. B	61. B	69. C
6. C	14. B	22. C	30. C	38. C	46. D	54. A	62. A	70. A
7. A	15. D	23. A	31. B	39. A	47. A	55. A	63. A	71. B
8. D	16. D	24. D	32. A	40. D	48. B	56. D	64. B	72. D

1. Littoral Right
2. Short-Form/Record Plat
3. Easement by Prescription
4. Real Estate
5. Conditions
6. Fructus Industriales
7. Proprietary Lease
8. Remainderman
9. Legal Life Estate
10. Severance
11. Immobility
12. Improvement
13. Percolating Water
14. Fee Simple Determinable
15. Right of Survivorship
16. Joint Tenancy
17. Appurtenance
18. Mortgage Lien
19. Encumbrance
20. Government Survey
21. Deed
22. Covenants, Conditions, Restrictions (CC&Rs)
23. Easement in Gross
24. Injunction
25. Conventional Life Estate
26. Tenant in Common
27. Accession
28. Fee Simple on Condition Subsequent
29. Bill of Sale
30. Partition Suit
31. Acre
32. Severalty
33. Personal Property
34. Escheat
35. Lien
36. Covenants
37. Freehold
38. Riparian Right
39. Equitable Lien
40. Section
41. Reversion
42. Right of Lateral Support
43. Land Trust
44. Easement Appurtenant
45. Concurrent Ownership
46. Common Elements
47. License
48. Tenants by the Entirety
49. General Lien
50. By Laws
51. Mechanic's Lien
52. Community Property
53. Cooperative
54. Datum
55. Fructus Naturales
56. Metes and Bounds
57. Allodial System
58. Timesharing
59. Bundle of Rights
60. Fee Simple Absolute
61. Township
62. Fixture
63. Condominium
64. Easement
65. Specific Lien
66. Situs
67. Estate in Land
68. Trust
69. Chattel
70. Life Estate Pur Autre Vie
71. Encroachment
72. Real Property

Exercise 1

1. L	3. H	5. D	7. I	9. K	11. F
2. C	4. A	6. B	8. E	10. G	12. J

Exercise 2

1. C	3. B	5. E	7. J	9. K	11. D
2. F	4. I	6. A	8. H	10. G	

Exercise 3

1. N	5. H	9. B	13. G
2. J	6. E	10. L	14. I
3. M	7. D	11. K	15. A
4. O	8. F	12. C	

Exercise 4

1. E	3. K	5. D	7. L	9. O	11. I	13. N	15. J
2. A	4. C	6. B	8. G	10. H	12. M	14. F	

Exercise 5

1. D	3. J	5. C	7. F	9. E	11. L	13. K	15. N
2. A	4. I	6. G	8. H	10. B	12. M	14. O	

Section 6 Answer Key:

1. Possession – Regardless of interest owned, all parties have an equal right to possess

2. 1. A limited partner has limited liability to his investment only - 2. A limited partner does not participate in the management of the business

3. M - odification A - ttachment R - elationship between the parties I - ntention A - greement

4. Cooperative

5. Items such as a swimming pool and parking lot shared by condo owners as tenants in common

6. Land Trust

7. No, only in tenants by the entirety

8. Tenants by the entirety

9. Whether the property is separate or marital property

10. 1. Cannot partition in tenancy by the entirety - 2. Tenants by the entirety is for married couples only - 3. None of the tenants by the entirety can sell or transfer their interest without consent

11. Joint Tenants or Tenants by the entirety

12. When one tenant dies, his share automatically passes to the surviving tenant

13. One

14. One owner or one entity

15. Possession, Interest, Time, Title

16. To prevent transfer of ownership of a property pending a lawsuit

17. Merger, Release, Prescription, Abandonment, Necessity, Expiration of Purpose

18. Grant, Reservation, Implication, Prescription, Condemnation, Agreement, Necessity

19. 1. License – Permission; Easement – Creates an interest - 2. License – can be oral; Easement – writing - 3. License – revocable; Easement – irrevocable - 4. License – friend, neighbor; Easement – company

20. 1. One person builds his home over the property line of an adjacent home - 2. A tree limb from one home infringes over the property line of another home

21. 1. Appurtenant - 2. In Gross

22. Judgment or Federal Income Tax

23. Mortgage - Property Tax - Mechanic's - Vendee's

24. Encroachment, Covenants, Conditions, Liens, Easements

25. Police Power, Eminent Domain, Taxation, Escheat

26. Any estate where a lesser estate is being given such as a Fee Simple Determinable or Life Estate, but not in a Fee Simple Absolute because the entire estate is being given away

27. Fee Simple Absolute, Fee Simple Determinable, Fee Simple Condition Subsequent, Life Estate

28. Quantity, Quality, and Duration of one's interest in a property

29. Disposition, Possession, Use/Control, Enjoyment

30. 43,560

31. Datum

32. Survey

33. Improvements, Situs, Scarcity, Fixed Investment

34. Immobility, Indestructibility, Non-Homogeneity

35. Immobility

36. Fence, Pool, Water Rights (any right, interest, benefit, or improvement that runs with the land)

37. The level at which percolating water is found

38. Severance

39. Attachment

40. The adjacent landowner's right to have any extractions done in a manner that doesn't damage his land

41. A fixture that is personal property but operates an item of real property (remote control for a garage door opener or projector)

42. Situs

SECTION 7 ANSWERS:

1. D. The mortgage on the property does not change the trade fixtures from being personal property if removed prior to the expiration of the lease

2. D. The last survivor of either a joint tenancy or tenancy by the entirety will own the property in severalty. Deeds can be signed by either party in a Joint Tenancy but need both parties in a Tenancy by the Entirety and in a Tenancy by the Entirety, partition suits are not allowed

3. B. An easement by necessity is created with the seller sells property in a way to deprive the buyer access. In such case, the court could grant such an easement

4. B. Emblements (crops) are always considered to be personal property. Appurtenances, Tenements, and Attachments are all considered to be real property

5. C. A general lien would not be appropriate at this point because Mary is at the beginning of the lawsuit. The most appropriate action would be to seek an attachment lien so that assets are not transferred pending the lawsuit. Because an attachment lien is a specific encumbrance, both A and B are also correct. If Mary wins, then a general lien would be appropriate

6. B. The example describes a classic timeshare where one may be deeded a week or given a right to use a week for a stated period of time. In exchange the person will pay an upfront fee and a maintenance fee throughout his ownership

7. D. Life estate tenants are "LIKE" owners of the property for the time that they are alive. However, once the person passes, the property reverts to the owner. Because a life tenant doesn't FULL ownership rights and because there is a reversion, they are not given the entire estate. So, while they can sell their interest in the life estate, they cannot sell the property

8. B. Neither party in a tenants by the entirety can partition the property while married. On divorce, they can remain owners of the property, but the title would have to be changed to tenants in common or joint tenancy

9. A. Mechanic's Liens (liens on behalf of someone who has improved a property) can still be filed by the subcontractor even if the general contractor has been paid the full amount. There is no rule that it must be brought within 3-months, and these are specific, not general liens

10. C. The first question here is how they owned the property. Until we know that, we cannot answer the question. So, the correct answer will hinge upon that. If the property was owned as Joint Tenants, then B and D would not come into play at all. A would be the second-best answer here but one cannot not know if A is true without knowing C

11. B. From the dominant estate's standpoint, he is benefiting from the easement. He now has access, and his property value has increased. The easement is appurtenant to his property

12. A. Joint Tenancy requires the unities of title (PITT). Once those unities are broken, the new owner is a tenant in common with the other owners who still have a joint tenancy. A person also does not need consent to sell their interest in a joint tenancy while they are alive

13. C. The TV will be determined to be a fixture. It doesn't matter that Denzel did not intend to leave it, informed prospects that he would not leave it, or that it was freestanding. The only thing that matters is the law and what is in the contract. Because Denzel modified the cabinet to receive the TV, it is a fixture. The only way he can now take it is if the seller agrees to amend the contract

14. B. A trade fixture is an item installed by the business tenant. They can be removed prior to the expiration of the lease because they are personal property. However, when the landlord installs the item, it is not considered a trade fixture and must be left by the tenant

15. D. Coop owners do not own the units they reside in. They have a proprietary lease on the unit of their choice through the purchase of shares in the cooperative. Any share owner who wishes to leave the coop may do so, but the new share owner must be approved by the cooperative

16. C. Property Tax liens always have priority over others. Because a special assessment is a form of a property tax, it has priority. Federal income tax liens never have priority. They are treated the same as all other liens in terms of recordation date

17. D. Attachment liens are filed to prevent someone from transferring property out of his name pending a lawsuit. It is the only lien that prevents conveyance of property

18. C. Both Emblements and Trade Fixtures are personal property. A. is real and personal, B. is real and personal, D. is real and personal

19. B. An inheritable estate without conditions

20. C. All encumbrances do not affect property specifically. Some are because of a lawsuit in which case, in order to enforce, one must find or hope that the debtor has real or personal property. In this case, Mechanic's Lien, Deed Restrictions, and Encroachment all affect the property, but Judgments are a type of lien that must be enforced by finding real or personal property of the debtor

21. C. Surveys are utilized to delineate property boundaries as well as identify encroachments

22. A. A limited partner is not responsible for the day-to-day activities and as such, has limited liability

23. A. Of those listed, only a reservation is created by written document. Prescription is open and continuous use; Necessity would be created by a court when necessary to get access; Implication is also created by a court when it makes sense in that circumstance

24. C. A tenancy for years is any date certain. It doesn't matter how long. Here, the end date is July 31, 2010, so it is a date certain

25. D. Liens are paid in order of priority. Most priority is because of recordation. However, certain liens (property taxes) always have priority. Because a special assessment is a property tax lien, it will be paid first. Because the mortgage was recorded prior to any other lien, it will be paid right after the special assessment. The federal income tax lien which doesn't have any special priority will be paid last

26. A. Mrs. Jones gave her neighbor a license and all licenses are revocable at any time. Further, all licenses terminate on sale of the property. While easements in gross also terminate upon the sale of the property, this is not an easement. The use of the terms (easement grants must be in writing) and neighbor (suggesting a friendly relationship, not a sale) help us to determine that this was a license

27. A. Because Mary modified the deck to receive the pool, the pool is now considered a fixture. When a person marries two pieces to function together, the free-standing item will most likely have to remain with the property

28. D. Because the unities of title (PITT) have been broken, the new owner (Jim) is now a tenant in common with John and Jill who are still joint tenants. Consent to transfer an interest is not necessary

29. D. Ownership that abuts a river or stream is a riparian right and those owners own to the center of the river or stream

30. B. Real Property since modification under the fixture test will consider free standing items real property when the two items have been married to work together

Chapter 5: Transfer of Title

Section 1: *Outline*

I. Title Transfer – an exploration of deeds, title, and ownership

A. Title – right of ownership and the evidence of that right. When title changes hands, it is called **alienation**

    1. Involuntary Transfers of Title – without the owner's consent

Transfers by Natural Causes

    a. Accretion – gradual build-up of the land from wind or water. The deposited material is called **alluvium**

    b. Reliction (or dereliction) – **increase** in the land **when the water recedes.** The newly exposed land now belongs to the riparian owner

    c. Erosion – The gradual loss of land

    d. Avulsion – The violent or sudden loss of land due to a flood, earthquake, or hurricane

Transfers by Operation of Law

    a. Condemnation – legal action by the government to take property by eminent domain

    b. Intestate succession – when the property owner dies without a will (**intestate**), the estate will be distributed to heirs by **laws of descent and distribution**

    c. Community Property – each spouse owns half of the marital property upon divorce

    d. Adverse Possession – when one person (squatter) **openly, continuously, and without permission** occupies another's land for the **statutory time period,** after bringing a **quiet title action**, he could be awarded title in this manner

        i. Tacking – adding one's time to a previous occupant to meet the statutory time period

        ii. Color of Title – shortening the adverse possession time period by some appearance of ownership (new roof, paying taxes)

    e. Forfeiture of Title – Fee Simple Determinable – Breach of the condition will result in a **reversion** or **remainder** without court action

Transfers by Court Action

    a. Partition Sale – a concurrent owner (not a tenant by the entirety) asks the court to solve the disagreement regarding separation of the property

    b. Foreclosure Sale – a court ordered procedure for sale of the property to satisfy the debts of the owner

    c. Quiet Title Action – court awards title to someone after proof of ownership; also used to clear clouds when a person is unavailable

      d. Forfeiture of Title – Fee Simple Condition Subsequent – Breach of the condition will require a court action for the **reversion** or **remainder** to take place

  2. **Voluntary Transfers of Title** – with the owner's consent

      a. Transfer by Government Patent or Public Grant – **patent** is the document used when the government conveys land to a private individual

      b. Transfer by Will – **Testator** writes the **Last Will and Testament**, dies **Testate**, and names an **executor. Real property** is a **devise** to be received by a **devisee. Personal Property** is a **legacy or bequest** to be received by a **legatee.** Will modifications require a **Codicil.** When real property is conveyed after death, transfer is by executor's deed

        i. Formal Will – a typed or pre-printed instrument usually prepared by an attorney
        ii. Holographic Will – will entirely handwritten, dated, and signed by testator
        iii. Nuncupative Will – will made orally, in **expectation of impending death**, effective only for the disposition of personal property

      c. Transfer by Gift- A **gift deed (voluntary deed)** is used to gift property to a relative. The phrase "for love and affection" is known as **good consideration**

      d. Transfer by Sale – voluntary transfer of property

II. Deeds – A written instrument that conveys an interest in the property to the person who accepts it.

The person conveying the interest is called the **grantor (giver)** and the person receiving the interest is the **grantee (receiver)**

Requirements for a Valid Deed Conveyance:

1. **Must Be in Writing** (Statute of Frauds)
2. **Grantor Must Be Named and be Legally Competent** – Legal age, sound mind, and **genuine assent** (free will). A **guardian** would be necessary to transfer property for a minor or impaired person
3. **Grantee Must Be Named** - legal competency is not required
4. **Consideration** – exchange of promises
5. **Legal Description** – Metes and Bounds, Government Survey, Recorded Plat
6. **Granting Clause (Words of Conveyance)** – must clearly express the **grantor's intent** and identify the type of interest being granted such as easement, fee simple estate or some lesser estate
7. **Signature of the Grantor(s)** – only the grantor is required to sign
8. **Delivery and Acceptance** – title is conveyed when a properly executed deed is **delivered** to and **accepted** by the **grantee** or the grantee's agent (Doctrine of Relation Back) during the **grantor's lifetime.** Acceptance can be **express** or **implied.**

Typical (but not essential) Deed Provisions

1. **Date** – not necessary but customary
2. **Habendum Clause** – describes the quantity and duration of the estate being granted. Should mirror the granting clause
3. **Reservation and Exceptions – Reservation** – reserving **(USE)** of something on the property; **Exception** – excluding some physical portion of the property **(TITLE)** being granted

Covenants of Title – the grantor promises that certain conditions of the title exist

1. **Covenant of Seisin** – the grantor does own the property and has a right to convey it
2. **Covenant Against Encumbrances** – there are no encumbrances except those specifically mentioned in the deed
3. **Covenant of Quiet Enjoyment** – the grantee will not suffer interference from others having superior claim to title
4. **Covenant of Warranty Forever** – obligates the grantor to compensate the grantee for any loss suffered in defending the title from past claims

5. **Covenant of Further or Future Assurances** – obligates the grantor to produce any document that might be needed to perfect the title. If an error in a deed is found, a **correction deed (deed of reformation)** may be necessary

Legal Aspects of Deeds

   a. **Seal** – actual seal is no longer required but it is a good idea to use corporate seal

   b. **Attestation-** act of witnessing the grantor's signature and signing the deed as a witness

   c. **Acknowledgment** – formal declaration made by the grantor in the presence of an authorized official, usually a notary, that the deed is being signed voluntarily

Types of Deeds – when properly executed, delivered, and accepted, all deeds serve to convey that grantor's interest in the property

1. **Warranty Deeds** – guarantees good title to the property and contains all 5 covenants of title

   a. **General Warranty Deed** – the grantor is promising to guarantee the title from when the property was constructed even if not owned by the grantor during that period

   b. **Special Warranty Deed (Limited Warranty Deed)** – same as a general warranty except that the warranties only protect against defects while the grantor owned the property

2. **Grant Deed** – limited to the covenants of Seisin and Encumbrance

3. **Bargain and Sale Deed** – promises that title to the property is being conveyed but contains no warranties about the condition of the title

4. **Quitclaim Deed** – conveys any interest in the property that the grantor **might have.** There are no warranties, either express or implied. The grantor may not even have an interest to convey. Most often used to clear clouds

5. **Special Purpose Deeds**

   a. **Gift Deed** – property given by gift

   b. **Deeds of Trust (Trust Deeds)** – used in some states in place of a mortgage lien. When the loan is satisfied the trustee signs a **deed of reconveyance (See Finance Module)**

   c. **Deed of Reformation (Correction Deed)** – used for correcting mistakes in another deed

   d. **Court Ordered Deeds** – when an officer of the court is used to convey title such as a **sheriff's deed, deed in foreclosure, tax deed or deed in partition**

   e. **Deeds Executed by Court Appointed Representatives** – i.e., guardian's deed, executor's deed, and administrator's deed

III. Title Protection – Insurance against title encumbrances

1. **Constructive Notice** – knowledge that one is presumed by law to have, even though there is no actual knowledge of the fact. The first to give this notice is the owner of the property – **moving in, recording the deed, cultivating the land**

2. **Actual Notice** – knowledge acquired through what has been seen, heard, read, or observed by making reasonable and diligent inquiry into logical sources of information

3. **Recording**

   a. **Constructive Notice** – gives the whole world notice of the interest the document represents

   b. **Priority of Lien order** – the lien recorded first is most often paid first

   c. **Requirements for Recording** – state laws regulate the requirements of documents that are to be recorded. Acknowledgment and attestation are often required to record documents

   d. **Recording of the deed is not required for validity**

   Two systems to locate a parcel:

     1. **Tract Index** – provides a map where each parcel of land is given a number which refers to a reference book

     2. **Grantor-Grantee index** – alphabetical list of all grantors and grantees for each calendar year

4. **Methods of Title Protection**

   a. **Title Reports** – lawyer or title company is retained to issue a report on either the complete history of a title or the records dating back a specified number of years

      1. **Chain of title** – recorded instruments revealing a continuous link of ownership from the original grant to the present owner
      2. **Abstract of title** – a condensed history of the title
      3. **Cloud on the title** – a **title defect** that would include any claim, lien or encumbrance that impairs the title
      4. **Quiet title action** –**removing a cloud** on the title when the interests are adverse, or the person is unavailable
      5. **Certificate of title** – similar to an abstract

   b. **Title Insurance** – **Protects against** what happened in the **past** not against what happens in the future. Both recorded and unrecorded defects are covered but they must exist when the policy is issued. One-time premium usually paid at closing

      1. **Lender's Policy** – protects the lender (loan amount) against loss due to a title defect and it is valid as long as there is an outstanding balance on the loan
      2. **Owner's Policy** – protects the owner's equity in the property. Protection lasts for as long as the owner or heirs have an interest or any obligation regarding the property

Section 2: *Vocabulary*

Abstract of Title: A condensed history report of the chain of title

Accretion: Buildup of land through wind and water

Acknowledgment: A signor's declaration made before an authorized person

Actual Notice: Direct knowledge that one has because he saw, heard, or read it

Adverse Possession: An open, notorious, exclusive, and continuous way of gaining title to property

Alienation: Transfer of Title by will, gift, deed

Alluvion: The soil that has been deposited on the shore resulting from accretion

Attestation: A witness' certification of validity

Avulsion: Sudden change in land mass due to a violent weather act

Chain of Title: All recorded and unrecorded instruments revealing the history of ownership

Cloud on Title: Title defect including any claim, lien, or encumbrance

Color of Title: Shortens the adverse possession time frame with proof of additional information

Constructive Notice: Knowledge that one is presumed to have

Covenants of Title: Promises in the deed made by the grantor certifying that certain conditions of title exist

Deed: A document to Transfer Real Property

Dereliction: Increase in Land when water recedes

Erosion: The gradual wearing away of land as a result of wind or water

Executor: A person named in the will designated to carry out its terms

Exception: The exclusion of a physical portion of the property being granted

Grantor: A person that conveys an interest in real property by deed

Grantee: A person who receives an interest in real property by deed

Holographic Will: A handwritten will by a testator

Intestate: A person who died without a will

Laws of Descent and Distribution: Law that determines how property is transferred after intestate death

Nuncupative Will: Oral Will in expectation of impending death

Probate Court: A court that determines the validity of a will and the rightful heirs

Quitclaim Deed: A voluntary transfer, without warranties, that conveys the grantor's interest to the grantee

Quiet Title Action: Court Action to Acquire Legal Title in one's name

Recording: The act of entering documents concerning title to a property into the public records

Reservation: Conveyance of property but retention of something on it

Statute of Frauds: Governs the enforceability of real estate contracts

Tacking: A theory that allows two parties to add time together to gain adverse possession

Testator: A person who dies with a will

Warranty Deed: A deed that guarantees clear title to the buyer through covenants

Section 3: *Recall Multiple Choice*

1. **Excluding a physical portion of the property being granted**
   A. Reservation
   B. Exception
   C. Dedication
   D. Effective

2. **A person named in the will designated to carry out its terms**
   A. Executor
   B. Devisee
   C. Testator
   D. Intestate

3. **Promises that the grantor makes certifying that certain conditions of title exist**
   A. Warranty Deed
   B. Abstract of Title
   C. Certificate of Title
   D. Covenants of Title

4. **A person who receives an interest in real property by deed**
   A. Grantee
   B. Grantor
   C. Testator
   D. Devisee

5. **Direct knowledge that one has because he saw, heard, or read it**
   A. Actual Notice
   B. Constructive Notice
   C. Statute Of Frauds
   D. Habendum Clause

6. **A person that conveys an interest in real property by deed**
   A. Grantor
   B. Intestate
   C. Grantee
   D. Testator

7. **Shortens adverse possession time frame with proof of additional information**
   A. Chain of Title
   B. Cloud on Title
   C. Color of Title
   D. Abstract of Title

8. **A court that determines the validity of a will and the rightful heirs**
   A. Grant Deed
   B. Probate Court
   C. Small Claims Court
   D. Statute Of Frauds

9. **Title defect including any claim, lien, or encumbrance**
   A. Abstract of Title
   B. Cloud on Title
   C. Color of Title
   D. Chain of Title

10. **A voluntary transfer, without warranties, that conveys the grantor's interest**
    A. Special Warranty Deed
    B. Bargain And Sale Deed
    C. Quitclaim Deed
    D. Warranty Deed

11. **A condensed history report of the chain of title**
    A. Constructive Notice
    B. Abstract of Title
    C. Chain of Title
    D. Cloud on Title

12. **Died without a will**
    A. Executor
    B. Escheat
    C. Intestate
    D. Testator

13. **Sudden change in land mass due to a violent weather act**
    A. Accretion
    B. Avulsion
    C. Alienation
    D. Erosion

14. **A person who dies with a will**
    A. Testator
    B. Intestate
    C. Executor
    D. Grantor

15. **The soil that has been deposited on the shore as a result of accretion**
    A. Erosion
    B. Accretion
    C. Reservation
    D. Alluvion

16. **Buildup of land through wind and water**
    A. Accretion
    B. Attestation
    C. Erosion
    D. Avulsion

17. **Document to Transfer Real Property**
    A. Title
    B. Executor
    C. Deed
    D. Devise

18. Conveyance of property but keeps use of something on it
   A. Condemnation
   B. Exception
   C. Reservation
   D. Consideration

19. A signor's declaration made before an authorized person
   A. Codicil
   B. Constructive Notice
   C. Consideration
   D. Acknowledgment

20. Witness certification of validity
   A. Recording
   B. Attestation
   C. Dereliction
   D. Acknowledgment

21. Handwritten Will
   A. Abstract of Title
   B. Holographic Will
   C. Constructive Notice
   D. Nuncupative Will

22. Oral Will in expectation of impending death
   A. Abstract of Title
   B. Nuncupative Will
   C. Quiet Title Action
   D. Constructive Notice

23. Court Action to Acquire Legal Title in one's name resulting from adverse possession
   A. Constructive Notice
   B. Abstract Of Title
   C. Quiet Title Action
   D. Owner's Title Policy

24. Adding time to another in Adverse Possession
   A. Recording
   B. Tacking
   C. Codicil
   D. Avulsion

25. Knowledge that you're presumed to have
   A. Constructive Notice
   B. Actual Notice
   C. Correction Deed
   D. Abstract Of Title

26. Governs the enforceability of real estate contracts
   A. Statute of Limitations
   B. Statute of Frauds
   C. Actual Notice
   D. Habendum Clause

27. **Increase in Land when water recedes**
    A. Erosion
    B. Dereliction
    C. Attestation
    D. Avulsion

28. **Transfer of Title by will, gift, deed**
    A. Condemnation
    B. Alienation
    C. Avulsion
    D. Accretion

29. **The gradual wearing away of land as a result of wind or water**
    A. Erosion
    B. Avulsion
    C. Accretion
    D. Adverse Possession

30. **All recorded and unrecorded instruments revealing the history of ownership**
    A. Lender's Title Policy
    B. Abstract of Title
    C. Cloud on Title
    D. Chain of Title

31. **The act of entering documents concerning title to a property into the public records**
    A. Avulsion
    B. Exception
    C. Recording
    D. Accretion

32. **Law that determines transfer of property after intestate death**
    A. Recording Laws
    B. Right of Survivorship
    C. Laws or Escheat
    D. Laws of Descent and Distribution

33. **Open, Notorious, Exclusive, Continuous way of gaining title to property**
    A. Eminent Domain
    B. Probate Court
    C. Escheat
    D. Adverse Possession

34. **A deed that guarantees a clear title to the buyer through covenants**
    A. Guardian's Deed
    B. Quitclaim Deed
    C. Warranty Deed
    D. Grant Deed

Section 4: *Recall Fill-In*

1. Knowledge that you're presumed to have

_____

2. Conveyance of property but keeps use of something on it

_____

3. Handwritten Will

_____

4. Governs the enforceability of real estate contracts

_____

5. Witness certification of validity

_____

6. A person who dies with a will

_____

7. Died without a will

_____

8. Excluding a physical portion of the property being granted

_____

9. A condensed history report of the chain of title

_____

10. The gradual wearing away of land as a result of wind or water

_____

11. A person that conveys an interest in real property by deed

_____

12. Title defect including any claim, lien, or encumbrance

_____

13. The soil that has been deposited on the shore as a result of accretion

_____

14. Sudden change in land mass due to a violent weather act

15. Court Action to Acquire Legal Title in one's name after adverse possession

16. A voluntary transfer, without warranties, that conveys the grantor's interest

17. Document to Transfer Real Property

18. Adding time to another in Adverse Possession

19. Promises that the grantor makes certifying that certain conditions of title exist

20. A person named in the will designated to carry out its terms

21. A person who receives an interest in real property by deed

22. A court that determines the validity of a will and the rightful heirs

23. A signor's declaration made before an authorized person

24. Buildup of land through wind and water

25. A deed that guarantees a clear title to the buyer through covenants

26. Open, Notorious, Exclusive, Continuous way of gaining title to property

27. Increase in Land when water recedes

28. Transfer of Title by will, gift, deed

_____

29. All recorded and unrecorded instruments revealing the history of ownership

_____

30. Could shorten adverse possession time frame with proof of additional information

_____

31. The act of entering documents concerning title to a property into the public records

_____

32. Oral Will in expectation of impending death

_____

33. Law that determines transfer of property after intestate death

_____

34. Direct knowledge that one has because he saw, heard, or read it

_____

Section 5: *Matching*

A   Color of Title

B   Accretion

C   Intestate

D   Attestation

E   Exception

F   Alienation

G   Deed

H   Reservation

I   Tacking

J   Holographic Will

K   Quiet Title Action

L   Statute of Frauds

1 _____ Buildup of land through wind and water

2 _____ Adding time to another in Adverse Possession

3 _____ Conveyance of property but keeps use of something on it

4 _____ Court Action to Acquire Legal Title in one's name

5 _____ Died without a will

6 _____ Document to Transfer Real Property

7 _____ Excluding a physical portion of the property being granted

8 _____ Governs the enforceability of real estate contracts

9 _____ Handwritten Will

10 _____ Can shorten adverse possession time frame

11 _____ Transfer of Title by will, gift, deed

12 _____ Witness certification of validity

A   Dereliction   1 _____   A voluntary transfer, without warranties, that conveys the grantor's interest

B   Avulsion   2 _____   All recorded and unrecorded instruments revealing the history of ownership

C   Nuncupative Will   3 _____   Deed that guarantees clear title through covenants

D   Adverse Possession   4 _____   Increase in Land when water recedes

E   Quit Claim Deed   5 _____   Knowledge that you're presumed to have

F   Constructive Notice   6 _____   Law that determines transfer of property after intestate death

G   Chain of Title   7 _____   Open, Notorious, Exclusive, Continuous way of gaining title to property

H   Recording   8 _____   Oral Will in expectation of impending death

I   Warranty Deed   9 _____   Sudden change in land mass due to a violent weather act

J   Cloud on Title   10 _____   Entering title Documents into the public record.

K   Intestate Succession   11 _____   Title defect including any claim, lien, or encumbrance

A   Abstract of Title   1 _____   A condensed history report of the chain of title

B   Acknowledgment   2 _____   A court that determines the validity of a will and the rightful heirs

C   Actual Notice   3 _____   A person named in the will designated to carry out its terms

D   Alluvion   4 _____   A person that conveys an interest in real property by deed

E   Covenants of Title   5 _____   A person who dies with a will

F   Erosion   6 _____   A person who receives an interest in real property by deed

G   Executor   7 _____   A signor's declaration made before an authorized person

H   Grantee   8 _____   Direct knowledge that one has because he saw, heard, or read it.

I   Grantor   9 _____   Promises that the grantor makes certifying that certain conditions of title exist

J   Probate Court   10 _____   The gradual wearing away of land as a result of wind or water

K   Testator   11 _____   The soil that has been deposited on the shore as a result of accretion

Section 6: *Analysis Fill-In*

1. What is the difference between a quit claim deed and a bargain and sale deed?

    _____

2. What is title insurance for?

    _____

3. Why is constructive notice important?

    _____

4. What does the grantee always receive from the grantor in a quit claim deed?

    _____

5. How many warranties are contained in a quit claim deed?

    _____

6. What is the difference between a limited warranty and general warranty deed?

    _____

7. What are the 5 covenants of title?

    _____

8. What is the difference between a Reservation and an Exception?

    _____

9. Who must sign a deed?

    _____

10. What type of property can be given away in a nuncupative will?

    _____

11. What law indicates that deeds must be in writing to be enforceable?

    _____

12. When is title conveyed from grantor to grantee:

    _____

13. A handwritten will is also known as:

    _____

14. What is a Chain of Title?

_____

15. What type of deed would be used to clear a cloud when the party is available?

_____

16. What type of action would be brought to clear a title cloud when the party is unavailable?

_____

17. How does adverse possession differ from prescriptive easement?

_____

18. What are the adverse possession elements?

_____

19. Name two operation of law property transfers:

_____

20. When would an avulsion occur?

_____

21. Give an example of Accretion:

_____

22. Give two ways to voluntarily alienate property:

_____

23. Give two ways to alienate property by Court Action:

_____

24. Give an example of Dereliction:

_____

25. What are the three ways to give constructive notice?

_____

Section 7: *Analysis Multiple Choice*

1. **Which of the following is NOT included in the covenants of a warranty deed?**
   A. Execution sale
   B. Quiet enjoyment
   C. Warranty forever
   D. Warranty of seizin

2. **For over 20 years, a private school has been using an empty lot next to the school for a ball field. The owner of the lot recently sold it and the new owner is demanding the school stop using the lot. The school might claim title to the lot by using:**
   A. The doctrine of laches
   B. Eminent Domain
   C. An easement appurtenant
   D. Adverse possession

3. **If a grantor dies before the property is received by the grantee but the deed is delivered to the grantee's agent. Can the agent still give the property to the grantee?**
   A. Yes, because the doctrine of relation back allows the transfer to take place after death of the grantor
   B. No, because the grantor died before the grantee received the deed
   C. Yes, because it was delivered to and accepted by the grantee
   D. No, it must be given directly to the grantee

4. **In order for there to be a valid deed conveyance, the deed must be:**
   A. Signed by the grantee
   B. Accepted by the grantor
   C. Recorded by the grantee
   D. Delivered to the grantee

5. **In which situation might a Cloud on title result if searched in 2021?**
   A. All documents were properly recorded from the time from which the building was constructed
   B. A grantee took title in a fictitious name and reconveyed the property in that name
   C. A lien recorded in 2002 wasn't satisfied until 2018
   D. A title search reveals that in 2010, a defective legal description was recorded

6. **John sells a property to Jim and puts a reservation in the deed. What did he most likely reserve?**
   A. Title to part of the land
   B. Use of the lake on the land
   C. A reversionary interest in the land
   D. A remainder interest in the land

7. **Carla is the seller on a piece of property that Ron is purchasing. The title examiner goes to the county courthouse to perform the title search. The examiner can't remember the seller's name of the property, but he does remember the address to the property. He should use the:**
   A. Grantor Grantee Index
   B. Tract Index
   C. Torrens System
   D. Survey System

8. Carol is the purchaser on a single-family home. She is taking a loan on the property. At the closing, Carol is at the point of purchasing title insurance. She purchases a lender's policy but declines to purchase an owner's policy. Three years after Carol moves in, it is discovered that she has an income tax debt. The IRS has been attempting to collect this debt for 10 years and when it discovers that Carol owns a house, it puts a tax lien on the property. Carol contacts her title insurance company, to which they respond:
   A. Because all purchasers have a four-year period of time after closing to purchase a policy, if she does so now, they will cover her
   B. Carol would have been covered had she purchased an owner's policy
   C. While title insurance covers items from the past, it doesn't cover act of the current owner of the property
   D. While the title insurance would cover Carol for her debts, it does not cover taxes that have priority over the insurance

9. Title to real estate can be voluntarily transferred by:
   A. Sale, Patent, Will, Gift
   B. Sale, Operation of Law, Foreclosure, Gift
   C. Will, Gift, Operation of Law, Court Action
   D. Will, Patent, Gift, Foreclosure

10. There are a number of different taxes that occur in a real estate transaction. Which taxes are charged at the closing based upon the sales price of the home?
   A. Transfer Taxes or Deed Stamps
   B. Intangible Taxes
   C. Ad Valorem Taxes
   D. Special Assessment Taxes

11. The purchaser of a home is requesting that the seller provide the purchaser with a home warranty at closing. If the seller agrees, the purchaser will be protected if there are:
   A. Title Claims against the property
   B. Mechanical Problems with the HVAC
   C. Tree Damage from a Storm
   D. A neighbor falling on the lawn

12. The deed that provides the greatest liability to the grantor is:
   A. General Warranty Deed
   B. Limited Warranty Deed
   C. Bargain and Sale Deed
   D. Quit Claim Deed

13. Mary is selling Jane her home. At the closing, Mary signs the deed. She then transfers the deed to Jane and Jane accepts it. Jane then records the deed. Two months later, Jane moved into the home. At what point was title conveyed?
   A. When Jane signed the deed
   B. When Mary transferred the deed and Jane accepted it
   C. When Jane recorded the deed
   D. When Jane moved into the home

14. **John purchases a home where the closing takes place on January 18, 2019. Immediately after the closing, John goes on vacation but doesn't record the deed. Several years pass and John finds the deed in one of his briefcases and decides to record it on May 20, 2022. Will John be allowed to record it?**
    A. No, recording the deed must happen immediately after closing to give notice of ownership
    B. Yes, John can record the deed at any time, but may be subject to claims from others who gave constructive notice of ownership
    C. No, John's failure to record the deed placed a cloud on the title, so he now can't record it until the clouds are removed
    D. Yes, John can record the deed, but must include an explanation as to what occurred between 2019 and 2022

15. **John and Mary entered into an agreement where Mary is purchasing John's home for $300,000. They decide that it isn't necessary to put the agreement or the deed in writing. John gives his oral intent to transfer the property to Mary, she pays him, and Mary moves in. John dies three weeks later and he has heirs. Which of the following is true:**
    A. The transfer of the property is invalid because it was not in writing
    B. The transfer of the property is valid and it didn't need to be in writing for validity
    C. The transfer of the property is invalid since John had heirs
    D. The transfer of the property is valid because Mary paid John for the property

16. **In 2022, John puts his home on the market and found a buyer. John purchased the home in 1998. When a title search was done by the potential purchaser, it was discovered that in 2018, there was a judgment placed on the home because John didn't pay his VISA bill. What would be the best way for John to have this problem corrected so that the buyer can move forward immediately?**
    A. Go to his title company and have them resolve the issue
    B. Inform the title company that he paid the VISA bill and show them proof
    C. File a lawsuit against VISA for failing to inform John in a timely manner
    D. Pay the VISA bill now and have VISA issue a document releasing the judgment

17. **Fatima sold a property to Delilah on 4/5. Delilah immediately left the closing and went on vacation for exactly two weeks. When Fatima noticed that Delilah had left without moving in on 4/17, she resold the same property to Mark. Mark decided to go over to the property to check it out and return to his old home to pack. Delilah returned from vacation on 4/19 and began having work done on the outside of the home to include landscaping, siding, exterior lighting, but she totally forgot that she needed to record her deed. On 4/23, Mark recorded his deed. Who owns the property?**
    A. Fatima because there is no indication that any of the deeds are in writing
    B. Mark because he was the first to record the deed
    C. Delilah because she was the first to cultivate the land
    D. Delilah because although Mark recorded the deed first, she purchased the property first

18. **Derrick is selling his home. He signs the deed over to the buyer, but didn't have it notarized. In anticipation of closing, he gives it to his attorney and tells his attorney that he will meet him at the closing the next day. Derrick dies that night unbeknownst to anyone. Can his attorney complete the closing since the deed was already delivered to him?**
    A. No, the attorney cannot complete the closing because it must be delivered to the grantee while Derrick is alive
    B. Yes, because the attorney had specific instructions from Derrick
    C. Yes, because the attorney had no idea that Derrick died, he can complete the closing
    D. No, because the deed has to be notarized before transfer

19. **Delia is selling her home to David, who happens to be a minor, but who just won $2,000,000 in a lottery. Delia signs the deed over to the David and David moves into the property. A month after the closing Delia wants to declare the sale void and states that the deed was invalid because minors cannot be grantees. Will Delia be able to get out of the transaction?**
    A. Yes, because minors cannot be grantees to property
    B. Yes, because a deed granted to a minor is void
    C. No, because minors can be grantees, but the closing happened too long ago
    D. No, because minors can be grantees and only the minor can void the contract

20. **An attorney handling a closing for Mr. and Mrs. Jones sends a title researcher to the local county courthouse to examine the title on a home the Jones' are purchasing. After the attorney receives the information, he writes a report to the title company giving a rendition of the title documents that were on file. This opinion is called:**
    A. Chain of Title
    B. Abstract of Title
    C. Color of Title
    D. Cloud on Title

21. **A licensee is listing a rural property. The property was owned by a woman who is now deceased. The woman had six grown children. Two of the sons are listing the property for sale. Before completing the listing agreement, the licensee should do which of the following?**
    A. Check the woman's will to ascertain who the heirs are
    B. Require all six children to sign quitclaim deeds
    C. Have the woman's attorney sign a release of title
    D. Check the ownership of record

Chapter 5 Answers

1. B	5. A	9. B	13. B	17. C	21. B	25. A	29. A	33. D
2. A	6. A	10. C	14. A	18. C	22. B	26. B	30. D	34. C
3. D	7. C	11. B	15. D	19. D	23. C	27. B	31. C	
4. A	8. B	12. C	16. A	20. B	24. B	28. B	32. D	

1. Constructive Notice
2. Reservation
3. Holographic Will
4. Statute of Frauds
5. Attestation
6. Testator/Testate
7. Intestate
8. Exception
9. Abstract of Title
10. Erosion
11. Grantor
12. Cloud on Title
13. Alluvium/Alluvion
14. Avulsion
15. Quiet Title
16. Quit Claim Deed
17. Deed
18. Tacking
19. Warranties/Covenants of Title
20. Executor
21. Grantee
22. Probate Court
23. Acknowledgment
24. Accretion
25. Warranty Deed
26. Adverse Possession
27. Dereliction/Reliction
28. Alienation
29. Chain of Title
30. Color of Title
31. Recording
32. Nuncupative Will
33. Laws of Descent/Intestate Succession
34. Actual Notice

Exercise 1

1. B	3. H	5. C	7. E	9. J	11. F
2. I	4. K	6. G	8. L	10. A	12. D

Exercise 2

1. E	3. I	5. F	7. D	9. B	11. J
2. G	4. A	6. K	8. C	10. H	

Exercise 3

1. A	3. G	5. K	7. B	9. E	11. D
2. J	4. I	6. H	8. C	10. F	

1. Neither contain any warranties, but a bargain and sale deed guarantees conveyance whereas a quit claim deed does not

2. Protection from loss due to defects in the title

3. The first party to give constructive notice is the homeowner

4. Whatever interest the grantor had in the property

5. None

6. Both contain all covenants of title, but a limited warranty deed only warrants items from when the current grantor owned the property

7. Seizin, Encumbrance, Further Assurance, Enjoyment, Warranty Forever

8. A reservation goes to USE – the grantor sells the entire tract but wants to continue to use the barn whereas an exception goes to TITLE – the grantor doesn't want to sell the entire tract so he excepts a portion of it from the grant

9. Grantor

10. Personal Property, Legacy, Bequest

11. Statute of Frauds

12. When the grantor signs and delivers the deed to the grantee or the grantee's agent while the grantor is alive

13. Holographic

14. All recorded and unrecorded documents on a parcel

15. Quit Claim

16. Quiet Title

17. The elements are essentially the same but with adverse possession, the attempt is to acquire title. With a prescriptive easement, the goal is continued use

18. Open, continuous, without permission, for the statutory period of time

19. Intestate Succession, Community Property, Condemnation, Adverse Possession, Fee Simple Determinable

20. As a result of a sudden or violent weather action (earthquake, hurricane)

21. Beach water pushing the sand onto the land

22. Gift, Deed, Sale, Patent

23. Fee Simple on Condition Subsequent, Foreclosure, Quiet Title, Partition

24. Beach tide going out and exposing additional land

25. Recording, Cultivating the land, Moving into a property

Section 7 Answers:

1. A. Execution of sale is a term used with the court orders a sheriff sale, could be after a foreclosure or tax sale

2. D. Adverse Possession is a claim made when one entity or person (here, the private school) attempts to take title of property of another openly, continuously and without permission, for the statutory period of time. Here, because the school has used the empty lot for 20 years as a ball field, it will attempt to claim title by adverse possession

3. A. Doctrine of relation back indicates that as long as the deed is delivered to the agent while the grantor is alive, it is the same as delivery to the grantee

4. D. All valid deed conveyances must be delivered to the grantee. There is no requirement that deeds be recorded, although it is a good idea to record a deed

5. D. A defective legal description that wasn't corrected is a cloud on title. The 2002 lien was satisfied in 2018 and the search occurred in 2021. So, there is not cloud at search. Further, all grantees are allowed to take title in fictitious names as long as reconveyed in that same fictitious name

6. B. Reservations always go to the USE of something on the land. The seller might sell the property, but wish to continue use of something. He would do so by reservation

7. B. The tract index would be the best one used here if the address of the property is known

8. C. Carol wouldn't be covered by an owner's policy in this instance since it wasn't an unexpected event and it was one that she would be responsible for

9. A. Sale, Patent, Will, Gift. Operation of Law, Foreclosure, and Court Action are not voluntary transfers

10. A. Anytime a deed is transferred from one person to another, a tax must be paid when that new deed is recorded. It is based on the sales price of the home

11. B. Home warranties typically would cover the mechanical breakdown of items in the home. Title claims would be covered by the title insurance, the tree damage and the neighbor falling would both be covered by the homeowner's insurance

12. A. The General Warranty deed provides the greatest liability to the grantor and gives the greatest protection to the grantee since all 5 covenants are given by the grantor to the grantee

13. B. Title is conveyed when the deed is delivered and accepted by the grantee

14. B. There is no requirement that a deed must be recorded. However, on recording there may be other items that were recorded on the title between 2019 and 2022. Most will probably not be a problem unless there was another ownership claim (recording, moving in, cultivating the land)

15. B. The property transfer is valid and as long as there is no challenge by the heirs, it will remain that way. Contracts and Deeds for an interest in real estate must be in writing to be enforceable, but they can still be performed. So, as long as this issue doesn't need to be taken to court, the parties can perform as agreed

16. D. John's best course of action is to pay the VISA bill and have the company issue documentation to that effect. That documentation will clear the cloud off of the title. He is not entitled to go to his title company because they will not handle issues for him that he is responsible for, and showing proof doesn't release the judgment

17. C. Delilah began cultivating the land on 4/19 which was 4 days prior to Mark recording the deed. Because of that, she is the first to give constructive notice and now owns the property

18. A. A valid deed transfer requires delivery and acceptance by the grantee while the grantor is alive

19. D. Delia will not be able to void the contract because grantees can be incompetent and only the minor would be able to void the sale in any event

20. B. The synopsis of the title history is called an abstract of title. It is provided to the title company so that it can decided whether to insure the title of the home

21. D. All licensees should check the ownership of record to ascertain that they are dealing with correct parties who can sign the listing and make a decision

Chapter 6:
Land Use Controls and Regulations

Section 1: *Outline*

Land use controls and regulations – a closer look at governmental power

A. Government rights in land

   1. Property taxes and special assessments

     Real Property Taxes – Most privately-owned land is subject to real estate taxes based on the value of property (**ad valorem taxes**)

     The Ad Valorem Tax Process
     i. **Budget** – the taxing authority must prepare an annual budget estimating needed income for coming year
     ii. **Appropriation** – legislature must figure out where to get the money and how to spend it
     iii. **Levy** – taxing authority determines how taxes will be imposed on individuals and property
     iv. **Assessment** – tax assessor determines the market value of parcel of property. An assessment rate is then applied to the market value
     v. **Appeal** – property owner can appeal his assessment to the board of arbitration
     vi. **Equalization** – board of equalization can create equalization factors to ensure fairness across jurisdictions.
     vii. **Tax Rate** – total amount of budget needed/total of assessed values (assessment roll) = tax rate (the rate at which all taxpayers will pay)
     viii. **Tax Calculations** – Assessed Value of home x Tax Rate (MILL RATE) = Property Tax Bill
     ix. **Tax Exemptions** – deducted from the assessed value to lower the tax bill.
       Homestead, Senior, Disabled
     x. **Tax abatement** – temporary suspension of property taxes to encourage economic development
     xi. **Tax Collection** – unpaid taxes become a lien on the property and take precedence over all other liens. A delinquent taxpayer may have a **right to redeem** property before the tax sale (**equitable right**) or after the tax sale (**statutory right**) by paying all outstanding taxes and penalties

     Special Assessments – a tax imposed only those who receive the benefit from the improvement

   2. Eminent domain, condemnation, escheat

   Encumbrances – external limitation placed on either the title or the use of property which can diminish it value. Can be public or private

Public Encumbrances – (PETE)

a. **Police Power** – right of the government to enact laws regulating the safety, health, morals, and general well-being of the community. **No compensation**

b. **Eminent Domain** – power to take private property for public use when **just compensation** has been paid

c. **Taxation** – ad valorem or special assessment taxes

d. **Escheat** – the state's right to take property where no heirs exist

B. Government controls

1. Zoning and master plans

Zoning – An organized effort to provide for the orderly growth of the community. Regulates how each parcel of land may be used and the density, the height and bulk of buildings and in some cases architectural styles and other aesthetics.

Master plan – drafted at the local level and serves as a blueprint for future development by dividing the community into **Land use districts**: commercial, residential, industrial, multi-family, recreational, and conservation, and historic. **Buffer zones** separate incompatible uses between these districts.

- If **zoning conflicts** with **deed restrictions**, the **strictest** prevails.
- **Zoning Change (difficult)** – Filing a rezoning petition, give notice to neighbors, attend a public hearing, board recommends a new local zoning ordinance
- **Variance Request (easier)** – Can be requested to allow use for a purpose that does not comply with current zoning; to one specific parcel or person. Can be temporary or permanent. Must show hardship.

Types of Zoning:

- **Down-Zoning** – rezoning a parcel to a lower density or less profitable use
- **Spot-Zoning** – to permit a small area to have a use inconsistent with the surrounding area
- **Aesthetic Zoning** – specifies that architectural styles must be compatible.
- **Bulk Zoning** – designed to limit population growth and density. Uses floor area ratio (FAR) and setbacks
- **Directive Zoning** – used to encourage the highest and best use of the land.
- **Incentive Zoning** – award-based system that encourages developers to meet certain physical, social, or cultural benefits.
- **Exclusionary Zoning** – requiring large lots and house where people could naturally afford.

Zoning is **NOT RETROACTIVE**. It only moves forward. Any existing structures are now **non-conforming** or **grandfathered** and can continue legal use

2. Building codes – regulations designed to set the standards for construction materials, method, and safety procedures.

- Plans must be provided to the building inspector and once approved, a building permit is issued and work can begin
- Each phase must be inspected
- If the building inspector finds something not in compliance, it can be **abated** (work stopped, torn down)
- After final inspection, a **Certificate of Occupancy/Completion** is issued to occupy the premises

3. Regulation of special land types

Flood zones – Areas that have a greater chance of flooding as designated by FEMA; Owners with loans are required to have a special insurance policy

Wetlands – Areas that are flooded by water all, most, or much of the time

4. Regulation of environmental hazards

a. **Types of hazards**

<u>**Lead Paint Hazard Reduction Act**</u> – **Aimed at protecting children from ingesting lead** – A soft metal that can cause problems in children under 6.

- On all homes built before 1978, a lead-based paint disclosure must be included with the contract
- Does not indicate that lead is present, just that the house was constructed prior to 1978
- Gives the buyer 10 days to inspect for lead
- Seller must provide copies of any reports available dealing with the presence of lead
- Agent to provide a "Protect Your Family from Lead in Your Home" pamphlet
- There is no requirement to abate the lead from the home

<u>**Mold**</u> – moist areas of the home – bathrooms, kitchens
<u>**Asbestos**</u> – a chemical that causes cancer found in basements or cellar wrapping of HVAC system, flooring, roofing
<u>**Radon**</u> – A radioactive material that comes through the foundation of a home

b. Abatement and mitigation

The RRP Rule (Renovation, Repair and Paint) – Only a trained certified lead-based paint contractors can perform work.
Other rules relating to mitigation – state specific

c. Restrictions on contaminated property

Under **CERCLA**, certain properties containing hazardous waste are prevented from being sold unless the waste is cleaned, and property inspected

C. Private controls

1. Deed Conditions or Restrictions

Conditions – usually found in deeds, conditions differ from covenants because they **don't** usually **have** any **time limits** but they-run with the land indefinitely
Private Restrictions – limitations on the use of one's property in other to protect the rights of others. When private restrictions conflict with zoning laws, **the stricter will always prevail.** Private restrictions against public policy or the sale of property will not be enforced; private agreements between two parties that restricts the use of property such as in a Fee Simple Determinable or a restriction placed on the property such as size, color, maintenance

2. Covenants, Conditions, and Restrictions (CC&Rs) – legally binding; generally used in condominiums or subdivisions; recorded in the county; contains property use restrictions, such as only for residential use, no pets, no investors, or only tan paint colors

Covenant - a promise made in a sales contract, lease or deed that specifies the property will or will not be used in a certain manner. The grantor or other parties can file an **injunction** to stop a prohibited use. If parties unduly delay in taking proper legal action, they could be prevented due to **laches**

3. Homeowners association regulations – covers items that wouldn't be included in the CC&Rs because they may change over time such as pool closes at 10:00 pm Monday-Wednesday

D. Capital Gains

Capital Gains – profit an investor makes from selling an asset for more than it was purchased.
Cost Basis – the cost including any repairs or improvements
Sales Price – Basis = Capital Gains.
Tax relief Act of 1997 – may exempt a homeowner if they own the home as primary residence for 2 of the last 5 years. $500k married filing jointly and $250k single
1031 Exchange – An IRS tax provision that allows investors to exchange property held for productive use for a like-kind property in order to defer taxes on sale to a later date

Section 2: *Vocabulary*

1031 Exchange: A tax provision that permits investors to defer capital gains taxes to a later date

Ad Valorem Property Tax: The property tax bill based on the assessed value of the property multiplied by the tax rate

Assessment Rate: Percentage applied to the market value of property to determine the assessed value

Assessment Value: The market value of the property multiplied by the assessment rate

Board of Arbitration: The board that hears property owner ad valorem property tax assessment challenges

Buffer Zone: A strip of land intended to separate incompatible uses

Building Codes: Laws that specify the minimum standards for construction

Building permit: Permission from the building department to improve the property in accordance with the building codes

Bulk Zoning: Controls population density and avoids overcrowding

Capital Gains: The taxes on the profit an investor makes when selling an asset

Certificate of Occupancy: Issued by the building department after inspection of construction if done in accordance with the building permit

Condemnation: The legal process to exercise an eminent domain right

Conditions: Limitations placed in deeds through the type of estate granted to control the property's future use

Cost Basis: The original purchase price of a property together with any investment put into it

Covenants: Legally binding promises for which the parties become liable

Down Zoning: Rezoning from a high density to a low-density use

Eminent Domain: Power of a government to take private property for public use with just compensation

Escheat: The reverting of property to the State when no heirs or owners can be found

Exclusionary Zoning: Requires large lots or contains minimum square foot requirements

Flood Zones and Maps: Areas determined by Federal Emergency Management Agency (FEMA) as likely to flood

Homestead Exemption: A reduction in the assessed value of property for owner occupants

Intangible tax: A tax paid at closing on any new mortgage loan

Land-use Districts: Areas in a community which are classified according to use

Master Plan: A plan done by the local zoning board to guide the physical development of an area

Mill: An expression of tax rate based in 1000s

Non-Conforming Use: A property allowed to continue a prior use even though not permitted by the new zoning law

Police Power: The power to regulate for the general welfare, health, safety, and morals of the community

Restrictions: General limits on use of the land

Right of Redemption: The debtor's legal right to pay the default amount or repurchase the property after a foreclosure or tax sale

Special Assessment Taxes: A property tax levied against only those property owners who have benefited from the improvement

Spot Zoning: Rezoning of a parcel or group of parcels to permit a use different from neighboring properties

Tax Abatement: The elimination of real estate property tax for a certain time period

Tax Relief Act of 1997: Exempts homeowners from the payment of capital gains taxes under certain conditions

Transfer Tax: A conveyance tax paid at closing on the sales price of the home

Wetlands: A lowland area, such as a marsh or swamp, that is saturated with moisture during parts of the year

Zoning Ordinance: Classifying land for growth, use, and development

Zoning Setback: No building can be constructed within the stated minimum distances from the property line

Zoning variance: Approval to a particular property owner to deviate from an existing zoning regulation

Section 3: *Recall Multiple Choice*

1. **Percentage applied to the market value of property to determine the assessed value**
   A. Assessed Valuation
   B. Capitalization Rate
   C. Assessment Value
   D. Assessment Rate

2. **The legal process to exercise an eminent domain right**
   A. Condemnation
   B. Discrimination
   C. Depreciation
   D. Escheat

3. **An expression of tax rate based on 1000s**
   A. Assessment Roll
   B. HART
   C. PITI
   D. Mill

4. **A conveyance tax paid at closing on the sales price of the home**

A. **Value Added Tax**
   B. Capital Gains
   C. Transfer Tax
   D. Intangible Tax

5. **Areas determined by Federal Emergency Management Agency (FEMA) as likely to flood**
   A. Do not Call Registry
   B. Statute Right of Redemption
   C. Building Codes
   D. Flood Zones and Maps

6. **A parcel or group of parcels is rezoned to permit a use different from neighboring properties**
   A. Bulk Zoning
   B. Spot Zoning
   C. Directive Zoning
   D. Aesthetic Zoning

7. **Classification of land for growth, use, development**
   A. Building Codes
   B. Escheat
   C. Tax Abatement
   D. Zoning

8. **The elimination of real estate property tax for a certain period of time**
   A. Homestead Exemption
   B. Assessment Roll
   C. Tax Abatement
   D. Tax Reassessment

9. **A set of laws, rules and regulations that specify the minimum standards for construction**
   A. Police Power
   B. Eminent Domain
   C. Building Permit
   D. Building Codes

10. **A tax provision that permits investors to defer capital gains taxes to a later date**
    A. 1131 Exchange
    B. 1031 Exchange
    C. Transfer Tax
    D. Enabling Acts

11. **Approval to a particular property owner to deviate from an existing zoning regulation**
    A. Exclusionary zoning
    B. Zoning variance
    C. Spot zoning
    D. Zoning setback

12. **Areas in a community which are classified according to use**
    A. Zoning Setback
    B. Down Zoning
    C. Spot Zoning
    D. Land-use Districts

13. **No building can be constructed within the minimum distances from the property line**
    A. Zoning Variance
    B. Cost Basis
    C. Zoning Setback
    D. Building Permit

14. **Requires large lots or minimum square foot requirements**
    A. Exclusionary Zoning
    B. Bulk Zoning
    C. Spot Zoning
    D. Incentive Zoning

15. **Controls population density and avoids overcrowding**
    A. Aesthetic Zoning
    B. Incentive Zoning
    C. Spot Zoning
    D. Bulk Zoning

16. **A lowland area, such as a marsh or swamp, that is saturated with moisture during parts of the year**
    A. Water Frontage
    B. CERCLA
    C. Riparian
    D. Wetlands

17. **Exempts homeowners from the payment of capital gains taxes under certain conditions**
    A. Federal tax act
    B. Tax Relief Act of 2002
    C. Tax Relief Act of 1997
    D. Revised Tax Act of 1997

18. **General Limits placed on land use**
    A. Condemnation
    B. Encroachment
    C. Restrictions
    D. Covenants

19. **Issued by the building department after inspection of construction in accordance with the building permit**
    A. Tax Certificate
    B. Building Codes
    C. Certificate of Occupancy
    D. Building Permit

20. **A strip of land intended to separate incompatible uses**
    A. Buffer Zone
    B. Assessment Roll
    C. Spot Zoning
    D. Police Power

21. **The reverting of property to the State when no heirs or owners can be found**
    A. Condemnation
    B. Police Power
    C. Escheat
    D. Tax Abatement

22. **The market value of the property multiplied by the assessment rate**
    A. Market Value
    B. Assessment Value
    C. Economic Value
    D. Appraised Value

23. **A tax paid at closing on any new mortgage loan**
    A. Note tax
    B. Intangible tax
    C. Transfer tax
    D. Tax certificate

24. **The original purchase price of a property together with any investment put into it**
    A. Cost Basis
    B. Carryover Basis
    C. Capital Gain
    D. Assessment Value

25. **A property tax levied against only those property owners who have benefited from the improvement**
    A. Ad Valorem Taxes
    B. Assessment Roll
    C. Property Taxes
    D. Special Assessment Taxes

26. **The power to regulate for the general welfare, health, safety, and morals of the community**
    A. Building Permit
    B. Escheat
    C. Police Power
    D. Eminent Domain

27. **The board that hears property owner ad valorem property tax assessment challenges**
    A. Commissioner of Insurance
    B. Office of Administrative Law
    C. Board of Equalization
    D. Board of Arbitration

28. **Power of a government to take private property for public use with just compensation**
    A. Cost Basis
    B. Escheat
    C. Eminent Domain
    D. Police Power

29. **The taxes on the profit an investor makes when selling an asset**
    A. Transfer Tax
    B. Taxable Income
    C. Tax Abatement
    D. Capital Gains

30. **The property tax bill that is based on the assessed value of the property multiplied by the tax rate**
    A. Ad Valorem Property Tax
    B. Income Tax
    C. Assessment Rate
    D. Sales Tax

31. **Rezoning from a high density to a low-density use**
    A. Bulk Zoning
    B. Down Zoning
    C. Zoning Variance
    D. Spot Zoning

32. **Permission from building department to improve the property in accordance with the building codes**
    A. Certificate of occupancy
    B. Building permit
    C. Police power
    D. Building codes

33. **A comprehensive plan done by the local zoning board to guide the long-term physical development of a particular area**
    A. Eminent Domain
    B. Building Codes
    C. Police Power
    D. Master Plan

34. **Legally binding promises for which the parties become liable**
    A. Conditions
    B. Escheat
    C. Condemnation
    D. Covenants

35. **Limitations placed indeed through the type of estate granted to control the property's future use**
   A. Definitions
   B. Consideration
   C. Conditions
   D. Condemnation

36. **A reduction in the assessed value of property for owner occupants**
   A. Depreciation
   B. Homestead Exemption
   C. Mrs. Murphy Exemption
   D. Tax Abatement

37. **A property can continue prior use even though the new zoning law doesn't permit it**
   A. Spot Zoning
   B. Enabling Acts
   C. Buffer Zone
   D. Non-Conforming Use

38. **The debtor's legal right to pay the default amount or repurchase the property after a foreclosure or tax sale**
   A. Right of Redemption
   B. Deed in Lieu of Foreclosure
   C. Equitable Redemption
   D. Equity of Redemption

Section 4: *Recall Fill-In*

1. A property can continue prior use even though the new zoning law doesn't permit it

_____

2. The legal process to exercise an eminent domain right

_____

3. Issued by the building department after inspection of construction in accordance with the building permit

_____

4. No building can be constructed within the minimum distances from the property line

_____

5. A parcel or group of parcels is rezoned to permit a use different from neighboring properties

_____

6. Exempts homeowners from the payment of capital gains taxes under certain conditions

_____

7. Legally binding promises for which the parties become liable

_____

8. The reverting of property to the State when no heirs or owners can be found

_____

9. A reduction in the assessed value of property for owner occupants

_____

10. The market value of the property multiplied by the assessment rate

_____

11. General limits on land use

_____

12. Limitations placed indeed through the type of estate granted to control the property's future use

_____

13. The property tax bill that is based on the assessed value of the property multiplied by the tax rate

_____

14. An expression of tax rate based on 1000s

15. A strip of land intended to separate incompatible uses

16. Controls population density and avoids overcrowding

17. The taxes on the profit an investor makes when selling an asset

18. The elimination of real estate property tax for a certain period of time

19. A property tax levied against only those property owners who have benefited from the improvement

20. A lowland area, such as a marsh or swamp, that is saturated with moisture during parts of the year

21. A set of laws, rules and regulations that specify the minimum standards for construction

22. Power of a government to take private property for public use with just compensation

23. Rezoning from a high density to a low-density use

24. Classification of land for growth, use, development

25. A tax paid at closing on any new mortgage loan

26. The original purchase price of a property together with any investment put into it

27. Approval to a particular property owner to deviate from an existing zoning regulation

28. Permission from building department to improve the property in accordance with the building codes

29. A tax provision that permits investors to defer capital gains taxes to a later date

30. A comprehensive plan done by the local zoning board to guide the long-term physical development of a particular area

31. The debtor's legal right to pay the default amount or repurchase the property after a foreclosure or tax sale

32. The power to regulate for the general welfare, health, safety, and morals of the community

33. Percentage applied to the market value of property to determine the assessed value

34. A conveyance tax paid at closing on the sales price of the home

35. Requires large lots or minimum square foot requirements that certain people are barred

36. Areas determined by Federal Emergency Management Agency (FEMA) as likely to flood

37. The board that hears property owner ad valorem property tax assessment challenges

38. Areas in a community which are classified according to use

Section 5: *Matching*

A	Special Assessment Taxes	1 _____	A conveyance tax paid at closing on the sales price of the home
B	Assessment Value	2 _____	A parcel or group of parcels is rezoned to permit a use different from neighboring properties.
C	Flood Zone Maps	3 _____	A property tax levied against only those property owners who have benefited from the improvement
D	Certificate of Occupancy	4 _____	A tax provision that permits investors to defer capital gains taxes.
E	Mill	5 _____	An expression of tax rate based on 1000s
F	Condemnation	6 _____	Approval to a particular property owner to deviate from an existing zoning regulation
G	Covenants	7 _____	Areas determined by Federal Emergency Management Agency (FEMA) as likely to flood
H	1031 Exchange	8 _____	Issued by the building department after inspection of construction in accordance with the building permit
I	Transfer Tax	9 _____	Legally binding promises for which the parties become liable
J	Zoning Variance	10 _____	Power of a government to take private property for public use with just compensation.
K	Police Power	11 _____	The legal process to exercise an eminent domain right
L	Eminent Domain	12 _____	The market value of the property multiplied by the assessment rate
M	Spot Zoning	13 _____	The power to regulate for the general welfare, health, safety and morals of the community

A   Down Zoning   1 _____   A comprehensive plan done by the local zoning board to guide the long-term physical development of a particular area

B   Building Codes   2 _____   A set of laws, rules and regulations that specify the minimum standards for construction

C   Escheat   3 _____   Controls population density and avoids overcrowding

D   Tax Relief Act   4 _____   Exempts homeowners from the payment of capital gains taxes under certain conditions

E   Assessment Rate   5 _____   No building can be constructed within the minimum distances from the property line

F   Bulk Zoning   6 _____   Percentage applied to the market value of property to determine the assessed value

G   Zoning Setback   7 _____   Requires large lots or minimum square foot requirements

H   Tax Abatement   8 _____   Rezoning from a high density to a low-density use

I   Master Plan   9 _____   The elimination of real estate property tax for a certain time period

J   Capital Gains Tax   10 _____   The original purchase price of a property together with any investment put into it

K   Cost Basis   11 _____   The property tax bill that is based on the assessed value of the property multiplied by the tax rate

L   Exclusionary Zoning   12 _____   Property reverts to the State when no heirs or owners can be found

M   Ad Valorem Tax   13 _____   The taxes on the profit an investor makes when selling an asset

A   Restrictions   1 _____   A lowland area, such as a marsh or swamp, that is saturated with moisture during parts of the year.

B   Right of Redemption   2 _____   A property can continue prior use even though the new zoning law doesn't permit it

C   Buffer Zone   3 _____   A reduction in the assessed value of property for certain homeowners

D   Wetlands   4 _____   A strip of land intended to separate incompatible uses

E   Conditions   5 _____   A tax paid at closing on any new mortgage loan

F   Intangible Tax   6 _____   Areas in a community which are classified according to use

G   Non-Conforming Use   7 _____   Classifying land for growth, use, development

H   Land Use Districts   8 _____   Limitations placed in a deed to control the property's future use

I   Building Permit   9 _____   Limits the use of the property such through the deed or contract

J   Zoning   10 _____   Permission from building department to improve the property in accordance with the building codes

K   Board of Arbitration   11 _____   The board that hears property owner ad valorem property tax assessment challenges.

L   Homestead Exemption   12 _____   The debtor's legal right to pay the default amount or repurchase the property when there's a foreclosure or tax sale.

Section 6: *Analysis Fill-In*

1. What is the rule regarding capital gains tax when it's an investor vs. a homeowner?

_____

2. If zoning wanted to separate uses between a residential area and industrial area, it should use a:

_____

3. Allowing one particular area to operate as commercial when the entire area is residential is an example of:

_____

4. What is the difference between a zoning law and a building code?

_____

5. What is another term for a non-conforming use?

_____

6. On what amount would an investor pay capital gains tax if he purchased a property for $150,000, invested $90,000 into it, paid attorney's fees of $5,000 and sold it for $300,000?

_____

7. What's the difference between an equitable right of redemption vs. a statutory right of redemption?

_____

8. Which right of redemption ALWAYS allows a right to redeem?

_____

9. Define Assessment value:

_____

10. How do you calculate assessment value?

_____

11. What is the difference between ad valorem and special assessment taxes?

_____

12. Define Homestead Exemption:

_____

13. If the taxpayer is entitled to an exemption, how is it applied to the property tax?

_____

14. **Where would a property owner go if they are unhappy with the property assessment?**

_____

15. **Give an example of exclusionary zoning?**

_____

16. **What is another name for a certificate of occupancy?**

_____

17. **Who issues a certificate of occupancy?**

_____

18. **Define tax abatement:**

_____

19. **Difference between a transfer tax and intangible tax:**

_____

20. **What's the difference between zoning and eminent domain?**

_____

Section 7: *Analysis Multiple Choice*

1. **Which would be an example of a special assessment tax?**
   A. Raising funds for a new county courthouse
   B. Increased wages for police offices
   C. Building a new school in the county
   D. Putting a stop sign at the entrance of a 500-home subdivision

2. **The state is allowed to utilize its right of police power to:**
   A. Take private property as long as it's for public use
   B. Require 4 x 4 posts when building a deck
   C. Take property that doesn't have any heirs
   D. Impose Taxes on a single-family residence

3. **The purpose of a building permit is to:**
   A. Demonstrate compliance with restrictive covenants
   B. Demonstrate compliance with the subdivision's CC&Rs
   C. Demonstrate an intent to comply with the type of use of property
   D. Demonstrate an intent to comply with regulations for improvements

4. **The owner of a property containing Lead Based Paint is ordered by the court to have the lead removed. This would be called an order of:**
   A. Removal
   B. Abatement
   C. Injunction
   D. Restriction

5. **The local jurisdiction has just completed its newest master plan for the area. This document would show:**
   A. Uses of every individual property in the jurisdiction
   B. Time frame of the schedule of all planning to occur at the local level
   C. The definitive structure of what is to be built in the community
   D. Overall comprehensive goals of the community, including guidance on future development

6. **The county decides to take over a property from Ms. Jones to expand the roadway at the rear of the property. Ms. Jones does not have any heirs. The county is exercising his right of:**
   A. Police Power and Ms. Jones owner is entitled to compensation
   B. Escheat and Ms. Jones is not entitled to compensation
   C. Escheat and Ms. Jones is entitled to compensation
   D. Eminent Domain and Ms. Jones is entitled to compensation

7. **The city decides to take Ms. Smith's property for the purpose of building a new school and playground on it. The court action that the city will bring in this circumstance would be:**
   A. Quiet Title
   B. Eminent Domain
   C. Adverse Possession
   D. Condemnation

8. **The building department would NOT have jurisdiction over:**
   A. John wants to put a new deck on his property
   B. Jane wants to remove a wall in her living room
   C. Jack wants to use part of his basement for a barber shop
   D. Jill wants to install new siding on the detached garage of her property

9. The 500-home subdivision HOA is noticing that there are too many cars at each home and parking in the subdivision is becoming an issue. It decides to amend its CC&Rs to state that no house can have more than 3 cars parked in front of it at any one-time. However, the local zoning ordinance states that each house can have 4 cars parked in front of it at any one-time. Ten of the homeowners file a lawsuit against the HOA. Who wins?
   A. The HOA because the strictest rule/law will prevail
   B. The HOA because it has power to change the CC&Rs to anything it wishes
   C. The owners all changes to the CC&Rs must have the consent of all homeowners
   D. The owners because they are grandfathered into the zoning law

10. Subdivision restrictive covenants:
   A. Can only be enforced by the developer only
   B. Do not have to be renewed after a specified time
   C. Do not transfer to new homeowners
   D. Can be removed by all consenting landowners of the subdivision

11. Jackson purchased a bowling alley in the city. One year later, the zoning law changed to residential. Can Jackson continue to operate the bowling alley?
   A. Yes, it is now considered a non-conforming use
   B. Yes, because he had no knowledge that it would be changed to residential
   C. No, since the zoning changed, he can no longer operate the bowling alley
   D. No, because the area will become residential, and the bowling alley will not conform to the area

12. Certain disclosures must be made to a purchaser if a property was built prior to 1978? These include:
   A. Asbestos disclosure
   B. Lead Paint disclosure
   C. Mold disclosure
   D. Radon disclosure

13. All of the following are false about Lead Based Paint Except:
   A. It can cause harm to young children who ingest it
   B. It is only present in residential properties
   C. It is no longer used in residential properties, but is used in commercial properties
   D. It was outlawed in 1974

14. John bought a property and got a $6,000 quote for a new deck. However, the building inspector came out and indicated that there was a new code and that there are additional materials that must be used for the deck. The new materials brought the cost up to $12,000. Does John have any recourse?
   A. No. He cannot collect the money because there is no right to compensation when the government exercises his police power
   B. Yes. He can sue the county's building department for the money
   C. No. Because John should've known that building code
   D. Yes. He is entitled to be compensated by the building department

15. The McArthur's are selling their home. They have occupied the home since they bought it 20 years ago for $150,000. They have done various repairs throughout the course of the 20 years totaling $200,000. The property is sold for $830,000. After the closing, they receive a 1099 for the $480,000 profit that must be reported to the IRS. They were under the impression that they wouldn't have to pay any taxes on the home. Are they correct in this assumption?
   A. No, the McArthur's will have to pay taxes on $180,000
   B. No, the McArthur's will have to pay taxes on $680,000
   C. Yes, because they only made a $480,000 profit, they will be exempt from taxes
   D. Yes, because all homeowners are exempt from capital gains taxes

16. A husband and wife have owned a property for 6 years and they have occupied it for the last four. They bought the property for 320,000 and sold it for 650,000. On what amount would they pay in capital gains tax?
    A. Zero
    B. $510,000
    C. $20,000
    D. $290,000

17. The county is trying to figure out the ad valorem tax rate to be paid by all property owners in the county. Mr. Brown is unhappy with the assessment attributed to his home. She should appeal to:
    A. Board of Equalization
    B. Board of Arbitration
    C. Tax Assessor's Office
    D. County Tax Commissioner

18. In which situation will the county least likely grant a variance?
    A. A family wants to temporarily place a mobile home on their property after their home burned down
    B. A family wishes to build an in-ground pool in violation of the setback lines
    C. A builder who wants to put a store on the edge of a subdivision zoned residential
    D. A builder requests to build a fence on a property 6 inches higher than the law allows due to the contour of the land

19. To qualify as a tax-deferred 1031 exchange, a property must be
    A. A principal residence
    B. Held for productive use in trade or business
    C. Financed through a federal institution
    D. Amortized over a 30-year period

20. Mary hasn't paid her property taxes in over a year and the county has put a lien on her property. The county will be selling the lien at a tax sale next week. What can Mary do? *
    A. Pay all of the taxes prior to the sale under an equitable right of redemption
    B. Pay all of the taxes prior to the sale under a statutory right of redemption
    C. Nothing, it is too late to do anything at this point
    D. Sue the county and prevent them from selling the lien

21. A husband and wife have owned a property for 5 years and they have occupied it for the last three. They bought the property for 290,000 and sold it for 810,000. On what amount would they pay in capital gains tax?
    A. Zero
    B. $510,000
    C. $20,000
    D. $290,000

22. You are the agent selling a property that was built in 1972, what are your obligations regarding lead?
    A. Tell the buyer that lead is on the premises since the property was built in 1972
    B. There are no further obligations relating to lead since the property was built in 1972 and not 1973
    C. Have the buyer and seller fill out a lead-based paint disclosure and have the seller test for lead
    D. Allow the buyer an additional 10 days to inspect for lead and ensure that the lead paint disclosure is signed by both parties

Chapter 6 Answers

1. D	6. B	11. B	16. D	21. C	26. C	31. B	36. B
2. A	7. D	12. D	17. C	22. B	27. D	32. B	37. D
3. D	8. C	13. C	18. C	23. B	28. C	33. D	38. A
4. C	9. D	14. A	19. C	24. A	29. D	34. D	
5. D	10. B	15. D	20. A	25. D	30. A	35. C	

1. Nonconforming
2. Condemnation
3. Certificate of Occupancy
4. Setbacks
5. Spot Zoning
6. Tax Relief Act of 1997
7. Covenants
8. Escheat
9. Homestead Exemption
10. Assessed Value
11. Restrictions
12. Conditions
13. Ad Valorem Taxes
14. Mil
15. Buffer Zone
16. Bulk Zoning
17. Capital Gain
18. Tax Abatement
19. Special Assessment
20. Wetland
21. Building Codes
22. Eminent Domain
23. Down Zoning
24. Zoning
25. Intangible Tax
26. Cost Basis
27. Variance
28. Building Permit
29. 1031 Exchange
30. Master Plan
31. Right of Redemption
32. Police Power
33. Assessment Rate
34. Transfer Tax
35. Exclusionary Zoning
36. Flood Zone
37. Board of Arbitration
38. Land Use Districts

Exercise 1

1. I	3. A	5. E	7. C	9. G	11. F	13. K
2. M	4. H	6. J	8. D	10. L	12. B	

Exercise 2

1. I	3. F	5. G	7. L	9. H	11. M	13. J
2. B	4. D	6. E	8. A	10. K	12. C	

Exercise 3

1. D	3. L	5. F	7. J	9. A	11. K
2. G	4. C	6. H	8. E	10. I	12. B

1. An investor pays capital gains on all profits; an owner-occupied homeowner for two of the last 5 years gets an exemption if he's single of $250,000 of gain and $500,000 if married

2. Buffer Zone

3. Spot Zoning

4. Zoning goes to how property is to be used; Building codes go to who property will be improved

5. Grandfathered

6. $300,000-$245,000 = $55,000

7. An equitable right comes prior to court invention; a statutory right comes after court intervention

8. Equitable Right of Redemption

9. The amount of property value that the government uses to calculate ad valorem taxes

10. Multiply the market value by the assessment rate

11. Ad valorem is assessed to everyone who owns a property in the county; special assessments are only assessed to those who receive a benefit

12. A reduction in property taxes for owner occupants

13. It is taken off of the assessed value of the property

14. Board of Arbitration

15. An area that requires all houses to be 10,000 square feet

16. Certificate of completion

17. Building Department

18. Suspension of property taxes for a specified period to encourage economic development

19. Transfer tax is based on sales price; Intangible tax is based on loan amount

20. Zoning is a police power of the government; Eminent domain is a taking

SECTION 7 ANSWERS:

1. D. Special assessment taxes are only levied against those who receive the benefit. Homeowners in the 500-home subdivision are the only ones benefiting from the stop sign and will be the only one to pay for it. All other answers will be levied against ad valorem taxes

2. B. Require 4 x 4 posts when building a deck

3. D. Building permits regulate improvements on the property and the homeowner who correctly applies for and is issued one demonstrates an intent to comply with those regulations

4. B. Abatement is the removal of lead. In a broader sense, it can be used in different contexts, but it generally means the removal or lessening

5. D. The master plan is a fluid plan that outlines the goals of the community in terms of its future development direction

6. D. Eminent Domain since the county want to expand the roadway at the rear of the property and Ms. Jones is entitled to compensation. It doesn't matter that she doesn't have heirs as she is still alive

7. D. The city would be exercising its right under Eminent Domain but the legal action that it would bring is called Condemnation

8. C. Jack wants to use his property in a way that would not be zoned. The building department has jurisdiction over improvements. The zoning board has jurisdiction over use

9. A. The HOA would prevail here because the stricter of the private restriction/public restriction will always prevail. The HOA probably cannot change any rule it wishes and it probably doesn't need consent from all homeowners either. Further, the zoning law didn't change, so, the grandfathering clause is inapplicable

10. D. Restrictive covenants can be removed if all landowners of the subdivision agree to dissolve the covenants. Covenants must be renewed and transfer to all new homeowners

11. A. Zoning is not retroactive. All existing structures prior to a zoning change can remain in existence

12. B. The law requires that a lead-based paint disclosure be made to the purchaser any time a property was built before 1978 to make the party aware that there may be lead. It doesn't require that the seller abate the lead, only that he discloses the possibility of lead

13. A. The concern with lead-based paint is that it can harm young children who ingest it. Thus, it must be disclosed in all properties built before 1978. That is the year that it was outlawed in both residential and commercial properties

14. A. Because building codes are an exercise of police power, there is no entitlement to compensation

15. C. The McArthur's fulfilled the requirement of the Tax Reinvestment Act. Married couples who profit from homes that they have lived in and owned for at least 2 of the last 5 years will be exempt from the first $500,000 of profit. Here, they purchased the home for $150,000 and put $200,000 into it. They then sold it for $830,000 so their profit is $480,000. Since that amount is less than $500,000, they won't pay any taxes on the property

16. A. Married couples who have lived in and owned their home for at least 2 of the last 5 years get a $500,000 profit exemption from capital gains. Here, the total profit on the sale was $330,000, but since they have a $500,000 exemption, they won't pay capital gains

17. B. Appeals relating to property assessments are brought to The Board of Arbitration

18. C. Variances are exceptions to current zoning and are given to the person applying for the variance rather than to the property itself. It would often be a small change as opposed to something that will affect an entire area. It also does not change the current zoning. Of the examples, the store on the edge of a subdivision zoned residential would have the greatest impact on the area and will be the least like approved for a variance

19. B. A 1031 exchange is a way for investors to defer income taxes until a much later date. There are many rules such as on any sale, the investor must find a like kind property to buy, cannot touch the proceeds but must bring in a qualified intermediary, and the properties must be used in a trade or business

20. A. Most, if not all states, will have an equitable right of redemption in this situation. Since the county has not sold the property yet (statutory right of redemption), she would be entitled to pay all taxes prior to the sale

21. C. Married couples who have lived in and owned their home for 3 of the last 5 years get a $500,000 profit exemption from capital gains. Here, the total profit on the sale was $520,000, but since they have a $500,000 exemption, they will only pay capital gains on $20,000

22. D. The agent/seller has the obligation to disclose lead potential in any home that was built prior to 1978. The obligations include providing a disclosure that the house may have led, that the purchaser has a 10 day right to inspect, and there is no requirement to abate the lead

Chapter 7: Leasing and Property Management

Section 1: *Outline*

I. <u>Leases</u> – <u>a contractual agreement between the parties and a conveyance of property from landlord to tenant</u>

    A. Landlord and Tenant – the lease, which can be in writing or verbal, is the document that provides for the transfer of rights from landlord (**lessor**) to tenant (**lessee**). The lessor is the fee simple owner and retains a **leased fee estate** that is **reversionary**. The lessor grants the lessee a temporary right of exclusive possession of property, called a **leasehold** estate or tenancy. There are four basic types of leasehold estates:

        1. Leasehold Estates:

            a. Estate for Years (Tenancy for Years) – grants to the tenant exclusive possession and use of the property for a specific time period. No notice is required to terminate. Sale or death of either the landlord or the tenant does not terminate the lease. Its terms are binding on the heirs and any new landlord

            b. Estate from Period to Period (Periodic Tenancy) – the payment of each rent renews the time period unless either the landlord or the tenant gives notice to terminate. Sale or death of either the landlord or the tenant does not terminate the lease and the terms are binding on the new landlord

            c. Estate at Will (Tenancy at Will) – landlord allows the tenant to occupy the property for an unspecified and uncertain time period. It is temporary and permissive in nature. It is not assignable and ends if the property is sold or if either party dies

            d. Estate at Sufferance (Tenancy at Sufferance) –tenant will not leave after being given notice to vacate. Also known as a **holdover tenant** which differs from a trespasser in that this right to occupy was once legal. The landlord has the option of filing a legal action of **ejectment** to have the tenant removed

        2. Requirements for a Valid Lease – since a lease is both a contract and an instrument of conveyance, it must meet both the contractual and deed elements

            a. Consideration – exchange of promises
            b. Assent – mutual (meeting of the minds) and Genuine (free will)
            c. Legal Capacity – of sound mind and not a minor
            d. Lawful Purpose – not illegal
            e. In Writing as Required by Law – Statute of Frauds
            f. Description of the Premises – Metes and Bounds, Short-Form, Government Survey
            g. Lease Term – dates of possession
            h. Signature, Delivery and Acceptance – signed by the landlord and delivered to the tenant for acceptance

3. **Rights and Obligations of the Parties to a Lease**

   a. **Possession and the Right to Enter** – once the tenant takes possession, the landlord is not allowed to enter the premises without the tenant's permission unless the lease states otherwise

   b. **Quiet Enjoyment** – implied promise that the tenant will not be disturbed or evicted because of a defective title

   c. **Use of Premises** – **restrictive covenants** – premises can only be used for certain purposes or **protective covenants** – prohibiting a certain use

   d. **Rent** – **Contract rent** – amount stated in the lease. **Market rent** – amount the market will bear

   e. **Taxes and Insurance** – landlord is responsible for paying ad valorum taxes, special assessments, and property insurance unless the lease provides otherwise

   f. **Repairs and Maintenance** – tenants must keep leased property in good condition and not commit **waste.** The landlord provides an **implied warranty of habitability** – minimum level of livability

   g. **Injury to be Tenant** – landlord can be liable for tenants' or guests' injury if it resulted from landlord's negligence

   h. **Improvements** – the landlord is not obligated to improve the premises. Tenant can make **leasehold improvements** only if approved by the landlord

   i. **Security Deposits** – security deposits are not essential and are only collected for two reasons:

      1. To ensure lease fulfillment
      2. To ensure that the property will be returned in satisfactory condition

4. **Transfer of Landlord Rights**

   a. Landlord does not need tenant's permission to sell the leased property

   b. Tenant's possession serves as constructive notice to a subsequent owner that he must honor the lease

   c. If the lease was arranged before mortgage, the **lease prevails** and cannot be terminated without a **subordination clause**

   d. Foreclosure – **Receiver clauses** and **Owner's Rent clauses** allow the lender to appoint a receiver to manage the property pending the lawsuit. A **non-disturbance agreement** indicates that the lender promises not to cancel any lease in the event of foreclosure

5. **Transfer of Tenants Rights**

   a. **Assignment** – is a transfer by the tenant (**assignor**) of **all** remaining leasehold rights and interests to another person (**assignee**). The assignee becomes the tenant and accepts the responsibility to pay rent to the landlord; all other terms of the lease remain the same; the assignor remains secondarily liable

   b. **Sublease** – is a transfer by the tenant (**sublessor**) of **some** of the rights and interests to another person (**sublessee**). The sublessee pays rent to the original tenant and has no liability to the landlord. This arrangement is called a **sandwich lease**

   c. **Mortgaging the Leasehold Estate** – the leasehold estate may be used by a tenant as security for a loan

6. **Lease options (Unilateral Contracts)**

   a. **Option to Renew** – gives the tenant the right to extend the lease for another term at a set price

   b. **Option to Buy** – gives the tenant the right to buy at a set price within a designated time period

   c. **Right of First Refusal** – assures the tenant of the right to buy the leased premises IF the landlord **EVER** decides to sell the property. Price is not set until the option is exercised

7. **Types of Leases**

   a. **Gross lease** – aka **flat** or **straight** lease. All-inclusive payment from tenant. The landlord is responsible for the property taxes, insurance, repairs, and maintenance

   b. **Net Lease** – the tenant pays a fixed rental amount <u>plus</u> all or a specifically defined net for taxes, insurance, maintenance, and repairs

   c. **Graduated Leases** - landlord in a long-term lease acquires some necessary protection against rising costs and inflation by including an **escalator clause** in the agreement

1. **Step-up Lease** – provides rent increases in predetermined amounts
2. **Index lease** – periodic rent adjustments based on changes to a designated economic index
3. **Escalator lease** – applies to a lease in which rent increases are tied to certain operating costs
4. **Reappraisal lease** – reappraisal at certain intervals to adjust rents to market conditions
5. **Percentage Lease** – most used in malls, it provides that the tenant pay a fixed minimum or base rent plus a percentage of either gross sales, gross profits, or net profit
6. **Ground Lease** – very long term rental of unimproved land in which permission granted to the tenant to build or make improvements
7. **Sale Leaseback** – a lease which occurs as part of a sale when the owner sells the property to an investor with an agreement to lease it back on a long- term basis
   Advantages to Buyer:
   Secure long-term investment, appreciation, equity growth
   Advantages to Seller:
   Acquisition of capital, no management, tax deductions
8. **The Occupancy (Move-In) Agreement** – an agreement which allows purchasers to occupy the property before the closing or seller to remain past closing

8. **Landlord's Remedies if the Tenant Defaults:**

   a. **Statutory Remedies**

      1. Sue for rental payments or damages
      2. Eviction/Unlawful detainer

   b. **Remedies provided in the lease** – additional remedies for default can be written in the lease

9. **Tenant's Remedies if the landlord Defaults:**

   a. Sue for damages
   b. **Constructive eviction** – if the landlord's actions or omissions leave the leased premises uninhabitable, the landlord has violated **the implied warranty of habitability** and the tenant can abandon the property and stop paying rent

10. **Termination of leases**

    a. **Expiration** – Tenancy for Years
    b. **Notice** – Periodic Tenancy and Tenancy at Will
    c. **Mutual Agreement (Surrender and Acceptance)**
    d. **Merger** – tenant buys the property from the landlord
    e. **Condemnation** – the govt exercises it right to eminent domain
    f. **Eviction** – Court action
    g. **Destruction of the Premises** – complete destruction
    h. **Death** – death of either party does not terminate a lease except in a **tenancy at will**

B. Property Management

1. **The Property Manager** – an agent with fiduciary responsibility to maintain, preserve and enhance the owner's investment in the property and to generate the highest possible net return from the property over its economic life
2. **The Management Contract** – establishes the agency relationship. The written agreement contains, at a minimum:

   a. **Name of the parties**
   b. **Property description** – complete legal description
   c. **Manager's authority and responsibility** – duties and scope of authority
   d. **Financial Reporting**
   e. **Management fee** – fixed amount or percentage of rents collected

3. **Functions of the Property Manager**

    a. **Develop a plan**

    b. **Marketing (Renting the space)**

    c. **Collecting Rents**

    d. **Keeping Tenants**

    e. **Property Maintenance**

    f. **Accounting and Reporting**

    g. **Sale of the Property** – terminates management contract

C. Community Association Management

Subdivision Homeowner Associations (HOAs)

    a. **Subdivision with no governing Homeowner association** – if one owner violates the covenants, it up to others to enforce

    b. **Subdivision with a Voluntary Homeowner Association** – association has the right to enforce covenants however enforcement can wane as community ages

    c. **Subdivision with Mandatory Association Membership** – recognized as the best option for maintaining an appealing community

D. Condominium Management

The Condominium Associations Power

1. Can tax owners in regular and/or special assessments
2. Adopt rules for reasonable use
3. Take legal action
4. Approve or disapprove physical alterations

Section 2: *Vocabulary*

Constructive Eviction: Tenant's claim that the landlord's actions impair his enjoyment of the leased premises

Eviction: The legal process of removing a tenant from a rental property

Graduated Lease: Long-term leases that include escalator clauses to protect the landlord against inflation

Gross Lease: A pay one price all-inclusive lease

Ground Lease: A lease of unimproved land that is accompanied by permission from the landlord for the tenant to improve the property

Implied Warranty of Habitability: Landlord warrants a minimum level of livability of the premises

Index Lease: The lease is tied to some external index that the tenant can access

Landlord/Lessor: The owner of a rental property

Lease: A legal contract defining the terms and conditions between landlord and tenant

Leased Fee Estate: The type of estate the landlord retains when property is leased to another

Leasehold: The interest that the tenant has in the leased premises

Merger: The tenant purchases the property from the landlord resulting in lease termination

Net Lease: An agreement for the tenant to pay a fixed rent plus a share of taxes, insurance, utilities, and maintenance

Non-Disturbance Clause: A clause that promises to honor all leases if the property is foreclosed

Occupancy Agreement: An agreement between the buyer and seller which changes the date for transfer of possession after closing

Percentage Lease: A lease where the tenant pays a base rent and a percentage of gross sales or profit

Periodic Tenancy: Any lease agreement that automatically renews with each rental period until either party gives notice of termination

Protective Covenant: A provision in a lease prohibiting certain uses of the property

Property Management Contract: The agency contract between an owner and a broker to manager real property

Receiver Clause: A provision which permits a court to appoint a receiver to manage income producing property

Restrictive Covenant: A provision in a lease indicating to the tenant the only permissible uses of the property

Sale Leaseback: An owner sells property to an investor and signs a long-term lease to remain in possession

Security Deposit: Paid to a landlord to ensure lease compliance

Step-up lease: The rent is fixed for the initial part of the term, then adjusts upward in predetermined amounts

Sublease: The transfer of part of the term of a lease to someone else

Subordination Clause: Permits a later placed mortgage or lease to take priority over an earlier one

Surrender and Acceptance: Termination of a lease by mutual agreement of the landlord and the tenant

Tenant/Lessee: The person in possession of a rental property under contract with the lessor

Tenancy at Sufferance: Created when a tenant who has been given notice to terminate fails to do so

Tenancy at Will: A permissive tenancy where the landlord allows the tenant to remain in possession for an unstated period

Tenancy for Years: A leasehold estate for any definite duration

Trade Fixture: An article owned by a tenant and attached to a rented space or building for use in conducting a business

Warranty of Quiet Enjoyment: Landlord's warranty that the tenant won't be disturbed by a claim of superior title

Section 3: *Recall Multiple Choice*

1. **The tenant purchases the property from the landlord terminating the lease**
   A. Acquisition
   B. Merger
   C. Sublease
   D. Leasehold

2. **The type of estate the landlord retains when property is leased to another**
   A. Fee Simple Estate
   B. Net Lease
   C. Leasehold Estate
   D. Leased Fee Estate

3. **The general agency contract between a broker and an owner of property**
   A. Sales Contract
   B. Lease
   C. Listing Contract
   D. Property Management Contract

4. **The person in possession of a rental property under contract with the lessor**
   A. Tenant/Lessee
   B. Index Lease
   C. Owner /lessee
   D. Gross Lease

5. **A pay one price all-inclusive lease**
   A. Ground Lease
   B. Gross Lease
   C. Percentage Lease
   D. Net Lease

6. **A provision in a lease prohibiting certain uses of the property**
   A. Protective Covenant
   B. Subordination Clause
   C. Receiver Clause
   D. Escalator Clause

7. **A lease of unimproved land that is accompanied by permission from the landlord for the tenant to improve the property**
   A. Ground Lease
   B. Net Lease
   C. Percentage Lease
   D. Gross Lease

8. **An agreement for the tenant to pay a fixed rent plus a share of taxes, insurance, utilities, and maintenance**
   A. Gross Lease
   B. Net Lease
   C. Ground Lease
   D. Percentage Lease

9. **The transfer of part of the term of a lease to someone else**
   A. Gross Lease
   B. Net Lease
   C. Assignment
   D. Sublease

10. **Long-term leases that include escalator clauses to protect the landlord against inflation**
    A. Net Lease
    B. Graduated Lease
    C. Gross Lease
    D. Percentage Lease

11. **An agreement between the buyer and seller which changes the date for transfer of possession**
    A. Occupancy Agreement
    B. Proprietary Lease
    C. Non-disturbance Agreement
    D. Lease Agreement

12. **The lease is tied to some external index that the tenant can access**
    A. Graduated Lease
    B. Percentage Lease
    C. Gross Lease
    D. Index Lease

13. **An article owned by a tenant and attached to a rented space or building for use in conducting a business**
    A. Net Lease
    B. Trade Fixture
    C. Real Property
    D. Lease

14. **A permissive tenancy where the landlord allows the tenant to remain in possession for an unstated period**
    A. Receiver Clause
    B. Tenancy at Will
    C. Tenancy for Years
    D. Percentage Lease

15. **A legal contract defining the terms and conditions between landlord and tenant**
    A. Lease
    B. Periodic Tenancy
    C. Assignment
    D. Ejectment

16. **The rent is fixed for the initial part of the term, then adjusts upward in predetermined amounts**
    A. Ground lease
    B. Step-up lease
    C. Escalator lease
    D. Gross lease

17. **Landlord warrants a minimum level of livability of the premises**
    A. Warranty of Quiet Enjoyment
    B. Covenant of Quiet Enjoyment
    C. Statute of Frauds
    D. Implied Warranty of Habitability

18. **The legal process of removing a tenant from a rental property**
    A. Ejectment
    B. Assignment
    C. Eviction
    D. Merger

19. **Tenant's claim that the landlord's actions impair a tenant's enjoyment of the leased premises**
    A. Tenancy At Sufferance
    B. Assignment
    C. Tenant/lessee
    D. Constructive Eviction

20. **A lease where the tenant pays a base rent and a percentage of gross sales or profit**
    A. Graduated Lease
    B. Percentage Lease
    C. Gross Lease
    D. Index Lease

21. **The owner of a rental property**
    A. Lessee/lessor
    B. Tenant/lessee
    C. Landlord/Lessor
    D. Market Rent

22. **Paid to a landlord to ensure lease compliance**
    A. Periodic Tenancy
    B. Escrow Account
    C. Security Deposit
    D. Percentage Lease

23. **An owner sells property to an investor and signs a long-term lease to remain in possession**
    A. Index Lease
    B. Percentage Lease
    C. Sandwich Lease
    D. Sale Leaseback

24. **A leasehold estate for any definite duration**
    A. Step-up Lease
    B. Periodic Tenancy
    C. Net Lease
    D. Tenancy for Years

25. **A provision which permits a court to appoint an independent receiver to manage income producing property**
    A. Alienation Clause
    B. Defeasance Clause
    C. Receiver Clause
    D. Brundage Clause

26. **A provision in a lease indicating to the tenant the only permissible uses of the property**
    A. Leasehold
    B. Lease
    C. Subordination Clause
    D. Restrictive Covenant

27. **Any lease agreement that automatically renews with each rental period until either party gives notice of termination**
    A. Gross Lease
    B. Periodic Tenancy
    C. Tenancy At Sufferance
    D. Net Lease

28. **Created when a tenant who has been given notice to terminate fails to do so**
    A. Tenancy at Sufferance
    B. Assignment
    C. Periodic Tenancy
    D. Constructive Eviction

29. **Permits a later placed mortgage or lease to take priority over an earlier one**
    A. Net Lease
    B. Lease
    C. Subordination Clause
    D. Restrictive Covenant

30. **A clause that promises to honor all leases if the property is foreclosed**
    A. Receiver Clause
    B. Subordination Clause
    C. Non-Disturbance Clause
    D. Sublease

31. **Tenant's interest created by a lease**
    A. Sublease
    B. Easement
    C. Leasehold
    D. Merger

32. **Termination of a lease by mutual agreement of the landlord and the tenant**
    A. Rescission and Acceptance
    B. Surrender and Acceptance
    C. Release and Acceptance
    D. Release and Surrender

33. **Landlord's warranty that the tenant won't be disturbed by a superior claim of occupancy**
    A. Warranty of further Assurance
    B. Implied Warranty of Habitability
    C. Warranty of Quiet Enjoyment
    D. Right of First Refusal

Section 4: *Recall Fill-In*

1. A provision in a lease prohibiting certain uses of the property

   _____

2. The tenant purchases the property from the landlord terminating the lease

   _____

3. The rent is fixed for the initial part of the term, then adjusts upward in predetermined amounts

   _____

4. Any lease agreement that automatically renews with each rental period until either party gives notice of termination

   _____

5. A provision which permits a court to appoint an independent receiver to manage income producing property

   _____

6. A permissive tenancy where the landlord allows the tenant to remain in possession for an unstated period

   _____

7. The legal process of removing a tenant from a rental property

   _____

8. A lease where the tenant pays a base rent and a percentage of gross sales or profit

   _____

9. A pay one price all-inclusive lease

   _____

10. Created when a tenant who has been given notice to terminate fails to do so

    _____

11. The lease is tied to some external index that the tenant can access

    _____

12. A legal contract defining the terms and conditions between landlord and tenant

    _____

13. Tenant's interest created by a lease

    _____

14. An agreement between the buyer and seller which changes the date for transfer of possession

15. An owner sells property to an investor and signs a long-term lease to remain in possession

16. An article owned by a tenant and attached to a rented space or building for use in conducting a business

17. The type of estate the landlord retains when property is leased to another

18. Landlord warrants a minimum level of livability of the premises

19. A lease of unimproved land that is accompanied by permission from the landlord for the tenant to improve the property

20. The person in possession of a rental property under contract with the lessor

21. A leasehold estate for any definite duration

22. Tenant's claim that the landlord's actions impair a tenant's his ability to remain in the leased premises

23. Permits a later placed mortgage or lease to take priority over an earlier one

24. The owner of a rental property

25. The general agency contract between a broker and an owner of property

26. Long-term leases that include escalator clauses to protect the landlord against inflation

27. Paid to a landlord to ensure lease compliance

28. Termination of a lease by mutual agreement of the landlord and the tenant

_____

29. A clause that promises to honor all leases if the property is foreclosed

_____

30. A provision in a lease indicating to the tenant the only permissible uses of the property

_____

31. An agreement for the tenant to pay a fixed rent plus a share of taxes, insurance, utilities, and maintenance

_____

32. Landlord's warranty that the tenant won't be disturbed by a superior claim of occupancy

_____

33. The transfer of part of the term of a lease to someone else

_____

Section 5: *Matching*

A   Landlord/Lessor   1 _____   The owner of a rental property

B   Percentage Lease   2 _____   A clause that promises to honor all leases if the property is foreclosed

C   Periodic Tenancy   3 _____   A lease where the tenant pays a base rent and a percentage of gross sales or profit

D   Gross Lease   4 _____   A pay one price all-inclusive lease

E   Sublease   5 _____   A permissive tenancy where the landlord allows the tenant to remain in possession for an unstated period

F   Tenancy at Will   6 _____   An article owned by a tenant and attached to a rented space or building for use in conducting a business

G   Subordination Clause   7 _____   Any lease agreement that automatically renews with each rental period until either party gives notice of termination

H   Trade Fixture   8 _____   Landlord's warranty that the tenant won't be disturbed by a superior claim of occupancy

I   Leasehold   9 _____   Permits a later placed mortgage or lease to take priority over an earlier one

J   Warranty of Quiet Enjoyment   10 _____   The tenant's interest in a lease

K   Non-Disturbance Clause   11 _____   The transfer of part of the term of a lease to someone else

A   Tenant/Lessee

1 _____   A leasehold estate for any definite duration

B   Restrictive Covenant

2 _____   A legal contract defining the terms and conditions between landlord and tenant

C   Graduated Lease

3 _____   A provision in a lease indicating to the tenant the only permissible uses of the property

D   Lease

4 _____   A provision which permits a court to appoint an independent receiver to manage income producing property

E   Receiver Clause

5 _____   An agreement for the tenant to pay a fixed rent plus a share of taxes, insurance, utilities, and maintenance

F   Step-Up Lease

6 _____   An owner sells property to an investor and signs a long-term lease to remain in possession

G   Tenancy for Years

7 _____   Created when a tenant who has been given notice to terminate fails to do so

H   Tenancy at Sufferance

8 _____   Long-term leases that include escalator clauses to protect the landlord against inflation

I   Net Lease

9 _____   The general agency contract between a broker and owner of property

J   Sale Leaseback

10 _____   The person in possession of a rental property under contract with the lessor

K   Property Management Contract

11 _____   The rent is fixed for the initial part of the term, then adjusts upward in predetermined amounts

A   Ground Lease   1 _____   A lease of unimproved land that is accompanied by permission from the landlord for the tenant to improve the property

B   Surrender and Acceptance   2 _____   A provision in a lease prohibiting certain uses of the property

C   Merger   3 _____   An agreement between the buyer and seller which changes the date for transfer of possession

D   Security Deposit   4 _____   Landlord warrants a minimum level of livability of the premises

E   Eviction   5 _____   Paid to a landlord to ensure lease compliance

F   Constructive Eviction   6 _____   Tenant's claim that the landlord's actions impair a tenant's enjoyment of the leased premises

G   Protective Covenant   7 _____   Termination of a lease by mutual agreement of the landlord and the tenant.

H   Occupancy Agreement   8 _____   The lease is tied to some external index that the tenant can access.

I   Index Lease   9 _____   The legal process of removing a tenant from a rental property.

J   Implied Warranty of Habitability   10 _____   The tenant purchases the property from the landlord terminating the lease

K   Leased Fee Estate   11 _____   The type of estate the landlord retains when property is leased to another

Section 6: *Analysis Fill-In*

1. Which lease is not assignable?

_____

2. What is the difference between a tenancy at will and periodic tenancy in terms of notice to end the lease?

_____

3. What is the difference between a tenancy for years and periodic tenancy in terms of notice to end the lease?

_____

4. What is the most likely situation where a net lease would be used?

_____

5. What is the most likely situation where a gross lease would be used?

_____

6. What is the difference between a Tenancy for Years and Tenancy at Will if the landlord dies?

_____

7. When does a lease have to be in writing to be valid?

_____

8. A very long-term lease where the lessee has permission to improve the property himself is called:

_____

9. When does a lease have to be in writing to be enforceable?

_____

10. Name 4 Ways to terminate a lease:

_____

11. Name 4 requirements of a valid lease:

_____

12. Name two reasons why a seller would do a sale leaseback?

_____

13. When a tenant purchases the property from the landlord resulting in termination of the lease, it is called:

_____

14. **Property management agency agreements always ends when?**

_____

15. **Give an example of constructive eviction:**

_____

16. **Occupancy agreements are used when?**

_____

17. **What is a step-up lease?**

_____

18. **Name a type of option contract:**

_____

19. **What's the difference between a lease assignment and a sublease in terms of liability?**

_____

20. **A change in the order of priority of liens would require what clause?**

_____

21. **Give one reason why a landlord would collect a security deposit:**

_____

22. **You cannot use this space for a barber shop is an example of what type of covenant?**

_____

23. **What two implied promises does a landlord make to a tenant?**

_____

24. **This type of lease is all-inclusive (pay one price):**

_____

25. **This lease doesn't require notice to terminate:**

_____

26. **This lease is tied to the landlord's operating costs:**

_____

Section 7: *Analysis Multiple Choice*

1. **One would expect a property manager to understand aspects of managing a property except:**
   A. Acquiring and keeping tenants
   B. Investing the principal's funds into accounts
   C. Hold the rents in trust for the principal
   D. Ensuring the property through vendor relationships

2. **Ms. Millie's cookies has a lease in the local shopping mall. Her lease agreement states that she is to pay $13.00 per square foot for the space and a portion of her net sales to the landlord on a quarterly basis. This type of lease is:**
   A. Gross Lease
   B. Net Lease
   C. Ground Lease
   D. Percentage Lease

3. **Mel, who is handicapped, decides to rent a unit from Heather in her 10 story apartment building. Mel requires that the building have a ramp placed in the lobby so that he can use his wheelchair to get to the elevator. Heather allows Mel to construct the ramp but wants to place a provision in the lease that states that Mel must bear the cost to remove the ramp once he departs the premises. Is Heather allowed to do this under the ADA?**
   A. No. The ADA requires that the landlord bear the cost of removal of the ramp
   B. Yes. While Heather must allow Mel to live there, Heather can require that he remove the ramp on departure
   C. Yes. While the ADA doesn't even require that Heather rent to Mel. Because she chooses to do so, she can make him remove the ramp
   D. No. Since the building is now ADA complaint, the ramp must remain

4. **Malia has an apartment in Maia's building. Malia has 4 dogs that she does not do a good job in taking care of. The dogs often go to the bathroom on the newly installed carpet. Before the lease expires, Maia has to come into the apartment to do a repair and he sees the carpet as well as several doors scratched up. Maia sues Malia and claims:**
   A. Constructive Eviction
   B. Waste
   C. Laches
   D. Breach of the implied warranty of habitability

5. **Madeleine is a tenant in Dale's 25-unit rental property. Madeleine's set a fire in the bathroom. As a result, some of the units in the building were completely destroyed and some only had minimal damage. Can all of the tenants terminate their leases?**
   A. Yes, because any destruction of property allows lease termination
   B. Maybe, it depends on the language of the leases
   C. No, only the tenants whose apartments were completing destroyed can terminate their leases
   D. Yes, all tenants, except Madeleine can terminate their leases

6. **John is a tenant in Larry's building. John continually asked Larry to speak with the tenants above John. He complains that they are excessively loud, stomping on the floor, and has loud parties. After 4 months of not being able to sleep, John asked Larry one more time to handle the situation. When Larry refuses, John decides to leave the apartment and sues Larry for:**
   A. Breach of the implied covenant of quiet enjoyment
   B. Constructive eviction
   C. Breach of the duty to assist with tenant issues
   D. Laches for failure to do something in the first month

7. **Ensuring that the entry hallways to an apartment building are clean and appealing is an example of:**
    A. Routine Maintenance
    B. Preventative Maintenance
    C. Corrective Maintenance
    D. Not considered to be a type of maintenance

8. **An owner hired a broker to manage his property. He should expect that the broker:**
    A. Maintain loyalty and have knowledge about hazard insurance
    B. Maintain obedience and have knowledge about investment strategy
    C. Keep him informed of only material matters and have knowledge about hazard insurance
    D. Commingle funds and have knowledge about rental rates in the area

9. **When managing property, which of the following actions is legal?**
    A. Refusing to rent to families with children
    B. Placing all families with children in the same building
    C. Collecting larger security deposits from prospective tenants with support animals
    D. Refusing to rent to people with a criminal record

10. **Which of the following is subject to the Statute of Frauds?**
    A. Six - month lease for an apartment
    B. Tenancy at will
    C. Two year - lease for real property
    D. Month to month rental

11. **When a landlord rents property to a tenant:**
    A. Landlord has a leased fee estate that is reversionary
    B. Landlord has a leasehold estate that is a remainder
    C. Landlord has a leased fee estate that is a remainder
    D. Landlord has a leasehold estate that is reversionary

12. **What estate is created when a tenant's lease has expired and he did not vacate the premises as agreed in the lease**
    A. An estate at sufferance
    B. A remainder estate
    C. A reversionary estate
    D. A leasehold estate

13. **The owner of an investment property died on May 31st. Can the property manager collect the rent checks that are due on April 1st?**
    A. Yes, because leases do not expire on death of the landlord
    B. No, because the agency terminated on the owner's death
    C. No, because all leases expire at the death of the landlord
    D. Yes, because 30 days have not passed since the owner's death so the next lease payment is due

14. **Notice is needed to terminate most leasehold estates. Which leasehold estate does not normally require notice to terminate?**
    A. Tenancy in sufferance
    B. Tenancy in common
    C. Tenancy for years
    D. Tenancy at will

15. Which of the following does not normally terminate a lease?
   A. Constructive Eviction
   B. Actual Eviction
   C. Death of the landlord
   D. Condemnation of the property

16. Bob entered into a property management agreement with Broker Jim. The agreement most likely indicates that Broker Jim will be paid:
   A. A Net Amount after Bob earns a certain amount
   B. A percentage of last year's income
   C. A percentage of this year's potential income
   D. A percentage of this year's income

Chapter 7 Answers

1. B	5. B	9. D	13. B	17. D	21. C	25. C	29. C	33. C
2. D	6. A	10. B	14. B	18. C	22. C	26. D	30. C
3. D	7. A	11. A	15. A	19. D	23. D	27. B	31. C
4. A	8. B	12. D	16. B	20. B	24. D	28. A	32. B

1. Protective Covenant
2. Merger
3. Step-Up Lease
4. Periodic Tenancy
5. Receiver Clause
6. Tenancy at Will
7. Eviction
8. Percentage Lease
9. Gross (Flat, Straight) Lease
10. Tenancy at Sufferance
11. Index Lease
12. Lease
13. Leasehold
14. Occupancy Agreement
15. Sales Leaseback
16. Trade Fixture
17. Lease Fee Estate
18. Implied Warranty of Habitability
19. Ground Lease
20. Tenant
21. Tenancy for Years
22. Constructive Eviction
23. Subordination Clause
24. Landlord
25. Property Management Agreement
26. Escalator Leases
27. Security Deposit
28. Surrender and Acceptance
29. Non-disturbance Clause
30. Restrictive Covenant
31. Net Lease
32. Implied Warranty of Quiet Enjoyment
33. Sublease

Exercise 1

1. A	3. B	5. F	7. C	9. G	11. E
2. K	4. D	6. H	8. J	10. I	

Exercise 2

1. G	3. B	5. I	7. H	9. K	11. F
2. D	4. E	6. J	8. C	10. A	

Exercise 3

1. A	3. H	5. D	7. B	9. E	11. K
2. G	4. J	6. F	8. I	10. C	

1. Tenancy at Will

2. Nothing. They both require the same notice as required by the law

3. The tenancy for years doesn't require notice, but the periodic tenancy does

4. Commercial Real Estate

5. Residential Real Estate

6. The tenant's rights are not affected in a tenancy for years, but in a tenancy at will, the lease terminates

7. Never

8. Ground Lease

9. If it cannot be performed within a year

10. Name 4 Ways to terminate a lease:
    1. Expiration of the term – Tenancy for years
    2. Notice – Periodic Tenancy, Tenancy at Will
    3. Mutual Agreement – Both landlord and tenant agree to terminate
    4. Merger – Tenant purchases the property from the landlord
    5. Condemnation – The government exercises its eminent domain right
    6. Eviction – Actual (Landlord) or Constructive (Tenant) can terminate the lease
    7. Destruction – The property is completely destroyed
    8. Death of the landlord or tenant – Tenancy at Will

11. Name 4 requirements of a valid lease:
    Consideration (Exchange of Promises)
    Assent (Mutual and Genuine)
    Legal Capacity (Legally Competent)
    Legal Purpose (Cannot be for illegal purposes)
    Description (Adequate Legal Description)
    Statute of Frauds (If over a year)
    Signature, Delivery and Acceptance (Landlord signs and delivers, Tenant accepts)
    Term of Lease (Type of Lease)

12. To get capital, to lessen management responsibilities, to lessen maintenance responsibilities, to get tax deductions

13. Merger

14. The Property is sold

15. The landlord has refused to repair the hot water tank and it's been a month without the tenant having hot water

16. The transfer of possession is not going to occur at closing

17. A lease that starts at one rate and goes up in predetermined amounts

18. Option to buy, option to lease, right of first refusal

19. In an assignment, the assignee is liable to the landlord, but the sublessee never has liability

20. Subordination

21. Ensure the tenant doesn't breach the lease; Ensure that the property is returned in original condition

22. Protective Covenant

23. Warranty of Habitability and Warranty of Quiet Enjoyment

24. Gross

25. Tenancy for years

26. Escalator Lease

SECTION 7 ANSWERS:

1. B. A property manager is not expected to invest the principal's funds, only to hold them in trust for the principal

2. D. Percentage leases are typically in shopping malls and the tenant pays a base rent plus a percentage of sales or profit, depending on landlord preference

3. B. The ADA requires that Heather allow the ramp to be installed, but also allows Heather to make Mel bear the cost of removal upon departure

4. B. Waste occurs when one person in possession of another person's property engages in acts which diminish the value of the property. Constructive eviction is a claim made by a tenant. Laches is when a person fails to bring a claim and the breach of habitability is when a landlord fails to repair items in a lease arrangement

5. B. Whether a tenant can terminate a lease lies in the lease itself. Most leases will contain a complete destruction clause allowing termination. However, there is no specific rule either way. Further, with respect to Madeleine, it would additionally depend on if she is prevented from termination due to an intentional act

6. B. Constructive Eviction occurs when the landlord positively or negatively makes it impossible for the tenant to live in the rented premises. It is not a quiet enjoyment claim as that goes to disputes of title

7. A. Routine Maintenance are classified as those items that are continually done on a daily basis, such as picking up trash in the hallways and parking lot. Preventative Maintenance is done so that items do not break and Corrective Maintenance is done after the item fails

8. A. One should expect that the broker property manager has knowledge about hazard insurance. He doesn't need to have knowledge of investment strategy, should keep the owner apprised of all matters, and should not commingle funds

9. D. A property manager can refuse to rent to criminals because they have no protection under fair housing. Note that a manager cannot refuse to rent to families with children or place them all in the same building

10. C. Statue of Frauds explains which contracts must be in writing to be enforceable. With respect to leases, only a lease over a year has to be in writing

11. A. When a landlord rents property to a tenant, he retains a leased fee estate. Leaseholds are the tenant's estate. It is also reversionary in that the landlord will get it back once the tenant departs

12. A. An estate or tenancy at sufferance results when a tenant stays past the expiration of the lease or if the landlord has requested that the tenant vacate the premises. The tenant is also known as a holdover tenant

13. B. Even though leases do not expire on the death of the landlord, when the principal dies, the agency is automatically terminated. Thus, the manger no longer has authority to collect the rent from the tenants

14. C. A tenancy for years doesn't require notice to terminate given that it already has a stated end date

15. C. Death of the landlord or the tenant does not normally terminate a lease. The heirs of each party are responsible

16. D. Property Managers are usually paid a percentage of income in the year in which they work for the company

Chapter 8:
Valuation and Market Analysis

Section 1: *Outline*

I. <u>Principles of Valuation and Appraisal</u> – <u>An in-depth look at how property is valued</u>

A. Principles of Valuation and Appraisal

1. **Comparative Market Analysis (CMA)** or **Broker Price Opinion (BPO)**, accomplished by comparing the subject property to similar homes that have recently sold or are on the market

2. **History of the Appraisal Profession** – The Appraisal Foundation, created in 1987, was founded to regulate the profession. It is comprised of **The Appraisal Standards Board** – implements procedures for a competent appraisal through standards and ethical conduct identified in the **Uniform Standards of Professional Appraisal Practice (USPAP) and Appraisal Qualifications Board** – requirements necessary to acquire and maintain licensure and certification

3. **Types of Appraisers: Staff Appraisers** – employed by lending institutions and **Fee Appraisers** – self-employed persons who perform on an individual basis for a negotiated fee. **Fee can never be based on the estimate of value**

4. **Need for Appraisals** – to solve a problem or answer questions about value. Some situations requiring professional appraisals:

   a. Contracts for the sale of property
   b. Lending institutions before making a real estate loan
   c. Insurance agents before insuring a property
   d. Lawyers before handling property settlements, estates and litigating certain lawsuits
   e. Investors
   f. Under eminent domain properties must be appraised before acquiring and paying just compensation

Value Defined – what a property is worth or what it might sell for on the open market. A property may have different values at the same time. The purpose for the appraisal determines which value the appraiser is seeking, the type of value. Some values that may be estimated include:

   a. **Assessed value:** ad valorum taxes
   b. **Condemnation Value:** just compensation for Eminent Domain
   c. **Going Concern Value:** worth of ongoing business
   d. **Insured Value:** replacement value for insurance policy
   e. **Investment Value:** worth of a property to an investor
   f. **Liquidation Value:** a sale within a specific limited time
   g. **Salvage Value:** worth of a property dismantled and moved

Market value – the most probable selling price in an **arm's length transaction.** Essentially, each party receives equal value. It is an estimated price one can hope to achieve, based on relevant and factual information. The 4 requirements of an arm's length transaction include:

    a. Payment must be in cash or cash equivalents
    b. Open market exposure for a reasonable period of time relative to the current market
    c. Parties are motivated relative to the current market
    d. Parties are typically knowledgeable relative to the current market

        1. Market Price – is the actual money paid, the selling price
        2. Cost – a historical concept, the sum of all past expenses that have gone into bringing a property into being. <u>It usually has no bearing on present or future market value</u>

Prerequisites to value – in order for property to have value, 4 basic elements must be present (<u>DUST</u>).

    a. Demand – an actual need or desire with the ability to pay
    b. Utility – usefulness, item must have some purpose
    c. Scarcity – there is a short supply relative to demand
    d. Transferability – the ability for ownership to be easily conveyed form one person to another

Economic Principles of Value – basic economic concepts that form the foundation of appraisals methods and procedures. These are interrelated:

    a. Principle of Supply and Demand – value results from the interaction of the supply available and the extent of the demand; As one goes up, the other goes down
    b. Principle of Highest and Best Use – the legal use of a property that is likely to produce the greatest net return over a given period of time
    c. Principle of Substitution – often sets the upper limit on the value of a piece of property. Properties that provide the same or similar utility are considered substitutes. The value of one property tends to be set by the price of an equally desirable substitute
    d. Principle of Conformity – property achieves its highest potential value if it has a reasonable similarity to the social, economic and architectural make-up of the neighborhoods
    e. Principle of Change – each neighborhood goes through a cycle of change over time

        1. Development phase: a period of growth, expansion and rising property values
        2. Phase of stability of equilibrium: growth ends and value levels off
        3. Phase of decline or disintegration: deterioration sets in and values fall. Can be the beginning of new development phase

    f. Principle of Progression and Regression

        1. Principle of Regression – the most expensive house loses value because of its association with less valuable properties
        2. Principle of Progression – the least expensive property in the neighborhood gains value because it is located near properties of greater quality; Unearned Increment

    g. Principle of Competition – When demand exceeds supply, new suppliers jump into the market to meet the demand
    h. Principle of Increasing and Decreasing Returns

        1. Principle of Increasing Returns – a dollar spent on remodeling will add at least a dollar of value to the property
        2. Principle of Decreasing Returns – a dollar spent on remodeling will not add at least a dollar of value to the property, resulting in over improvement

    i. Principle of Contribution – The value an item adds to the property when present vs what it detracts when absent

    j. Principle of Anticipation – a property's value is based not only on what it consists of today but on whatever expectation there might be for future income and benefits

Factors Influencing Value

    a. Location – The sum of all factors is situs
    b. Size and Shape
    c. Depth tables
    d. Soil Characteristics
    e. Key lots
    f. Assemblage – process of combining adjoining parcels into one tract. If the tract results in an increase in value **plottage** occurs

B. The Appraisal Process

1. Define the Problem

    a. Identify the Property – legal description
    b. Identify the Rights and Interests to be Evaluated – usually looking for the value of a fee interest but sometimes evaluates a lesser or partial estate
    c. Identify the Appraisal Objective and the Value Sought – the appraiser should know the client's objective in seeking an appraisal
    d. Date of Value Estimate – majority of appraisals seek the current value that is recorded as the date of inspection. However, the date can be a retrospective, prospective or current date

2. Make a Preliminary Study

    a. Data Needed and Sources of Date – depends on the type of property to be evaluated and the objectives of the appraisal. Mostly, the appraiser needs general market as well as specific property data
    b. Personnel Needed – may need help form other professionals, i.e., engineers, cost estimators, lawyers
    c. Time Needed – estimate of time needed for assignment
    d. Decide on the Fee – should be established with client before proceeding

3. Gather Data – Data must be verified and recorded as it is gathered

    a. General Data – all the external sources that affect value. 4 major forces are constantly at work and create the overall market in which the property is located (**PEGS**):

        1. Physical – visible physical factors that may be either natural or man-made
        2. Economic – available economic opportunities
        3. Governmental – govt regulations i.e., zoning, building codes, police and fire protection, taxes and schools
        4. Social – the demographics or characteristics and customs of the people living within the community

    b. Specific Data – a thorough inspection of the subject property site and improvements yields data on all characteristics of property. Appraisers measure the exterior of a structure to determine the **gross living area (GLA)**. GLA is the square footage above grade, heated, enclosed and finished

4. Analyze Data – three separate approaches for analysis. All three can be used if they are relevant, each as a check on the others

    a. The Sales Comparison or Market Data Approach
    b. The Cost or Replacement Approach
    c. The Income or Capitalization Approach

5. Reconciliation and Final Estimate – a weighted factoring based on judgment and experience of the appraiser
6. Prepare Appraisal Report

    a. Letter of Opinion – an informal report. Usually in a business letter. States the opinion of value as of a certain date and identifies the property

    b. Short-Form Report – generally used by lending institutions and the government. Consist of pre-printed checklists on which the appraiser records data. <u>The short-form or summary is most often used in real estate</u>

    c. Narrative Report – the most comprehensive report. Usually required for appraising commercial property or as evidence in legal cases

C. The Three Appraisal Approaches

I. Sales Comparison or Market Data Approach – estimates value by comparing the property being appraised with similar properties (comparable). Based on the principle of substitution, it's the most commonly used approach for residential property

    a. Data Sources for Market Analysis – sales data for comparable properties can mainly be found from multiple listing, lending institutions, brokers, attorneys, public records and other appraisers

    b. Selecting Comparables – since no two properties are exactly alike. 3 to 5 comparables should be used and those that require the fewest and smallest amount of adjustment. The comparables should be:

        1. Recent

        2. Similar – should be near the subject property and in similar social and economic environment

        3. Sold under similar market conditions – should represent sales that accounted in free and competitive trading

    c. Making Adjustments – adjustments are made so that comparables will be as similar to the subject property as possible. <u>Never make any adjustment to the subject property</u>

        1. CIA – <u>C</u>omparable <u>I</u>nferior <u>A</u>dd. When a <u>comparable</u> property is <u>inferior</u> to the subject property, add to the value of the comparable

        2. CBS – <u>C</u>omparable <u>B</u>etter <u>S</u>ubtract. When a <u>comparable</u> property is <u>superior</u> to the subject property, subtract from the value of the comparable

    d. Reconciliation – more weight or emphasis is placed on the indicated values of the most similar properties

II. The Cost or Replacement Cost Approach Mainly used for special purpose properties, new properties or in any situation where comparables and income data is lacking. The basic cost procedure involves three steps:

    a. Estimate Replacement Cost New

        1. Comparative Unit Method

            a. Square foot method – calculates the square footage of the property

            b. Cubic foot method – calculates the cubic feet of the property

        2. Unit in place method – calculates the cost of <u>each component</u> of the building such as floors, walls, roof, plumbing, electrical systems and HVAC

        3. Quantity survey method – Provides a detailed breakdown of everything that goes into a building

    b. Estimate Accrued Depreciation – The loss in value of improvements over time

    c. Land does not depreciate. If it makes economic sense to fix the source of depreciation it is said to be **curable** (the cure cost less than the value added), otherwise it is **incurable** (the cure cost more than the value added)

        1. Types of Depreciation

            a. Physical Deterioration – occurs form normal wear and tear, by exposure to the elements, or by lack of proper maintenance of the property; mostly curable

            b. Functional Obsolescence – inadequate, over-adequate or out of date improvements in the property. Items that are considered obsolete and do not meet current market expectations; can be curable or incurable

            c. Economic Obsolescence – based on forces outside the property and beyond the owner's control. Mostly incurable

        2. Calculating Depreciation – not an exact science, it involves the subjective opinion of the appraiser

    a. Accrued depreciation – the total lump sum dollar amount the property has depreciated form the time the structure was built until the date of appraisal

    b. Actual age – historical age

    c. Effective age – how old the property appears

    d. Physical life – how long a structure, with normal maintenance, will remain physical sound

    e. Economic life – how long the property will remain economically productive

    f. Remaining economic life – number of years at the time of the appraisal that the property will remain economically productive

c. Estimate Land Value – appraiser estimates the land value as if it were vacant and available for improvements to its highest and best use. A comparison to comparable and takes place which can be based on square footage, front footage or acreage

<u>Replace Cost New – Depreciation = Depreciated Value of the improvements</u>
<u>Depreciated Value of the Improvements + Estimated Land Value = Estimated Value by Cost Approach</u>

III. The Income Approach – Interested in quantity of income that will be provided, quality of income stream and durability (how long) of the income stream

    a. Capitalization Approach – uses net operating income to project an estimate of value

        1. Projecting net Operating Income (NOI) – The appraiser's projections are based on a one-year period. Does not include income taxes, depreciation or debt service

            a. Potential Gross Income (PGI) (<u>annual</u>) – assumes 100% rent at market rate

            b. Vacancy and Collection losses (V&C) – due to vacancy and uncollected rent

            c. Effective Gross Income (EGI) = PGI – V&C

            d. Expenses and Reserve for replacement – expenses are those items that are paid for or repaired frequently. Reserves are those longer term items that will eventually require replacements such as air conditioners or roofs (EXP)

            e. Net Operating Income (NOI) = EGI - EXP

        2. Select an Appropriate Capitalization Rate – the return that a prudent investor would demand if the property were to be purchased today

        3. Convert the NOI and the Cap Rate into an Estimate of Value:

        Capitalization formula: $V = I/R$

        I = Net Operating Income (NOI)
        R = Capitalization Rate
        V = Value

    b. The Gross Rent Multiplier/Gross Income Multiplier

        1. Gross Rent Multiplier (GRM) is used in appraisal of residential properties which are 1-4 families

            a. Divide each comparable's sales price by its monthly rent to determine the GRM

            b. Multiply the subject property's estimated monthly market rent by the indicated GRM

            c. Comps Sales Price / Comps Gross <u>Monthly</u> Rent = GRM Subjects Monthly Market Rent x GRM = Subject's Value

        2. Gross Income Multiplier (GIM) used in determining the value in small commercial and residential properties of 5 units or more

            a. Divide each comparable's sales price by the annual income to determine the GIM

            b. Multiply the subject property's estimated total annual income by the indicated GIM

            c. Comps Sales Price / Comps Gross <u>Annual</u> Income = GIM Subjects Annual Gross Income x GIM = Subject's Value

Section 2: *Vocabulary*

Appraisal: Estimate or opinion of value by a qualified person

Appreciation: The increase in value of an asset over time

Assemblage: The act of combining individual lots, resulting in one larger lot

Comparable: A property being utilized to assist in valuing the subject property

Cost or basis: The total investment made into the property up until today

Debt Service: The monthly loan payment on a property

Depreciation: The loss in value of the improvements over time

Economic Obsolescence: Depreciation that is caused by factors external to the property

Functional Obsolescence: Depreciation that results when the property is not to contemporary standards

Gross Living Area: The above ground, enclosed, heated, and finished area of a property

Key Lot: One that joins to the rear of a corner lot and is undesirable without assemblage

Market Price: The amount that the property sold for in an arm's length transaction

Market Value: The amount the property should sell for in an arm's length transaction

Over-Improvement: Investing more money in a structure than one may expect to recapture

Physical Deterioration: Depreciation that results from normal wear and tear

Principle of Anticipation: Based on a property's current value and the expectation of future income and benefits

Principle of Progression: The least expensive property gains value because it's located near greater value properties

Principle of Regression: The most expensive property loses value because it's located near lesser value properties

Principle of Substitution: Comparable properties set the upper limit on the value of neighboring properties

Principle of Supply and Demand: The price is determined by the available supply and demand for the item

Plottage: The increase in value resulting from the assemblage of two or more adjacent lots into one larger lot

Plottage Increment: The unit increase in value after assembling properties

Quantity Survey Method: Estimating replacement cost by calculating the cost of all of materials and labor used in the improvements

Reconciliation: Assigning a certain weight to each comparable based upon its similarities to the subject property

Replacement Cost: The cost to replace using new materials of like quality, but that serve the same purpose

Reproduction Cost: The cost to replace using exact replicas of what was damaged

Reserves for Replacements: Saving monthly for long-term items that will require replacement

Subject property: The property that the appraiser is currently seeking a value for

Unearned Increment: The increase in value due to outside forces, rather than personal efforts of the owner

Unit in Place Method: Estimating replacement cost by calculating the cost of all of the major components in the structure

Section 3: *Recall Multiple Choice*

1. **Estimating replacement cost by calculating the cost of all of the major components in the structure**
   A. Quantity Survey Method
   B. Replacement Cost
   C. Unit in Place Method
   D. Cost Approach

2. **A property being utilized to assist in valuing the subject property**
   A. Appraisal
   B. Comparable
   C. Market Value
   D. Relevant

3. **The least expensive property gains value because it's located near greater value properties**
   A. Market Value
   B. Principle of Competition
   C. Principle of Increasing Returns
   D. Principle of Progression

4. **A lot that joins to the rear of a corner lot and is undesirable by itself**
   A. Specific Data
   B. Key Lot
   C. Effective Age
   D. Economic Life

5. **The cost to replace using new materials of like quality, but serve the same purpose**
   A. Reproduction Cost
   B. Functional Obsolescence
   C. Replacement Cost
   D. Market Value

6. **Depreciation that is caused by factors external to the property**
   A. The Neighborhood Cycle
   B. Economic Life
   C. Economic Obsolescence
   D. Functional Obsolescence

7. **Depreciation that results when the property is not to contemporary standards**
   A. Replacement Cost
   B. Physical Deterioration
   C. Economic Obsolescence
   D. Functional Obsolescence

8. **The total investment made into the property up until today**
   A. Comparable
   B. Effective age
   C. Cost or basis
   D. Principle of change

9. **The amount that the property actually sold for in an arm's length transaction**
   A. Market Value
   B. Market Price
   C. Market Economy
   D. Assessed Value

10. **Depreciation that results from normal wear and tear**
    A. Functional Obsolescence
    B. Curable Depreciation
    C. Physical Life
    D. Physical Deterioration

11. **The unit increase in value after assembling properties together**
    A. Reproduction Cost
    B. Plottage Increment
    C. Salvage Value
    D. Unearned Increment

12. **The price is determined by the available supply and demand for the item**
    A. Principle of Conformity
    B. Principle of Change
    C. Principle of Increasing Returns
    D. Principle of Supply and Demand

13. **Estimate or opinion of value by a qualified person**
    A. Appraisal
    B. Appreciation
    C. Assessed Value
    D. Market Value

14. **The act of combining individual lots, resulting in one larger lot**
    A. Market Value
    B. Assemblage
    C. Reconciliation
    D. Plottage

15. **The amount the property should sell for in an arm's length transaction**
    A. Market Price
    B. Salvage Value
    C. Market Value
    D. Replacement Cost

16. **The loss in value of the improvements over time**
    A. Amortization
    B. Market Value
    C. Depreciation
    D. Salvage Value

17. **The cost to replace using exact replicas of what was damaged**
    A. Reproduction Cost
    B. Replacement Cost
    C. Market Value
    D. Effective Age

18. **The increase in value of an asset over time**
    A. Appraisal
    B. Plottage
    C. Appreciation
    D. Assemblage

19. **The increase in value due to outside forces, rather than personal efforts of the owner**
    A. Unearned Increment
    B. Plottage Increment
    C. Market Value
    D. Assessed Value

20. **When an owner invests more money in a structure than the owner may expect to recapture**
    A. Economic Life
    B. Physical Deterioration
    C. Functional Obsolescence
    D. Over-Improvement

21. **The above ground, enclosed, heated, and finished area of a property**
    A. Gross Finished Area
    B. Gross Living Area
    C. Gross Building Area
    D. Gross Rent-able Area

22. **Comparable properties set the upper limit on the value of neighboring properties**
    A. Principle of Increasing Returns
    B. Principle of Regression
    C. Principle of Substitution
    D. Principle of Change

23. **The property that the appraiser is currently seeking a value for**
    A. Target property
    B. Sold property
    C. Subject property
    D. Comparable property

24. **Assigning a certain weight to each comparable based upon its similarities to the subject property**
    A. Reconciliation
    B. Comparable
    C. Plottage
    D. Appraisal

25. **Takes into consideration a property's value on the expectation of future income and benefits**
    A. Principle of Change
    B. Principle of Progression
    C. Principle of Supply and Demand
    D. Principle of Anticipation

26. **The most expensive property loses value because it's located near lesser value properties**
    A. Principle of Conformity
    B. Principle of Change
    C. Principle of Regression
    D. Principle of Progression

27. There is an increase in value resulting from the assembling two or more adjacent lots into one larger lot
  A. Appreciation
  B. Key Lot
  C. Assemblage
  D. Plottage

28. The monthly loan payment on a property
  A. Replacement Cost
  B. Debt Ceiling
  C. Special Revenue
  D. Debt Service

29. Saving on a monthly basis for long-term items that must be replaced
  A. Mortgage Payments
  B. Vacancies and Collection Losses
  C. Reserves for Replacements
  D. Cost or Basis

30. Estimating replacement cost by calculating the cost of all of materials and labor used in the improvements
  A. Unit In Place Method
  B. Reproduction Cost
  C. Replacement Cost
  D. Quantity Survey Method

Section 4: *Recall Fill-In*

1. Assigning a certain weight to each comparable based upon its similarities to the subject property:

    _____

2. A property being utilized to assist in valuing the subject property:

    _____

3. Depreciation that results when the property is not to contemporary standards:

    _____

4. Depreciation that is caused by factors external to the property:

    _____

5. Principle that states: The price is determined by how much someone wants the item and how much is available:

    _____

6. The amount that the property actually sold for in an arm's length transaction:

    _____

7. The increase in value due to outside forces, rather than personal efforts of the owner:

    _____

8. The act of combining individual lots, resulting in one larger lot:

    _____

9. Estimate or opinion of value by a qualified person:

    _____

10. Principle that states: A property's Value is based on the expectation of future income and benefits:

    _____

11. Principle that states: The most expensive property loses value because it's located near lesser valued properties:

    _____

12. Saving on a monthly basis for long-term items that must be replaced:

    _____

13. Estimating replacement cost by calculating the cost of all of materials and labor used in the improvements:

    _____

14. The loss in value of the improvements over time:

_____

15. Principle that states: The least expensive property gains value because it's located near greater valued properties:

_____

16. The total investment made into the property up until today:

_____

17. The amount the property should sell for in an arm's length transaction:

_____

18. The cost to replace an item using new materials of like quality, but serve the same purpose:

_____

19. When an owner invests more money in a structure than the owner may expect to recapture:

_____

20. The cost to replace an item using exact replicas of what was damaged:

_____

21. A lot that joins to the rear of a corner lot and is undesirable by itself:

_____

22. There is an increase in value from assembling two or more adjacent lots into one larger lot:

_____

23. The monthly loan payment on a property:

_____

24. The unit increase in value after assembling properties together:

_____

25. The above ground, enclosed, heated, and finished area of a property:

_____

26. Depreciation that results from normal wear and tear:

_____

27. Principle that states: Comparable properties set the upper limit on the value of neighboring properties:

_____

28. The increase in value of an asset over time is also known as:

_____

29. The property that the appraiser is currently seeking a value for is known as:

_____

30. A way of estimating replacement cost by calculating the cost of all of the major components in the structure:

_____

Section 5: *Matching*

A   Market Price

1 _____   The amount that the property actually sold for in an arm's length transaction

B   Subject Property

2 _____   A lot that joins to the rear of a corner lot and is undesirable by itself

C   Functional Obsolescence

3 _____   A property being utilized to assist in valuing the subject property

D   Key Lot

4 _____   Comparable properties set the upper limit on the value of neighboring properties

E   Principle of Supply and Demand

5 _____   Depreciation that results when the property is not to contemporary standards

F   Gross Living Area

6 _____   Estimate or opinion of value by a qualified person

G   Comparable

7 _____   The above ground, enclosed, heated, and finished area of a property

H   Plottage Increment

8 _____   The amount the property should sell for in an arm's length transaction

I   Principle of Substitution

9 _____   The increase in value of an asset over time

J   Depreciation

10 _____   The loss in value of the improvements over time

K   Appraisal

11 _____   The price is determined by the available supply and demand for the item.

L   Appreciation

12 _____   The property that the appraiser is currently appraising

M   Over Improvement

13 _____   The unit increase in value after assembling properties together

N   Market Value

14 _____   When an owner invests more money in a structure than the owner may expect to recapture

EXERCISE 2

A   Unit in Place Method   1 _____   Assigning a certain weight to each comparable based upon its similarities to the subject property

B   Physical Deterioration   2 _____   Depreciation that is caused by factors external to the property

C   Principle of Anticipation   3 _____   Depreciation that results from normal wear and tear

D   Reconciliation   4 _____   Estimating replacement cost by calculating the cost of all of the major components in the structure

E   Principle of Regression   5 _____   Takes into consideration a property's value on the expectation of future income and benefits.

F   Replacement Cost   6 _____   The act of combining individual lots, resulting in one larger lot.

G   Assemblage   7 _____   The cost to replace using exact replicas of what was damaged

H   Debt Service   8 _____   The cost to replace using new materials of like quality, but serve the same purpose

I   Economic Obsolescence   9 _____   The increase in value due to outside forces, rather than personal efforts of the owner.

J   Unearned Increment   10 _____ The increase in value resulting from the assemblage of two or more adjacent lots into one larger lot.

K   Cost or Basis   11 _____ The least expensive property gains value because it's located near greater value properties

L   Principle of Progression   12 _____ The monthly loan payment on a property

M   Plottage   13 _____ The most expensive property loses value because it's located near lesser value properties

N   Reproduction Cost   14 _____ The total investment made into the property up until today.

Section 6: *Analysis Fill-In*

1. Give an example of economic obsolescence:

_____

2. Define incurable depreciation:

_____

3. Give an example of when an appraiser would use a short-form report:

_____

4. Name at least two items that are never included when calculating NOI?

_____

5. Give an example of when an appraiser would use a narrative report:

_____

6. If the appraiser needed to value a 200-unit income producing apartment building, what is the most likely appraisal approach that he would use?

_____

7. The appraiser needs to value a church, what approach to value would the appraiser use?

_____

8. Name the three approaches to value that an appraiser uses?

_____

9. How does an appraiser select a comparable?

_____

10. Define curable depreciation:

_____

11. Name the three types of depreciation:

_____

12. What is the first step in appraisal process?

_____

13. Name any 5 of the Appraisal Principles of Value:

_____

14. What is the Net Operating Income formula?

_____

15. Name two types of properties where the appraiser would use the replacement cost approach?

_____

16. When is the Market Data Approach most used?

_____

17. What are the steps to calculate value under the replacement cost approach?

_____

18. On the market data approach, what adjustment would be made if the comparable had one more bedroom than the subject?

_____

19. What is the Gross Rent Multiplier formula?

_____

20. What is the capitalization formula (visualize the T)?

_____

21. Define Arm's Length transaction (Hint: There are 4 elements):

_____

22. What are the four prerequisites to value?

_____

23. What is the difference between an expense and reserve for replacements?

_____

24. What is the significance of land when calculating depreciation?

_____

25. Define Depreciation:

_____

26. Give an example of an expense item:

_____

27. Give an example of a reserve for replacement item:

_____

28. Give an example of functional obsolescence:

_____

29. Give an example of physical deterioration:

_____

Section 7: *Analysis Multiple Choice*

1. Your agent takes you out on a Saturday and you see many houses that are similar in your chosen subdivision. You decided that you will select the lowest priced home. Under which economic principle did you make your selection?
   A. Anticipation
   B. Supply and Demand
   C. Substitution
   D. Competition

2. You are an investor and have a one family residence in a neighborhood of similar properties. You learn that another investor sold the property their property two weeks ago for $325,000 that was renting for $1,800 per month. You decide that you may want to sell yours also based upon the price the other investor received. Your property is currently rents for $2,100. What approach would the appraiser utilize?
   A. Gross Income Multiplier and your value would be lower
   B. Capitalization Approach and your value would be lower
   C. Gross Rent Multiplier Approach and your value would be higher
   D. Gross Income Multiplier Approach and your value would be higher

3. Which of the following is an example of incurable functional obsolescence?
   A. Sagging Floors in a home
   B. A Leaking roof in a home
   C. A home that has 5 bedrooms and one bath
   D. A kitchen where all of the appliances are white

4. When calculating Net Operating Income for the Capitalization Approach, what items are NOT a part of that calculation?
   A. Potential Gross Income
   B. Depreciation
   C. Expenses
   D. Property Taxes

5. When calculating Net Operating Income (NOI) under the Capitalization Approach, what would be the final step in the formula before arriving at NOI?
   A. Subtract Expenses from Effective Gross Income
   B. Subtract Expenses from Potential Gross Income
   C. Subtract Vacancies and Collection Losses from Potential Gross Income
   D. Subtract Depreciation from Effective Gross income

6. When an appraiser selects comparable, he should select:
   A. 3-5 and those requiring the fewest adjustments
   B. As many as he can find that are close to the comparable in terms of similarity
   C. 3-5 that are the closest in distance to the subject
   D. The ones that were closest in price to the subject

7. What would be the most likely approach that an insurance company would use in valuing a property?
   A. Market Data Approach
   B. Reproduction Cost Approach
   C. Replacement Cost Approach
   D. Gross Income Multiplier

8. **What would be the most appropriate appraisal report for a condemnation action?**
   A. Narrative Report
   B. Letter of Opinion
   C. Short-Form Report
   D. It depends on the appraiser

9. **What is meant by the term Condemnation Value of a property?**
   A. The value after the city condemns a dilapidated property
   B. The value of the property for eminent domain purposes
   C. The value of a property right before it is torn down
   D. The value of a property dismantled and moved

10. **There are three vacant lots next to each other in a residential area. None are perfect for a home build. Each lot individually is $10,000. The builder decides to combine the lots to make them more appealing. After combining, the lots are now worth $45,000**
    A. The builder has assembled the lots
    B. The builder has assembled the lots, but did not get pottage
    C. The builder has assembled the lots and did get pottage
    D. No assemblage occurred

11. **The replacement cost approach would be most appropriate when valuing:**
    A. A public library
    B. A 20-unit investor-owned apartment building
    C. A single-family residence
    D. A storage business with 40 units

12. **The appraiser is valuing a one family residential property with 3 bedrooms and 2 baths. The appraiser has located a comparable. It is 2 bedrooms and 3 baths and sold for $230,000. A bedroom is worth $4,000 and a bathroom is worth $5,000. How much will the subject sell for?**
    A. $234,000
    B. $226,000
    C. $229,000
    D. $231,000

13. **Market value of a property is determined by:**
    A. The actual selling price
    B. The most probable selling price between neighbors
    C. The price after applying an assessment rate
    D. The most probably selling price in an arm's length transaction

14. **In which situation would an appraisal most likely be required?**
    A. A purchaser is obtaining financing to purchase a home
    B. An insurance agent is insuring a residential property
    C. A lawyer is settling an estate
    D. An investor is purchasing a 20-unit apartment building with cash

15. **An EXAMPLE of the principle of substitution would be:**
    A. Appraising two properties that are equal to one another
    B. A theory that a comparable establishes the upper limit of prices in a certain neighborhood
    C. Two homeowners exchanging parcels with each other
    D. The inability to sell a higher priced home in an area of lower price homes

16. **An appraiser is valuing a property with 5 bedrooms 3 baths. The comparable has 4 bedrooms and 4 baths. The appraiser will:**
    A. Adjust the subject upward for bedrooms but downward for baths
    B. Adjust the comp upward for bedrooms and downward for baths
    C. Adjust the subject downward for bedrooms but upward for baths
    D. Adjust the comp downward for bedrooms and upward for baths

17. **An appraiser is asked to appraise a 3-story commercial building. What is the first step in the appraisal process?**
    A. Identify the Problem
    B. Go to the building
    C. Determine the number of appraisers necessary
    D. Set the fee

18. **An Appraisal is _____ and are primarily utilized to __**
    A. A determination of value; assure the bank that the property is worth the sales price
    B. An opinion of value; solve a problem or answer a question concerning value
    C. An opinion of value; assure the bank that the property is worth the sales price
    D. A determination of value, solve a problem or answer a question concerning value

19. **A lender explains to an appraiser that his assignment is contingent upon the appraiser coming up with a specific number. What should the appraiser do?**
    A. Accept the assignment if he believes that he can reach that number
    B. Accept the assignment but tell the lender that there is no guarantee that he can reach that number
    C. Refuse to accept the assignment as it would violate the Uniform Standards of Appraisal Practice
    D. Refuse to accept the assignment and report the lender to the local police department

20. **A homeowner wishes to install a huge swimming pool with a slide to the cost of $250,000. Her home is valued at $300,000 in a neighborhood of similar homes and the swimming pool will raise her property taxes by $4,000 more than the other homes in the neighborhood. What two valuation principles would suggest that this may not be a good idea?**
    A. Regression and Economic Obsolescence
    B. Progression and Economic Obsolescence
    C. Regression and Functional Obsolescence
    D. Progression and Functional Obsolescence

21. **You live in a neighborhood where the high property taxes lead to less houses being sold in the neighborhood. This is an example of:**
    A. Principle of Regression
    B. Principle of Progression
    C. Economic Obsolescence
    D. Economic Deterioration

22. **You are on the board of trustees of a large museum. The real estate market is booming and you want to make sure that your insurance policy is up to date and would cover any damage to the building in the event of a fire. You commission an appraisal of the property. Which appraisal method does the appraiser indicate she will use to complete your appraisal?**
    A. The gross rent multiplier and/or gross income multiplier method
    B. The income and/or capitalization method
    C. The replacement cost method
    D. The market data and/or comparison approach method

23. **What happens when plottage occurs?**
    A. The planning board allows the re - zoning which results in an increase in value of the land
    B. The HOA is successful in forcing the homeowner to stop building in violation of the building codes which maintains the value of everyone's land
    C. Assemblage took place which results in a larger tract of land with no increase in value but an increase in marketability
    D. Assemblage took place which results in a larger tract of land and an increase in value

24. **The least expensive property in the neighborhood gains value because it is located near properties of greater value is called:**
    A. The principle of anticipation
    B. The principle of substitution
    C. The principle of progression
    D. The principle of regression

25. **Producers enter and leave the market based on market conditions and opportunities. If too many producers enter the market the resulting conditions may be that:**
    A. Housing prices will remain stable
    B. Interest rates will remain stable
    C. Existing housing prices may fall
    D. Existing housing prices may rise

Chapter 8 Answers

1. C	5. C	9. B	13. A	17. A	21. B	25. D	29. C
2. B	6. C	10. D	14. B	18. C	22. C	26. C	30. D
3. D	7. D	11. B	15. C	19. A	23. C	27. D	
4. B	8. C	12. D	16. C	20. D	24. A	28. D	

1. Reconciliation
2. Comparable
3. Functional Obsolescence
4. Economic Obsolescence
5. Principal of Supply and Demand
6. Market Price
7. Unearned increment
8. Assemblage
9. Appraisal
10. Principle of Anticipation
11. Principle of Regression
12. Reserves for Replacements
13. Quantity Survey Method
14. Depreciation
15. Principle of Progression
16. Cost Basis
17. Market Value
18. Replacement Cost
19. Over-Improvement
20. Reproduction Cost
21. Key Lot
22. Plottage
23. Debt Service
24. Plottage Increment
25. Gross Living Area
26. Physical Deterioration
27. Principle of Substitution
28. Appreciation
29. Subject Property
30. Unit in Place Method

Exercise 1

1. A	3. G	5. C	7. F	9. L	11. E	13. H
2. D	4. I	6. K	8. N	10. J	12. B	14. M

Exercise 2

1. D	3. B	5. C	7. N	9. J	11. L	13. E
2. I	4. A	6. G	8. F	10. M	12. H	14. K

1. Property next to a prison, over-improvement for the area, high taxes

2. The cost of the repair is more than the value received

3. Residential Real Estate

4. Depreciation, Debt Service, Income Taxes

5. Condemnation Actions, Estate Sales, Tax Sales, Commercial Real Estate

6. Capitalization Approach

7. Replacement Cost Approach

8. Market Data Approach, Replacement Cost Approach, Income Approach (Capitalization and Gross Rent Multiplier/Gross Income Multiplier)

9. Near the Subject, Like the Subject in terms of neighborhood amenities and similarities

10. The cost of the repair is less than the value

11. Economic, Functional, Physical

12. Define the Problem

13. Contribution, Substitution, Highest and Best Use, Supply and Demand, Anticipation, Increasing/Decreasing Returns, Progression/Regression, Competition, Conformity, Change

14. What would be the formula if you had to figure out the Net Operating Income for a property?
    Potential Gross Income
    − Vacancy/Collection
    = Effective Gross Income
    − Expenses and Reserves for Replacements
    = NOI

15. New Construction, Unique, No comparable, Insurance

16. Residential Property

17. What are the steps to calculate value under the replacement cost approach?
    Calculate Replacement Cost
    - Depreciation
    + Land

18. Subtract the price of a bedroom from the comparable

19. Comp Sales Price/Comp Monthly Rent = Multiplier x Subject Monthly Rent

20. NOI/V x R

21. 1. Payment in Cash or its equivalent - 2. Open Market Exposure - 3. Parties are equally motivated - 4. Parties have equal knowledge

22. Demand, Utility, Scarcity, Transferability

23. An expense is something that occurs more often (less than a year); A reserve is savings for those items that will break at some point (more than a year)

24. Land is not a part of the calculation because it doesn't depreciate

25. Loss in value of improvements over time

26. Leaking Toilet

27. New Air Conditioning System

28. A house with 5 bedrooms and one bathroom

29. A house with a leaky roof

Section 7 Answers:

1. C. Substitution is the economic principle that states when items are considered to be substitutes of one another (houses in the same subdivision), the lowest priced one will always sell first. Anticipation is when the appraiser values based on future income, Supply and Demand states that when Supply is up, prices are down and vice versa and Competition states that when new producers enter the market and it becomes over-saturated, profits and prices when eventually fall

2. C. The appraiser would most likely use Gross Rent Multiplier to compare the sales prices with the rental rates of both properties and because the subject property has a higher rent, using this formula, it will have a higher value

3. C. Functional obsolescence goes to how the home functions to today's standards and it is incurable when the cost to cure it is more than the added value. Sagging floors and a leaking roof are physical and the kitchen with white appliances is functional but not incurable

4. B. When calculating NOI, Depreciation, Debt Service on the property, and Income Taxes are never a part of the calculation

5. A. The NOI formula requires that we start with Potential Gross Income and subtract Vacancies and Collection Losses to get to Effective Gross Income and then subtract expenses from that to get to NOI

6. A. An appraiser would always be looking for 3-5 comparables and those that are most like the subject in terms of features, area, amenities, etc

7. C. The insurance company always uses replacement cost to give like kind materials as reproduction cost would be too expensive

8. A. Narrative report is the most complete report and is used in most actions other than regular residential

9. B. The value of property under eminent domain - the right of the government to take private property for public use when just compensation is given. Condemnation is the action the government would use. So, condemnation value would be the value given to the homeowner when the property is taken under the government's eminent domain right

10. C. Putting the lots together is assemblage, and if there is an increase in value, plottage also occurs

11. A. The replacement cost approach would be most appropriate when valuing a public library since there wouldn't be a comparable to use the Market Data Approach and there wouldn't be any income to use the Income Approach

12. C. The rule is that we only adjust the comparable to get the price of the subject. Here, the comp sold for $230,00. It is Inferior when speaking bedrooms (2 v 3) so we add a bedroom price to it (Comp Inferior Add) of $4,000. We are now at $234,000, but it is better when speaking of bathrooms (3 v 2) so we subtract a bathroom price (Comp Better Subtract) of $5,000 to get to $229,000

13. D. Market value can only occur if there is an arm's length transaction (people who don't know each other and the market sets the price)

14. A. The most likely situation would be the bank financing the purchase. Given that the bank has an interest in the property, it would want to be assured that its investment is secured

15. D. The best example would be the inability to sell a home that is priced too high. B. Represents the definition, but the question asks for an example

16. B. We never touch the subject. The comp is adjusted upward for the bedrooms since it is inferior and downward for baths since it is better

17. A. The first step in most situations would be to identify and evaluate the problem that one is presented with

18. B. An appraisal is an opinion of value intended to solve a problem or answer a question concerning value. It is not a determination, but an opinion by a qualified person

19. C. No appraiser should accept an assignment contingent upon that appraiser having to reach a specific number. That would be a violation of the appraisal standards and ethics

20. A. This is a classic example of Regression (best house in the neighborhood) where similar houses pull the value down of the subject. Also, the high taxes and over improvement of the home for the neighborhood are external forces to the property resulting in Economic Obsolescence

21. C. Economic obsolescence is when external forces cause the property to depreciate. High property taxes, leading to slower sales would be an example. Economic obsolescence is often incurable because the owner has little control over changing the thing causing the depreciation

22. C. The replacement cost approach is used when the properties are new, unique, or there is no comparable available. Because a museum is a unique property that would have no comparable, it is more appropriately appraised under the cost approach

23. D. Plottage is defined as the increase in value that occurs after assemblage

24. C. Progression occurs when the smallest or least priced property in the neighborhood gains value because it is closed to higher priced properties

25. C. When too many producers enter a market to fill a need, prices will drop because of increased competition

Chapter 9: Financing

Section 1: *Outline*

I. <u>Introduction</u> – The study of how money moves through the financial system

A. The Federal Reserve Bank ("The Fed") – The Fed has control over all chartered banks that choose to protect their depositor's funds (up to $ 250,000) using the FDIC. The Fed influences interest rates:

    1. by changing the discount rate it charges to member banks

    2. by changing the reserve requirements

    3. by buying and selling US treasuries

B. Financing Instruments

    1. The Use of Property as Security for a Loan

        a. Pledged – offering the property as collateral

        b. Hypothecation – allowing the borrower to possess and control the property while a loan is on it

        c. Right of redemption – defines whether the borrower can redeem the property **Equity of redemption** – between default and before the sale. **Statutory Right of Redemption** – after the sale

    2. Evidence of the Debt: Promissory Note (Debt Instrument) – a contract serving as evidence of the debt where the borrower makes a promise to pay. It is a **negotiable instrument** where the holder of it can transfer the right to collect the debt to another. The buyer of the note is the **holder in due course.** If more than one person signs, they are **jointly and severally liable**

    3. Security Instrument: Title Theory State (Security Deed) – the **security deed** conveys **legal title** to the lender. The borrower retains **equitable title.** A **defeasance clause** in the deed obligates the lender to cancel the debt once paid

    4. Security Instrument: Lien Theory States (Mortgage) – a contract in which the **mortgagor (borrower)** pledges real property as security for a loan. The mortgagee (lender) places a lien on the property which acts as the collateral. Should be signed by the same parties who signed the note. Once repaid, the lender issues a **satisfaction**

    5. Security Instrument: Trust Deed State (Trust Deed) – primarily Title Theory, but a third-party trustee is brought in to hold the deed. The **trustor** (borrower) conveys title to the **trustee (naked title)** who holds it for the **beneficiary** (lender). The title is **reconveyed** to the trustor upon payment

C. Lender's Remedies Upon Default

    1. Judicial Foreclosure – begins with the lender filing suit **(lis pendens)** and requesting the court to allow it to sell the property to repay the debt

    2. Non-Judicial Foreclosure (Foreclosure by Power of Sale) – allows a lender to foreclose on a property without filing a lawsuit as long as a power of sale clause is present

3. **Strict Foreclosure** – The court establishes a time period for the borrower to satisfy the debt. If debt is not satisfied, the lender takes title

4. **Deed in lieu of Foreclosure (Friendly Foreclosure)** – the borrower voluntarily conveys title to the lender

5. **Short Sale** – Borrower cannot sell the property for the amount owed to the bank. The bank agrees to release the lien for the sale price

I. Typical Provisions in a Loan Agreement

1. **Mortgage or Granting Clause** – In lien theory states, the mortgaging clause pledges the property as security for the debt. In title theory states, the granting clause conveys title to the lender or trustee

2. **Defeasance Clause** – in title theory states, allows the borrower to defeat the security instrument by paying the debt

II. Borrowers' covenants to protect the Lender's Interest:

1. **Covenant to pay indebtedness** – will pay debt as agreed

2. **Covenant to pay taxes** – will pay property taxes and special assessments

3. **Covenant to pay insurance** – will keep the property insured against damage

4. **Covenant of good repair** – will keep property in good condition and not abandon it

5. **Covenant against removal** – promise not to remove or destroy any improvements

6. **Covenant of property inspection** – will allow lender the right to inspect property

7. **Covenant to acknowledge indebtedness** – the borrower agrees to sign an **estoppel certificate** that acknowledges the loan balance

8. **Covenant to pay legal expenses** – borrower will pay legal expenses if in default

III. Clauses that Protect the Lender in a Default

1. **Acceleration (Due on Default) Clause** – default on any required payment or other covenants in the loan documents makes the entire loan due and payable in full

2. **Receiver Clause** – allows the court to appoint a receiver to maintain and manage the property after default and prior to foreclosure

3. **Owner's Rent Clause** – obligates the owner occupant to pay rent to receiver while remaining in possession

4. **Alienation (Due on Sale) Clause** – allows the lender to demand the entire loan balance due when title to the property is transferred; seeks to prohibit loan assumptions

5. **Escalation Clause** – allows the lender to increase the interest rate at certain times or for certain reasons

6. **Prepayment Clause** – Informs the borrower of any penalties if the loan is paid off early

7. **Condemnation Clause** – if property is condemned, the just compensation must be used to pay off the loan

8. **Exculpatory Clause** – the mortgaged property becomes the lender's only security for the debt and the lender's right to a deficiency judgment in other property is waived

9. **Subordination Clause** – the holder of the loan that is first recorded agrees to a subordinate position to an anticipated lien that will be recorded later

IV. Classification by Method of Payment

1. **Straight-Term Mortgage (Term Loan)** – one that allows the borrower to make periodic payments of interest only until maturity and then pay a **balloon payment**

2. **Amortized Mortgage Loans** – level periodic monthly payments of principal and interest

   a. **Fully amortized loan** – the balance of the loan is brought to zero at maturity

   b. **Partially amortized loan** – the terms fall short of completing the amortization process. At some predetermined time, the borrower must make a balloon payment

3. **Adjustable Mortgage Loan (ARM)** – allows the lender to adjust the rate of interest at stated intervals

   a. **Adjustment period** – establishes how often the rate can change

   b. **Index** – an external economic index

   c. **Margin** – the amount a lender will add to the index to determine rate

   d. **Caps** – limits the amount the interest rate will rise or fall, regardless of the index

4. **Graduated Payment Mortgage Loan (GPM)** – Monthly payments are reduced in the early years of the loan, in exchange for higher payments later. Results in **negative amortization** and decreased **equity**

5. **Interest Only loan** – the borrower pays interest only for the beginning years of the loan, it then converts to a fully amortized loan for the remaining term

6. **Buy downs** – someone, generally a builder, pays the lender a fee to provide a lower interest rate to the borrower in the first years

7. **Budget Mortgage Loan** – any loan where the borrower is required to pay the taxes and hazard insurance premium as part of the monthly payment. This is called PITI payment. The added amount is **impounded** to set up an **escrow account**

D. Classification of Mortgage Loans by Special Provisions

1. **Purchase Money Mortgage Loan** – seller financing that can either be a first or second mortgage

2. **Wraparound Mortgage Loan** – a second or junior mortgage, that includes the amount still owed in the first mortgage plus additional financing needed

3. **Reverse Annuity Mortgage (RAM)** – allows the elderly to borrow on their equity and receive funds in the form of monthly income

4. **Open-Ended Mortgage Loan** – a line of credit secured by the home. Interest is only paid on the amount in use

5. **Construction Loan** – covers the cost and materials and labor used in construction of a home. Disbursed in increments after inspection and assurance of lien waivers from subcontractors and suppliers

6. **Blanket Mortgage Loan** – more than one property provides the security for the loan. Must contain a **partial release** clause so that each parcel can be sold with clear title

7. **Package Mortgage Loan** – both real and personal property provide the security for the loan

E. Basic Loan Terms

1. **Principal** – amount borrowed from the bank

2. **Interest** – cost of the principal

3. **Maturity** – end of the loan where all interest and all principal is paid in full

4. **Loan To Value** – amount the bank will loan in relation to the home's sales price or appraised amount, whichever is lower. Expressed as a %

5. **Equity** – the borrower's unencumbered portion of the property

6. **Conventional Loans** – loans that are not backed by a government, but the bank's proprietary product

7. **Government Backed Loans** – loans that are backed by a government entity

F. Mortgage Insurance

1. **PMI** – Insurance issued by **conventional lenders** to ensure that the lender is paid the full amount of the loan if the buyer defaults. Often required if the down payment is less than 20%. The borrower usually pays a monthly premium for the coverage. Can be canceled by request once the equity reaches 20% and automatically once the equity reaches 22%

2. **MIP** – Insurance issued by **FHA** to ensure that the lender is paid the full amount of the loan if the defaults. Required on all FHA loans regardless of LTV. Paid at the closing Up Front MIP (**UFMIP**) but could be financed into the loan and monthly (**MMIP**) throughout the loan. Can never be canceled

G. Government Backed Loans

1. **FHA Insured Loans** – the Federal Housing Administration (FHA) does not make loans. Loans are made through approved lenders. FHA promises to reimburse the lender if the property cannot be sold at a sufficient price at foreclosure to pay the loan balance

   a. **Conditional commitment** – establishes the value of property, any required repairs and commits to insure the loan

   b. Owner-occupied residences only

   c. **Loan to value ratio** – maximum loan is 96.5% of the sales price or appraisal

   d. **Maximum Insurable Loan** – based on the median home prices in a given area

   e. **Interest Rates** – vary with the market

    f. Qualifying Ratios – more liberal than conventional loans, borrowers are qualified by ratios: mo. housing cost/mo. gross income **(FRONT END) and**

mo. housing cost + mo. payment obligations/gross income **(BACK END)**

    g. Assumption – complete qualification is required for an assumption and the buyer must be an owner occupant

    h. Prepayment Penalty – None

    i. Mortgage Insurance Premium (MIP) – UFMIP is 1.75% and MMIP is .85%

    j. Second Mortgages – permitted if 1st and 2nd do not exceed the maximum loan amount

    k. Seller Contributions – FHA permits the seller to provide financing concessions up to 6% of sales price or value, whichever is less

2. VA Guaranteed Mortgages – administered by the Department of Veterans Affairs (VA). VA loans come from approved private lenders. The VA **guarantees** the lender against loss under certain limitations. No insurance premium is charged to the borrowers

    a. Eligibility – designed for honorably discharged veterans and un-remarried spouses of veterans killed in the line of duty

    b. Certificate/Determination of Reasonable Value – establishes the value of property, any required repairs and commits to insure the loan

    c. Owner-occupied residences, farms, and mobile homes

    d. Loan to value ratio – maximum loan is 100% of the sales price or appraisal

    e. Maximum Insurable Loan – None, limits the protection

    f. Interest Rates – vary with the market

    g. Qualifying Ratios – more liberal than conventional loans, borrowers are qualified by ratios: mo. housing cost + mo. payment obligations/gross income **(BACK END)**

    h. Assumption – complete qualification is required for an assumption and the buyer must be an owner occupant, but could be a non-veteran

    i. Prepayment Penalty – None

    j. Mortgage Insurance Premium (MIP) – None

    k. Second Mortgages – permitted if 1st and 2nd do not exceed the certificate of reasonable value

    l. Seller Contributions – permits the seller to provide financing concessions up to 4% of sales price or value, whichever is less

    m. Certificate of Eligibility – establishes the veteran's eligibility and maximum guarantee

    n. Re-using the Entitlement – the veteran who has already used the entitlement must either pay off the first or, in case of an assumption, obtain a release from the lender by substituting another veteran or non-veteran

    o. Origination Fee – charged by lender and paid by borrower cannot exceed 1% of loan value

    p. VA Funding Fee – pays the administration costs of the VA loan program and may be financed or paid at the closing by the buyer or seller

H. Alternative Financing Techniques

    1. "Assuming" or Taking "Subject to" an Existing Loan

Assumption – the transfer of a loan to another; often requires an equity payment to the initial borrower. The assuming borrower becomes primarily liable for the loan to the lender, but the original borrower is ultimately liable. Risk can be mitigated by asking for a novation instead.

Selling "Subject to" an Existing loan – the existing loan is similar to assumption. The loan remains in place, and the buyer is in effect paying the seller for the equity. The buyer takes over the loan payments, but has no personal responsibility in the event of default the lender

    2. Land Contract – also called installment sale or contract for deed. Seller financing arrangement where the purchaser makes a down payment, receives possession of the property, and makes monthly payments to the seller, who retains legal title. The buyer gets equitable title **(See Contracts)**

3. **Sale and Leaseback** – A technique allow a business property owner to free up equity so that it can be used for working capital while retaining possession of the property. The property is sold to an investor who, in turn, promises to lease it back on a long-term basis, net basis **(See Leases)**

I. The Mortgage Market

Primary Sources of Loans – where a consumer would go to obtain a loan

    a. Savings and loan Associations (S&L's)
    b. Commercial Banks
    c. Mutual Savings Banks
    d. Mortgage Banking Companies
    e. Mortgage Brokers
    f. US Department of Agriculture
    g. Life Insurance Companies – participation loans
    h. Credit Unions
    i. Individual Lenders

Secondary Mortgage Market (Bank to Bank Only) – purpose is to purchase packages of notes to re-infuse the Primary Market with funds to continue loaning to consumers

    a. Federal National Mortgage Association (FNMA or Fannie Mae) – a private corporation, purchasing blocks of VA, FHA, and conventional loans
    b. Government National Mortgage Association (GNMA or Ginnie Mae) – created to take over some secondary market areas that were not necessarily profitable, but in the public interest, like financing subsidized housing for low-income citizens
    c. Federal Home Loan Mortgage Corporation (FHLMC or Freddie Mac) – a private corporation that favors conventional loans
    d. Other Secondary Markets – private buyers of mortgages on the secondary market, i.e., Mortgage Guaranty Insurance Company and other large corporations and endowment funds

J. Lending practices

    a. The Loan Application
    b. Appraisal
    c. Verifications and Credit
    d. Closing Cost

K. Federal Regulations

1. **Federal Equal Credit Opportunity Act** – prohibits discrimination in lending based on race, religion, sex, national origin, marital status, age, receipt of public assistance
2. **Federal Truth-In-lending Law** – aims to give consumers an opportunity to compare the costs of borrowing before committing to one lender, does not set fees

Compliance with Regulation Z – covered and requiring full disclosure:

    a. All loans up to $50,000 for personal, family or household purposes
    b. All residential real estate transactions involving credit, regardless of amount
    c. Residential mortgages loans for 2 to 4 family residential properties providing owner occupies one unit
    d. No commercial properties

Key required Disclosures

    a. Total Finance Charge – total of all the costs the lender will charge for loan over its entire life, including interest, loan fees, finder's fees, loan discount, service fee, and a premium for life insurance, if needed
    b. Annual percentage Rate – the **true interest rate** because it includes not only interest charged but also all the other costs of the loan expressed as annual interest figure

  c. Provide within 3 days of application and once delivered, cannot close for 7 days

  d. Advertising – Truth in lending law provides a "tell all or tell nothing" rule for advertising when credit is involved. If any specific "trigger terms" are used, all disclosures must be made

3. Real Estate Settlement Procedures Act (RESPA) – designed to inform of all closing costs prior to selecting a lender and requires certain disclosures within 3 days of application. Lender can only collect a credit report fee until the disclosures are made

  a. Good Faith Estimate – the borrower must be given a "good faith estimate" of loan closing costs

  b. Settlement cost Booklet – each loan applicant is to receive a copy of booklet "Shopping for Your Loan: HUD's Settlement Cost Booklet"

  c. Restrictions – RESPA prohibits: Kickbacks – no one in a federally related mortgage transaction may either give or receive kickbacks fees, or anything of value in exchange for referrals of settlement service business unless they constitute pay for services performed. **Unreasonable Impounds** – lender is only allowed to collect the amount necessary to pay the taxes and insurance when it becomes due and a 2-month cushion

  d. Uniform Settlement Statement (HUD-1) – may be requested one day prior to closing and provides an accounting of all final charges and credits to the buyer and the seller in the transaction; used in cash transactions

4. TRID (TILA RESPA Integrated Disclosure) – combined the elements of TILA and RESPA in one document. The first document is a LE (Loan Estimate) given 3 days after application. The second document is called a CD (Closing Disclosure) given 3 days before closing. Purpose is to compare the LE to the CD

L. Mortgage Fraud (Federal, but could be state specific laws)

1. Fraud for property or housing – occurs when the borrower provides misinformation about their financial status on a loan application to obtain a loan

2. Fraud for profit – also referred to as industry insider fraud and usually involves more than one person. In mortgage fraud for profit the perpetrators secures excess financing that is then pocketed as gain

Section 2: *Vocabulary*

Acceleration Clause: Allows the lender to demand that the loan be paid in full in case of default

Adjustable-Rate Mortgage (ARM): A property loan that has adjusts periodically based on an external index

Alienation Clause (Due on Sale Clause): A provision in a loan document requiring full payment of the debt upon any transfer of title to the property

Amortized Loan: A loan consisting of a level payment but with a portion of it going to principal and a portion going to interest

Annual Percentage Rate (APR): The true interest rate as required by TILA because it includes the simple interest rate, plus all other costs of the loan expressed as interest

Assumption: An agreement to take over and be responsible for another's loan

Balloon Payment: A final payment on a bank loan that is often considerably larger than the required periodic payments

Blanket Mortgage Loan: Multiple parcels provide the security for the loan

Budget Mortgage: The lender requires the borrower pay 1/12 of the property taxes and hazard insurance each month in addition to the loan payment

Certificate of Eligibility: Authorization of a Veteran's entitlement for a VA loan

Certificate of Reasonable Value (CRV): An appraisal issued by the Veterans Administration showing the property's current market value

Conditional Commitment: The FHA established appraisal amount, required repairs, and commitment to insure the loan

Construction Loan: A short-term, interim loan used to finance construction

Conventional Loan: A private sector loan which differs depending upon bank and product

Deed in Lieu of Foreclosure: The defaulting borrower returns the deed to the lender to avoid a foreclosure

Defeasance Clause: Indicates that the bank must convey title and cancel the borrower's debt once the loan has been repaid

Deficiency Judgment: A personal judgment entered against the borrower when a foreclosure sale does not produce sufficient funds to pay the entire loan

Discount Points: A one-time fee charged by the lender at closing that increases the lender's yield and reduces the borrower's interest rate over the life of the loan

Discount rate: The interest rate charged by the Federal Reserve Bank to its member banks

Equitable Title: The title held by a buyer under a land sale contract, contract for deed, or an installment sale agreement

Equity: The amount represented by the unencumbered portion of the property

Equity of Redemption: The right of a defaulting borrower to reclaim the property prior to final judicial intervention

Escalation Clause: Allows the lender to raise the existing interest rate at specified times during the loan

Exculpatory Clause: In the event of foreclosure, the bank will forgive any debt in excess of the collateral

Fannie Mae (FNMA): The largest purchaser of secondary mortgage market FHA and VA loans

Federal Equal Credit Opportunity Act: Federal law prohibiting discrimination against borrowers on the based on race, color, religion, sex, national origin, religion, marital status, age, or the receipt of public assistance

Federal Truth-in-Lending Act (TILA): Requires lenders to disclose the consumers' exact cost of credit within three days of a loan application

FHA (Federal Housing Administration) loan: A property loan made to a qualified borrower and that is insured by the Federal Housing Administration

Foreclosure: A legal procedure where, as a result of a borrower's default, the lender sells the property that was used as security for the debt

Freddie Mac (FHLMC): An independent agency that primarily purchases conventional loans in the secondary mortgage market

Ginnie Mae (GNMA): A federal agency that purchases Department of Housing and Urban Development, high risk, and subsidized housing loans in the secondary market

Good Faith Estimate (GFE): An estimate of all closing costs provided to a borrower within three days of the loan application as required by RESPA

Graduated Payment Mortgage: A loan where the payments are low in the early years, then rise to a higher level over time, often resulting in negative amortization

Hypothecation: Allowing a borrower to maintain possession and control of the property while the loan is being paid off

HUD-1 Uniform Settlement Statement: A statement of all closing expenses given to the borrower at least 1 day prior to closing

Impounds: The amount collected at closing and monthly to set up an escrow account

Interest: The cost of borrowing money

Interest Only Loan: Only requires the payment of interest for a stated time period and then converts to a fully amortized loan

Judicial Foreclosure: Court action granting the lender permission to sell a borrower's property at a public sale

Junior Mortgage: Any loan that has a lower lien position than another loan

Kickback: A payment made to someone who has facilitated a transaction, but who did not perform an actual service

Land Contract: Seller financing where the title is not transferred to the purchaser until all payments are made

Lis Pendens: A recorded legal document giving constructive notice that an action (generally a foreclosure) has been filed against the property

Lien Theory State: The lender secures property by placing a lien on it until the debt is repaid

Loan-to-Value Ratio (LTV): The maximum loan the lender will provide to the borrower for the purchase of a home

Mortgage: The security instrument used to create the lien on the property in a lien theory state

Mortgage Guaranty Insurance Corporation (MGIC): An insurance company that issues private mortgage insurance (PMI) on loans and also purchases secondary mortgage market notes

Mortgage Insurance Premium (MIP): The mortgage insurance premium paid by the borrower in an FHA transaction

Mortgage Satisfaction: Indicates that the bank must record a mortgage satisfaction when the buyer's loan is repaid

Naked Title: Title held by the trustee in a trust deed

Negative Amortization: The loan payment is not sufficient to cover the principal and interest due, causing the loan balance to increase, rather than decrease

Negotiable Instrument: The right to receive payments under a note can be freely transferred to another

Package Mortgage Loan: Both real and personal property provide the security for the loan

Partial Release Clause: Obligates the lender to release each parcel held as security in a blanket mortgage upon payment of a specified sum

Power of Sale Clause: Enables the lender to conduct a non-judicial foreclosure against the defaulting borrower

Purchase Money Mortgage: Given by the seller to the buyer to cover all or part of the purchase price of the property, but title is conveyed immediately, rather than after payment in full is made

Prepayment Clause: Indicates whether the loan can be paid off early and, if so, whether a penalty exists for early payment

Primary Mortgage Market: The market where lenders originate loans being made directly to the consumer

Private Mortgage Insurance (PMI): Insurance provided by a private carrier that protects a lender against a loss in the event of a foreclosure and deficiency

Promissory Note: A written and signed promise to pay a sum of money at a specified time and according to a specified schedule

Qualifying Ratios: Minimum %'s that are used to determine whether a borrower can qualify for a bank loan

Real Estate Settlement Procedures Act (RESPA): Requires that a borrower be given a Good Faith Estimate of all closing costs within 3 days of application

Receiver Clause: Permits a court to appoint a receiver to manage income producing property during a period of default

Reconveyance Deed: Used by a trustee under a deed of trust to return title to the trustor once the loan has been paid in full

Regulation Z (Truth in Lending Act): A provision of TILA which further explains it

Reverse Annuity Mortgage (RAM): Allows borrowers (aged 62 and older) to secure a loan against the equity in their home

Secondary Mortgage Market: Allows mortgagees to sell notes to acquire cash to make loans to consumers

Security Deed: A security instrument used in title theory states which conveys title to the lender until the debt is satisfied

Security Instrument: Demonstrates the lender's right to foreclose on a specific property of a defaulting borrower

Seller Concession/Contribution: An amount that the seller is allowed to contribute towards the purchaser's closing costs

Statutory Right of Redemption: The borrower's right redeem after the foreclosure or tax sale but prior to the end of the redemption period

Straight Term Loan: A loan in which only interest is paid during the term of the loan, leaving a large balloon payment of principal at maturity

Subject to sale: The buyer takes over the property subject to an existing loan, but does not agree to assume liability to the bank for the payments

Subordination Clause: The holder of an earlier loan permits a later loan to take priority of order

Subprime loans: High interest loans issued to borrowers with a poor credit history

Title Theory State: The lender secures property by taking legal title to it until the debt is repaid, while the borrower retains equitable title

Trust Deed (Deed of Trust): A security instrument where legal title is transferred to a trustee who holds it for the lender's benefit

VA Guaranteed Loan: A property loan made to a qualified veteran by an authorized VA lender, but that is partially guaranteed by the Department of Veterans Affairs

Section 3: *Recall Multiple Choice*

1. **The process of allowing a borrower to maintain possession and control of the property while the loan is being paid off**
   A. Hypothecation
   B. Interest
   C. Mortgage
   D. Foreclosure

2. **Loans issued to borrowers with poor credit history. These loans have a higher risk and thus, the terms are less favorable in terms of higher interest rates and fees**
   A. Subprime loans
   B. Conforming loans
   C. Participation loan
   D. Lifetime caps

3. **A written and signed promise to pay a sum of money at a specified time and according to a specified schedule**
   A. Partial Release Clause
   B. Lien Theory State
   C. Mortgage
   D. Promissory Note

4. **A state where the lender secures property by allowing the borrower to retain title to the property, but that title is encumbered by a lien placed on it until the debt is repaid**
   A. Lien Theory
   B. Foreclosure
   C. Land Contract
   D. Reconveyance Deed

5. **Both real and personal property provide the security for the loan**
   A. Package Mortgage Loan
   B. Private Mortgage Insurance
   C. Primary Mortgage Market
   D. Chattel Mortgage

6. **Requires that a borrower be given a Good Faith Estimate of all closing costs within 3 days of application; also states no kickbacks and no unreasonable impounds**
   A. Federal truth-in-lending act
   B. Real Estate Settlement Procedures Act
   C. Holder in due course
   D. Open ended mortgage loan

7. **A state where the lender secures property by taking title to it until the debt is repaid; the lender has legal title and the borrower has equitable title**
   A. Mortgage
   B. Promissory Note
   C. Foreclosure
   D. Title Theory

8. **A federal agency created to purchase Department of Housing and Urban Development, high risk, and subsidized housing loans**
    A. Conditional Commitment
    B. Ginnie Mae
    C. Open ended mortgage loan
    D. Federal truth-in-lending act

9. **The amount that the lender will provide to the borrower for the purchase of a home**
    A. Seller concession/contribution
    B. Loan-to-Value Ratio
    C. Foreclosure
    D. Secondary Mortgage market

10. **Allows borrowers (aged 62 and older) to take a loan against the equity in their homes**
    A. Package mortgage loan
    B. Closed mortgage
    C. Reverse Annuity Mortgage
    D. Wraparound mortgage

11. **A final one-time payment on a bank loan that is often considerably larger than the required periodic payments**
    A. Prepayment Clause
    B. Junior Mortgage
    C. Mortgage
    D. Balloon

12. **A one-time fee charged by the lender at closing that increases the lender's yield and reduces the borrower's interest rate over the life of the loan**
    A. Impounds
    B. Discount Points
    C. Mortgage
    D. Discount Rate

13. **A form of seller financing where the title is not transferred to the purchaser until all payments are made**
    A. Closed Mortgage
    B. Lien Theory State
    C. Land Contract
    D. Blanket Mortgage Loan

14. **A loan that only requires the payment of interest for a stated period of time and then converts to a fully amortized loan**
    A. Mortgage Loan
    B. Assumption Loan
    C. Interest Only Loan
    D. Conforming Loans

15. **The unencumbered portion of the property**
    A. Equity of Redemption
    B. Equity
    C. Mortgage
    D. Hypothecation

16. **The right to receive payments under a note can be freely transferred to another**
    A. Interest Only Loan
    B. Conforming Loans
    C. Negotiable Instrument
    D. Equitable Title

17. **The true interest rate required under TILA; it includes the simple interest rate, plus all other costs of the loan expressed as interest**
    A. Budget Mortgage Rate
    B. Annual Percentage Rate
    C. Lifetime Cap Rate
    D. Holder In Due Course

18. **A Law requiring lenders to disclose, within three days of a loan application, the consumers' exact cost of credit**
    A. Federal Reserve Bank
    B. Equal Credit Opportunity Act
    C. Real Estate Settlement Procedures Act
    D. Federal Truth-in-Lending Act

19. **The insurance premium paid by the borrower in an FHA transaction to ensure loan repayment**
    A. Private Mortgage Insurance
    B. Mortgage Insurance Premium
    C. Graduated Payment Mortgage
    D. Primary Mortgage Market

20. **A loan clause which indicates whether the loan can be paid off early and, if so, whether a penalty exists for early payment**
    A. Prepayment Clause
    B. Acceleration Clause
    C. Receiver Clause
    D. Defeasance Clause

21. **A loan where the payments are low in the early years and then rise to a higher level over time, often resulting in negative amortization**
    A. Budget Mortgage
    B. Balloon Payment
    C. Purchase Money Mortgage
    D. Graduated Payment Mortgage

22. **Any loan that has a lower lien position than another mortgage**
    A. Wraparound Mortgage
    B. Primary Mortgage Market
    C. Secondary Mortgage Market
    D. Junior Mortgage

23. **A vehicle for mortgagees to re-infuse the market with more cash so that they can continue to make loans to consumers**
    A. Loan-to-value Ratio
    B. Secondary Mortgage Market
    C. Open Ended Mortgage Loan
    D. Primary Mortgage Market

24. **Title held by the trustee in a trust deed situation**
    A. Equitable Title
    B. Reconveyance Deed
    C. Lien Theory State
    D. Naked Title

25. **A loan provision which enables the lender to conduct a non-judicial foreclosure against the defaulting borrower**
    A. Prepayment Clause
    B. Partial Release Clause
    C. Receiver Clause
    D. Power of Sale Clause

26. **The amount collected at closing and monthly to set up the borrower's escrow account**
    A. Hypothecation
    B. Discount Points
    C. Impounds
    D. Subprime Loans

27. **A loan given by the seller to the buyer to cover all or part of the purchase price of the property, but title is conveyed immediately, rather than after payment in full is made**
    A. Graduated Payment Mortgage
    B. Closed Mortgage
    C. Interest Only Loan
    D. Purchase Money Mortgage

28. **An amount that the seller is allowed to contribute towards the purchaser's closing costs**
    A. Mortgage Satisfaction
    B. Loan-to-value Ratio
    C. Interest Only Loan
    D. Concession/Contribution

29. **A clause in which the holder of an earlier loan permits a later loan to take priority of order**
    A. Straight Term Loan
    B. Subordination Clause
    C. Defeasance Clause
    D. Acceleration Clause

30. **The deed is given back to the lender by the defaulting borrower in order to avoid a foreclosure**
    A. Prepayment Clause
    B. Loan-to-Value Ratio
    C. Deed in Lieu
    D. Granting Clause

31. **A transfer of possession of real property in which the buyer takes the property subject to an existing loan, but does not agree to assume responsibility for the payments**
    A. Subject to sale
    B. Lifetime caps
    C. Strict foreclosure
    D. Closed mortgage

32. **A provision of TILA which further explains it. Rules relating to advertising and types of loans impacted**
    A. Alienation Clause
    B. Regulation Z
    C. Annual percentage rate
    D. Acceleration Clause

33. **The interest rate that the Federal Reserve Bank charges to its member banks to borrow money**
    A. Conforming loans
    B. Discount rate
    C. Mortgage
    D. Wraparound mortgage

34. **Court action granting the lender permission to sell a borrower's property at a public sale**
    A. Granting Clause
    B. Strict Foreclosure
    C. Junior Mortgage
    D. Judicial Foreclosure

35. **A provision in a blanket mortgage which obligates the lender to release each parcel held as security upon payment of a specified sum**
    A. Alienation Clause
    B. Trust Deed
    C. Mortgage Satisfaction
    D. Partial Release Clause

36. **A mortgage loan made to a qualified veteran by an authorized VA lender, but that is guaranteed to be partially repaid by the Department of Veterans Affairs**
    A. Conforming Loans
    B. Chattel Mortgage
    C. VA Guaranteed Loan
    D. Subprime Loans

37. **A clause that indicates that the bank must convey title and cancel the borrower's debt once the loan has been repaid**
    A. Defeasance Clause
    B. Mortgage Satisfaction
    C. Acceleration Clause
    D. Prepayment Clause

38. **A short-term, interim loan used to finance construction**
    A. Construction Loan
    B. Participation Loan
    C. Conforming Loans
    D. Assumption

39. **Occurs when the loan payment is not sufficient to cover the principal and interest due, causing the loan balance to increase, rather than decrease**
    A. Negative Amortization
    B. Subprime Loans
    C. Closed Mortgage
    D. Partially Amortized Loan

40. **Multiple parcels provide the security for the loan**
    A. Negative Amortization
    B. Chattel Mortgage
    C. Conventional Loan
    D. Blanket Mortgage Loan

41. **The cost of borrowing money**
    A. Foreclosure
    B. Open Mortgage
    C. Hypothecation
    D. Interest

42. **A loan consisting of a level payment for the stated loan period, with a portion of each payment going to principal and a portion going to interest**
    A. Wraparound Mortgage Loan
    B. Strict Foreclosure
    C. Amortized Loan
    D. Conforming Loans

43. **A loan provision that, in the event of foreclosure, the bank will forgive any debt in excess of the collateral**
    A. Exculpatory Clause
    B. Lien Theory State
    C. Prepayment Clause
    D. Acceleration Clause

44. **A payment made to someone who has facilitated a transaction or appointment, but who did not perform an actual service**
    A. Amortized Loan
    B. Kickback
    C. Beneficiary
    D. Land Contract

45. **A private sector loan which differs depending upon bank and product**
    A. Conforming Loans
    B. Blanket Mortgage Loan
    C. Mortgage Loan
    D. Conventional Loan

46. **An independent agency that primarily purchases conventional loans in the secondary mortgage market**
    A. Fannie Mae
    B. Loan-to-Value Ratio
    C. Freddie Mac
    D. Ginnie Mae

47. **Calculations that are used in determining whether a borrower can qualify for a bank loan**
    A. Loan To Value
    B. Qualifying Ratios
    C. Discount Rate
    D. Fannie Mae

48. **The mortgage market where lenders originate loans being made directly to the consumer**
    A. Open Mortgage
    B. Secondary Mortgage Market
    C. Primary Mortgage Market
    D. Budget Mortgage

49. **A property loan that is insured by the Federal Housing Administration**
    A. Participation loan
    B. Federal Housing Administration loan
    C. Deed in Lieu Of foreclosure
    D. Partially Amortized loan

50. **The right of a borrower in default to reclaim the property prior to final judicial intervention**
    A. Mortgage Satisfaction
    B. Trust Deed
    C. Closed Mortgage
    D. Equity of Redemption

51. **The document that the bank records after a mortgage is paid off in a lien theory state**
    A. Defeasance Clause
    B. Chattel Mortgage
    C. Mortgage Satisfaction
    D. Mortgage Guaranty Insurance Corporation

52. **A security instrument, used in title theory states which conveys title to the lender until the debt is satisfied**
    A. Reconveyance Deed
    B. Security Deed
    C. Lien Theory State
    D. Security Instrument

53. **A property loan that has adjusts periodically to reflect market conditions and is adjusted based on an external index**
    A. Closed mortgage
    B. Junior mortgage
    C. Adjustable-Rate Mortgage
    D. Reverse Annuity Mortgage

54. **A deed used by a trustee under a deed of trust to return title to the trustor once the loan has been paid in full**
    A. Lien Theory State
    B. Open Mortgage
    C. Naked Title
    D. Reconveyance Deed

55. **The FHA established appraisal amount, required repairs, and commitment to insure the loan**
    A. Deficiency Judgment
    B. Conditional Commitment
    C. Conventional Loan
    D. Granting Clause

56. **A security instrument wherein legal title in the real property is transferred to a trustee who holds it for the lender's benefit**
   A. Trust Deed
   B. Title theory state
   C. Adjustable-Rate Mortgage
   D. Equity of redemption

57. **The document demonstrating the collateral and giving the creditor the right to sell it to satisfy a debt in case of default**
   A. Defeasance Clause
   B. Promissory Note
   C. Negotiable Instrument
   D. Security Instrument

58. **A loan in which only interest is paid during the term of the loan, leaving the entire principal balance to be paid in a balloon payment at the end of the term**
   A. Partially Amortized Loan
   B. Mortgage
   C. Strict Foreclosure
   D. Straight Term Loan

59. **A statement of all closing expenses given to the borrower at least 1 day prior to closing**
   A. Real Estate Settlement Procedures Act
   B. HUD-1 Uniform Settlement Statement
   C. Hud-2 Uniform Settlement Statement
   D. Hud-6 Uniform Settlement Statement

60. **The largest purchaser of secondary mortgage market loans; most often FHA and VA loans**
   A. Ginnie Mae
   B. Fannie Mae
   C. Mortgage Guaranty Insurance Corporation
   D. Freddie Mac

61. **The borrower's right redeem after the foreclosure or tax sale but prior to the end of the redemption period**
   A. Adjustable-Rate Mortgage
   B. Security Deed
   C. Equitable Right of Redemption
   D. Statutory Right of Redemption

62. **A loan provision which permits a court to appoint a receiver to manage income producing property during a period of default**
   A. Power of Sale Clause
   B. Acceleration Clause
   C. Receiver Clause
   D. Title Theory State

63. **An agreement to take over and be responsible for another's loan**
   A. Loan-to-Value Ratio
   B. Assumption
   C. Interest Only Loan
   D. Mortgage Satisfaction

64. **Allows the lender to raise the existing interest rate at specified times during the loan**
    A. Defeasance Clause
    B. Exculpatory Clause
    C. Escalation Clause
    D. Acceleration Clause

65. **The title held by a buyer under a land sale contract, contract for deed, or an installment contract**
    A. Mortgage
    B. Equitable Title
    C. Security Deed
    D. Exculpatory Clause

66. **A personal judgment entered against the borrower when a foreclosure sale does not produce sufficient funds to pay the loan debt in full**
    A. Open Mortgage Judgment
    B. Deficiency Judgment
    C. Closed Mortgage
    D. Exculpatory Judgment

67. **Federal law which prohibits discrimination against borrowers on the basis of race, color, religion, sex, national origin, religion, marital status, age, or the receipt of public assistance**
    A. Federal Reserve Bank
    B. Real Estate Settlement Procedures Act
    C. Federal Truth-in-lending Act
    D. Federal Equal Credit Opportunity Act

68. **A loan clause that will allow the lender to demand that the loan be paid in full in case of default**
    A. Defeasance Clause
    B. Prepayment Clause
    C. Exculpatory Clause
    D. Acceleration Clause

69. **An appraisal issued by the Veterans Administration showing the property's current market value**
    A. Trust Deed
    B. Certificate of Reasonable Value
    C. Loan-to-Value Ratio
    D. Certificate of eligibility

70. **An insurance company that issues private mortgage insurance on loans and also purchases secondary mortgage market notes**
    A. Mortgage Guaranty Insurance Corporation
    B. Fannie Mae
    C. Freddie Mac
    D. Ginnie Mae

71. **The security instrument used by the lender to create the lien on the property in a lien theory state**
    A. Foreclosure
    B. Title Theory State
    C. Mortgage
    D. Hypothecation

72. **A loan where the lender requires that in addition to the monthly principal and interest payments, the borrower also pay 1/12 of the property taxes, and hazard insurance each month**
    A. Amortized Loan
    B. Interest Only Loan
    C. Closed Mortgage
    D. Budget Mortgage

73. **A legal procedure where, as a result of a borrower's default, the lender sells the property that was used as security for the debt**
    A. Foreclosure
    B. Closed Mortgage
    C. Mortgage
    D. Hypothecation

74. **Insurance provided by a private carrier that protects a lender against a loss in the event of a foreclosure and deficiency**
    A. Package mortgage loan
    B. Private Mortgage Insurance
    C. Primary Mortgage Market
    D. Mortgage Guaranty Insurance Corporation

75. **An estimate of all closing costs to be provided to a borrower within three days of the loan application as required by RESPA**
    A. Alienation clause
    B. Federal Truth-in-lending Act
    C. Good Faith Estimate
    D. Mortgage

76. **A provision in a loan document requiring full payment of the debt upon any transfer of title to the property to another**
    A. Sale Leaseback
    B. Partial Release Clause
    C. Alienation Clause
    D. Deed in Lieu of Foreclosure

77. **Endorsement from the Veterans Administration indicating the right of a veteran to obtain a VA loan and the amount of her entitlement**
    A. Trust Deed
    B. Certificate of Eligibility
    C. Foreclosure
    D. Title Theory State

78. **A recorded legal document giving constructive notice that an action (generally a foreclosure) has been filed against the property**
    A. Sale Leaseback
    B. Reconveyance Deed
    C. Lis Pendens
    D. Land Contract

Section 4: *Recall Fill-In*

1. A provision in a blanket mortgage which obligates the lender to release each parcel held as security upon payment of a specified sum

   _____

2. A transfer of possession of real property in which the buyer takes the property subject to an existing loan, but does not agree to assume responsibility for the payments

   _____

3. The interest rate that the Federal Reserve Bank charges to its member banks to borrow money

   _____

4. An independent agency that primarily purchases conventional loans in the secondary mortgage market

   _____

5. A mortgage loan made to a qualified veteran by an authorized VA lender, but that is guaranteed to be partially repaid by the Department of Veterans Affairs

   _____

6. The process of allowing a borrower to maintain possession and control of the property while the loan is being paid off

   _____

7. A state where the lender secures property by allowing the borrower to retain title to the property, but that title is encumbered by a lien placed on it until the debt is repaid

   _____

8. Calculations that are used in determining whether a borrower can qualify for a bank loan

   _____

9. The cost of borrowing money

   _____

10. Requires that a borrower be given a Good Faith Estimate of all closing costs within 3 days of application; also states no kickbacks and no unreasonable impounds

   _____

11. The right of a borrower in default to reclaim the property prior to final judicial intervention

   _____

12. Loans issued to borrowers with poor credit history. These loans have a higher risk and thus, the terms are less favorable in terms of higher interest rates and fees

---

13. Insurance provided by a private carrier that protects a lender against a loss in the event of a foreclosure and deficiency

---

14. The deed is given back to the lender by the defaulting borrower in order to avoid a foreclosure

---

15. A loan clause which indicates whether the loan can be paid off early and, if so, whether a penalty exists for early payment

---

16. A legal procedure where, as a result of a borrower's default, the lender sells the property that was used as security for the debt

---

17. Occurs when the loan payment is not sufficient to cover the principal and interest due, causing the loan balance to increase, rather than decrease

---

18. Allows borrowers (aged 62 and older) to take a loan against the equity in their homes

---

19. The bank must record this document when the buyer's loan is repaid in a lien theory state

---

20. A security instrument, used in title theory states which conveys title to the lender until the debt is satisfied

---

21. A loan where the payments are low in the early years and then rise to a higher level over time, often resulting in negative amortization

---

22. Federal law which prohibits discrimination against borrowers on the basis of race, color, religion, sex, national origin, religion, marital status, age, or the receipt of public assistance

---

23. An appraisal issued by the Veterans Administration showing the property's current market value

---

24. The percentage amount that the lender will provide to the borrower for the purchase of a home

_____

25. The title held by a buyer under a land sale contract, contract for deed, or an installment contract

_____

26. A one-time fee charged by the lender at closing that increases the lender's yield and reduces the borrower's interest rate over the life of the loan

_____

27. A loan provision which permits a court to appoint a receiver to manage income producing property during a period of default

_____

28. A statement of all closing expenses given to the borrower at least 1 day prior to closing

_____

29. Court action granting the lender permission to sell a borrower's property at a public sale

_____

30. A loan given by the seller to the buyer to cover all or part of the purchase price of the property, but title is conveyed immediately, rather than after payment in full is made

_____

31. A written and signed promise to pay a sum of money at a specified time and according to a specified schedule

_____

32. The mortgage market where lenders originate loans being made directly to the consumer

_____

33. A loan provision which enables the lender to conduct a non-judicial foreclosure against the defaulting borrower

_____

34. A payment made to someone who has facilitated a transaction or appointment, but who did not perform an actual service

_____

35. Any loan that has a lower lien position than another mortgage

_____

36. The borrower's right redeem after the foreclosure or tax sale but prior to the end of the redemption period

_____

37. A form of seller financing where the title is not transferred to the purchaser until all payments are made

_____

38. The amount collected at closing and monthly to set up the borrower's escrow account

_____

39. A clause that indicates that the bank must convey title and cancel the borrower's debt once the loan has been repaid

_____

40. A security instrument wherein legal title in the real property is transferred to a trustee who holds it for the lender's benefit

_____

41. An estimate of all closing costs to be provided to a borrower within three days of the loan application as required by RESPA

_____

42. Multiple parcels provide the security for the loan

_____

43. The largest purchaser of second mortgage market loans; most often FHA and VA loans

_____

44. A clause that allows the lender to raise the existing interest rate at specified times during the loan

_____

45. A vehicle for mortgagees to re-infuse the market with more cash so that they can continue to make loans to consumers

_____

46. A provision in a loan document requiring full payment of the debt upon any transfer of title to the property to another

_____

47. Endorsement from the Veterans Administration indicating the right of a veteran to obtain a VA loan and the amount of her entitlement

_____

48. Requires lenders to disclose, within three days of a loan application, the consumers' exact cost of credit

_____

49. An amount that the seller is allowed to contribute towards the purchaser's closing costs

_____

50. The insurance covering mortgage default in an FHA transaction

_____

51. A deed used by a trustee under a deed of trust to return title to the trustor once the loan has been paid in full

_____

52. The security instrument used by the lender to create the lien on the property in a lien theory state

_____

53. A loan clause that will allow the lender to demand that the loan be paid in full in case of default

_____

54. An agreement to take over and be responsible for another's loan

_____

55. A federal agency created to purchase Department of Housing and Urban Development, high risk, and subsidized housing loans

_____

56. The right to receive payments under a note can be freely transferred to another

_____

57. Both real and personal property provide the security for the loan

_____

58. A provision of TILA which further explains it. Rules relating to advertising and types of loans impacted

_____

59. A private sector loan which differs depending upon bank and product

_____

60. The true interest rate required under TILA; it includes the simple interest rate, plus all other costs of the loan expressed as interest

_____

61. A personal judgment entered against the borrower when a foreclosure sale does not produce sufficient funds to pay the loan debt in full

_____

62. A final one-time payment on a bank loan that is often considerably larger than the required periodic payments

63. A loan that only requires the payment of interest for a stated period of time and then converts to a fully amortized loan

64. An insurance company that issues private mortgage insurance on loans and also purchases secondary mortgage market notes

65. Title held by the trustee in a trust deed situation

66. A loan where the lender requires that in addition to the monthly principal and interest payments, the borrower also pay 1/12 of the property taxes, and hazard insurance each month

67. A short-term, interim loan used to finance construction

68. The unencumbered portion of the property

69. A property loan that has adjusts periodically to reflect market conditions and is adjusted based on an external index

70. A loan in which only interest is paid during the term of the loan, leaving the entire principal balance to be paid in a balloon payment at the end of the term

71. A state where the lender secures property by taking title to it until the debt is repaid; the lender has legal title, and the borrower has equitable title

72. A document demonstrating the collateral and giving the creditor the right to sell it in the event of default

73. A property loan made by an authorized FHA Lender to a borrower and that is insured by the Federal Housing Administration

74. **A clause in which the holder of an earlier loan permits a later loan to take priority of order**

---

75. **A loan provision that, in the event of foreclosure, the bank will forgive any debt in excess of the collateral**

---

76. **The FHA established appraisal amount, required repairs, and commitment to insure the loan**

---

77. **A loan consisting of a level payment for the stated loan period, with a portion of each payment going to principal and a portion going to interest**

---

78. **A recorded legal document giving constructive notice that an action (generally a foreclosure) has been filed against the property**

Section 5: *Matching*

A   Receiver Clause   1 _____   An independent agency that primarily purchases conventional loans in the secondary mortgage market

B   Lien Theory State   2 _____   The largest purchaser of second mortgage market loans; most often FHA and VA loans

C   Purchase Money Mortgage   3 _____   A loan made by the seller to the buyer but title is conveyed immediately, rather than after payment in full is made.

D   Mortgage   4 _____   A loan provision which enables the lender to conduct a non-judicial foreclosure against the defaulting borrower.

E   Power of Sale Clause   5 _____   A loan that only requires the payment of interest for a stated period of time and then converts to a fully amortized loan.

F   Escalation Clause   6 _____   A payment to someone who has not performed an actual service

G   Equity of Redemption   7 _____   A security instrument, used in title theory states which conveys title to the lender until the debt is satisfied

H   Interest Only Loan   8 _____   A vehicle for mortgagees to re-infuse the market with more cash so that they can continue to make loans to consumers.

I   Subprime Loans   9 _____   Clause that allows the lender to raise the existing interest rate at specified times during the loan

J   Prepayment Clause   10 _____   Indicates whether the loan can be paid off early or if there is a penalty

K   Interest   11 _____   A state where a lender secures property by placing a lien on it

L   Kickback   12 _____   Loans issued to borrowers with poor credit history and higher interest rates

M   Security Deed   13 _____   Permits a court to appoint a receiver to manage income producing property during a period of default

N   Freddie Mac   14 _____   The cost of borrowing money.

O   Fannie Mae   15 _____   The right of a borrower in default to reclaim the property prior to final judicial intervention

P   Secondary Mortgage Market   16 _____   The security instrument used by the lender to create the lien on the property in a lien theory state.

A   Equity

1 _____   A statement of all closing expenses given to the borrower at least 1 day prior to closing

B   Amortized Loan

2 _____   Both real and personal property provide the security for the loan

C   Private Mortgage Insurance

3 _____   The mortgage market where lenders originate loans being made directly to the consumer

D   Primary Mortgage Market

4 _____   A judgment against the borrower when a foreclosure sale does not produce sufficient funds to pay the loan

E   Promissory Note

5 _____   A level payment loan, with a portion of each payment going to principal and a portion going to interest

F   Package Mortgage Loan

6 _____   A private sector loan which differs depending upon bank and product.

G   Conditional Commitment

7 _____   A TILA provision that explains its rules relating to advertising and types of loans impacted

H   Title Theory State

8 _____   A written and signed promise to pay a sum of money at a specified time and according to a specified schedule

I   HUD-1 Settlement Statement

9 _____   An appraisal issued by the Veterans Administration showing the property's current market value.

J   Regulation Z

10 _____   Insurance that protects a lender against a loss in there is a deficiency from foreclosure

K   Annual Percentage Rate

11 _____   Loan requiring that the borrower part of the taxes and insurance each month

L   Deficiency Judgment

12 _____   The FHA established appraisal amount, required repairs, and commitment to insure the loan

M   Certificate of Reasonable Value

13 _____   The lender secures property by taking legal title to it until the debt is repaid

N   Loan to Value Ratio

14 _____   The percentage amount that the lender will provide to the borrower for the purchase of a home

O   Budget Mortgage

15 _____   The true interest rate under TILA to include all costs of the loan expressed as interest

P   Conventional Loan

16 _____   The unencumbered portion of the property

A   Negotiable Instrument   1 _____   A loan clause that will allow the lender to demand that the loan be paid in full in case of default

B   Alienation Clause   2 _____   A document recorded to give constructive notice a foreclosure is pending

C   Graduated Payment Mortgage   3 _____   A loan guaranteed by the Veteran's Administration

D   Lis Pendens   4 _____   A provision requiring full payment of the debt upon any transfer of the property

E   Good Faith Estimate   5 _____   Allowing a borrower to maintain possession and control of a property while the loan is being paid.

F   Hypothecation   6 _____   An estimate of closing costs required by RESPA

G   Naked Title   7 _____   Issues private mortgage insurance on loans and purchases secondary mortgage market notes.

H   Mortgage Guaranty Insurance Corporation   8 _____   Legal procedure where the property is sold due to default

I   Defeasance Clause   9 _____   Loan which often results in negative amortization since the early payments aren't sufficient

J   VA Guaranteed Loan   10 _____   Requiring lenders to disclose, within three days of a loan application, the consumers' exact cost of credit

K   Foreclosure   11 _____   The document recorded by the bank when the loan is repaid in a Lien Theory State

L   Federal Truth In Lending Act   12 _____   States the bank must convey title once the loan has been repaid.

M   Mortgage Satisfaction   13 _____   The deed is given back to the lender by the defaulting borrower in order to avoid a foreclosure.

N   Deed in Lieu of Foreclosure   14 _____   The right to receive payments under a note can be freely transferred to another.

O   Acceleration Clause   15 _____   Title held by the trustee in a trust deed situation.

A   Discount Points   1 _____   A clause in which the holder of an earlier loan permits a later loan to take priority of order

B   Assumption   2 _____   A deed used by a trustee under a deed of trust to return title to the trustor once the loan has been paid in full.

C   Reconveyance Deed   3 _____   A one-time fee charged by the lender at closing to lower the borrower's interest rate

D   Seller's Concession   4 _____   A property loan that is insured by the Federal Housing Administration

E   RESPA   5 _____   A provision in a blanket mortgage which obligates the lender to release each parcel held as security upon payment of a specified sum.

F   Certificate of Eligibility   6 _____   An agreement to take over a loan, but not agree to be responsible for the debt

G   Blanket Mortgage   7 _____   A short-term, interim loan used to finance construction

H   FHA   8 _____   An agreement to take over a loan and be responsible for the debt

I   Subject To   9 _____   An amount that the seller is allowed to contribute towards the purchaser's closing costs

J   Negative Amortization   10 _____   Endorsement from the Veterans Administration indicating the right of a veteran to obtain a VA loan and the amount of her entitlement.

K   Equitable Title   11 _____   Multiple parcels provide the security for the loan

L   Subordination Clause   12 _____   Occurs when the loan payment is not sufficient to cover the PI due, causing the loan balance to increase

M   Statutory Right of Redemption   13 _____   Requires that a borrower be given a Good Faith Estimate of all closing costs within 3 days of application

N   Partial Release Clause   14 _____   The borrower's right redeem after the foreclosure or tax sale but prior to the end of the redemption period.

O   Construction Loan   15 _____   The title held by a buyer under a land sale contract, contract for deed, or an installment contract

A	Security Instrument	1	_____	A federal agency created to purchase Department of Housing and Urban Development, high risk, and subsidized housing loans
B	Trust Deed	2	_____	A final one-time payment on a bank loan that is often considerably larger than the required periodic payments.
C	Federal Equal Credit Opportunity	3	_____	A form of seller financing where the title is not transferred to the purchaser until all payments are made
D	Qualifying Ratios	4	_____	A loan in which only interest is paid during the term and a balloon payment is due at the end
E	Balloon Payment	5	_____	A loan provision that, in the event of foreclosure, the bank will forgive any debt in excess of the collateral.
F	Reverse Annuity Mortgage	6	_____	A property loan that has adjusts periodically to reflect market conditions and is adjusted based on an external index
G	Discount Rate	7	_____	A security instrument wherein legal title in the real property is transferred to a trustee who holds it for the lender's benefit
H	Exculpatory Clause	8	_____	Allows borrowers (aged 62 and older) to take a loan against the equity in their homes
I	Mortgage Insurance Premium	9	_____	A document demonstrating the collateral and giving a creditor the right to sell it to satisfy a debt if there is a default
J	Junior Mortgage	10	_____	Any loan that has a lower lien position than another mortgage
K	Land Contract	11	_____	Calculations that are used in determining whether a borrower can qualify for a bank loan
L	Straight Term Loan	12	_____	Court action granting the lender permission to sell a borrower's property at a public sale
M	Ginnie Mae (GNMA)	13	_____	Prohibits discrimination in lending based on the protected classes
N	Adjustable-Rate Mortgage	14	_____	The amount collected at closing and monthly to set up the borrower's escrow account
O	Impounds	15	_____	The interest rate that the Federal Reserve Bank charges to its member banks to borrow money.
P	Judicial Foreclosure	16	_____	The insurance premium paid by the borrower in an FHA transaction in case of default

Section 6: *Analysis Fill-In*

1. Define Annual Percentage Rate (APR):

   _____

2. Where would you see a Defeasance Clause?

   _____

3. What type of state uses a Mortgage Satisfaction as a financing instrument?

   _____

4. Give an example of a Statutory Right of Redemption:

   _____

5. What is the purpose of a Power of Sale Clause?

   _____

6. Why does a bank need to put an Acceleration Clause into the loan documents?

   _____

7. Who benefits from Discount Points and why?

   _____

8. What is a Discount rate?

   _____

9. Define a Deed in Lieu of Foreclosure:

   _____

10. Why is a Fully Amortized Loan better than a straight loan for the borrower?

    _____

11. Who files a Lis Pendens and why?

    _____

12. Which loan will most likely result in Negative Amortization?

    _____

13. Give a situation where a buyer would hold Equitable Title:

    _____

14. What type of loan would have an Escalation Clause?

_____

15. Define Straight Term Loan:

_____

16. What's the difference between a Judicial and Non-Judicial Foreclosure?

_____

17. Why are Non-Judicial Foreclosures more likely in title theory states?

_____

18. Define a Budget Mortgage:

_____

19. Which right of redemption is ALWAYS allowed regardless of state?

_____

20. What's the difference between an interest only loan and a straight term loan?

_____

21. What is the difference between a Purchase Money Mortgage and a Land Contract?

_____

22. An Alienation Clause prevents the borrower from doing what?

_____

23. Who holds Naked Title in a Trust Deed?

_____

24. Name the three Security Instruments:

_____

25. Define Reverse Annuity Mortgage (RAM):

_____

26. Define a Promissory Note:

_____

27. Promissory Notes are _____, so they can be transferred to others.

_____

28. Can a Promissory Note be used to secure property?

29. What type of mortgage is tied to an external index?

30. Your loan requires a one-time payment at the end. What is that payment called?

31. This clause tells you if you can pay your loan off early:

32. Define Exculpatory Clause:

33. Multiple parcels provide the security for this type of loan:

34. Define Package Mortgage Loan:

35. What clause would allow the second mortgagee priority over the first mortgagee?

36. What is a Qualifying Ratio?

37. Difference between a Certificate of Reasonable Value and Conditional Commitment:

38. Define Assumption:

39. Private Mortgage Insurance vs Mortgage Insurance Premium?

40. Name three facts about the VA Loan Program:

41. Name three elements of an FHA loan:

42. What is a Conventional Loan?

_____

43. A vehicle for mortgagees to re-infuse the market with more cash so that they can continue to make loans to consumers:

_____

44. Name Three Secondary Mortgage Market Entities:

_____

45. What and who does the Federal Equal Credit Opportunity Act protect against?

_____

46. What law requires a Good Faith Estimate?

_____

47. Define Loan-to-Value Ratio:

_____

48. How long before closing should a borrower receive a HUD-1 Uniform Settlement Statement?

_____

49. What's the difference between an assumption and Subject to sale?

_____

50. What is the difference between Title Theory State vs Lien Theory State?

_____

51. What is the Primary Mortgage Market vs Secondary Mortgage Market?

_____

52. When would a Deficiency Judgment most likely occur?

_____

53. What loan requires a Partial Release Clause?

_____

54. What law does Regulation Z refer to?

_____

Section 7: *Analysis Multiple Choice*

1. **Marylou took out a conventional home loan from Bank of America 6 years ago. She wants to now move and allow her daughter to take over her loan by placing it in her daughter's name. Will she be able to do this?**
   A. As long as her daughter can qualify for the loan
   B. As long as the documents don't contain an alienation clause
   C. As long as the bank gives Marylou approval to transfer the loan
   D. As long as Marylou agrees to still be responsible for the debt

2. **Yolanda decides to sell her property to her cousin, Sue for $200,000. Their arrangement is that Sue will take the property subject to the existing mortgage with Wells Fargo as Yolanda travels the world. In this situation, if Sue doesn't make the monthly payments:**
   A. She is liable to Wells Fargo for the entire debt
   B. She is partially liable to Wells Fargo for the debt and Yolanda is partially responsible for the debt
   C. Only Yolanda is responsible to Wells Fargo for the debt
   D. Yolanda would be responsible only if Sue doesn't pay the debt

3. **Which of the following are true when financing is involved?**
   A. The mortgagee signs the note promising to pay the debt
   B. The beneficiary signs the trust deed
   C. The promissory note is security for the debt
   D. The mortgagor is the borrower

4. **When the Federal Reserve raises the discount rate on loans, it is most likely that:**
   A. Interest rates will go up, prices will go down, the market will slow down
   B. Interest rates will go down, prices will go up, the market will speed up
   C. Interest rates will go up, prices will go up, the market will speed up
   D. Interest rates will go down, prices will go down, the market will slow down

5. **What is the term used when a lender makes extremely high interest/high fee loans to certain borrowers utilizing deceptive and fraudulent practices?**
   A. Usury
   B. Predatory Lending
   C. Non-Conforming Loans
   D. Deficiency Loans

6. **What is the main difference between a land contract and a purchase money mortgage?**
   A. A land contract is seller financing and a purchase money mortgage is not
   B. Both are seller financing, but in a purchase money mortgage, title is transferred immediately
   C. A purchase money mortgage is seller financing and a land contract is not
   D. In a land contract the seller holds equitable title, but in a purchase money mortgage the buyer holds equitable title

7. **What is the greatest benefit of points to both the lender and the borrower?**
   A. Lowers interest rate for borrower; Increases yield for lender
   B. Lowers closing cost for borrower; Increases yield to lender
   C. Raises closing cost for borrower; decreases yield to lender
   D. Raises interest rate for borrower; decreases yield to lender

8. **What is the definition of Loan to Value?**
   A. It represents the ratio between the loan amount and the sales price of the property
   B. It represents the ratio between the down payment, closing costs, and sales price of the property
   C. It represents the ratio between the loan amount and appraisal amount of the property
   D. It represents the amount the bank will loan based on the sales price or appraised amount of the property

9. **What is the benefit of a buy-down (discount points)?**
   A. The purchaser gets a higher interest rate
   B. The purchaser pays more closing costs
   C. The purchaser pays less closing costs
   D. The purchaser gets a lower interest rate

10. **Under the Truth in Lending Act, the law requires banks to disclose:**
    A. All fees that will be necessary to close the loan
    B. The annual percentage rate of the loan
    C. The right to rescind in all loan transactions
    D. The interest rate of the loan

11. **The purchaser of a home with the sales price of $500,000 is going to put $50,000 down on it and take a conventional loan for the difference. The purchaser will most likely have a monthly payment that will include:**
    A. Principal, Taxes, Insurance, Title Insurance
    B. Principal, Interest, Taxes, Title Insurance, and Mortgage Insurance
    C. Principal, Taxes, Mortgage Insurance
    D. Principal Interest, Taxes, Hazard Insurance, and Mortgage Insurance

12. **The federal government has raised the discount rate again resulting in higher mortgage loan rates. John is a borrower and still wishes to purchase a home. He is hoping for a lower payment for at least the first two years since he expects a huge raise on his job after his 2-year probationary period is over. What type of mortgage will John most likely benefit from?**
    A. Adjustable-rate mortgage
    B. Amortized mortgage
    C. Graduated payment mortgage
    D. Straight term mortgage

13. **The Equal Credit Opportunity Act (ECOA) provides that the banks must treat people fairly when lending. It essentially follows fair housing but adds additional categories. What categories are added to the Equal Credit Opportunity Act**
    A. Age, Marital Status, Color
    B. Sexual Preference, Public Assistance, Color
    C. Sexual Preference, Age, Marital Status
    D. Age, Marital Status, Public Assistance

14. **The cost of the title insurance policy would most likely be included on what two documents?**
    A. TILA statement and Good Faith Estimate
    B. TRID Loan Estimate and TRID Closing Disclosure
    C. Equal Credit Opportunity Statement and HUD-1
    D. HUD-1 and TILA statement

15. **The bank has issued a clear to close on Sally's home set for October 15th. The bank sent an appraiser to the home on September 15th and the home appraised for the full price. Sally, however, never paid the appraiser and has decided to simply pay the appraiser at the closing. Is this permissible?**
    A. No, although some parties can be paid at closing, an appraiser cannot
    B. Yes, as long as the appraiser performed a service and his fee is included on the settlement statement
    C. No, all parties must be paid prior to closing
    D. Yes, as long as the Appraiser agrees, the Truth in Lending Act allows it

16. **Sally is obtaining a loan from a lender. The stated interest rate on the loan is 5.5% and Sally is seeking to lower the interest rate to 5%. Sally should request:**
    A. That the lender allows her to pay more of a down payment to lower the interest rate
    B. That the lender allows her to pay points on a monthly basis to lower the interest rate
    C. That the lender allows her to pay points up front to lower the interest rate
    D. That the lender lowers the interest rate to 5%

17. **RESPA requires that all borrowers be informed of the potential settlement costs of the loan within __ days of application for the loan**
    A. 1
    B. 7
    C. 3
    D. no specified date requirement

18. **Private Mortgage Insurance would most likely be required in the following situation:**
    A. Borrower takes an FHA mortgage with a 3.5% down payment
    B. Borrower is purchasing a home where the appraisal exceeds the sale price
    C. Borrower takes a conventional loan with 10% down
    D. Borrower takes a VA loan with 0% down

19. **Negative Amortization can occur in a loan:**
    A. Where the bank requires the borrower to pay more than what is due on the loan
    B. Where the payment doesn't cover the amount of principal and interest due on the loan
    C. Where the interest on the loan fluctuates
    D. Where the borrower makes an additional payment on the loan

20. **Marylou took out an FHA home loan from Bank of America 6 years ago. She wants to now move and allow her daughter to take over her loan. Will she be able to do this?**
    A. As long as her daughter can qualify for the loan
    B. As long as the documents don't contain an alienation clause
    C. As long as the bank gives Marylou approval to transfer the loan
    D. As long as Marylou agrees to still be responsible for the debt

21. **Marlene is purchasing a $400,000 home with a 20% down payment. The home appraises for $420,000. The bank will:**
    A. Will Base the loan on the $400,000
    B. Will Base the loan on the $420,000
    C. Will Base the loan on the $80,000
    D. Will Base the loan on 20% of the sales price

22. **John and Elda are now in their 70s. They wish to take out a loan on the equity of their home to travel, but don't want to make any payments on the loan since they are on a fixed income. The best loan product for them would be:**
    A. Reverse Annuity Mortgage
    B. Blanket Mortgage
    C. Home Equity Line of Credit
    D. Home Equity Loan

23. **In states that use Deeds of Trust as security instruments, who in the transaction holds naked title?**
    A. Lender
    B. Beneficiary
    C. Trustee
    D. Trustor

24. **Fannie Mae and Freddie Mac are agencies included in the secondary mortgage market. The purpose of this market is to:**
    A. Provide stability to the primary market
    B. Purchase loans from mortgagors
    C. Protect borrowers from predatory lending practices
    D. Provide liquidity to mortgage holders

25. **Conventional Loans are:**
    A. Insured by the bank
    B. A different loan product depending on bank
    C. Require that the borrower put 20% down
    D. Are never insured

26. **Bank A had a loan and 1st lien on a property that was occupied by a tenant. The homeowner then wanted to take a larger, second loan on the property. The second bank agrees to give the loan, but is insistent that the tenant sign a document containing a:**
    A. Non-Disturbance Clause
    B. Subordination Clause
    C. Occupancy Agreement
    D. Receiver Clause

27. **All of the following are the primary reasons why someone would be placed in an FHA product rather than a conventional product except**
    A. Lower Down Payment
    B. Lower Credit Score
    C. Lower Debt to Income Ratio
    D. Higher Debt to Income Ratio

28. **A veteran wants to apply for a VA loan. The veteran has no down payment and wants to purchase a property for $500,000. The veteran has a guarantee from the US government for $100,000. Will the bank be allowed to loan the $500,000 to the veteran**
    A. Yes, because he qualifies for a VA loan of $500,000
    B. No, but it can loan him the $100,000 that the government will guarantee
    C. No, because he doesn't have any down payment to obtain the VA loan
    D. Yes, if the bank determines that he qualifies for $500,000

29. **A veteran is attempting to move out of the area where he has a VA loan. He is considering allowing a non-veteran to take the loan over, but is concerned about whether it would be possible and whether he would continue to have liability. Which is true?**
    A. The veteran can allow a non-veteran to take over his loan and he won't have liability any longer
    B. The veteran cannot allow a non-veteran to take over his loan, but he wouldn't have liability if he could
    C. The veteran can allow a non-veteran to take over his loan, but he would still have liability
    D. The veteran cannot allow a non-veteran to take over his loan, but, if he could, he would still have liability

30. **A security deed is:**
    A. The mortgagee's security for the debt
    B. The mortgagor's security for the debt
    C. The promise to pay the debt
    D. Evidence of the debt

31. **A loan product where principal and interest is paid on a monthly basis with a balloon payment paid at maturity is most likely:**
    A. A Fully Amortized Loan
    B. A Partially Amortized Loan
    C. An Adjustable-Rate loan
    D. Any Amortized Loan

32. **A lender will usually qualify a borrower for a loan using:**
    A. The house debt and all other borrower debt
    B. Only the house debt
    C. The house debt and only Student Loan Debt
    D. The house debt, including closing costs and all other borrower debt

33. **A homeowner has a home loan on his property that he is unable to pay. He also cannot sell the property since he owes more to the bank than the property is currently worth. He contacts the bank. His best course of action would be to:**
    A. Allow the property to go into foreclosure
    B. File bankruptcy
    C. Request the bank approve a short sale
    D. Request that the bank allow a deed in lieu of foreclosure

34. **A borrower is seeking to obtain a loan to purchase a property. The borrower has limited credit and only a small down payment. It is most likely that the borrower will receive:**
    A. An FHA guaranteed loan from the government
    B. An FHA insured loan from the local bank
    C. A conventional loan with PMI attached to it
    D. A VA guaranteed loan from the government

35. **A borrower is seeking a loan for a house with a sales price of $550,000. He has already gone to the bank and submitted his W-2, bank statements, and credit report and is told to go and look for a house. The banking process proceeds in what order:**
    A. Pre-approval, Loan Estimate, Appraisal, Financing Approval, Closing
    B. Pre-approval, Loan Estimate, Financing Approval, Appraisal, Closing
    C. Loan Estimate, Pre-approval, Appraisal, Financing Approval, Closing
    D. Loan Estimate, Appraisal, Pre-approval, Financing Approval, Closing

36. **You are representing a buyer who is purchasing and financing 19 acres of undeveloped land. He plans to subdivide the land into smaller building lots, selling them one at a time after financing and constructing new builds on each parcel. What clause would the buyer ask the first bank to include in the mortgage?**
    A. A subordination clause
    B. A due on sale clause
    C. An exculpatory clause
    D. A habendum clause

37. **Which of the following is true about prepayment penalties on VA or FHA loans for single-family dwellings?**
    A. The VA requires a prepayment penalty of 2% of the outstanding loan balance
    B. The FHA requires a prepayment penalty of 2% of the original principal amount
    C. Both the VA and the FHA require prepayment penalties of 3% of the outstanding loan balance
    D. Neither the VA nor the FHA allows prepayment penalties

38. **Which of the following factors tends to increase the price of residential real estate in a given area?**
    A. A zoning change allowing a group home to be constructed in a subdivision
    B. A large manufacturing plant opening in the city
    C. Higher interest rates on home loans
    D. An overabundance of homes in a preferred area

39. **Which of the following are typical of FHA loans?**
    A. They are insured and incorporate a balloon payment
    B. They are insured and are fully amortized
    C. They are insured and are partially amortized
    D. None of the above

40. **When a mortgagor buys a discount point what effect does a loan discount point have for him/her?**
    A. It increases the monthly payment of the borrower
    B. It increases the cost of the loan on the secondary market
    C. It decreases the interest rate
    D. It decreases the closing costs

41. **When a borrower defaults on a mortgage, an acceleration clause allows the lender the option of**
    A. Attaching the borrower's personal property
    B. Demanding immediate payment of the entire loan balance
    C. Reporting the borrower to both the FHA and the VA
    D. Preventing conveyance of the mortgaged property

42. **Which of the following is generally income tax-deductible when owning a home?**
    A. Down payment on the property
    B. Major home improvements
    C. Points paid to obtain the loan
    D. Maintenance on the property

Chapter 9 Answers

1. A	10. C	19. B	28. D	37. A	46. C	55. B	64. C	73. A
2. A	11. D	20. A	29. B	38. A	47. B	56. A	65. B	74. B
3. D	12. B	21. D	30. C	39. A	48. C	57. D	66. B	75. C
4. A	13. C	22. D	31. A	40. D	49. B	58. D	67. D	76. C
5. A	14. C	23. B	32. B	41. D	50. D	59. B	68. D	77. B
6. B	15. B	24. D	33. B	42. C	51. C	60. B	69. B	78. C
7. D	16. C	25. D	34. D	43. A	52. B	61. D	70. A	
8. B	17. B	26. C	35. D	44. B	53. C	62. C	71. C	
9. B	18. D	27. D	36. C	45. D	54. D	63. B	72. D	

1. Partial Release Clause
2. Subject to
3. Discount Rate
4. Freddie Mac
5. VA loan
6. Hypothecation
7. Lien Theory
8. Qualifying Ratios
9. Interest
10. Real Estate Settlement Procedures Act (RESPA)
11. Equity of Redemption
12. Subprime Loans
13. Private Mortgage Insurance
14. Deed in Lieu of Foreclosure
15. Prepayment Clause
16. Foreclosure
17. Negative Amortization
18. Reverse Annuity Mortgage
19. Mortgage Satisfaction
20. Security Deed
21. Graduation Payment Mortgage
22. Federal Equal Credit Opportunity Act
23. Certificate of Reasonable Value
24. Loan to Value
25. Equitable Title
26. Discount Points
27. Receiver Clause
28. HUD-1 Settlement Statement
29. Judicial Foreclosure
30. Purchase Money Mortgage
31. Promissory Note
32. Primary Mortgage Market
33. Power of Sale Clause
34. Kickback
35. Junior Mortgage
36. Statutory Right of Redemption
37. Land Contract (Contract for Deed, Installment Sale Agreement)
38. Impounds
39. Defeasance
40. Trust Deed
41. Good Faith Estimate
42. Blanket Mortgage
43. Fannie Mae (FNMA)
44. Escalation Clause
45. Second Mortgage Market
46. Alienation (Due on Sale) Clause
47. Certificate of Eligibility
48. Truth in Lending Act
49. Seller Concession/Contribution
50. Mortgage Insurance Premium (MIP)
51. Reconveyance Deed
52. Mortgage
53. Acceleration Clause
54. Assumption
55. Ginnie-Mae (GNMA)
56. Negotiable Instrument
57. Package Mortgage
58. Regulation Z
59. Conventional Loan
60. Annual Percentage Rate
61. Deficiency Judgment
62. Balloon Payment
63. Interest Only Loan
64. Mortgage Guaranty Insurance Company (MGIC)
65. Naked Title
66. Budget Mortgage
67. Construction Loan
68. Equity
69. Adjustable-Rate Mortgage
70. Straight Loan
71. Title Theory State
72. Security Instrument
73. FHA loan
74. Subordination Clause
75. Exculpatory Clause
76. Conditional Commitment
77. Amortized Loan
78. Lis Pendens

Exercise 1

1. N	4. E	7. M	10. J	13. A	16. D
2. O	5. H	8. P	11. B	14. K	
3. C	6. L	9. F	12. I	15. G	

Exercise 2

1. I	4. L	7. J	10. C	13. H	16. A
2. F	5. B	8. E	11. O	14. N	
3. D	6. P	9. M	12. G	15. K	

Exercise 3

1. O	3. J	5. F	7. H	9. C	11. M	13. N	15. G
2. D	4. B	6. E	8. K	10. L	12. I	14. A	

Exercise 4

1. L	3. A	5. N	7. O	9. D	11. G	13. E	15. K
2. C	4. H	6. I	8. B	10. F	12. J	14. M	

Exercise 5

1. M	3. K	5. H	7. B	9. A	11. D	13. C	15. G
2. E	4. L	6. N	8. F	10. J	12. P	14. O	16. I

SECTION 6 ANSWERS:

1. The true interest rate required under TILA; it includes the simple interest rate, plus all other costs of the loan expressed as interest

2. In a security instrument (security deed). It indicates that the bank must convey title and cancel the borrower's debt once the loan has been repaid

3. Lien Theory States

4. A Lis Pendens was filed, and a foreclosure sale occurred

5. Allows the lender to conduct a non-judicial foreclosure against the defaulting borrower

6. Because without it, the defaulting borrower would only have to pay the amount he owes, not the entire loan

7. Both the lender – increases the yield and the borrower – lowers the interest rate over the loan

8. The interest rate that the Federal Reserve Bank charges to its member banks to borrow money

9. The deed is given back to the lender by the defaulting borrower to avoid a foreclosure

10. Because a Fully Amortized loan doesn't require a balloon payment

11. The bank, generally to give constructive notice that an action (generally a foreclosure) has been filed against the property

12. Graduated Payment Mortgage

13. Land Contract or a Purchase in a title theory state

14. Adjustable-Rate Mortgage

15. A loan in which only interest is paid during the term of the loan, leaving the entire principal balance to be paid in a balloon payment at the end of the term

16. Judicial - Court action granting the lender permission to sell a borrower's property at a public sale; Non-Judicial – no Court necessary as long as a Power of Sale clause is present

17. Because the title was never transferred to the borrower, so it allows a more expedited process

18. A loan where the lender requires that in addition to the monthly principal and interest payments, the borrower also pay 1/12 of the property taxes, and hazard insurance each month

19. Equitable Right of Redemption

20. Interest Only converts to an amortized loan but a straight term loan has a balloon

21. A loan given by the seller to the buyer to cover all or part of the purchase price of the property, but title is conveyed immediately, rather than after payment in full is made

22. A provision in a loan document requiring full payment of the debt upon any transfer of title to the property to another

23. Title held by the trustee in a trust deed situation

24. Trust Deed, Security Deed, Mortgage

25. Allows borrowers (aged 62 and older) to take a loan against the equity in their home

26. A written and signed promise to pay a sum of money at a specified time and according to a specified schedule

27. Negotiable Instruments

28. No, only a security instrument can do that

29. Adjustable-Rate Mortgage (ARM)

30. Balloon Payment

31. Prepayment Clause

32. A loan provision that, in the event of foreclosure, the bank will forgive any debt in excess of the collateral

33. Blanket Mortgage Loan

34. Both real and personal property provide the security for the loan

35. Calculations that are used in determining whether a borrower can qualify for a bank loan

36. Subordination Clause

37. CRV is used by the VA; Conditional Commitment is used by FHA. Both are appraisals

38. An agreement to take over and be responsible for another's loan

39. Both are Mortgage Insurance that protects the lender in case of default, but PMI is for conventional lenders and MIP is for FHA

40. Veterans or Un-remarried Spouses of Veterans, No Max Loan Amount, Maximum Guarantee Amount, No Prepayment Penalty or Alienation Clauses, no mortgage insurance; Guaranteed by the VA; zero down payment

41. Lower Credit Score, Higher Debt to Income, Lower Down Payment, Max Loan Amount, No Prepayment Penalty or Alienation Clause, Mortgage Insurance Premiums, 3.5% down payment, Insured by FHA

42. A private sector loan which differs depending upon bank and product

43. Secondary Mortgage Market

44. Fannie Mae (FNMA), Freddie Mac (FHLMC), Ginnie Mae (GNMA), MGIC

45. Prohibits discrimination against borrowers based-on race, color, religion, sex, national origin, religion, marital status, age, or the receipt of public assistance

46. RESPA requires a GFE to be provided within three days of loan application

47. The percentage amount that the lender will provide to the borrower for the purchase of a home

48. At least 1 day prior to closing

49. The buyer assumes liability in an assumption and the original purchaser moves to secondary liability, but in a subject to, the buyer does not agree to assume responsibility for the payments and liability remains with the original purchaser

50. A state where the lender secures property by taking title to it until the debt is repaid; the lender has legal title, and the borrower has equitable title vs. A state where the lender secures property by allowing the borrower to retain title to the property, but that title is encumbered by a lien placed on it until the debt is repaid

51. The mortgage market where lenders originate loans being made directly to the consumer. The secondary market is where mortgagees sell loans to re-infuse the market with money

52. As a result of a foreclosure action where the borrower still owes money

53. Blanket mortgage obligates the lender to release each parcel held as security upon payment of a specified sum

54. The Truth in Lending Act

Section 7 Answers:

1. B. An alienation clause would prevent anyone from taking over the bank loan

2. C. The parties arrangement is called a subject to loan assumption. In a subject to arrangement, Sue will never be responsible to Wells Fargo for the debt and Yolanda will remain responsible to Wells Fargo for the duration of the loan

3. D. The mortgagor is also known as the borrower in a loan transaction

4. A. The effect of higher discount rates would be higher interest rates to the consumer which will lower the prices and slow the market. If the rates go down, the market speeds up because the interest rates are lower and people have more buying power

5. B. The practice is called predatory lending and it is more common in areas where people may not be as educated relating to the loan process and have lesser credit than other borrowers

6. B. Both are seller financing, but in a land contract, title is not transferred to the borrower until all payments are made. With a purchase money mortgage, title is transferred immediately at closing and seller puts a lien on the property

7. A. When a borrower pays points, he is gaining a lower interest rate over the life of the loan. In exchange, the lender is increasing the yield (amount of money) it makes at closing

8. D. The loan to value is the amount the bank will provide to the lender based upon the sales price or the appraised amount of the property, whichever is lower

9. D. A buy-down is the same as paying points. The purchaser benefits by ensuring a lower interest rate over the life of the loan

10. B. The Truth in Lending Act requires that the annual percentage rate of the loan is disclosed to the borrower within 3 days of application. It does not require the interest rate on the loan because that number does not include all of the fees that are incurred as part of acquiring the loan

11. D. A home purchased with a 90% conventional loan will most like include a monthly payment of PITI and Mortgage Insurance. Title Insurance is paid one-time at the beginning of the loan

12. A. The best loan for John would be an adjustable-rate mortgage where his payments would be lower at the beginning of the loan. Adjustable-rate mortgages always start with a lower interest rate which will make his payments lower. It will adjust at the next adjustment period, but John will be making more money at that time

13. D. The ECOA added age, marital status, and the receipt of public assistance. The lender must not discriminate against these additional classes when writing a loan product

14. B. The most likely documents would be the TRID given at the beginning of the loan process and the TRID given at the end. These will contain all that is necessary to close including the cost of the title policy. This cost would not be included on a TILA statement. It would be included on a HUD-1. There is also no such item as an Equal Credit Opportunity statement

15. B. Under RESPA, as long as the party performed a service and it is included on the settlement statement, he can be paid at the closing

16. C. Points are paid one-time up front at closing to the lender in exchange for a lower interest rate over the life of the loan

17. C. RESPA requires that all borrowers receive a good faith estimate of closing costs (contained in TRID loan estimate) within 3 days of the initial loan application

18. C. The term Private Mortgage Insurance is only used in the case of a conventional loan. With FHA, we use Mortgage Insurance Premium and there is no insurance in a VA loan as the VA is a guarantor

19. B. Negative Amortization occurs when the required payment is not paid in full. Over time, this will result in the loan balance increasing rather than decreasing as is in the case of a regular amortization schedule

20. A. The only requirement here would be that the daughter qualify for the loan because all FHA loans are assumable. The documents cannot contain an alienation clause and the bank doesn't have to give Marylou approval to transfer. The daughter simply needs to be able to qualify

21. A. The bank will always base the loan on the sales price or appraisal amount of the home whichever is lower

22. A. A loan product made especially for the elderly. The bank will provide them with a loan off the home's equity and the loan will not be repaid until the last of either John or Elda pass

23. C. Naked Title is a term used to describe the type of title held by the Trustee during the term of the Trust

24. D. The secondary mortgage market exists to re infuse the primary market with money so that it will have additional funds to lend

25. B. Conventional loans differ depending on which bank issues it. The bank is not an insurer of these loans but instead go through an insurance company. Further, the down payment is dependent upon the loan

26. B. The second bank would require that the tenant who is in possession at the time of the loan subordinate to it so that the tenant no longer has priority over the bank. A subordination clause changes the order of priority between the parties

27. C. The FHA borrower is allowed a higher debt to income ratio. These factors are of course independent of the others, but for the most part, an FHA borrower would have more debt than a conventional borrower or at least it is allowed as part of the criteria

28. D. The VA doesn't place any limitations on the amount of loan the veteran can receive, but it will limit its exposure to the guaranteed amount of $100,000. If the bank determines that he qualifies for $500,000, the bank is entitled to loan him that amount

29. C. All VA loans are assumable, even by non-veterans, but the veteran would still have liability for the debt

30. A. The security deed provides the lender (mortgagee) with security that it can repossess the property should the borrower (mortgagor) not pay. The promise to pay and evidence of the debt would be contained in a promissory note

31. B. The loan is most likely partially amortized. This loan allows for the payment of principal and interest for some period of time, but at maturity, there is still a loan balance. That balance must be paid in one payment known as a balloon

32. A. The bank is most concerned with, after the closing, can the borrower pay for the home. Therefore, all house debt and the borrower's other debt is considered

33. C. The borrower's best course of action would be to request a short sale approval. This way, the borrower can negotiate a price with the new purchaser and perhaps with the lender. The lender wouldn't consider a deed in lieu in this circumstance because it would have to take the property back with all of the other liens on it. Allowance of foreclosure wouldn't be the best action for the borrower because he wouldn't be able to negotiate

34. B. The person will most likely be put into an FHA loan product given the lower down payment and lesser credit. Those loans are insured by FHA but administered by a local bank

35. A. Pre-approval (good candidate), Loan Estimate (within 3 days of application for a specific home), Appraisal, Financing Approval (clear to close), Closing

36. A. The buyer would ask for a subordination clause because he knows that the bank financing the new builds would require the clause before funding the loan

37. D. Prepayment penalties are not allowed in either VA or FHA loans

38. B. Prices tend to increase when demand increases. A large manufacturing plant will bring new workers into the area who will be searching for housing. The zoning change, higher interest rates, and an overabundance of home will all drive prices down

39. B. The Federal Housing Administration is the government organization that ensures FHA loans that have been given by the bank to FHA borrowers. These loans are government regulated and are fully amortized, typically over 30 years

40. C. A mortgagor (borrower) pays discount points one-time at the beginning of the loan in exchange for a lower interest rate over the life of the loan. Lower interest rate means a lower monthly payment and if anything, it would increase the closing costs

41. B. Demand the entire payment due in order to sue the person for foreclosure. Absent an acceleration clause, the bank would only be able to sue the person for the late payment, not the entire loan

42. C. Because interest payments are tax deductible and points are simply considered to be pre-paid interest, it is also tax deductible

Chapter 10: Property Disclosures

Section 1: *Outline*

Liability, Insurance, Disclosures – Property Protection and What must be disclosed

A. Liability – The same as finding one responsible

1. **Strict** – Liable regardless of fault or whether you intended to violate the law
2. **Primary vs Secondary** – Liability attaches to one party first and only attaches to the second party if the first doesn't perform
3. **Joint and Several** – All parties are liable at the same time, and each are liable 100%
4. **Vicarious** – Liability attaches because of the actions of another person

B. Insurance – Protection for unexpected items

1. **Hazard (Property)** – wind, water, theft, burglary, slip and fall, injury
2. **Title** – clouds that arise from something that happened in the past
3. **Mortgage** – protects the lender if the borrower does not pay the mortgage
4. **Flood** – protection for properties located in designated flood zones
5. **Errors and Omissions** – protects against errors made in one's profession
6. **General Liability** – protects against injuries on the premises or damages caused to another's property
7. **Home Warranty** – covers the cost of repairs or replacement of certain items that break within the home

C. Disclosures

1. **Lead Based Paint** – properties built before 1978, 10-day right to inspection, can be waived, no duty to abate the lead
2. **Latent Defects** – hidden; must be disclosed to 3rd parties
3. **Asbestos*** – used as an insulator and in building materials, check state laws
4. **Radon*** – radioactive gas that seeps through the foundation, check state laws
5. **Mold*** – occurs in high moisture areas, check state laws
6. **Property*** – seller provides and attaches to the contract pertinent information about the home
7. **Material Facts*** – those facts that a person would want to know, but cannot easily discover, check state laws

Section 2: *Vocabulary*

Asbestos: Minerals that are resistant to heat corrosion and have been used in insulation for pipes, floor tiles, and building materials

Flood Insurance: A policy that compensates for physical property damage resulting from flooding

Home Warranty Insurance: A policy issued to buyers of existing homes which covers mechanical breakdown of certain items

Homeowner's (or Hazard) Insurance: A policy that covers loss for burglary, water, fire, and liability

Latent Defect: A defect that cannot be easily discovered by ordinary inspection

Lead-Based Paint Hazard Reduction Act: A required to all purchasers of homes built prior to 1978

Material Fact: A significant fact, the knowledge of which, could change the outcome of the contract

Mold: A type of fungus that thrives in moist areas of a home

Patent Defect: A defect that can be easily discovered by ordinary inspection

Radon: A radioactive gas, that enters through the foundation of a home

Property Inspection: An examination of the physical condition of real property

Survey: A drawing of property that details the lot location, boundary lines, and other structures

Section 3: *Recall Multiple Choice*

1. **A disclosure must be provided to all purchasers on homes built prior to 1978**
   A. Lead-Based Paint Hazard Reduction Act
   B. Sherman Anti-Trust Act
   C. Clean Air Act
   D. Fair Housing Act

2. **Insurance that compensates for physical property damage resulting from flooding**
   A. Policy
   B. Lead-Based Paint Hazard Reduction Act
   C. Flood Insurance
   D. Title Insurance

3. **A defect that cannot easily be discovered by ordinary inspection**
   A. Procuring Cause
   B. Latent Defect
   C. Gradual Deterioration
   D. Material Fact

4. **A defect that can be easily discovered by ordinary inspection**
   A. Primary Liability
   B. Material Fact
   C. Patent Defect
   D. Strict Liability

5. **A radioactive gas, that enters through the foundation and that can cause lung cancer**
   A. Mold
   B. Radon
   C. Lead
   D. Asbestos

6. **A policy for buyers of existing homes which covers against breakage of certain items in the home**
   A. Flood Insurance
   B. General Liability Insurance
   C. Home Warranty Insurance
   D. Mortgage Insurance

7. **A type of fungus that thrives in moist areas of a home that could be a health hazard**
   A. Radon
   B. Asbestos
   C. Restore
   D. Mold

8. **Minerals that are resistant to heat corrosion and have been used in insulation for pipes, floor tiles, and building materials**
   A. Asbestos
   B. Mold
   C. Radon
   D. Lead

9. **An insurance policy that covers burglary, water fire, and liability**
   A. Homeowner's (or Hazard) Insurance
   B. Mortgage insurance
   C. Flood insurance
   D. General liability insurance

10. **An examination of the condition of real property**
   A. Agent's Diligent Visual Inspection
   B. Primary Liability
   C. Property Inspection
   D. Title Insurance

11. **A drawing of property that details the lot location, property lines, and other structures**
   A. Survey
   B. Questionnaire
   C. Sample
   D. Interview

12. **A significant fact, the knowledge of which, could change the outcome**
   A. Insurable Interest
   B. Material Fact
   C. Morale Hazard
   D. Primary Liability

Section 4: *Recall Fill-In*

1. A drawing of property that details the lot location, property lines, and other structures

_____

2. A radioactive gas, that enters through the foundation and that can cause lung cancer

_____

3. A significant fact, the knowledge of which, could change the outcome

_____

4. A defect that can be easily discovered by ordinary inspection

_____

5. A disclosure must be provided to all purchasers on homes built prior to 1978

_____

6. A defect that cannot easily be discovered by ordinary inspection

_____

7. An examination of the condition of real property

_____

8. Minerals that are resistant to heat corrosion and have been used in insulation for pipes, floor tiles, and building materials

_____

9. Insurance that compensates for physical property damage resulting from flooding

_____

10. A type of fungus that thrives in moist areas of a home that could be a health hazard

_____

11. An insurance policy that covers burglary, water fire, and liability

_____

12. A policy for buyers of existing homes which covers certain items in the home

_____

Section 5: *Matching*

A   Mold

1 _____   A defect that can be easily discovered by ordinary inspection

B   Flood Insurance

2 _____   A defect that cannot easily be discovered by ordinary inspection.

C   Lead Based Paint Reduction Act

3 _____   A disclosure must be provided to all purchasers on homes built prior to 1978.

D   Home Warranty Insurance

4 _____   A drawing of property that details the lot location, property lines, and other structures.

E   Patent Defect

5 _____   A policy for buyers of existing homes which covers certain items in the home

F   Material Fact

6 _____   A radioactive gas, that enters through the foundation and that can cause lung cancer.

G   Radon

7 _____   A significant fact, the knowledge of which, could change the outcome.

H   Latent Defect

8 _____   A type of fungus that thrives in moist areas of a home that could be a health hazard.

I   Property Inspection

9 _____   An examination of the condition of real property

J   Homeowners (Hazard) Insurance

10 _____   An insurance policy that covers burglary, water fire, and liability.

K   Survey

11 _____   Insurance that compensates for physical property damage resulting from flooding.

L   Asbestos

12 _____   Minerals that are resistant to heat corrosion used in insulation for pipes, floor tiles, and roofing

Section 6: *Analysis Fill-In*

1. A seller knows his home has Lead Based Paint because he had it tested 3 years ago. He is now selling. What are his obligations?

_____

2. A property is determined to have Lead Based Paint. What are the purchaser's options?

_____

3. What would be the best way to determine if there is an encroachment on a property?

_____

4. A purchaser is unhappy with the property inspection results. What are his choices?

_____

5. When does the property inspection most likely occur?

_____

6. When must a property be covered by flood insurance?

_____

7. Give one example of an item that a Homeowner's Warranty policy would cover?

_____

8. Name two hazards that Homeowner's (Hazard) insurance would most likely cover?

_____

9. Where would Radon most likely enter the home?

_____

10. You are representing a client on a transaction. Who would you have to disclose a patent defect to?

_____

11. You are representing a client on a transaction. Who would you have to disclose a latent defect to?

_____

12. Give one location where asbestos was used in a home?

_____

13. In which room(s) would mold most likely be found?

_____

14. When does a material fact have to be disclosed to a third party in most situations?

_____

15. What is the difference between a Latent and a Patent Defect?

_____

16. What is the difference between Homeowner's Insurance and a Home Warranty policy?

_____

17. Who, in the transaction, would you most likely have to disclose a material fact that can be discovered to?

_____

18. Who, in the transaction, would you most likely have to disclose a material fact that cannot be discovered to?

_____

Section 7: *Analysis Multiple Choice*

1. **Jackson is the listing agent on a home where he knows the current zoning is being changed to a less desirable use for prospective purchasers. Does Jackson have a duty to disclose what he knows about the zoning?**
   A. No, because all prospective purchasers are in a caveat emptor position and must find this information out themselves
   B. Only if the prospective purchaser is represented by another agent
   C. Yes, he must disclose this information because it is considered material
   D. No, and his failure to disclosure would not be considered misrepresentation

2. **You are selling a property where the zoning law has changed in the area and you are aware that a new school is being built across from the property you are selling. It has already been determined that the increased congestion will lower the property value by $30,000, but the seller doesn't want this information disclosed and specifically tells you not to do so. Should you disclose the information?**
   A. Yes, the information is material and must be disclosed
   B. No, the seller told you not to disclose and you have an obedience duty
   C. No, because failure to discuss zoning is simply misrepresentation
   D. Yes, you should disclose it because all property value changes must be disclosed

3. **A licensee was completing a listing with a seller as the seller's agent. When they were walking through the property together, the licensee noticed that new paneling had been installed in the basement. When asked, the seller told the licensee that there had been a leak in the basement wall, but the crack had been patched and the paneling installed. Therefore, the seller said it need not be discussed with a buyer. In this case, which of the following is most appropriate?**
   A. As an agent of the seller, the licensee should follow the seller's instructions and not disclose any defects
   B. Tell the buyer the basement had leaked but had been successfully repaired and was no longer a problem
   C. Tell the buyer the basement had leaked and there had been some repair work done, but the buyer is entitled to an inspection of the basement
   D. Since the licensee works for the seller, he cannot discuss with the buyer potential problems in the property

4. **A licensee was showing a buyer an older home built in 1976. The buyer was concerned about the possibility of lead-based paint having been used on the house even though the house had been recently painted. The licensee should tell the buyer:**
   A. That there is no law regulating this, but the buyer could require an inspection
   B. That the Residential Lead-Based Paint Reduction Act requires disclosure by the seller on houses built before 1978, and the buyer could require an inspection
   C. A lead-based paint disclosure is required on all houses built after 1978, but the buyer is entitled to an inspection if he chooses to have one
   D. That lead-based paint is no longer problematic as long as it has been painted over

5. **A managing broker requires his licensees to mention a particular lender to buyers. The broker has a financial interest in this particular mortgage lender. Which of the following should the licensee recommend to buyers?**
   A. Use this lender for the best rates
   B. Seek advice from an accountant before selecting a lender
   C. Contact other lenders in the area before contacting this lender
   D. Consider this lender, disclosing the broker's interest, and other lenders

6. **Able is a listing agent on a property. He informs his seller that a property disclosure form will be required for the listing. The seller fills out the form but does not want to mention a leak in the roof because it has already been repaired by a certified contractor. Able should advise the seller:**
   A. That he doesn't have to disclose that there was alien since it was repaired by a certified contractor
   B. That regardless of it being repaired, the seller must disclose the leak
   C. That the seller doesn't have to disclose the leak because it wasn't a material item
   D. That the seller, while not required to disclose a leak that has been repaired, should disclose it from an ethical standpoint

7. **Jill is the purchaser of a home. She has a 5 year old son. The home was built in 1970 and Jill decides that she does not wish to obtain a lead based paint inspection despite the disclosure that informs her that the house was built prior to 1978 and that she has 10 days to inspect. Is she permitted to waive this right?**
   A. No, Lead Based Paint is a federal law that requires an inspection if the home is built prior to 1978
   B. Yes, a Lead Based Paint inspection is an option given to the purchaser but the right can be waived
   C. No, in this case, Jill would have to inspect the property because she has a child under the age of 6
   D. Yes, because there were no reports given to her indicating that the home definitely has lead

8. **Tom, a buyer's agent, is showing a home to his client. Tom would have to disclose all of the following to his client except?**
   A. The school district just changed
   B. The air-conditioning unit is new
   C. The seller is moving out of state
   D. The seller is going bankrupt

9. **A home warranty will cover all of the following except:**
   A. Title defects of the seller
   B. Leaky roof in the home
   C. An in-ground swimming pool pump
   D. The washer and dryer left in the home by the seller

10. **A purchaser has decided to waive property inspection, but one day before closing, it is discovered that the property was built in 1970 and no lead-based paint disclosure was ever made to the purchaser. What is the probable outcome?**
    A. The purchaser will not be able to get out of the contract because he waived the right to inspect the property
    B. The purchaser will not be able to get out of the contract because this issue should have been raised by the purchaser sooner
    C. The purchaser can walk away because he cannot waive his right to inspect for lead
    D. The purchaser can walk away because he did not also waive the right to inspect for lead

11. **Jaleesa is the selling agent on a home where it is commonly known that a murder took place 10 years ago. Should the selling agent disclose the information her buyer?**
    A. Yes, because it is material and must be disclosed to her principal
    B. No, because since it is commonly known, there's no reason to disclose it
    C. No, unless the purchaser doesn't know about the murder
    D. Yes, since it is less than 12 years since the murder took place

12. Janice, a listing agent for a seller, Misty, who tells Janice that there was a flood in his basement two years ago due to a broken sump pump. Misty assures Janice that the repair was made and doesn't want Janice to mention it to any prospective purchasers? Because Janice wants to be obedient to her seller, she decides not to mention it. Two months after the sale, Janice is sued. Should Janice have revealed the leak?
    A. No, because she must always stay obedient to her principal
    B. No, because she must always stay loyal to her principal
    C. Yes, but only if she felt the seller was being less than truthful
    D. Yes, because although she must remain obedient to her principal, material facts must be disclosed

13. Julian purchased a new home from ABC Builders in 2021. After moving into the home in December 2021, Julian discovered that there are a couple of cracks in the basement foundation. It is now November 2022, Julian did not request that the builder provide a home warranty and since the property was new, he didn't get a home inspection. Julian immediately calls the builder and is told that:
    A. The builder will not cover the problem since Julian didn't have a home warranty
    B. Most likely, the builder will cover the problem since the cracks were found within a reasonable time
    C. Julian should sue the agent for negligence
    D. Julian's failure to inspect the property effectively waived his right to claim under any warranty

14. Melissa is representing a purchaser who just had a $500 inspection done on a property she is purchasing. Melissa put $5,000 earnest money down and the contract contained an inspection contingency. Several items were noted on the report totaling in excess of $10,000. The purchaser can do all of the following except:
    A. Ask the seller to pay for all of the repairs
    B. Ask the seller to pay for some of the repairs
    C. Inform the seller that she doesn't intend on closing and wishes her earnest money back
    D. Inform the seller that she would like to be reimbursed for the cost of the inspection

15. The purchaser performs an inspection on the home you have listed. The inspection reveals that several items need repair. There is an inspection contingency in the contract. The purchaser has the following options except:
    A. Ask the seller to repair the items
    B. Use his right to rescind to get out of the contract
    C. Ask the seller to provide a credit at closing for the items
    D. Have the home warranty company repair the items after closing

16. Which of the following would not have to be disclosed to a potential purchaser?
    A. A leaky roof which shows stains in the ceiling
    B. An underground leaky septic tank
    C. Structural damage under the deck of the property
    D. A recent flood in the property but that has been corrected

17. You are selling a property and there is a concern about black spores in the bathroom around the toilet. A property inspection is conducted and a problem is revealed. The inspector most likely found:
    A. Mold
    B. Asbestos
    C. Radon
    D. Rodents

18. You are representing a seller on a home where you overheard that the buyer, represented by another agent, loves the home and would pay $50,000 over asking price for it. Your seller receives several offers on the home. Should you reveal the information you overheard to your seller?
    A. No, it would be a violation of the law of agency to disclose the information
    B. No, it would be an unethical act under the license law to reveal the information
    C. Yes, because you are obligated to keep the principal informed of relevant matters in a transaction
    D. Yes, because your job is to get the seller the highest amount for his home and your information will guarantee that

19. Which of the following would most likely have to be disclosed to a prospective purchaser?

   A. The driveway is shared between neighbors
   B. The property is on 2 acres
   C. The property has a 2-car garage
   D. The property is in the Secret Heart school district

20. The purchaser of a home is requesting that the seller provide the purchaser with a home warranty at closing. If the seller agrees, the purchaser will be protected if there are:

   A. Title Claims against the property
   B. Mechanical Problems with the HVAC
   C. Tree Damage from a Storm
   D. A neighbor falling on the lawn

Chapter 10 Answers

1. A	3. B	5. B	7. D	9. A	11. A
2. C	4. C	6. C	8. A	10. C	12. B

1. Survey	5. Lead Based Paint Disclosure	9. Flood Insurance
2. Radon	6. Latent Defect	10. Mold
3. Material Fact	7. Property Inspection	11. Hazard/Homeowner's Insurance
4. Patent Defect	8. Asbestos	12. Home Warranty

Exercise 1

1. E	3. C	5. D	7. F	9. I	11. B
2. H	4. K	6. G	8. A	10. J	12. L

1. He must provide a disclosure but also provide the purchaser with a copy of the report

2. Rescind the contract or negotiate with the seller to see if an arrangement can be made or move forward with the closing

3. Have a survey performed

4. Rescind the contract or negotiate with the seller (as long as there is a contingency) to see if an arrangement can be made or move forward with the closing

5. At the beginning of the contract during due diligence

6. Properties located in flood zone that have a bank loan

7. Swimming Pool, HVAC system, Roof, Appliances

8. Burglary, Fire, Theft, Water Damage (broken pipe)

9. Foundation

10. Principal (client)

11. Principal (client), Third Party (customer)

12. Roof, Flooring, Heating System

13. Moist areas – Bathroom, Kitchen

14. When it cannot be discovered by the third party

15. Latent – cannot be discovered; Patent – can be discovered

16. Homeowner's covers hazards such as burglary and fire. Home Warranty covers items that require repair such as electrical, plumbing

17. Principal (client)

18. Principal (client), Third Party (customer)

1. C. Agents must disclose information to prospective purchasers if it is material to the transaction. A known zoning change would be information that the prospective purchaser would want to know in making his decision

2. A. You must disclose this information regardless of what the seller is telling you to do. The law requires disclosure of material information to purchasers. You are aware of the information and aware that it will decrease the value of the property so it must be disclosed

3. C. Even though there is a requirement to be obedient to the principal, it doesn't continue when the agent is supposed to disclose items that are required to be disclosed. The information relating to the leak was material and had to be disclosed despite the seller telling the agent not to disclose

4. B. Because the house was built prior to 1978, the buyer is entitled to a lead based paint disclosure and if there are reports of lead, the seller must turn those over to the buyer

5. D. Recommendations should always come with disclosures, any conflicts of interest, and an opportunity for the buyer to choose others. Three is recommended

6. B. Because the leak is a material item (one that could change the buyer's decision), it must be disclosed to the purchaser

7. B. The Lead Based Paint disclosure is required for all houses built prior to 1978, but there is no requirement that the purchaser inspect for lead. This right can be waived

8. C. Tom would not have to disclose that the seller is moving out of state because it doesn't necessarily have bearing on the sale. The seller's financial status certainly does and issues relating to the house, whether patent or latent, should be disclosed to clients

9. A. Home warranty programs are usually provided by the seller at closing and will cover items in the home that break due to mechanical issues. Home warranties do not cover title issues

10. D. The lead-based paint disclosure is separate from the property inspection disclosure. The purchaser is allowed 10 days to inspect for lead but can waive the opportunity. However, a disclosure must still be made to the purchaser. There is no indication that the lead inspection was waived and in fact, it was never disclosed which is a violation

11. A. All material information, whether known or not, must be disclosed to the principal by the agent

12. D. Obedience is a requirement from agent to principal. However, the obedience requirement ends once an agent is asked to do something in contradiction of his ethical obligation to disclose

13. B. Luckily for Julian, most states require a builder to provide a new home warranty on the property. Julian's failure to have a separate home inspection done would not negate this right. He further could not sue the agent because there was no indication that the agent did anything wrong

14. D. A purchaser choosing to get a property inspection who also has a contingency in the contract can ask the seller to pay for any or all of the repairs or rescind the contract. The purchaser is not entitled to recoup the cost of the inspection

15. D. A home warranty will not cover for items that are already known as defective. It is for items that unexpectedly break throughout the period of the policy

16. A. All latent (hidden) defects have to be disclosed. The leaky roof showing stains in the ceiling is a patent defect that doesn't have to be disclosed

17. A. Mold is typically found in moist areas of the home and is evident by black spores on walls

18. C. As an agent, you are obligated to keep your principal informed of any matter that affects the business at hand

19. A. All material items must be disclosed to a prospective purchaser. Because a shared driveway would be more difficult to discover, if the agent is aware, he would have to disclose it

20. B. Home warranties typically would cover the mechanical breakdown of items in the home. Title claims would be covered by the title insurance, the tree damage and the neighbor falling would both be covered by the homeowner's insurance

Chapter 11: Real Estate Calculations

Section 1: *Outline*

In this chapter, we are going to review a few simple math concepts to get you started, provide you with a quick reference guide to the essential math formulas, give you math examples with the solutions in an easy-to-understand format. If you have difficulty with math, don't fret, if you insulate your math score with content, you should still be able to pass your state exam given that math is only about 10% of the exam. In the end, if you can correctly answer 50% of the math questions, you are on your way to obtaining your license.

If you find you are truly having difficulty after your pre-license course and you just need more assistance (math anxiety) to get you over the top, consider purchasing my math prep course at: https://www.kjmethod.com/pricing-plans. A full blown math course is beyond the purview of this study guide, but I did want to provide several math practice problems and solutions.

Topically, the <u>most important math topics</u> on the both the PSI and Pearsonvue exams follow:

1. Square footage
2. Acreage total
3. Comparative Market Analysis (CMA)
4. **Capitalization**
5. **Assessed value and property taxes**
6. **Commissions/compensation**
7. **Interest**
8. **Loan to Value (LTV)**
9. **Discount points, and prepayment penalties**
10. **Purchase price and down payment**
11. Monthly Loan Amount (PITI)
12. **Net to the seller**
13. Cost to the buyer
14. Prorated items
15. Transfer tax (state specific)
16. **Return on investment (Profit)**

17. **Qualifying Ratios**

18. **Depreciation**

19. **Mortgage Insurance**

Items in **BOLD** can all be done with the Magic T* (see below) and for further video clarification, go here: https://www.youtube.com/watch?v=ZsOLLz6Q6RM

It's important that a student know how to convert between decimals, fractions, and percentages:

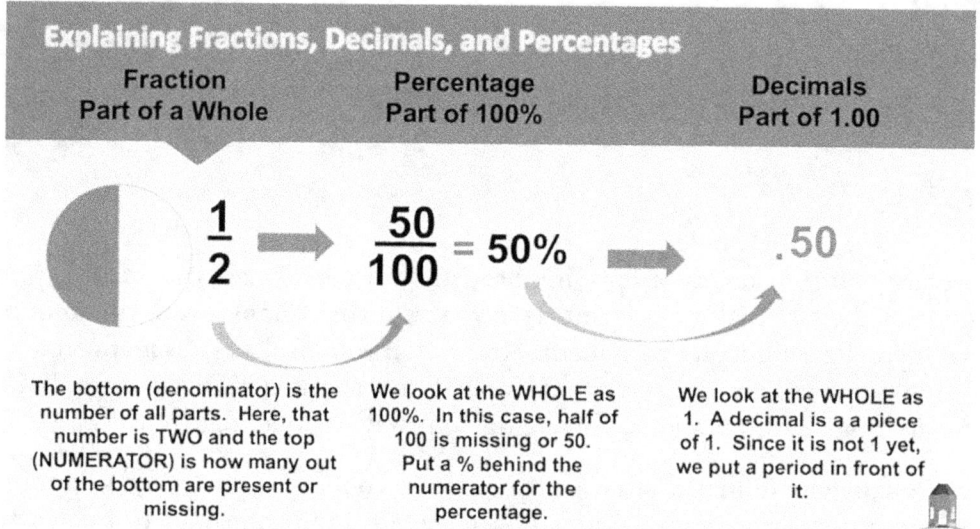

Conversion Practice

Fractions	Percentages	Decimals
$\frac{1}{4}$		
		.60
	$\frac{90}{100} = 90\%$	

Conversion Practice Solutions

Fractions	Percentages	Decimals
$\frac{1}{4}$	$\frac{25}{100} = 25\%$	.25
$\frac{6}{10} = \frac{3}{5}$	$\frac{60}{100} = 60\%$	.60
$\frac{9}{10}$	$\frac{90}{100} = 90\%$	.90

It's also important that students understand the Magic T to help solve real estate problems, especially those with math anxiety. It also helps those students dispense with formula memorization. Students who understand math may simply complete the problem without use of the Magic T.

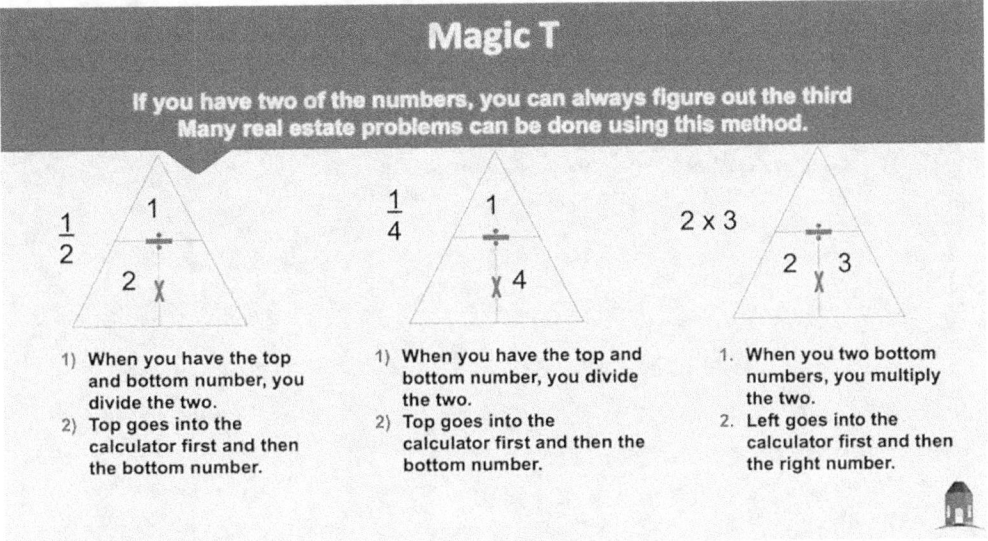

Once you understand the Magic T set up (top to bottom, divide, and left to right, multiply), simply put the numbers given to you in the appropriate place in the formula.

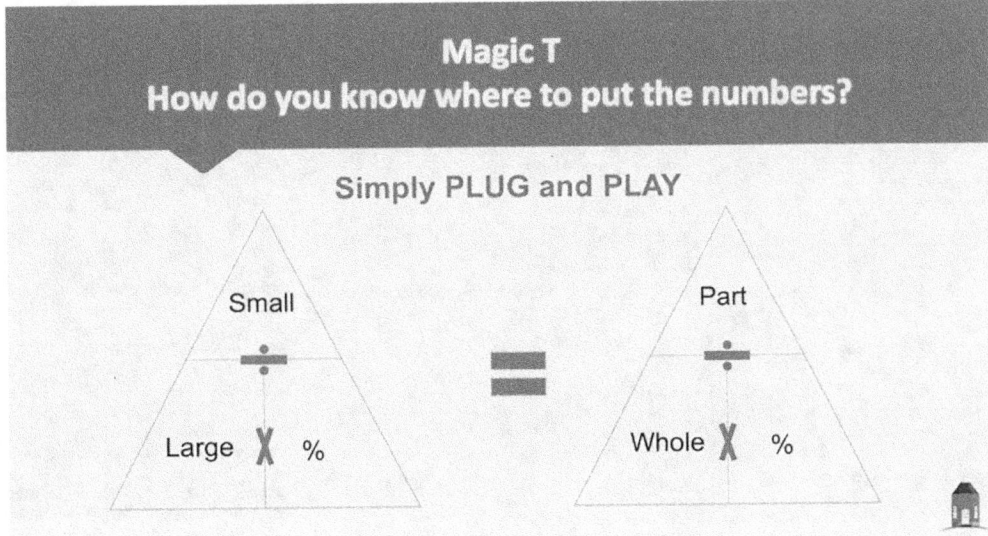

Essential Math Formulas

REAL ESTATE
MATH FORMULAS

A. Land Descriptions

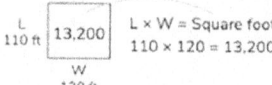

L × W = Square foot
110 × 120 = 13,200

Township = 36 square miles
Section = 1 square mile
Acre = 43,560 square feet

Conversion to Acres, Divide by 43,560 square feet

$$\frac{13,200}{43,560} = .30 \text{ of an acre}$$

B. Percentages, Fractions, Decimals

Fractions – Part of a whole
(Bottom represents the whole)

$\frac{1}{4}$ of 1 $= \frac{1}{4}$

$\frac{1}{2}$ of 1 $= \frac{1}{2}$

1 of 1 $= \frac{1}{1}$ or whole

Percentages – Part of a whole
(Based on 100%)

50% of 100%

25% of 100%

150% of 100%

Decimals – Part of a whole
(Based on 1)

.50 of 1

.25 of 1

1.25 of 1

C. Converting Fractions to Percentages to Decimals

HALF / TOP / but a period in front / WHOLE

$$\frac{1}{2} = \frac{50}{100} = 50\% = .50$$

Key: To go from Decimals to Percentages move the decimal two places to the right (.50 = 50%)

D. Magic T = Many real estate problems can be calculated this way without the need to memorize a formula

÷	PART	÷	SMALL
	TOTAL X %	=	LARGE X %

Because you're often given two of the numbers, simply place them correctly on the T to calculate the 3rd number.

= $6,000

$100,000 X 6%

$5,000

$50,000 X 10%

When going from Left to Right, **MULTIPLY**   When going from Top to Bottom, **DIVIDE**

E. Finance Math: Most calculations start with the Loan Amount (LTV%)

a. Calculate the Loan Amount
Sales Price × LTV % = Loan Amount

Loan Amount	
Sales Price	%
	LTV

b. Calculate the Down Payment
Sales Price × DP % = Down Payment Amount

Down Payment	
Sales Price	%
	DP

c. Calculate Discount Points
Loan Amount × Discount % = Loan Discount

Loan Discount	
Loan Amount	%
	Discount Points

Key: For every 1% the borrower pays at closing, he will get $1/8$% interest rate reduction over the life of the loan

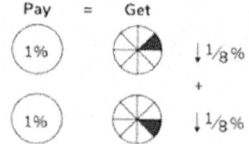

Pay	=	Get	
1%			↓$1/8$%
		+	
1%			↓$1/8$%

2 points (2% of loan) = $2/8$% ↓ interest rate reduction

d. Calculate Monthly Principal and Interest

$$\frac{\text{Loan}}{1000} = \boxed{\#} \times \text{Payment Factor Given}$$

e. Calculate Interest Only
Loan Amt × Interest Rate % = Annual Interest

Annual Interest	
Loan Amt	Interest Rate %

f. Calculate Principal Only

  Monthly Principal & Interest
– Monthly Interest
= Monthly Principal

g. Calculate Commissions
Sales Price × Commission % = Commission Amount

Commission Amt	
Sales Price	%
	Commission

h. Calculate PMI
Loan Amount × PMI % = Annual PMI

Annual PMI	
Loan Amt	%
	PMI

i. Buyer Loan Qualification
Front End Ratio (can you afford the house)

$$\frac{\text{Monthly House Obligations}}{\text{Monthly Gross Income}} = \text{Qualifying \%}$$

Monthly House Obligations	
Monthly Gross Income	Qualifying %

Back End Ratio (can you afford the house with other obligations)

$$\frac{\text{Monthly House Obligations + Other Monthly Debt}}{\text{Monthly Gross Income}} = \text{Qualifying \%}$$

Monthly House Obligations + Other Debt	
Monthly Gross Income	Qualifying %

j. FHA Calculation – Depending on the question, any of these steps can be involved in an FHA problem
LTV = 96.5%; UFMIP = 1.75%; MMIP = .85%

Step 1: Calculate the Loan Amount
Sales Price × LTV = Loan Amount

Loan Amount	
Sales Price	%
	LTV

Step 2: Get UFMIP Premium
Loan Amount × UFMIP % = UFMIP Premium

UFMIP Premium	
Loan Amount	UFMIP %

Step 3: Calculate the New Loan Amount
Loan Amount + UFMIP Premium = New Loan Amount

Step 4: Calculate the Annual MMIP Premium
New Loan Amount × MMIP % = Annual MMIP

Annual MMIP Premium	
New Loan AMT	MMIP %

Step 5: Calculate the Monthly MMIP Premium
Annual MMIP/12 Months = Monthly MMIP

F. Calculating Property Taxes

Step 1: Calculate Tax Rate

$$\frac{\text{Budget}}{\text{Assessed Value of All Properties}} = \text{Tax Rate \% or Mil Rate \%}$$

Budget		
Assessed Value Properties	Tax Rate %	Mil Rate %
	(.02) →	(20%)

Tax Rate and Mil Rate are different expressions of the same thing.

To go from Tax Rate → Mil Rate × by 1000

To go from Mil Rate → Tax Rate ÷ by 1000

Step 2: Calculate Property Tax by applying Tax Rate (Mil Rate) to Assessed Value of the home

a. Market Value × Assessment Rate = Assessed Value

Assessed Value	
Market Value	Assessment Rate

b. Assessed Value × Tax Rate % (Mil Rate %) = Annual Property Taxes

Annual Property Taxes	
Assessed Value	Tax Rate % (Mil Rate)

G. Net Listing Calculation

Sales Price × (100% – commission) = Seller's Net

Seller's Net	
Sales Price	100% – Commission

I. Prorations Rules

Step 1: Start all problems with a timeline

Step 2: Length of the timeline depends upon how often you make the payment (Taxes – 1 year; Rent – 1 month; Mortgage – 1 month)

Step 3: The timeline should start on the due date given and end one day before its next due. If there is no due date given, assume it is the 1st of the month or year

Step 4: Note the closing date on the timeline

Step 5: Sellers pays for all house expenses through closing: buyer begin to pay the day after closing

Step 6: Assume the bill is paid unless told otherwise

Step 7: When calculating taxes and insurance, use 365 days to get a daily rate. When calculating rent, use the number of days in the month where the rent is due

Step 8: When calculating interest, use 360 days to get a daily rate

Step 9: When calculating interest, both the buyer and seller pay for the closing date to each of their banks

Step 10: Seller always owes accrued interest; Buyer owes Prepaid interest except when he closes on the 1st of the month

Step 11: Debit = account reduction; Credit = account increase

H. Valuation Math

1. Market Data Approach (Residential Properties)

CBS (If the COMPARABLE is BETTER than the Subject, SUBTRACT from the comparable)
CIA (If the COMPARABLE is INFERIOR to the Subject, ADD to the comparable)

Never ADJUST the SUBJECT

2. Replacement Cost Approach (New Construction, Insurance, No Comparable)

Replacement Cost
– Depreciation
+ Land
=Value

a. Calculating Replacement Cost

L × W = 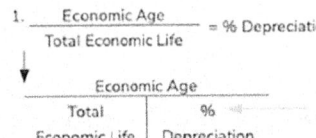 × Cost Factor
ex. 300 ft x 500 ft = 150,000 sq ft x $2.00 sqft = $300,000 replacement cost

b. Calculating Depreciation

i. Annual Depreciation (Straight Line)

$$\frac{\text{Replacement Cost}}{\text{Life in years}} = \text{Annual Depreciation}$$

ii. Age-Life

1. $\frac{\text{Economic Age}}{\text{Total Economic Life}}$ = % Depreciation

Economic Age	
Total Economic Life	% Depreciation

2. % Depreciation × Replacement Cost = Accrued Depreciation

Accrued Depreciation	
Replacement Cost	% Depreciation

c. Add Land (calculate the same as replacement cost)

3. Income Approach (Investment Properties)

a. Cap Rate Formula

Value × Cap Rate % = Net Operating Income

Net Operating Income	
Value	% Cap Rate

   Potential Gross Income
– Vacancies/Collections
= Effective Gross Income
– Expenses/Reserves for Replacements
= Net Operating Income

Gross Rent Multiplier (1-4 Family)

$\frac{\text{Sales Price Comparable}}{\text{Monthly Rent Comparable}} = \frac{\text{GRM}}{\boxed{\#}}$ × Monthly Rent Subject = Value Subject

Gross Income Multiplier (5+ Family/Commercial)

$\frac{\text{Sales Price Comparable}}{\text{Annual Income Comparable}} = \frac{\text{GRM}}{\boxed{\#}}$ × Annual Income Subject = Value Subject

Examples:

1. Taxes/Insurance Paid:

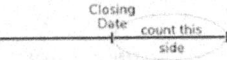

Divide by 365, start from day after closing, one year timeline, buyer debit, seller credit

2. Taxes/Insurance Unpaid (Arrears):

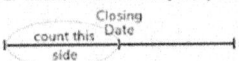

Divide by 365, start from due date to closing date, one year timeline, buyer credit, seller debit

3. Rent Paid, Count this Side:

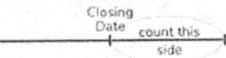

Divide by Days in Month, start from Day after closing, one month timeline, buyer credit, seller debit

4. Accrued Interest (Seller):

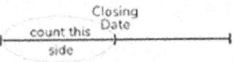

Divide by 360, start from due date to closing date, one month timeline, seller debit, bank credit

5. Prepaid Interest (Buyer):

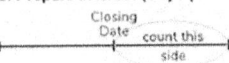

Divide by 360, start from closing date to end of the month, one month timeline, buyer debit, bank credit, unless buyer closes on the 1st = No calculation

Section 2: *Math Problems*

1. Joseph had property totaling 856,000 square feet. He sold 1/4 of the property to Mary. How many acres did he sell Mary?
   A. 8.2 acres
   B. 7.1 acres
   C. 13 acres
   D. 4.9 acres

2. Jane has two properties on a main access road that she owns and wants to combine them to sell to a developer. The first property has 150 feet of frontage on the main road and is 800 feet in length. The other property only has 100 feet of road frontage and is also 800 Feet deep. How many acres does Jane own?
   A. 3.5 Acres
   B. 4.6 Acres
   C. 2.2 Acres
   D. 4 Acres

3. A sales associate has 2.7 acres listed at .25 cents per square foot. What is the asking price?
   A. $29,000
   B. $28,500
   C. $29,403
   D. $31,485

4. A lot measuring at 300' x 700' is sold at a price of $5,000 per acre. What was the selling price?
   A. $23,160
   B. $23,288
   C. $24,105
   D. $24,623

5. A 100-acre parcel is divided into 16 lots. How many square feet are contained in each lot?
   A. 274,300
   B. 274,126
   C. 272,250
   D. 273,200

6. A buyer borrows $220,000 after putting 20% down on a home. What was the purchase price of the property?
   A. $275,000
   B. $264,000
   C. $300,000
   D. $280,000

7. Sara is purchasing a home for $150,000 and putting down 20% to eliminate PMI from her mortgage payment. What is her down payment?
   A. $20,000
   B. $25,000
   C. $30,000
   D. $35,000

8. John wants to purchase a home for $300,000. The bank agrees to a 70% LTV, but John only has 20% down and needs to borrow the rest. How much would John have to borrow?
    A. $3,000
    B. $30,000
    C. $20,000
    D. $10,000

9. Mr. Smith is purchasing a $500,000 home and the lender offers to give Mr. Smith an 85% loan. How much is the bank willing to loan Mr. Smith?
    A. not enough information in the question
    B. $410,000
    C. $425,000
    D. $400,000

10. Jane is going to make a large home purchase of $900,000. But she has to go to the bank to get the loan. The bank agrees to loan her 80% LTV on the first $500,000 of value and 60% LTV on the balance of value. What is Jane's down payment amount?
    A. $200,000
    B. $260,000
    C. $225,000
    D. $250,000

11. A mortgagee has been quoted a factor of 11.80 for a 90% LTV 30-year conventional loan at 9.5% annual interest. On a $250,000 loan, how much would the monthly principal and interest be?
    A. $1,979.17
    B. $2,655.00
    C. $2,950.00
    D. $2,083.33

12. Approximately how much principal would be paid for the first month on a $200,000 loan with a factor of 8.52 and an interest rate of 9.5%
    A. $121
    B. $1,583
    C. $170
    D. Cannot calculate without knowing the term of the mortgage

13. Using the chart below, if John has an amortized 15-year loan for $320,000 at 4% interest, what is his monthly PI payment

Rate	10 year	15 year	30 year
4%	10.00	7.25	4.3
5%	10.71	7.61	5.1
6%	11.02	7.99	5.5

    A. $3,220
    B. $2,320
    C. $3,320
    D. $2,220

14. John and Mary are purchasing a home with a sales price of $236,000 and will make a down payment of $22,000. They will take a 10-year loan with a payment factor of $10.10 at a 6% interest rate. What is their monthly payment on the loan?
    A. $2,086
    B. $2,384
    C. $1,860
    D. $2,161

15. On the loan above, if they kept it for the entire 10 years and paid it off, how much did they separately pay in principal and interest?
    A. $259,368 P, $236,000 I
    B. $214,000 P, $45,368 I
    C. $236,000 P, $22,000 I
    D. $214,000 P, $36,500 I

16. If a loan of $300,000 has a factor of 5.85 and an interest rate of 6%. How much interest is paid in the first month?
    A. $2,340
    B. $2,000
    C. $1,500
    D. $900

17. A home buyer is obtaining a fully amortized loan in the amount of $170,000. The bank has given him 2 options, a 15-year loan at 6% interest or a 30-year loan at 7% interest rate. What is the difference in the monthly payments?
    A. $141.67
    B. $192.40
    C. $93.24
    D. $249.20

18. Seller & Buyer agree to a $210,000 purchase price. The property appraises for $212,000. Buyer is obtaining a 30 fixed rate loan with 10% Down Payment and a 6% interest rate. What is the buyer's 1st monthly interest payment?
    A. $945
    B. $990
    C. $899
    D. $845

19. Assume you borrow $150,000 at 8% for 15 years on a straight loan. How much interest will be paid if the loan is paid off at the scheduled maturity date?
    A. $150,000
    B. $180,000
    C. $200,000
    D. $210,000

20. On a loan balance of $12,485, the next monthly payment will include $117.80 to be applied to interest. What is the interest rate on the loan?
    A. 11.32%
    B. 12%
    C. 9.6%
    D. 10.9%

21. What is the present balance of an 8.75% loan if the next monthly interest payment is $1,531.25?
    A. $190,000
    B. $401,000
    C. $342,000
    D. $210,000

22. The bank tells Mrs. Jones that she must bring 5 months of taxes and 3 months of insurance premium to her closing. Her tax bill is $3,000 and her insurance bill is $1,250. How much will Mrs. Jones have to bring to set up her escrow account?
    A. $354.17
    B. $1,250
    C. $3,000
    D. $1,562.50

23. Ms. Smith is closing on a new loan on March 5 and the bank is requiring her to bring 5 months of escrow funds to her closing so that her taxes and insurance can be paid when they are due on September 9. If Ms. Smith's tax bill is $4,000. How much will her monthly escrows be? And when will her first escrow payment be made after the closing?
    A. $1,666.67; May 1
    B. $4,000; April 1
    C. $4,000; May 1
    D. $1,667.67; April 1

24. Jane's bank is requiring that she bring 4 months of tax escrows to closing. Her tax bill is $5,000. How much would she have to bring to the closing if the bank is also requiring that it have a two-month cushion just in case her taxes go up?
    A. $2,500
    B. $1,666.67
    C. $833.34
    D. $5,000

25. Mr. Samuels sold his home and paid an 8% commission to their realtor. Assuming no other fees, if he walked away from the sale with $480,000, about how much did their house sell for?
    A. $521,739
    B. $500,300
    C. $518,400
    D. $498,000

26. Jim wants to net $75,000 from the sale of his home. He owes $85,000 on the mortgage and $9,000 in expenses on the sale. He will owe his broker 7.5% commission on the sale. What should we list the home for?
    A. $181,000
    B. $180,100
    C. $182,703
    D. $181,675

27. Jennifer netted $35,000 on the sale of her house. She also had closing costs of $6,000 and owed on a $185,000 loan. The commission on the sale was 7%. What was the sales price?
    A. $240,000
    B. $243,011
    C. $244,100
    D. $243,500

28. **Courtney has a gross monthly income of $4,100 and a $45 monthly Visa card payment, a $255 monthly car payment, a $150 monthly student loan payment and a Dillard's credit card with $25 minimum monthly payment. Her monthly mortgage payment is estimated to be $695 for principal and interest, $240 month for property taxes, and $50 a month for hazard insurance. What is her Total Debt Service Ratio?**
   A. 24.0%
   B. 29.4%
   C. 21.6%
   D. 35.6%

29. **Mark has a gross monthly income of $2,400 and his proposed PITI loan payment is $740 including Mortgage Insurance of $67 and monthly taxes of $145. What is his housing expense ratio (front end)?**
   A. 30.8%
   B. 33.6%
   C. 36.9%
   D. 39.7%

30. **Your buyer has gross annual income of $120,000, and the following monthly fixed expenses: Credit Card Debt of $400, Car Payment of $625 Child Support of $500. If the house they are looking at has a monthly housing expense of $2,000, what are their qualifying ratios?**
   A. 35.25% upfront/20% back end
   B. 20% upfront/35.25% back end
   C. 1.6% up front/2.9% back end
   D. 2.9% up front/1.6% back end

31. **Mary is applying for a 90% conventional loan with monthly payments including principal, interest, taxes, and insurance of $1,260. Her annual income is $50,400 and her currently monthly obligations include a car loan of $325 per month and a student loan at $150 per month. Based on the information given, which of the following statements is INCORRECT?**
   A. Her front-end ratio is 30%
   B. Her back-end ratio is 41.3%
   C. The total debt used to calculate the back-end ratio is $1,735
   D. Mary will qualify for the loan if the lender uses ratios of 33% and 38%

32. **You sold a house is sold for $255,000. Your broker will receive a commission of 3% of the sale price and your affiliation agreement with your broker states you'll receive 60% of the broker's commission as compensation. How much compensation will you receive?**
   A. $4,950
   B. $3,060
   C. $7,650
   D. $4,590

33. **You sold a house and received a compensation check for $8,400. Your agreement with your broker is to split commissions 60/40. If the listing broker and selling broker split the 7% listing commission 50/50, what did the house sell for?**
   A. $28,000
   B. $280,000
   C. $400,000
   D. $5,600

34. A seller has a listing contract for a 6% commission rate. If he lists his home for $170,000 and sells his home for $160,000 with $4,000 in seller paid closing cost and the buyer's agent will receive 3% compensation, how much will the total commission be for the sale of his home?
    A. $6,000
    B. $9,360
    C. $9,600
    D. $4,800

35. If a Coop real estate agent received a commission check at closing for $3,900 and the MLS showed a 3% co-op commission, which was 50% of the total commission. What was the sale price of the home?
    A. $120,000
    B. $125,000
    C. $130,000
    D. $135,000

36. A seller lists his home with Sally's brokerage who gets 5.5% commission. The home is listed for $435,000. Another agent brings a buyer who offers $420,000. The offer is accepted, and the two companies equally split the commission. Sally gets 60% of the commission with her brokerage. How much does Sally get?
    A. $6,930
    B. $4,620
    C. $11,550
    D. $$23,100

37. John purchased a home for $310,000 with a 90% conventional loan. His bank charged him $7,500 for loan discount points. How many discounts points did Michael pay for?
    A. 2.7 points
    B. 4.1 points
    C. 3.2 points
    D. 1.5 points

38. Buyer is purchasing a home for $100,000 with a 15% down payment. The lender charges 2 points. How much in total does the buyer need to bring to closing for this loan?
    A. $15,000
    B. $85,000
    C. $1,700
    D. $16,700

39. Jim is purchasing a home for $125,000 and is putting a down payment of 20% towards the purchase. Jim is being charged 2 points to buy down his interest rate. How much will the buy down cost him at closing?
    A. $1,000
    B. $1,500
    C. $2,000
    D. $2,500

40. The buyer was required to pay a loan discount of $4,000. The loan balance was $80,000. How many points did the lender require?
    A. 5
    B. 4
    C. 6
    D. 3

41. A borrower is offered an interest rate of 7% on a home loan, but the borrow wishes an interest rate of 6 5/8%, how many points would the borrower have to pay to get to the desired rate?
    A. 4
    B. 3
    C. 5
    D. 2

42. A building owner nets $10,500 each month which represents a 9% cap rate. What is the approximate value of the building?
    A. $116,667
    B. $1,400,000
    C. $13,850.000
    D. $450,000

43. If an investor wishes to sell his building at a 10% cap rate, what price would you place on the building if his building had semi-annual gross income of $500,000 and operating expenses of 42% of gross income?
    A. $1,000,000
    B. $520,000
    C. $5,800,000
    D. $420,000

44. If you own a building free and clear that is worth $125,000 and want an annual return of 12%, what net income is needed each month?
    A. $1,250
    B. $1,200
    C. $1,000
    D. $1,125

45. A property has a gross annual income of $24,000 and monthly expenses of $500. It has been valued at $175,000. What is the capitalization rate?
    A. 10.3
    B. 11.3
    C. 10.8
    D. 11.8

46. A high-rise office building has a gross quarterly income of $255,000. The annual expenses are 48% of the gross income. What is the approximately dollar amount of net income?
    A. $489,000
    B. $132,600
    C. $530,400
    D. $1,020,000

47. A retail store building was evaluated at $285,000 using a 10% capitalization rate. What would be the value of the building if a 12% capitalization rate was used?
    A. $237,500
    B. $227,500
    C. $215,000
    D. $356,200

48. John has 5 apartments renting at $800 per month and 2 parking spaces renting at $50 per month. His vacancies are 5% and he also has expenses of 40%. How much is his building valued at if using a 6% cap rate?
    A. $450,000
    B. $467,400
    C. $413,000
    D. $356,000

49. A comparable residential property recently sold for $162,000. The monthly market rent was determined to be $1,200. If the subject property rents for $1,300 monthly, what is the value of the subject property?
    A. $196,290
    B. $149,500
    C. $175,500
    D. $167,500

50. Sally bought a piece of residential property that was currently being rented at $990 per month. Comparable properties in that area are operating on a 125 GRM. Based on the comparables, what is the value of Sally's property?
    A. $123,750
    B. $125,500
    C. $123,450
    D. $124,800

51. The owner of a commercial building wants to list her property. Eleven years ago, she paid $1,550,000 and put numerous improvements into the building. She tells you that the expenses on the building are 45% and the gross income is $16,500 per month. A comparable in the area recently sold for $1,950,000 with a gross annual income of $165,000. What would you list the property for?
    A. $1,550,000
    B. $1,675,000
    C. $2,340,000
    D. $1,950,000

52. A 20-unit comparable apartment building next door to yours recently sold for $2,000,000 with a monthly income of $30,000. Your property rents for $40,000 a month. What would be the value of your property?
    A. $2,666,667
    B. $2,000,000
    C. $3,434,000
    D. $3,125,890

53. Your buyer bought a home for $325,000 with a maximum FHA loan. The lender has quoted an up-front MIP of 1.75% and an annual MIP of .93%. Approximately how much UFMIP will be added to the loan?
    A. $319,113
    B. $5,488
    C. $2,968
    D. $2,648

54. A purchaser is borrowing with an FHA loan of $273,000. The UFMIP is 1.75% of the loan amount and the MIP is .85% of the loan amount. What is the total monthly MIP payment to be added to the loan?
    A. $196.76
    B. $212.34
    C. $144.78
    D. $942.00

55. Ray purchased a home for $140,000 with a 10% down payment and financing the remaining amount with a conventional loan. He will have a PMI charge of 0.62% per year, added to his monthly mortgage. If the property was listed for $149,900 and appraises for $144,000, How much PMI will be included in his 1st monthly payment?
    A. $74.40
    B. $72.33
    C. $65.10
    D. $77.49

56. Jude is applying for loan on a property with a purchase price of $135,000. On an FHA loan she is putting down the minimum of 3.5%. The property appraised for $136,000 and has an assessed value of $82,000 for taxes. With a MIP Charge of 1.35% for the first year of her loan, what will her monthly MIP payment be for her 1st mortgage payment?
    A. $153.00
    B. $146.56
    C. $151.87
    D. $92.25

57. The sales price of $192,000 and the buyer is getting a 90% loan. The lender has quoted a rate of .62% annual for PMI. The buyer's monthly PMI obligation would be:
    A. $99.20
    B. $89.28
    C. $107.18
    D. $105.80

58. You purchased a home that is valued at $275,000. The taxing authority has an assessment rate of 55% with a tax rate of $3.18 per 100. What amount would be added to your budget mortgage payment to pay for your monthly tax bill?
    A. $4,809.75
    B. $1,512.50
    C. $480.97
    D. $3,545

59. Hamilton County has a tax rate of 4 mils for the parks. A buyer is purchasing home for $150,000 and it has an assessed value of $110,000. What will this levy for the parks cost him per year?
    A. $440.00
    B. $50.67
    C. $600.00
    D. $36.67

60. A property has a value of $350,000 and an assessment rate of 29%. If the tax rate is 92 mills, what is the annual property tax?
    A. $9,191
    B. $9,156
    C. $9,287
    D. $9,338

61. If a property is taxed at $4,125 and the assessed value is $225,000, what is the mills?
    A. 18.3
    B. 19.7
    C. 19.1
    D. 17.9

62. The value of a property is $147,000. The properties are assessed at 60% and the mil rate is $51.47 per $1000. What is the *monthly* property tax bill?
    A. $498
    B. $542
    C. $379
    D. $415

63. The county assesses all parcels at 50% and needs $700,000 from real property to contribute to the county shortage. The market value of all properties in the county is $70,000,000. What is the county tax rate?
    A. .02
    B. .03
    C. .025
    D. .04

64. The sale of a home closed on October 16th. Insurance for the home is $500 for the current year and have been paid in advance by the seller. How much does the buyer owe the seller for these fees if the buyer pays for the day of closing? Use a 30-day month and a 360 days per year. Round to nearest cent
    A. $104.16 buyer debit, seller credit
    B. $106.95 buyer debit, seller credit
    C. $397.22 buyer debit, seller credit
    D. $397.22 seller credit, buyer debit

65. Property taxes are $900 per year and run from January 1 until the end of the year. The closing date is May 12
    A. $325.48 buyer debit, seller credit
    B. $325.48 seller debit, buyer credit
    C. $574.52 seller debit, buyer credit
    D. $574.52 buyer debit, seller credit

66. The insurance premium was $803 for the year, has been paid in advance by the seller and the policy begins January 1. If the closing date is November 8 and the buyer wishes to assume the policy, what are the prorations? Closing date goes to the buyer
    A. $684.20 debit buyer, credit seller
    B. $118.80 debit buyer, credit seller
    C. $226.45 debit buyer, credit seller
    D. $684.20 debit seller, credit buyer

67. The annual tax bill is $1,324 and the taxes have been paid. If the closing takes place on December 5th, how will the tax bill be prorated
    A. The buyers will receive a property tax credit at closing of $94.31
    B. The buyers will receive a property tax credit at closing of $122.96
    C. The sellers will receive a property tax credit at closing of $94.31
    D. The buyers will pay property taxes of $1,324 to the sellers at closing

68. The house insurance bill for the calendar year $1,290 and have been paid. The property sells and closing takes place on June 10. When the taxes are prorated, which of the following is the correct settlement statement entry?
    A. Credit to the seller $720.99
    B. Credit to the buyer $720.99
    C. Credit to the buyer $569.01
    D. Credit to the seller $569.01

69. The hazard insurance premium of $1,825 was paid on March 16. The house was sold on August 29th. What adjustment would you make on the net to seller sheet?
    A. Credit Seller $990
    B. Credit Seller $930
    C. Credit Buyer $830
    D. Credit Buyer $825

70. Insurance is due on April 8 and the sale closed on December 5. The cost for insurance for the year is $415. What are the prorations?
    A. Credit Seller $127.80
    B. Credit Seller $138.71
    C. Credit Buyer $144.00
    D. Credit Buyer $152.00

71. Taxes are due on September 15th and the tax payment is $3250. Closing is to take place on June 10th. What is the tax proration?
    A. Credit Seller $2395.21
    B. Credit Seller $854.79
    C. Credit Buyer $2106.25
    D. Credit Buyer $823.20

72. A property is sold and closes on April 15th. The taxes of $5,475 have not been paid. What adjustment would you make in this transaction?
    A. Debit Seller $1,575
    B. Debit Seller $3,900
    C. Credit Buyer $3,900
    D. Credit Buyer $5,475

73. Annual taxes of $3,650 have not been paid when the house sells on April 23rd. What adjustment would be made on the settlement statement? Use a 360-day calendar
    A. Credit Seller 113 days
    B. Debit Seller 113 days
    C. Credit Seller 252 days
    D. Debit Seller 252 days

74. Property taxes are $876 per year and are due February 26. If property taxes are paid in arrears and the closing date is May 12, how will this appear on the Settlement Sheet? Use a 365-day calendar
    A. $182.40 debit seller, credit buyer
    B. $693.60 debit seller, credit buyer
    C. $486.25 debit seller, credit buyer
    D. $537.48 debit seller, credit buyer

75. The rent of $1,100 was due on April 1 and paid to Landlord #1 and the closing date is April 19 when Landlord #2 will purchase the property. What are the prorations?
    A. Credit Seller $318.00
    B. Credit Seller $697.67
    C. Credit Buyer $343.30
    D. Credit Buyer $403.33

76. Rent is due on January 20 and the sale closed on February 5. The rent is $1550. What are the prorations?
    A. Credit Seller $500.00
    B. Credit Seller $550.00
    C. Credit Buyer $700.00
    D. Credit Buyer $850.00

77. A seller has an existing loan of $92,000 at 7% interest. Closing is scheduled for July 25. How much accrued interest would the seller owe at closing?
    A. $441.10
    B. $447.22
    C. $429.33
    D. $0

78. The Smiths sold their home on December 5. Their payoff was $84,150 at 8.75% interest. How much was the entire payoff to the bank?
    A. $84,252.27
    B. $84,150.33
    C. $156.76
    D. $228.43

79. The seller is closing on May 13th and his mortgage payment is due on the 5th of every month. How many days of accrued interest will he owe?
    A. 9
    B. 10
    C. 8
    D. 26

80. The borrower is closing on August 17th. Her new loan is going to be $146,530 at 9%. How much prepaid interest will she owe?
    A. $541.96
    B. $549.49
    C. $555.62
    D. $562.34

81. Borrower is closing his loan on April 1. His new loan amount will be $246,000 at 5% interest. How much prepaid interest will be collected from the borrower at closing?
    A. $1,025
    B. $1,100
    C. $0
    D. $34.17

82. An appraiser has valued a commercial building at $500,000 using the cost approach to appraising. She has determined that the building had a useful life of 50 years when it was built 19 years ago. What would the appraiser place as a current value of the building?
    A. Cannot calculate without knowing the effective age of the building
    B. $190,000
    C. $10,000
    D. $310,000

83. The ground floor of a home measures 40x50; the second floor also measures 40x50, but the basement is ½ the size of the ground and second floors. The appraiser has determined that the price is $60 per square foot for both the ground and second floors, but that the basement is $30 per square foot. Depreciation is determined to be $30,000 and the land is valued at $50,000. What would be the appraiser's value for this property?
    A. $340,000
    B. $199,000
    C. $211,000
    D. $290,000

84. Jane and Joe are having a property appraised that they bought one year ago. The property is a warehouse. Its dimensions are 250 front feet x 250 side feet, with a height of 10 feet. The cost per cubic foot is $2.00. The property has a useful life of 20 years. The land that the property sits on is valued at $35,000. What would be the value of the property?
    A. $1,222,500
    B. $1,265,000
    C. $1,134,000
    D. $1,076,000

85. You sold a house a year ago for $225,000. The owner calls to tell you they are looking to sell the house. Property is the area has been increasing at an annual rate of 8%. Based on this information what would you estimate the house to be worth in today's market?
    A. $232,000
    B. $225,800
    C. $243,000
    D. $234,000

86. 2.A property was purchased for $20,000 in 2005. It was just sold for a total gain of $2,500. What was the percent of profit?
    A. 10.5%
    B. 11.5%
    C. 12.5%
    D. 13.5%

87. A developer purchased two lots totaling 3,000 square feet for $42,000. The developer subdivided the lots into three equal sized lots and sold them for $20 per square foot. How much profit did the developer make if he sold all three lots?
    A. 30%
    B. 43%
    C. 36%
    D. cannot tell from the problem given

88. John rehabbed a piece of property during COVID but lost money on it. He purchased the property for $246,000, put another 30,000 into the property, but was only able to sell it for $262,000. What was his % loss?
    A. -5.1%
    B. -6.3%
    C. -4.7%
    D. 6.3%

Chapter 11 Solutions

1. **D. 4.9 acres - Solution:** *Multiply 856,000 square feet x 25% = 214,000 square feet; Divide 214,000 square feet by 43,560 = 4.91 acres*

2. **B. 4.6 Acres - Solution:** *150x800= 120,000 + 100x800 = 80,000 = 200,000 /43,560 = 4.59 acres*

3. **C. $29,403 - Solution:** *2.7 x 43,560 = 117,612 square feet x .25 = $29,403*

4. **C. $24,105 - Solution:** *300 x 700 = 210,000 square feet/43,560 = 4.821 acres x $5,000 = $24,104.5*

5. **C. 272,250 - Solution:** *100 acres x 43,560 = 4,356,000 square feet/16 lots = 272,250 square feet*

6. **A. $275,000 - Solution:** *If the borrower put 20% down, the loan was 80%. $220,000/.80=$275,000*

7. **C. $30,000 - Solution:** *$150,000 x .20 = $30,000*

8. **B. $30,000 - Solution:** *Short way to look at this is John is short 10%. $300,000 x .10 = $30,000 or he has 90% x $300,000 = $270,000*

9. **C. $425,000 - Solution:** *$500,000 x .85 = $425,000*

10. **B. $260,000 - Solution:** *$500,000 x .80 = $400,000 (1st part of the loan) + $400,000 (balance of value) x .60 = $240,000 (2nd part of the loan) = $640,000 total loan. $900,000-$640,000 = $260,000 down payment*

11. **C. $2,950.00 - Solution:** *$250,000/1,000 = 250 x $11.80 = $2,950.00 Principal and Interest payment; Ignore the interest rate in these problems. You don't need it when given the factor to calculate the Principal and Interest*

12. **A. $121 - Solution:** *1st calculation: $200,000/1,000 = 200 x 8.82 = $1,704.00 Principal and Interest, 2nd calculation: $200,000 x 9.5%= $19,000 year interest/12 = $1,583.33 month JUST INTEREST. Subtract $1,704-$1,583.33= $120.60. You needed the interest rate in this one because they wanted you to calculate JUST INTEREST so you can give them JUST PRINCIPAL*

13. **B. $2,320 - Solution:** *$320,000/1000 = 320 x $7.25 = $2,320 per month*

14. **D. $2,161 - Solution:** *$236,000-$22,000 = $214,000 Loan Amount; $214,000/1,000 = 214 x $10.10 = $2161.40; IGNORE the Interest Rate again because they want the total payment*

15. **B. $214,000 P, $45,368 I - Solution:** *$2,161 month x 120 months (10 years) = $259,320 total payments of Principal and Interest; Since $214,000 was principal (amount borrowed), the rest must be interest $259,320-$214,000=$45,368*

16. **C. $1,500 - Solution:** *$300,000 x 6% = $18,000/12 = $1,500. On this one, you ignore the 5.85 because they don't want to know the entire monthly payment or the principal. You are just looking for interest*

17. **A. $141.67 - Solution:** *1st calculation: $170,000 x 6% = $10,200/12 = $850.00; 2nd calculation: $170,000 x 7% = $11,900/12 = $991.67. Subtract the two numbers: $991.67-$850.00=$141.67*

18. **A. $945 - Solution:** *$210,000 x .90 = $189,000; $189,000 x .06 = $11,340 year/12 = $945 month*

19. **B. $180,000 - Solution:** *$150,000 x 8% = $12,000 year x 15 years = $180,000. Remember, no principal is paid on a straight loan, so the interest stays the same throughout*

20. **A. 11.32% - Solution:** *Convert the monthly interest to yearly $117.80 x12 = $1,413.60 year. Divide $1,413.60/$12,485 = 11.32%*

21. **D. $210,000 - Solution:** *Convert the month interest to yearly $1531.25 x 12 = $18375/8.75%=$210,000*

22. **D. $1,562.50 - Solution:** *$3,000/12 = $250.00 per month; $1250/12=$104.17 per month. $250.000 x 5 months = $1,250.00 + $104.17x3 months = $312.50 = $1,562.50*

23. **A. $1,666.67; May 1 - Solution:** *$4,000/12 = $333.33 month x 5 months = $1666.67 and her first payment would be on May 1 since she is closing on March 5*

24. **A. $2,500 - Solution:** *$5,000/12 = $416.67 month x 4 months = $1666.67 + $833.34 (2 additional months) = $2,500*

25. **A. $521,739 - Solution:** *$480,000/92% = $521,739. This is essentially a reverse net listing. We know what the person walked away with, and we know the commission. But don't forget that 100%-8% goes into the formula*

26. **C. $182,703 - Solution:** *$75,000 net + $85,000 mortgage + $9,000 expenses = $169,000/92.5% (100%-commission) = $182,703*

27. **B. $243,011 - Solution:** *$35,000 net + $185,000 loan payoff + $6,000 closing costs = $226,000/93% = $243,011*

28. **D. 35.6% - Solution:** *Total Debt is the back-end ratio which is all monthly payments towards the home as well as any other monthly debt divided by gross monthly income: $695+$240+$50 (house debt) = $985.00 + $45+$255+$150+$25 (other debt) = $475.00. **$985+$475**=$1,460 month total/$4100 monthly gross income = 35.6%*

29. **D. 39.7% - Solution:** *Housing expense is the Front End: $740+$67+$145 = $952/$2,400 = 39.67%*

30. **B. 20% upfront/35.25% back end** - *Solution: Front End: $2,000/$10,000 (monthly income) = 20%; Back End: $2,000 + $400+ $625+ $500 = $3,525/$10,000 = 35.25%*

31. **D. Mary will qualify for the loan if the lender uses ratios of 33% and 38%** - *Solution: Front End: $1,260/$4,200 = 30%; Back End: $1,260 +$325 +$150 = $1,735/$4,200 = 41.31%. Mary will not qualify if the required numbers are 33% and 38% because she is over on the Back End ratio*

32. **D. $4,590** - *Solution: $255,000x.03 (broker receives) = $7650.00 x .60 = $4,590 (you receive)*

33. **C. $400,000** - *Solution: You must work this one backwards. The original commission for your office was $8,400/.60 = $14,000 and that was half of the entire commission of 7%. So, the entire commission was $28,000/7% = $400,000*

34. **C. $9,600** - *Solution: Testing that you understand that commission is on Sales Price. Total commission: $160,000 x 6% = $9,600. Nothing else in the question matters*

35. **C. $130,000** - *Solution: If the co-op agent received $3,900, the entire commission was $7,800/.06 = $130,000*

36. **A. $6,930** - *Solution: $420,000 x .055 commission = $23,100 total commission x .50 = $11,550 to each agency. Then Sally's split is $11,550 x .60 = $6,930*

37. **A. 2.7 points** - *Solution: $310,000 x 90% = $279,000 loan amount; $7,500/$279,000 = 2.68% which is the same as 2.7 points*

38. **D. $16,700** - *Solution: $100,000 x 85% = $85,000 loan x 2% = $1,700. Add $15,000 down payment and the total would be $16,700*

39. **C. $2,000** - *Solution: $125,000 x 80% (100% - down payment = loan) = $100,000 loan amount x 2% (points) = $2,000*

40. **A. 5** - *Solution: $4,000/$80,000 = 5% or 5 points*

41. **B. 3** - *Solution: The borrower wants to go from 7% to 6 5/8%. Each 1/8% that the borrower goes down, he will pay 1 point. To go from 7% to 6 7/8% is 1 point. To go from 6 7/8% to 6 6/8% is 1 point. To go from 6 6/8% to 6 5/8% is 1 point. So, a total of 3 points*

42. **B. $1,400,000** - *Solution: $10,500 x 12 = $126,000/9% = $1,400,000*

43. **C. $5,800,000** - *Solution: $500,000 x 2 = $1,000,000 annually x .42 = $420,000 expenses. $1,000,000-$420,000 = $580,000 (NOI)/10% = $5,800,000*

44. **A. $1,250** - *Solution: $125,000 x 12% = $15,000 year/12 = $1,250 monthly*

45. **A. 10.3** - *Solution: $24,000 - $500 x 12 = $6,000 (expenses) = $24,000-$6,000 = $18,000/$175,000 = 10.29%*

46. **C. $530,400** - *Solution: $255,000 x 4 annual = $1,020,000 x 48% = $489,600. $1,020,000-$489,600 = $530,400*

47. **A. $237,500** - *Solution: $285,000 x 10% = $28,500 what it looks like now; $28,500/12% = $237,500 if you were to sell it, just move the net income*

48. **B. $467,400** - *Solution: First calculate NOI: 5 x $800 x 12 = $48,000 (rent) + 2 x $50 x 12 (parking) = $1,200 for a total of $49,200 PGI – 5% vacancy =$46,740 – 40% expenses = $28,044 Net Operating Income; $28,044/6% (cap rate) = $467,400 Value*

49. **C. $175,500** - *Solution: Step 1. $162,000/$1,200 month = 135 GRM; Step 2: 135 GRM x $1,200 month = $175,500*

50. **A. $123,750** - *Solution: GRM is already calculated. Just multiply it by the monthly rent: $990 x 125 GRM = $123,750*

51. **C. $2,340,000** - *Solution: The only numbers that are important are sales price of the comp, annual income of the comp and annual income of the subject. The rest are there to throw you off. This is still a GIM problem $1,950,000/$165,000 annual income = 11.82 GIM x $198,000 ($16,500 Mo x 12 {need annual income}) = $2,340,000*

52. **A. $2,666,667** - *Solution: $2,000,000/$360,000 (based on a year) = 5.555 x $480,000 (based on a year) = $2,666,667*

53. **B. $5,488** - *Solution: $325,000 x 96.5% (max FHA loan) = $313,625 Loan Amount; $313,625 x 1.75% = $5,488. You don't need the .93%*

54. **A. $196.76** - *Solution: $273,000 x 1.75% = $4,778; $273,000 + $4,778 (add UFMIP to loan) = $277,778 x .85% = $2,361/12 = $196.76 per month*

55. **C. $65.10** - *Solution: $140,000 x 90% (if down payment is 10%) = $126,000 x .62% (PMI charge) = $781.20/12 = $65.10. The only thing that matters is the sales price*

56. **B. $146.56** - *Solution: $135,000 x 96.5% = $130,275 (loan) x 1.35% (MIP) = $1759/12 = $146.56 monthly. Only purchase price is relevant*

57. **B. $89.28** - *Solution: $192,000 x 90% = $172,800 x .62% = $1071.36/12 = $89.28*

58. **A. $4,809.75** - *Solution: $275,000 x 55% = $151,250 assessed value. $151,250/$100 = $1512.50 x $3.18 = $4,089.75*

59. **A. $440.00** - *Solution: $110,000 x .004 (mil rate converted to tax rate) = $440.00 or leave it in mils $110,000/1000 = $110 x 4 = $440.00*

60. **D. $9,338** - *Solution: $350,000 x .29 = $101,500 assessed value; $101,500 x .092 (mil rate converted to tax rate) = $9,338 annual property taxes*

61. **A. 18.3** - *Solution: $4,125 ÷ $225,000 = .0183 (to convert, move decimal 3 spaces to the right or multiply by 1000) = 18.3 mills*

62. **C. $379** - *Solution: $147,000 x .60 = $88,440 assessed value; $88,440 x .05147 (converted to tax rate) = $4,552 annual property taxes; $4,552 ÷ 12 = $379 monthly property taxes*

63. **A. .02 -** *Solution: $70,000,000 x 50% = $35,000,000 Assessed Value of all properties; $700,000 (need)/$35,000,000 (assessed value) = .02 tax rate*

64. **A. $104.16 buyer debit, seller credit -** *Solution: Since the taxes were paid for the entire year by the seller, the buyer owes the seller from October 16th- December 31st since buyer has the day of closing. All months have 30 days since we are told to use a 360-day calendar. The total number of days is October (14+1=15); November (30); December (30) for a total of 75 days. $500/360=$1.39-day x 75 = $104.16 buyer debit, seller credit*

65. **D. $574.52 buyer debit, seller credit -** *Solution: The buyer will owe the seller from May 13-December 31. Total number of days is May (18+1), June (30), July (31), August (31), September (30), October (31), November (30), December (31) = 233 days. $900 ÷ 365 = $2.47 per day x 233 days = $574.52*

66. **B. $118.80 debit buyer, credit seller -** *Solution: Buyer has the closing date and owes the seller from November 8-December 31. Nov (22+1) and December (31) = 54 days. $803 ÷ 365 = $2.20 daily rate x 54 = $118.80 debit buyer, credit seller*

67. **C. The sellers will receive a property tax credit at closing of $94.31 -** *Solution: If you understand these problems, you can answer this one without doing any math. We know the sellers will receive a credit for a small amount so that eliminates all answers except C. Here is the math: Seller will be credited from December 6-31 (25+1 or 26 days). $1,324/365=$3.63x26 days = $94.31 seller credit, buyer debit*

68. **A. Credit to the seller $720.99 -** *Solution: Buyer owes the seller from June 11-December 31 = June (19+1), July (31), Aug (31), Sep (30), Oct (31), Nov (30), Dec (31) = 204 days. $1,290/365 = $720.99 buyer debit, seller credit*

69. **A. Credit Seller $990 -** *Solution: The timeline is March 16-March 15 of the next year. Buyer would owe seller from August 30th-March 15th. August 30-31 (1+1), Sept (30), October (31), November (30), December (31), January (31), February (28), March 1st-15th (15) = 198 days. $1,825/365 = $5 x 198 days = $990*

70. **B. Credit Seller $138.71 -** *Solution: The timeline is April 8th-April 7th of the next year. Buyer would owe seller from December 6th-April 7th. December 6-31 (25+1), January (31), February (28), March (31), April 1st – April 7th (6) = 122 days. $415/365 = $1.14 x 122 days = $138.71*

71. **B. Credit Seller $854.79 -** *Solution: The timeline is September 15th-September 14th. Buyer would owe seller from June 11th-September 14th, June 11th-30th (19+1) = 20, July (31), August (31), September 1st – September 14th (14) = 96 days; $3,250/365 = $8.90 x 96 days = $854.79*

72. **A. Debit Seller $1,575 -** *Solution: Seller did not pay taxes for the time she was there. January 1st-April 15th. Jan (31), Feb (28), Mar (31), Apr (15) = 105 days. $5,475/365 = $15 x 105 days = $1,575 Debit Seller*

73. **B. Debit Seller 113 days. -** *Solution: January 1 – April 23 = Jan (30), Feb (30), Mar (30), Apr (23) = 113 Seller Debit*

74. **A. $182.40 debit seller, credit buyer -** *Solution: Seller is responsible from February 26 – May 12 since the problem didn't say taxes cover a calendar year. Feb (2+1) March (31), April (30), May (12) = 76 days; $876 ÷ 365 = $2.40 daily rate x 76 days = $182.40 debit seller, credit buyer*

75. **D. Credit Buyer $403.33 -** *Solution: Buyer (Landlord #2) takes over on April 20 and will be entitled to a credit for April 20-30 (10+1) = 11 days. $1,100/30 = $36.67 x 11 days = $403.33 Buyer Credit*

76. **C. Credit Buyer $700.00 -** *Solution: Buyer (Landlord #2) takes over on February 6 and will be entitled to a credit for February 6-February 19 (13+1) = 14 days. $1,550/31 (divide by number in the month that the rent is paid in [January] = $50 x 14 days = $700 Buyer Credit*

77. **B. $447.22 -** *Solution: July 1-July 25 is 25 days. $92,000 x 7% = $6,440/360 = $17.89 per day x 25 days = $447.22 Accrued interest*

78. **A. $84,252.27 -** *Solution: December 1 – December 5 = 5 days of accrued interest. $84,150 x 8.75%=$7,363/360=$20.45 per day x 5 = $102.27 accrued interest + $84,150 = $84,252.27*

79. **A. 9 -** *Solution: He will owe from May 5th-May 13th (only the timeline changed) = 8+1 or 9 days*

80. **B. $549.49 -** *Solution: August 17th-31st (yes, borrower has the closing day when talking interest) or 14+1 =15 days. $146,530 x 9%=$13,188/360 = $36.63 day x 15 = $549.49 prepaid interest collected at the closing*

81. **C. $0 -** *Solution: Because the borrower is closing on the 1st of the month, his new loan doesn't have prepaid interest*

82. **D. $310,000 -** *Solution: $500,000/50 = $10,000 per year depreciation x 19 (total accrued depreciation) = $190,000. $500,000 - $190,000 = $310,000 left. Since we don't have a land value given, that is the current value*

83. **D. $290,000 -** *Solution: 40 x 50 = 2,000 (ground and second); basement is 1,000 (1/2 the size). 2000 x $60 = $120,000 x 2 (ground and second) = $240,000 + $30,000 (1,000 x $30 basement). Replacement cost = $270,000 - $30,000 (Depreciation) + $50,000 (Land) = $290,000*

84. **A. $1,222,500 -** *Solution: 250 x 250 x 10 = 625,000 cubic feet x $2.00 = $1,250,000 (replacement cost)/20 years (useful life) = $62,500 per year in depreciation (only been in existence one year). $1,250,000 - $62,500 = $1,187,500 + $35,000 land = $1,222,500*

85. **C. $243,000 -** *Solution: Essentially, we are asking, what would be the price if it increased 8%? We would take 100% of the property ($225,000) and increase it by 8% for a total of 108% or 1.08 (different expression). $225,000 x 1.08 = $243,000*

86. **C. 12.5% -** *Solution: What you made or lost/What you paid, $2,500/$20,000 = 12.5%*

87. **B. 43% -** *Solution: The developer made $60,000 on the three lots (3,000 x $20), but he paid $42,000. $18,000 made/42,000 paid = 42.8%*

88. **A. -5.1% -** *Solution: $246,000+$30,000 = $276,000; $262,000-$276,000 = -$14,000/$276,000 = -5.1%*

Chapter 12:
Comprehensive Examinations

Comprehensive Examination 1

1. The purchaser requests that as a contingency of entering into the contract, the seller provide a home warranty on home he is selling. The seller agrees and prior to the closing, the HVAC system in the home breaks down. The seller is now that he agreed to provide the home warranty. He contacts the home warranty company, and they explain that they will not pay for the repair. Who is correct?
   A. The seller because he agreed to provide the home warranty to the purchaser
   B. The home warranty company since the property will not be covered until the closing
   C. The home warranty company since HVACs are never covered by these policies
   D. The seller since the policy is effective as soon as the contract is signed

2. A licensee was taking an upper income bracket listing from a seller. The seller told her that they had lived in the neighborhood a long time, had many friends there, and wanted to be selective about who bought their house. The licensee was to tell them the race and nationality of anyone making an offer. How should the licensee respond to this requirement?
   A. She should refuse to do so by explaining she would not always know the people making the offer
   B. She should refuse to do so and explain that the seller's instruction could be a violation of federal law
   C. She could take the listing as it is legal as long as no discriminatory advertising is used
   D. She should agree to it because, as the agent of the seller, the licensee has the duty of obedience to the seller's instructions

3. A licensee was showing a third-party buyer an older home built in 1976. The buyer was concerned about the stains on the ceiling in the upstairs bedroom. The licensee never mentioned the stains, but they were apparently from a roof leak that had been repaired. The licensee should tell the buyer:
   A. That he could put in an offer with the opportunity to inspect the roof and determine his next move
   B. That he doesn't have to worry about the roof leaks as it had been repaired
   C. That it is a good house and if he waits too long, it will be gone
   D. That he should offer less than the asking price to account for the roof stain repair

4. Your agent takes you out to look at house and you notice that there aren't many houses on the market. Yet, the prices are significantly higher than normal. Which economic principle would explain this?
   A. Anticipation
   B. Supply and Demand
   C. Substitution
   D. Competition

5. **Augusta National Golf Club has several rental units on its property for PGA golfers only. The charge for this housing is only $30 per night. Is this policy a violation of federal fair housing?**
   A. Yes, because once a price is charged, the exemption is lost
   B. Yes, because all housing must be open to everyone
   C. No, unless they are discriminating based on race
   D. No, since Golf Clubs always have an exemption

6. **An apartment building specializing in housing for 65 and older has made it clear that no children under the age of 18 would be allowed to reside there. Is this permissible?**
   A. Yes, as long as 80% of the occupants are 55 and older
   B. Yes, this exemption applies to housing of persons 62 and older
   C. No, because discrimination against children is never allowed
   D. Yes, because there was notice before taking applications

7. **A mortgage broker contacts a bank on behalf of his client who is perfect by all banking standards. The bank, however, refuses to look at the client's credit profile, stating that the zip code where the property is located has a high percentage of crime and property values. Due to the increased risk, the bank policy is that it doesn't loan in that area. This is an example of:**
   A. Blockbusting, but it would be legal in this circumstance
   B. Redlining, and it is never legal
   C. Redlining, but it is legal here, due to the bank's increased risk
   D. Blockbusting and it is never legal

8. **A licensee is listing a property. The property was owned by a couple, both of whom are now deceased. The couple has three children who are at the listing appointment. Before completing the listing agreement, the licensee should do which of the following?**
   A. Check the probate records for the family
   B. Require all three children to sign quitclaim deeds
   C. Ensure that all three children sign the listing agreement
   D. Check the ownership of record even though all children are there

9. **A broker decides to place all funds that he receives as payment for commission into his personal account rather than his business account. Has he committed any violation of the license law?**
   A. Yes, he is committing the act of commingling funds
   B. Yes, he is committing the act of conversion
   C. No, because conversion is not a violation of the license law
   D. No, because the license law is not concerned with these funds

10. **A broker advertises a property to have the most beautiful backyard that he has ever seen. The buyer purchases the property based on the broker's assertions. When the backyard of the month contest comes around, the buyer doesn't win. He sues the broker for false advertising. What is the result?**
    A. The purchaser should have checked out the other backyards before purchasing
    B. The "most beautiful backyard" is considered puffing
    C. The "most beautiful backyard" could reasonably be interpreted as being the most beautiful
    D. The broker engaged in false advertising

11. **There has been an influx of children moving into a neighborhood that was formerly all elderly. You represent an elderly buyer couple. You showed them the one property in that neighborhood for sale, but you inform them about the influx of children. Were your actions appropriate?**
    A. Yes, because you owe a fiduciary duty to your client
    B. No, you have violated fair housing by discussing this information with them
    C. No, because you limited their choices of homes they wanted to see
    D. Yes, because your elderly client has an exception from fair housing

12. **Malia has an apartment in Maia's building. Malia has 4 dogs that she does not do a good job in taking care of. The dogs often go to the bathroom on the newly installed carpet. Before the lease expires, Maia has to come into the apartment to do a repair and she sees the carpet as well as several doors scratched up. Maia sues Malia and claims:**
    A. Constructive Eviction
    B. Waste
    C. Laches
    D. Breach of the implied warranty of habitability

13. **Under which circumstance can a real estate contract be considered voidable?**
    A. One of the parties was a minor at the time of signing
    B. If the contract was made on a Sunday
    C. If the contract does not include a legal property description
    D. If the contract was signed without witnesses

14. **Pepper had a car accident in 2020. She wanted to sue then, but failed to do so and got busy. She didn't sue until 2023. At that time, we learned that all witnesses either died or could not be found. The court refuses to hear her case stating that she should've sued earlier on the basis of:**
    A. Violation of Statue of Frauds
    B. Violation of Doctrine of Laches
    C. Violation of Statue of Limitations
    D. Violation of Operation of Law

15. **When a contract is dependent upon the successful completion of some prior act or condition**
    A. Assignment
    B. Contract
    C. Contingency
    D. Consideration

16. **When a party uses a position of trust or confidence to induce another to enter into a contract**
    A. Duress
    B. Undue Influence
    C. Innocent Misrepresentation
    D. Mutual Mistake

17. **Which of the following scenarios would most likely result in a suit for constructive fraud?**
    A. A buyer lies about the ability to obtain a loan large enough to purchase the house
    B. The broker mistakenly tells the buyer that the house is 4,000 square feet
    C. The seller intentionally tells the buyer that he fixed the air conditioner when he didn't
    D. The broker conceals from the buyer that the basement leaks during bad rainstorms

18. **Jessica has been hired by Mr. and Mrs. Smith to sell their home. After successfully closing on the property, what happens to the agency relationship?**
    A. It automatically continues for any future transactions
    B. It is terminated upon the successful closing of the sale
    C. Jessica must confirm the termination in writing
    D. The Smiths must hire Jessica again when and if they want to buy another home

19. **An Asian family requests to see properties in only Asian neighborhoods, but you refuse because you believe that you would be violating fair housing. Have you committed a fair housing violation?**
    A. Yes, an agent must demonstrate full obedience to their principal
    B. Yes, this is an example of blockbusting and is not permitted under the fair housing law
    C. No, while an agent should follow the principal's instructions, he should not if it violates any law
    D. Yes, because the agent is obligated to show them properties in any neighborhood they wish

20. **Sally is the listing agent on a home. Mary, an agent, brings a prospective purchaser, John, who Mary is representing. John happens to notice that there are several African American children playing in the playground near the house. So, John asks Mary if she could tell him what the demographics are in the neighborhood. Mary is uncomfortable at this line of questioning, but she understands her role as a fiduciary to her principal. Mary's best reply would be:**
    A. The local school district would probably have that information
    B. That she can find out the information and provide it
    C. It doesn't matter because those children are from another neighborhood
    D. Any discussion of neighborhood demographics is against the law

21. **Tom, a buyer's agent, is showing a home to his client. Tom would have to disclose all of the following to his client except**
    A. The school district just changed
    B. The air-conditioning unit is new
    C. The seller is moving out of state
    D. The seller is going bankrupt

22. **Broker Frank tells his client Alice that he has the authority to negotiate prices on her behalf and accepts an offer on her behalf. However, Alice has not given him explicit permission to do so. What could be the consequence of Frank's actions?**
    A. Frank can legally negotiate as he sees fit
    B. Alice must honor any agreements that Frank makes
    C. Frank will definitely be liable for acting outside of his authority
    D. Frank could be liable unless Alice ratifies Frank's actions

23. **On February 1, a licensee with ABC Realty takes a 3-month exclusive right-to-sell listing on a house. On March 1, the licensee moves out of state and inactivates his license. What happens to this listing?**
    A. It is automatically terminated
    B. It becomes an open listing contract
    C. It is voidable by the owner because the licensee is no longer active
    D. It remains a valid exclusive right-to-sell listing contract with ABC Realty

24. **The purchaser of a home is requesting that the seller provide the purchaser with a home warranty at closing. If the seller agrees, the purchaser will be protected if:**
    A. The home catches fire due to arson
    B. Plumbing Problems causing the sinks to back up
    C. A claim on the title
    D. A person slipping and falling on the property

25. **John bought a property and got a $6,000 quote for a new deck. However, the building inspector came out and indicated that there was a new code and that there are additional materials that must be used for the deck. The new materials brought the cost up to $12,000. Does John have any recourse?**
    A. No. He cannot collect the money because there is no right to compensation when the government exercises his police power
    B. Yes. He can sue the county's building department for the money
    C. No. Because John should've known that building code
    D. Yes. He is entitled to be compensated by the building department

26. **To qualify as a tax-deferred 1031 exchange, a property must be**
    A. A principal residence
    B. Held for productive use in trade or business
    C. Financed through a federal institution
    D. Amortized over a 30-year period

27. **You need to contact a prior client who is on the Do Not Call Registry. Can you contact them?**
    A. Yes, as long as its prior to 9 PM and for up to 18 months since your last transaction with them
    B. Yes, as long as its prior to 9 PM and for up to 3 months since your last transaction with them
    C. No, because they are already on the Do Not Call Registry, you cannot call them
    D. Yes, if you have first received permission to call them and then you cannot call past 8 PM

28. **Mandisa is listing a property that has a crack in an underground storage tank. The seller wants to list the property "AS IS" and indicate in the listing that the low sales price reflects the condition of the home. Can Mandisa list the home?**
    A. No, it would be innocent misrepresentation to list the home "AS IS"
    B. Yes, as long as all problems with the house are disclosed in the listing
    C. Yes, but any latent defects still have to be disclosed to the purchaser despite the "AS IS"
    D. No, houses can't be listed on the MLS when there are known problems with the house

29. **Jill is the purchaser of a home. She has a 5-year-old son. The home was built in 1970 and Jill decides that she does not wish to obtain a lead-based paint inspection despite the disclosure that informs her that the house was built prior to 1978 and that she has 10 days to inspect. Is she permitted to waive this right?**
    A. No, Lead Based Paint is a federal law that requires an inspection if the home is built prior to 1978
    B. Yes, a Lead Based Paint inspection is an option given to the purchaser, but the right can be waived
    C. No, in this case, Jill would have to inspect the property because she has a child under the age of 6
    D. Yes, because there were no reports given to her indicating that the home definitely has led

30. **Able is a listing agent on a property. He informs his seller that a property disclosure form will be required for the listing. The seller fills out the form but does not want to mention a leak in the roof because it has already been repaired by a certified contractor. Able should advise the seller:**
    A. That he doesn't have to disclose that there was a leak since it was repaired by a certified contractor
    B. That regardless of it being repaired, the seller must disclose the leak
    C. That the seller doesn't have to disclose the leak because it wasn't a material item
    D. That the seller, while not required to disclose a leak that has been repaired, should disclose it from an ethical standpoint

31. **A licensee plans to send out an e-mail offering his services. According to the CAN-SPAM Act, the licensee must**
    A. Include only the brokerage firm's name in the "Reply-To" line
    B. E-mail individuals who have given prior permission to be e-mailed
    C. Hire a company to market services
    D. Tell recipients how to opt out of receiving future e-mail

32. **An owner has been asked to grant a 60-day option to purchase a property. When should the purchase price be decided?**
    A. Upon creation and signing of the option to purchase
    B. When the buyer decides to exercise his option
    C. At any time during the 60-day option period
    D. Within the last 10 business days of the 60-day option period

33. **Michael has paid $5,000 for a 90-day option on a piece of land. With regards to the option, which of the following statements is FALSE?**
    A. Michael is not obligated to buy the land during the first 90 days
    B. Michael is obligated to buy the land during the first 90 days
    C. Michael's option money belongs to the optionor even if Michael doesn't buy
    D. Michael's option is a unilateral executory contract

34. **The term parole evidence refers to the law that states:**
    A. All real estate contracts must be in writing
    B. Oral agreements will be given effect over written agreements
    C. Written agreements will be given effect over oral agreements
    D. Only those items that were specifically discussed with be given effect by the court

35. **What type of contract is created when a buyer and seller agree to and fully sign a purchase and sale agreement?**
    A. An express bilateral executory contract
    B. An express unilateral executory contract
    C. An express bilateral executed contract
    D. An express unilateral executed contract

36. **Kevin and Laura enter into a contract for the sale of Kevin's beachfront cottage. A week before the closing, a hurricane destroys the cottage. What is the status of the purchase and sale agreement?**
    A. The contract is still valid and Kevin must rebuild the cottage
    B. The outcome will be determined by the language of the contract
    C. The contract is terminated due to impossibility of performance
    D. Laura can rescind the contract and get her earnest money deposit back

37. **Judy and Rob are a married couple, and they decide to purchase a home in a neighborhood that is 50 miles from where they currently reside. They orally enter into a contract with the seller, Mary. Judy and Rob pay Mary $5,000 in earnest money for a closing that is to take place in three weeks. When the time comes to close the loan, Mary is nowhere to be found. Judy and Rob sue Mary. What is the probable result?**
    A. Statute of Frauds prevents Judy and Rob from seeking relief in court
    B. The contract between Judy and Rob and Mary is invalid
    C. Parol Evidence prevents the court from determining who should get the earnest money
    D. If Judy and Rob bring a quit claim action, they should be able to have the court award the property to them

38. **Four persons own a 20-room mansion as tenants in common. Two of the owners decide to liquidate their assets. Can this legally be done?**
    A. Yes, because tenants in common may liquidate their portions of the assets if at least half of the co-owners agree to do the same
    B. Yes, because each co-owner has a separate legal title to the undivided interest
    C. No, because there is only one title to a property
    D. No, because a co-owner's interest terminates only at death

39. **Which of the following is an easement appurtenant?**
    A. A shared driveway
    B. A party wall
    C. A pathway over adjoining property leading to a lake
    D. All of the above

40. **Owner A has a house with a view of a nearby lake. When the neighboring property, which fronts the lake, decides to sell, owner A might lose the view because of new construction. Which of the following can owner A due to preserve her scenic view?**
    A. Purchase an easement from the owner of the lake front property
    B. File a suit of inverse condemnation once construction begins on the lake front property
    C. Build an encroachment onto the lake front property that will preserve the view
    D. Seek a writ of execution from the local civil court

41. **Which of the following is NOT included in the covenants of a warranty deed?**
    A. Execution sale
    B. Quiet enjoyment
    C. Warranty forever
    D. Warranty of seizin

42. **A property owner moved from a farm he owned in fee simple to live in another country. He continued to pay taxes on the property and kept the title clear. Did he violate his rights of private ownership?**
    A. Yes, because his abandonment constituted waste
    B. Yes, because his abandonment restricted the use of the land
    C. No, because he has not abandoned the property as long as the taxes are paid
    D. No, because the right to abandon a property is included in fee simple ownership

43. **Kim Grant purchased property under the name Kim Howe. Later Grant, using the name Howe, sold the property to Lange. Does Lange hold legal title to the property?**
    A. Yes, because Grant conveyed to Lange an equitable interest in the property
    B. Yes, because Grant's use of an assumed name did not invalidate the deed
    C. No, because Grant's use of an assumed name invalidated the deed
    D. No, because Grant should have used both the names Grant and Howe in the deed in order to convey title

44. **Can the holder of a life estate sell the property to a neighbor?**
    A. No, the interest in life estate can be sold, but not the property
    B. Yes, as long as the neighbor is aware that the original owner is entitled to any income from the land
    C. No, because a life estate can never be transferred but must revert to the original owner
    D. No, because a life estate can only be inherited

45. **A company that was incorporated in one state buys property in another state. Which statement about this transaction is always true?**
    A. The company is subject to regulation only in the state in which it was incorporated
    B. The company is subject to regulation in both states involved in that particular transaction
    C. The company's stockholders must approve purchases of real estate
    D. The corporation may not take title to the property in its own name

46. **Which of the following would NOT be entitled to a mechanic's lien?**
    A. A laborer
    B. A subcontractor
    C. A cooperating broker
    D. An architect

47. **Which of the following is (are) always true about liens?**
    A. A mortgage lien affects only the parcel of real property in which the mortgagor lives
    B. A judgment lien affects all of the debtor's real and personal property
    C. A mechanic's lien affects all of the debtor's real and personal property
    D. A mortgage lien always have priority on the property that the loan is taken out on

48. **Which of the following is not considered an encumbrance on a parcel?**
    A. A mechanic's lien on new construction
    B. A contractual covenant
    C. A deed restriction
    D. An easement on the servient tenement

49. **A property has a restriction forbidding use of the property for commercial purposes. The zoning ordinance for the area would permit a business on the property. Can a business be operated from the house?**
    A. Yes, because deed restrictions can only apply to the type of building or construction and not to its use
    B. Yes, because the zoning ordinance takes precedence over the deed restriction since it is less restrictive
    C. No, because the deed restriction takes precedence over the zoning ordinance since it is more restrictive
    D. No, because deed restrictions are always valid for twenty-five years

50. **A deed restriction in a subdivision had created a community playground that used a few square feet from the rear of every owner's lot. An owner has begun making plans to convert the rear half of his lot to a garden. The plans would require the removal of park equipment. A neighbor objects to these plans. The neighbor should:**
    A. Do nothing since an individual landowner has no authority to enforce deed restrictions
    B. Apply for a court injunction against the owner's plans
    C. Inform the owner that the playground is community property
    D. File a lis pendens as soon as possible

51. **A tenant leases a lake side lot. Upon arriving at the lot to begin sunbathing, the tenant finds her landlord there, selling hot dogs and attracting a constant crowd to the lot. Apparently, the landlord does this every Saturday and Sunday. Under which of the following justifications could the tenant refuse to pay rent on this lot?**
    A. Constructive eviction
    B. Unlawful detainer
    C. Tenancy in common
    D. Zoning variance

52. **Which of the following statements about the statute of frauds is true?**
    A. It protects the purchaser against unknown liens on the property
    B. It requires that monetary consideration accompany offers to purchase to ensure serious intent
    C. It requires that a sales contract for real property be in writing to be enforceable
    D. It is used to prevent people from selling property that they do not own

53. **Which of the following statements about options is FALSE?**
    A. The option's fulfillment can be made conditional upon changes in zoning
    B. The option must be in writing in order to be enforceable
    C. The option may be revoked by the optionor
    D. The option is not usually obligated to purchase or lease the property

54. **A farm owner has no surviving family but has prepared a will. After she dies, is there any chance that her property will be disposed of by escheat?**
    A. Yes, because she has no surviving family
    B. Yes, but only if her property is acquired by eminent domain
    C. No, unless the will is defective or no one to take under her will can be found
    D. No, because only residential property is subject to escheat

55. **After the statutory period of possession, what does an adverse possessor actually do to acquire title?**
    A. File an action to quiet title
    B. Execute an estoppel certificate
    C. Record a writ of attachment
    D. Exercise the right of eminent domain

56. **A prospective buyer submits an offer to purchase a home for $83,500. The seller signs the offer, changes the price to the original listing price of $83,750, and initials that change. When the original offer has again been delivered to the prospective buyer, it:**
    A. Has been legally accepted
    B. Is a bilateral contract
    C. Has been terminated
    D. Is executable

57. **Which of the following means of transferring real property is most likely to be used by an occupant of the property who is under color of title?**
    A. A quitclaim deed
    B. A land contract
    C. A general warranty deed
    D. Adverse possession, and a quiet title action

58. **In which situation do we refer to the term "good consideration"?**
    A. Laws of Descent
    B. Accession
    C. Adverse possession
    D. Gift Deed

59. **Which of the following would most likely be an example of police power being exercised by a local government?**
    A. Passing stringent zoning restrictions dealing with the use of specific properties
    B. Controlling traffic flow by law officers at a football game
    C. Requiring the registration of deeds in order to assess their validity
    D. Imposing certain speed limits within the town limits

60. **An owner builds a recreation room onto her house. Her neighbor feels the new addition will violate setback lines established in city zoning codes. Does the neighbor have the right to request an injunction to stop construction?**
    A. No, an injunction may be obtained only by the city planning and zoning commission
    B. No, the neighbor forfeited this right when the owner began construction
    C. Yes, but only if a majority of homeowners in the neighborhood sign a petition supporting the neighbor's action
    D. Yes, under these circumstances the neighbor may justifiably ask for an injunction

61. **A broker described the boundaries of a property to a prospective buyer without informing her that the boundaries described were not exact. After purchasing the property, the new owner extended a fence within the described boundaries as told to her. A neighbor then brought an injunction against the new owner because the fence extended beyond the actual property boundaries. Can the broker be held liable for misrepresentation?**
    A. Yes, because the broker must present a lot and block survey before closing
    B. Yes, because the broker knew the boundaries that she cited could be false
    C. No, because the broker's description was oral
    D. No, because the prospective buyer is responsible for obtaining a survey before closing

62. If an agent breaches his fiduciary responsibilities to the principal, what actions can be taken against the agent?
    I. The principal may bring a civil suit to recover losses
    II. The agent's license may be revoked by the state
    Ill. The state may rescind all contracts negotiated by the agent with other principals during the past year
    A. I only
    B. II only
    C. I and II only
    D. I, II, and Ill

63. What does the law of agency govern?
    A. The rights and duties of principals, agents, and third parties
    B. The rights and duties of sponsoring brokers and salespersons
    C. The rights and duties of listing and cooperating brokers
    D. The licensing requirements for brokers and salespersons

64. The owner of an apartment building has just signed a management contract with a real estate firm. In this situation, has an agency been formed?
    A. No, because an agency is formed only with a listing agreement between a seller and a real estate broker
    B. No, because an agency with a broker is formed only in situations of buying and selling, not managing, real estate
    C. Yes, because an agency is formed whenever one-party delegates to another the right to act on his/her behalf in certain business transactions
    D. Yes, because the agreement between a property owner and a property manager creates a universal agency

65. An owner listed her house at $85,000 and wanted a $15,000 down payment. She told her broker not to bother her with offers below the listed price. Several weeks later, the broker was asked by a prospective buyer to present a written offer for $80,000 with a $10,000 down payment. If the broker presents this offer, has she violated the obligation of an agent to her principal?
    A. No, because a broker has every right to attempt to collect the commission agreed to in the listing contract
    B. No, because a broker is required to present all written offers to the principal
    C. Yes, because the broker has failed to follow the specific instructions of the principal
    D. Yes, because the offer is clearly below the terms of the listing

66. For which of the following reasons could a salesperson's real estate license be suspended or revoked?
    I. Paying a portion of his/her commission to someone who provided a valuable lead, but who is not yet licensed
    II. Being convicted of a felony
    Ill. Not disclosing a dual agency to a principal
    A. I only
    B. II only
    C. Ill only
    D. I, II, and Ill

67. Which of the following is NOT a duty of a listing agent to his/her client?
    A. Producing a ready, willing, and able buyer
    B. Inquiring about the financial condition of the prospective buyer
    C. Advertising the property to the client's best advantage
    D. Conducting a title search to be certain that the client's property title is clear

68. **A broker signed a sixty-day exclusive right-to-sell listing contract with an owner. After one week of advertising and showing, the house was not sold, and the owner lists the property with another broker. The second broker found a buyer one week later. Which statement about this situation is probably correct?**
    A. The owner owes two full commissions, one to each broker, because both contracts are enforceable
    B. The owner owes a full commission to the first broker only, because, since he already had a contract with her, the contract with the second broker is void
    C. The owner must give the commission to the first broker who must give half to the second broker
    D. The owner must give the commission to the second broker only, because the broker selling the home earns the commission no matter how many contracts are involved

69. **A broker and a seller signed a standard listing agreement. Which of the following would be among the acts that the broker was appointed to perform under the term of this listing?**
    I. Locate a ready, willing, and able buyer for the real property
    II. Sell, trade, or convey title to the real property
    III. Prepare the documents necessary to close the sale of the real property
    A. I only
    B. Ill only
    C. II or III only
    D. I, II, or III

70. **Which of the following is true about a liquidated damages clause in regard to an earnest money deposit?**
    A. If, after the offer is accepted, the buyer does not fulfill his/her obligations, the buyer may forfeit the earnest money as liquidated damages
    B. If, after the offer is submitted, the broker places the earnest money in a trust or escrow account, that broker can be subject to license revocation
    C. If, after the offer is accepted and before closing, the seller wants custody of the deposit, the broker can give it to the seller as liquidated damages
    D. None of the above

71. **In which of the following instances may a principal be liable to a broker for damages?**
    A. When the broker misrepresents the property to a prospective buyer
    B. When the principal allows a broker other than the listing broker to show the property
    C. When the broker terminates the listing contract after the contract has been signed
    D. When the principal revokes the agency formed by an exclusive right-to-sell listing contract before the termination date

72. **Which of the following may be used as the fee of a property manager?**
    A. A fixed monthly payment
    B. A fee based on gross rentals
    C. A fixed fee plus incentive bonuses
    D. All of the above

73. **Which of the following is NOT an example of steering?**
    A. An attempt to exclude black clients from one community by failing to show properties there
    B. An attempt to attract Hispanic prospects to a community composed primarily of Hispanic homeowners
    C. An effort to induce white homeowners to sell when a black purchaser moves into their neighborhood
    D. An effect to prevent an Asian client from moving into a neighborhood composed primarily of white homeowners

74. **A loan for the sale of a two-family residence would probably be covered by the federal Real Estate Settlement Procedures Act (RESPA) if the:**
    A. Loan was from a federally insured saving and loan association
    B. Loan was of the type not purchased by the Federal National Mortgage Association
    C. Residence was part of a 45-acre farm
    D. Loan was a second mortgage

75. **A seller is selling his only house. He will neither advertise the property nor use a broker's services. Can the seller legally refuse to sell the property to a member of a racial minority?**
    A. Yes, because the seller has not used the services of a real estate broker
    B. Yes, because the seller has not used racially discriminatory advertising or a broker's services
    C. No, because such discriminatory action is prohibited
    D. No, because the seller owns fewer than three houses

76. **The practice of capitalizing a property's net income is based upon the investor's need to:**
    A. Have a reasonable return on the investment based on similar risk and return
    B. Conform to the federal Real Estate Settlement Procedures Act
    C. Procure replacement costs
    D. Have a tax-sheltered income

77. **Which statement best describes why neighborhood analysis is important to the informed real estate agent?**
    A. Buyers want to know if neighborhood racial balance exists
    B. It can help determine an estimation of value
    C. The agent is often required to testify before zoning boards as to such matters
    D. The agent must include details of such an analysis in the listing contract

78. **Depreciation is caused by which of the following?**
    A. Physical Deterioration
    B. Functional obsolescence
    C. Economic obsolescence
    D. All of the above

79. **Which of the following trends can affect demand for housing?**
    A. Increase in the population
    B. Age of the population
    C. Migration of the population
    D. All of the above

80. **Which of the following is usually caused by a poor floor plan in a house?**
    A. Physical curable deterioration
    B. Physical incurable deterioration
    C. Economic incurable obsolescence
    D. Functional incurable obsolescence

81. **An appraiser performs an appraisal of an apartment building that earns $25,000 per year. The appraisal approach that should usually be given the most weight is:**
    A. The cost approach
    B. The income approach
    C. The market data approach
    D. None of the above

82. **If a buyer wishes a high initial equity investment in a house, which of the following should the buyer seek as part of the mortgage terms on the house?**
    A. The shortest mortgage term available
    B. The longest mortgage term available
    C. The smallest down payment
    D. The largest down payment

83. **A veteran wants to buy a house for which the owner will accept no less than $80,000. The Veterans Administration certifies the market value of this house to be $75,000. Which of the following is true about how the veterans may use VA-guaranteed financing to buy this house?**
    A. The veteran may not use VA-guaranteed financing to buy this house
    B. The veteran may pay the amount in excess of the VA-certified value from his savings account and use VA-guaranteed financing to buy this house
    C. The veteran may pay the amount in excess of the VA-certified value with a second mortgage and use VA-guaranteed financing to buy this house, as long as the interest rate of the second mortgage is higher than that of the VA-guaranteed mortgage
    D. The veteran must use a second mortgage to pay the amount in excess of the VA-certified value if he is to use a VA-guaranteed mortgage to buy this house, regardless of the interest rate of the second mortgage

84. **Which of the following must be present for a mortgage to exist?**
    1. A debt
    2. A source of equity
    3. A pledge of property
    4. A receiver clause
    A. #1 only
    B. #1 & #3 only
    C. #2 & #3 only
    D. #2 & #4 only

85. **A veteran has paid in full his/her VA-guaranteed mortgage of 1976 origin and has sold the originally mortgaged property. The veteran now holds no interest in any real property, mortgaged or un-mortgaged. Can the veteran obtain another VA-guaranteed mortgage at this time?**
    A. Yes, but a veteran can receive only two VA-guaranteed mortgages in his/her lifetime, receiving the second one only after the first one has been paid in full
    B. Yes, because the veteran's entitlement is fully restored if that veteran has paid off all prior VA mortgages and sold all such mortgaged properties
    C. No, because a veteran can use his/her VA entitlement only once, regardless of whether the veteran ever amortizes that mortgage loan
    D. No, because a veteran can use his/her VA entitlement only once, regardless of whether the veteran ever sells the mortgaged property

86. **The term finance charge as used in Regulation Z does NOT include which of the following?**
    A. Loan fees and loan-finders' fees
    B. Insurance premiums for mortgage protection insurance
    C. Discount points and service charge
    D. Recording fees and title insurance premiums

87. **Which of the following companies issues private mortgage insurance?**
    A. Veterans Administration
    B. Mortgage Guaranty Insurance Corporation
    C. Federal Housing Authority
    D. Farmer's Home Administration

88. **Which of the following statements about FHA-insured loans on single-family homes is FALSE?**
   A. Interest rates on FHA loans are set by the market
   B. The borrower is allowed to prepay the loan without penalty
   C. The maximum loan amount is set by FHA
   D. The borrower might not be required to make a down payment

89. **Which of the following does NOT result when the Federal Government raises interest rates on home loans?**
   A. The Federal Reserve System increases the reserve requirements of member banks
   B. Housing demand decreases
   C. The debt-to-income ratio are increased to maintain mortgage loan payments
   D. The number of potential home buyers is reduced

90. **Which of the following are directly or indirectly involved as loan package purchasers in the secondary mortgage market?**
   1. Government National Mortgage Association
   2. FHA and VA
   3. Federal National Mortgage Association
   4. Federal Home Loan Mortgage Corporation
   A. #1 & #3 only
   B. #1, #2, & #4 only
   C. #1, #3 & #4 only
   D. #2, #3 & #4 only

Comprehensive Examination 2

1. **Can a broker take a listing where the seller decides that he wants to discriminate against Muslims?**
   A. Yes, because Muslims are not a protected class
   B. No, because discrimination is never tolerated
   C. No, because Muslims are in a protected class
   D. Yes, but just make sure to not show the home to Muslims

2. **Can a listing agent ever use a church or religious building in its advertisement for a property?**
   A. Yes, as long as the agent doesn't name the church
   B. No, churches cannot be used in ads under any circumstances as it violates fair housing
   C. No, unless the advertisement has been approved by the broker
   D. Yes, if the agent refers to the church for direction clarity only, not preference

3. **The county is trying to figure out the ad valorem tax rate to be paid by all property owners in the county. Mr. Brown is unhappy with the assessment attributed to his home. She should appeal to:**
   A. Board of Equalization
   B. Board of Arbitration
   C. Tax Assessor's Office
   D. County Tax Commissioner

4. **Under what circumstances can a real estate agent legally contact a person listed on the Do Not Call Registry?**
   A. The agent can contact any person on the registry at any time if it relates to a property sale
   B. The agent can contact a former client for up to 18 months after the last business transaction
   C. The agent can contact a person on the registry at any time as long as given written permission
   D. The agent can never contact a person on the registry

5. **A broker is holding funds for his seller in a trust account. During this period of time, a judgment is entered against the broker and the creditor is attempting to collect. The broker owes $37,000 and has $30,000 of it in his operating account. After seizing that account, the creditor goes after the trust account to get the balance of the funds. Will the creditor be able to attach that account?**
   A. Yes, but only for the $7,000 that it is owed
   B. No, trust accounts cannot be attached unless it was for the client's funds
   C. No, trust accounts can never be attached
   D. Yes, but only with notice to all parties involved

6. **John is the owner of a 4-family house where he lives upstairs. He rents out all other units. He places an ad in the local newspaper for one of the downstairs rentals. The ad is answered by a young, handicapped person. The person tells John that he would need a ramp installed in order to be able to move into the premises. The ramp is going to cost about $10,000. John decides that the ramp cost too much and decides not to rent to the person. Can John do this?**
   A. Yes, because John would have to bear the cost of the ramp
   B. Yes, because John doesn't have to rent to a handicapped person
   C. No, since John wouldn't have to bear the cost of the ramp, he must rent to the person
   D. No, because discrimination is never tolerated

7. **Which could cause a broker to be in violation of the Sherman Anti-Trust Act?**
   A. Your broker keeps all the earnest money deposits in a safe in his office
   B. Your broker encourages you to violate fair housing laws to sell more real estate
   C. Your broker meets with other brokers and sets commission rates for the area
   D. Your broker accepts money from attorneys for closing services referrals

8. **Which of the following best describes steering?**
   A. A licensee sells a property to a family with six children in a predominately older neighborhood
   B. A lending institution refuses to lend mortgage money within certain areas due to the ethnic make-up of the area
   C. Because of a prospect's national origin, an individual selling her own property advises the prospect that the property is sold when it is not
   D. A licensee shows prospects of a particular race properties only in areas populated by families of the same race

9. **Which of the following is generally income tax-deductible in-home ownership?**
   A. Down payment on the property
   B. Major home improvements
   C. Points paid to obtain the loan
   D. Maintenance on the property

10. **Which of the following is NOT true about inducing sellers to sell in certain neighborhoods?**
    A. It only applies to race
    B. It applies to all protected classes
    C. It is activity normally engaged in by a sale agent
    D. It is also known as blockbusting

11. **Which of the following scenarios will NOT qualify for an exemption under the Federal Fair Housing Law?**
    A. A homeowner refuses to rent a room in her home to a male resident
    B. John refuses to rent an apartment in his 4-family residence to a family with young children
    C. A property owner using an agent refuses to rent to a family with young children
    D. A membership only club provides housing exclusively to its male members, yet allows club membership to women

12. **You are the agent selling a property that was built in 1972, what are your obligations regarding lead?**
    A. Tell the buyer that led is on the premises since the property was built in 1972
    B. There are no further obligations relating to lead since the property was built in 1972 and not 1973
    C. Have the buyer and seller fill out a lead-based paint disclosure and have the seller test for lead
    D. Allow the buyer an additional 10 days to inspect for lead and ensure that the lead paint disclosure is signed by both parties

13. **Jenna is an independent contractor work with Cityscape Realty. Which of the following can Cityscape not enforce against Jenna**
    A. Jenna is required to attend weekly team meetings at the agency office
    B. Jenna must adhere to the agency's code of ethics
    C. Jenna must avoid engaging in discriminatory practices
    D. Jenna must use agency software for managing client's interactions

14. **Harry offers to purchaser Janeesha's house for $350,000. Janeesha sends the offer back with a counteroffer for $375,000. Harry signs the $375,000 offer and is about to send it back to Janeesha. In the meantime, another offer comes into Janeesha for $375,000 which is the amount that she wants for the home. She accepts that second offer. Harry sues. Who wins?**
    A. Harry because Janeesha needed to give Harry time to respond
    B. Harry because he signed the $375,000 offer
    C. Janeesha since she wasn't notified of Harry's acceptance prior to accepting the second offer
    D. Janeesha because a seller can accept an offer anytime she wishes

15. Jalen is purchasing a home from an elderly seller, Bee. Bee's husband died two years ago and used to take care of all matters relating to the home. Jalen asks Bee whether the home is on septic or sewer to which she mistakenly responds that it is on sewer. Jalen is happy about this response because he does not want to live in a house which is on septic. After the closing, Jalen finds out that the house is indeed on septic, and he wants to get out of the contract. Assuming this was information that he couldn't find out on his own, his contract is:
    A. Void due to fraud
    B. Voidable due to innocent misrepresentation
    C. Void due to negligent misrepresentation
    D. Voidable due to constructive fraud

16. Jamie, as buyer, and Suzanne, as seller enter into a purchase and sale agreement where they are both represented by real estate agents. The offer had gone back and forth throughout the negotiations until the parties settled on the material terms. Once that occurred, both parties were sent digital documents for their signatures. Before closing, Jamie decides that she doesn't want to purchase the property and states that she is not in breach since no one followed up to obtain her actual signature. Suzanne sues her. What is the result?
    A. The contract is valid, but it is unenforceable because her signature wasn't in writing
    B. The contract is valid and enforceable because digital signatures are the same as written ones
    C. The contract is enforceable since it is in writing, but not valid without a written signature
    D. The contract is both invalid and unenforceable since a written signature is required for but

17. John and Jill enter into a contract where Jill is supposed to purchase John's house on New Year's Eve. She gave him $10,000 in earnest money. On Christmas Day, the house is destroyed by fire. The most probable result is:
    A. The contract may give Jill the right to cancel the sale
    B. Jill can automatically get out of the contract
    C. Jill is entitled to her earnest money back
    D. Jill will not have to purchase due to a supervening illegality

18. John, as seller, agrees to give Jane a period within which to purchase his property. Jane pays John $5,000 for him to do so and agrees to a purchase price of $500,000 should she choose to purchase the property. This is an example of:
    A. A unilateral contract
    B. A bilateral contract
    C. An executed contract
    D. A right of first refusal

19. Judy and Rob are a married couple, and they decide to purchase a home in a neighborhood that is 50 miles from where they currently reside. They make several promises to each other regarding the sale with the seller, Mary. When they put their negotiations in writing, however, certain of the promises are mistakenly left out of the purchase and sale contract. Judy argues that a promise is a promise and Mary argues that she doesn't have to honor the promises because they're not in writing. What law will the court use in determining who is correct?
    A. Statute of Limitations
    B. Parol Evidence
    C. Statue of Frauds
    D. Laches

20. Julius makes an offer to purchase a home from Peter. The parties negotiate for some time, and they plan to put in all into writing on Friday. However, Peter dies on Thursday. What is the effect of Peter's death?
    A. Peter's death will have no effect because they already negotiated the terms
    B. Peter's death will terminate the negotiations, meaning that there is no contract
    C. The promises made can be enforced by Peter's heirs
    D. The contract is not enforceable because it wasn't put in writing

21. **Maggie and Don enter into a contract where Don, as seller, inserts the clause next to the closing date: December 14, 2022 "time is of the essence". Both party's sign. What does the addition of this clause mean?**
    A. That Don is agreeing that he will close by December 14, 2022
    B. That all parties must meet each contract deadlines by December 14, 2022
    C. That whoever fails to close on December 14, 2022, is in breach
    D. That the parties should shoot for closing around December 14, 2022

22. **Mary attempts to purchase Janice's home, but the bank will not loan Mary the money. Mary and Janice enter into an agreement where Mary will pay Janice $1,200 per month for the home for a period of 20 years, but for that period of time, Mary will just have possession and equitable title in the property. This arrangement is called:**
    A. Land Contract
    B. Contract for Deed
    C. Installment Sale Agreement
    D. All of the above

23. **Mary is a seller and has signed an exclusive right to sell listing agreement with Todd, as broker. Mary is seeking an offer of $400,000 and wants to close the sale in 30 days. Todd brings a buyer who offers $390,000 and will close in 30 days. Mary agrees to that price, but at the closing, she fails to pay Todd. Todd sues. Will he win?**
    A. No, because he didn't bring a ready willing and able buyer to meet the terms
    B. No, because although he brought a buyer, it was for less than Mary was asking
    C. Yes, unless Mary can prove that Todd wasn't responsible for bringing the buyer
    D. Yes, since Mary entered into the contract even though it was for less than asking price

24. **During an open house, agent Derek verbally promises buyer Elaine that he will represent her interests in purchasing the property without signing any formal agreement. What type of agency could be created as a result?**
    A. No agency could be formed without a written agreement
    B. A dual agency is automatically created
    C. An implied agency may be formed based on Derek's actions and promises
    D. A general agency has been established

25. **The buyer and seller agree to a purchase price of $450,000 but during the time of the contract, the purchase price is reduced to $425,000 because the inspection revealed many issues. The new price is done by:**
    A. Amendment to the contract
    B. Addendum to the contract
    C. Exhibit to the contract
    D. Additional signatures on the main contract

26. **The president of a loan bank wants to sell her home. She instructs her agent to inform all potential buyers that banks will be curtailing their mortgage lending for the rest of the year which is untrue.. Hearing this, several people make offers immediately. The president enters into a contract with one of those buyers. The contract is:**
    A. Void
    B. Voidable
    C. Valid
    D. Valid but unenforceable

27. **The Statute of Frauds indicates that certain contracts be in writing to be enforceable. Which contracts?**
    A. All real estate contracts and all leases
    B. All real estate contracts and some leases
    C. Some real estate contracts and some leases
    D. Some real estate contracts and all leases

28. **If a seller breaches a real estate purchase contract, what remedy is typically NOT available to the purchaser?**
    A. Suing for specific performance to enforce the sale
    B. Seeking monetary damages for losses incurred
    C. Claiming punitive damages for emotional distress
    D. Terminating the contract and receiving a refund of the earnest money

29. **Which of the following scenarios would most likely result in a suit for constructive fraud?**
    A. A buyer lies about the ability to obtain a loan large enough to purchase the house
    B. The broker mistakenly tells the buyer that the house is 4,000 square feet
    C. The seller intentionally tells the buyer that he fixed the air conditioner when he didn't
    D. The broker conceals from the buyer that the basement leaks during bad rainstorms

30. **What does Regulation Z cover?**
    A. Real property loans for agricultural, investment and residential property and advertising rules
    B. Real property loans for residential and personal family and household loans
    C. Mrs. Murphy's law on discrimination and advertising rules
    D. Settlement costs of real property loans

31. **The most important function of the secondary mortgage market is to:**
    A. Provide loans to consumers
    B. Provide lenders with additional cash
    C. Borrow funds from the Fed
    D. Sell treasury certificates

32. **Mr. Smith decides to sell his home to Ms. Jones and also finance the purchase price under a land contract. Prior to completion of the contract, Ms. Jones defaults on the loan. Mr. Smith is protected to a certain extent because:**
    A. Ms. Jones never had possession and control of the premises
    B. Ms. Jones had legal title to the property, so all Mr. Smith must do is foreclose on her
    C. Ms. Jones only had equitable title to the property so it's easier to foreclose on her
    D. There isn't enough information about their contract to know

33. **If a borrower wanted to have no responsibility for a deficiency in the event of foreclosure what clause would the mortgagor want in the loan agreement?**
    A. An exculpatory clause
    B. A due on sale clause
    C. An alienation clause
    D. A hold harmless clause

34. **A VA loan has which of the following benefits?**
    A. Lower monthly payments but does have PMI
    B. Lower initial cash reserves and no PMI
    C. Lower down payment and no PMI
    D. Lower escrows but does have PMI

35. **A loan that has a constant payment of principal and interest for the first couple of years, but provides for a balloon payment at maturity is called:**
    A. A fully amortized loan
    B. A straight term loan
    C. A graduated payment loan
    D. A partially amortized loan

36. **A home equity line of credit is always**
   A. For a 30-year term
   B. Fully tax deductible
   C. A secured loan
   D. Available on rental property

37. **A buyer has been pre-approved for a loan up to $300,000. The buyer plans to make a down payment of 20% on a property. The buyer will most likely apply for which of the following types of mortgage loans?**
   A. FHA
   B. VA
   C. USDA
   D. Conventional

38. **A buyer bought a home from an owner. The owners agreed to owner-finance the property. The parties agreed to amortize the loan over a 15-year period. The buyer became the owner of record of the property, and the seller had a lien against the property. What type of instrument was used to purchase the property?**
   A. A loan assumption
   B. A land contract
   C. A purchase money mortgage
   D. A contract for deed

39. **A builder is buying a large tract of land to develop. Which clause in the mortgage would be most helpful for the builder to have included in the mortgage so he can sell off each house as it's finished without having to pay off the entire mortgage**
   A. Exculpatory clause
   B. Partial release clause
   C. Prepayment clause
   D. Escalation clause

40. **Mary decides to purchase a hot tub for her home. She builds a custom-made gazebo around it. She later decides to sell her home and wants to take both the hot tub and gazebo with her. Will she be able to do so?**
   A. She won't be able to take the hot tub or gazebo because the hot tub is going to be considered part of the gazebo
   B. She will be able to take the hot tub, but not the gazebo
   C. She won't be able to take the hot tub, but can take the gazebo
   D. She can take both the hot tub and gazebo

41. **Four people bought an investment property together, each having an equal ownership interest. They took title in such a manner that if one died, he could leave his one-fourth interest to his heirs. How did they take title to the real estate?**
   A. Joint tenants with the right of survivorship
   B. Tenancy by the entirety
   C. Tenants in common
   D. A limited partnership

42. **A business tenant leased a small building and installed metal shelves to display his products. Near the time for the lease to expire, the tenant decided to move to a larger building and wanted to take the metal shelving. Is the tenant allowed to take the shelving when he moves?**
   A. No, the shelves are attached to the property so they must stay with the property
   B. No, the shelves are trade fixtures and must remain with the building
   C. Yes, the shelves become personal property and must be removed by the tenant
   D. Yes, the shelves are trade fixtures and can be removed as long as it is done before the expiration of the lease

43. **Mary purchases a condominium unit on a lake that comes with title to two parking spaces and a boat ramp. Her use of the lake is a _ right and the parking spaces are considered ___**
    A. Littoral, Appurtenances
    B. Littoral, Easements in Gross
    C. Littoral, Encumbrances
    D. Littoral, Covenants

44. **John is purchasing a home. When he first viewed the property, the seller had a free-standing mirror that was customized to fit into a built-in bookshelf. After the closing, John realized that the mirror was gone. He reviewed his contract and saw that there was no mention either way of the mirror. He sued the seller. Who will most likely win?**
    A. The seller since the freestanding mirror was considered personal property
    B. John since the freestanding mirror would be considered a fixture since it was adapted to the bookshelf
    C. John since the parties would have had to agree that the seller can take the mirror
    D. The seller since there was no mention of it either way in the contract

45. **Ann owned an easement footpath across neighboring property. Ann allowed the local school children to use the path to walk to and from school for 10 years in a state that only requires 8 years to acquire an easement. After 10 years, Ann became interested in raising dogs, so she fenced in her entire property and did not provide for a gate to the footpath. What is the probable result of this action?**
    A. The children have a prescriptive easement regardless of the new fence
    B. The children's prescriptive easement ended when Ann put the fence up
    C. Ann could not give the children a prescriptive easement since she didn't own the property
    D. Ann abandoned the easement by putting the fence up

46. **A fee simple determinable places certain limitations on property. Such grants are:**
    A. Public encumbrances that affect use through contractual covenants
    B. Public encumbrances that affect the title through contractual conditions
    C. Private encumbrances that affect the title through deed covenants
    D. Private encumbrances that affect the title through deed conditions

47. **August's father, now deceased, built a custom free-standing bookshelf into the wall at August's home. When showings begin, there is no mention of the bookshelf in the listing because the agent assumed it was free standing and personal property. August removes the bookshelf before closing and is sued by the purchaser and August then sues the brokerage. What is the probable result?**
    A. August probably wins his lawsuit with the purchaser, and loses in his lawsuit with the brokerage
    B. August probably wins his lawsuit with the purchaser, and wins this lawsuit with the brokerage
    C. August probably loses his lawsuit with the purchaser, and wins in his lawsuit against the brokerage
    D. August probably loses his lawsuit with the purchaser, and loses his lawsuit against the brokerage

48. **Client Janet verbally informs her agent, Bob, that she no longer requires his services. When is the revocation effective?**
    A. Immediately, if Janet provides a valid reason
    B. Once Bob agrees to the revocation
    C. Only after Janet signs a document revoking the agency
    D. Immediately, unless the agency contract says otherwise

49. **An apartment complex owner advertises units for rent stating "Ideal for mature couples", "safe and quiet", "no kids environment", "located near a popular church landmark". Which aspect of this advertisement likely violates fair housing?**
    A. Ideal for mature couple
    B. Located near a popular church landmark
    C. No kids environment
    D. Safe and quiet

50. **You have an investor seller who wants you to list his property which needs many repairs. He tells you he's upside down in the property and therefore wants you to list the property for sale "as is". Should you list it?**
    A. Yes, it's perfectly ok as long as you list the property is listed in the MLS system with "AS IS" in bold letters
    B. Yes, fixer - uppers are often sought after by flippers
    C. Yes, but you should make sure all known defects are disclosed to the buyers
    D. No, "as is" sales are not allowed by the Real Estate Commission

51. **You are an agent at ACME real estate. You want to switch to another brokerage but you have 3 transactions that haven't closed yet. How will you be compensated on those three transactions?**
    A. You will receive ½ payment for those transactions on leaving the brokerage
    B. Since you will not be at ACME when the transactions close, you will be paid in advance upon leaving
    C. You will move the transactions over to the new brokerage
    D. The contract signed with ACME when you first started will determine how those transactions are handled

52. **Real estate agent Sarah receives an earnest money check on Friday evening from her client, John for a property purchase. According to the law, when should the check be deposited with Sarah's broker?**
    A. Within 5 business days of receiving it
    B. As soon as possible, but most likely Monday Morning
    C. By Saturday Morning
    D. After the purchase agreement is signed by both parties

53. **Your broker authorizes you to sign contracts on his/her behalf. How is this authorization given to you?**
    A. The State Real Estate Commission issues this right under both the Agency and License Laws
    B. The employment or affiliation agreement you signed with your broker
    C. The Exclusive Right to Sell Listing Agreement
    D. By a separate Power of Attorney given to you by your broker

54. **Your sister asks you to help her sell her home. Which would be an act that might be illegal?**
    A. She lists with you and 2 other brokers
    B. She lists with you, but she puts her own for sale sign in the side yard
    C. She tells you that your commission will be anything over her loan payoff of $59,750
    D. She tells you she will not accept a contract from anyone over 65 years old

55. **Jane works for John Apple Realty. Mary works for the same company. Jane has a third party/customer that puts an offer on a house that is listed by Mary. Jane:**
    A. Is a designated agent representing the seller
    B. Is a dual agent representing both her customer and the listing agent
    C. Represents the buyer since she put the offer in for him
    D. Represents the seller since John Apple represents the seller

56. **An agent representing the seller, fails to discover crumbling wallboard on the basement ceiling. After the sale, the third-party buyer sues the agent for not disclosing the clearly visible problem to him. The agent:**
    A. Is guilty of intentional misrepresentation
    B. Is guilty of negligent misrepresentation
    C. Is not guilty of any wrongdoing
    D. Is guilty of fraud

57. **Real estate agent Linda Martinez is representing a seller, Robert Yang, who just accepted an offer on his home. However, Linda continues to receive interest from other potential buyers. What should Linda do regarding the offers?**
    A. Inform the new inquirers that the property is under contract
    B. Ignore any new inquires as accepting a backup offer is against the real estate regulations
    C. Take all backup offers and inform them that their offers will be considered if the current deal falls through
    D. Have Mr. Yang accept as many additional offers as possible

58. **What is a warranty deed?**
    A. A deed that conveys the grantor's interest to the grantee
    B. A deed that guarantees clear title to the buyer through covenants
    C. A deed where a court must determine the validity of a will and the rightful heirs
    D. A deed that contains two covenants of title

59. **What is the difference between reservation and exception?**
    A. A reservation goes to use of the property, and an exception goes to title of the property
    B. A reservation goes to title of the property and an exception goes to use of the property
    C. They are the same in that you can reserve and except the same piece of land
    D. They are the same in that you can't reserve and except the same piece of land

60. **The closing date is approaching on the sale of a property to a buyer who is represented by a licensee. Although the sellers have both signed the sales contract, the buyer's licensee learns that a relative of the sellers may have a title claim to this property. In this situation, the licensee should**
    A. Ignore the existence of the relative because if a title claim is not asserted before the closing, the buyer can experience no future title problems
    B. Ask the listing licensee to advise the seller to contact an attorney
    C. Advise the buyer to contact an attorney in preparation to sue for specific performance
    D. Inform both the sellers and the buyers that the closing cannot occur

61. **During a title search for a property owned by Samantha which would most likely result in a cloud on the title?**
    A. Samantha recently paid off the mortgage and a satisfaction was filed
    B. The property taxes for the current year have been paid in full
    C. A detailed and accurate survey of the property was completed last year
    D. A previous deed in the chain of title was signed by an unauthorized representative of the owner

62. **Thomas signed a deed transferring ownership to Clara Smith. Before he could deliver the deed to Clara, Thomas passed away. What is the effect of the death?**
    A. The transfer is void because Thomas did not deliver the deed before dying
    B. The transfer is valid since there was an intent to deliver the deed
    C. The property goes to Thomas' heirs
    D. Clara could claim the property if Thomas told her that he would transfer it to her

63. **Michael has been using a pathway through his neighbor, Lisa's property for the last 15 years. Lisa was aware of this but never gave Michael explicit permission to use the pathway. Michael wants to sue for adverse possession. What does he have to prove?**
    A. Michael paid Lisa for use of the pathway
    B. Michael's use of the pathway was without Lisa's permission
    C. Lisa knew about Michael's use but did nothing
    D. Michael's use was continuous, open, and without Lisa's permission

64. **There are a number of different taxes that occur in a real estate transaction. Which taxes are charged at the closing based upon the sales price of the home?**
    A. Transfer Taxes or Deed Stamps
    B. Intangible Taxes
    C. Ad Valorem Taxes
    D. Special Assessment Taxes

65. **Title to real estate can be voluntarily transferred by:**
    A. Sale, Patent, Will, Gift
    B. Sale, Operation of Law, Foreclosure, Gift
    C. Will, Gift, Operation of Law, Court Action
    D. Will, Patent, Gift, Foreclosure

66. **Functional obsolescence will produce a loss in value. Which of the following may be curable functional obsolescence?**
    A. A house that has very small bedroom closets
    B. Outdated appliances
    C. An oil-fired system where natural gas is standard
    D. Worn carpeting

67. **A major employer leaves an area, taking most of its employees with it to the new city. Most properties in the area were left abandoned, won't sell, and are now in disrepair. This is an example of:**
    A. Physical Deterioration
    B. Economic Obsolescence
    C. Functional Obsolescence
    D. External Obsolescence

68. **There are three vacant lots next to each other in a residential area. None are perfect for a home build. Each lot individually is $10,000. The builder decides to combine the lots to make them more appealing. After combining, the lots are now worth $45,000**
    A. The builder has assembled the lots
    B. The builder has assembled the lots, but did not get pottage
    C. The builder has assembled the lots and did get pottage
    D. No assemblage occurred

69. **What would be the most appropriate appraisal report for a condemnation action?**
    A. Narrative Report
    B. Letter of Opinion
    C. Short-Form Report
    D. It depends on the appraiser

70. **When calculating Net Operating Income for the Capitalization Approach, what items are NOT a part of that calculation?**
    A. Potential Gross Income
    B. Depreciation
    C. Expenses
    D. Property Taxes

71. **Sally purchased a property in an area where house sales are very slow due to the location near a chicken factory. Therefore, property values are depressed in that area. This is an example of:**
    A. Incurable Functional Obsolescense
    B. Curable Functional Obsolescense
    C. Incurable Physical Deterioration
    D. Incurable Economic Obsolescense

72. You are an investor and have a one family residence in a neighborhood of similar properties. You learn that another investor sold the property their property two weeks ago for $325,000 that was renting for $1,800 per month. You decide that you may want to sell yours also based upon the price the other investor received. Your property is currently rents for $2,100. What approach would the appraiser utilize?
    A. Gross Income Multiplier and your value would be lower
    B. Capitalization Approach and your value would be lower
    C. Gross Rent Multiplier Approach and your value would be higher
    D. Gross Income Multiplier Approach and your value would be higher

73. The purchaser performs an inspection on the home you have listed. The inspection reveals that several items need repair. There is an inspection contingency in the contract. The purchaser has the following options except:
    A. Ask the seller to repair the items
    B. Use his right to rescind to get out of the contract
    C. Ask the seller to provide a credit at closing for the items
    D. Have the home warranty company repair the items after closing

74. Which of the following must be disclosed by an agent to a third party (customer)?
    A. Leaky roof that has left stains on the bathroom ceiling
    B. Warp flooring in front of the kitchen
    C. Three broken windows
    D. A damaged septic tank

75. Which of the following would not have to be disclosed to a potential third party (customer) purchaser?
    A. A leaky roof which shows stains in the ceiling
    B. An underground leaky septic tank
    C. Structural damage under the deck of the property
    D. A recent flood in the property but that has been corrected

76. You are representing a seller on a home where you overheard that the buyer, represented by another agent, loves the home, and would pay $50,000 over asking price for it. Your seller receives several offers on the home. Should you reveal the information you overheard to your seller?
    A. No, it would be a violation of the law of agency to disclose the information
    B. No, it would be an unethical act under the license law to reveal the information
    C. Yes, because you are obligation to keep the principal informed of relevant matters in a transaction
    D. Yes, because your job is to get the seller the highest amount for his home and your information will guarantee that

77. You are selling a home where you are the listing agent. When should you make your agency disclosure to the potential purchaser?
    A. When the agreement with the seller is signed
    B. Immediately before the parties go to closing
    C. Prior to allowing his agent to the property
    D. At the time of signing the contract

78. Janice is an agent selling a property where the zoning laws have changed and Janice is aware that a new shopping center is being built across the street that will lower the property value. The seller doesn't want Janet to disclose this information. What should Janice do?
    A. Disclose the information because there is a duty to do so regardless of the seller's wishes
    B. Not disclose because of the obedience duty to the seller
    C. Not disclose the information because a change in zoning is not a material fact
    D. Disclose the information because it would be the right thing to do

79. **Mel, who is handicapped, decides to rent a unit from Heather in her 10-story apartment building. Mel requires that the building have a ramp placed in the lobby so that he can use his wheelchair to get to the elevator. Heather allows Mel to construct the ramp but wants to place a provision in the lease that states that Mel must bear the cost to remove the ramp once he departs the premises. Is Heather allowed to do this under the ADA?**
    A. No. The ADA requires that the landlord bear the cost of removal of the ramp
    B. Yes. While Heather must allow Mel to live there, Heather can require that he remove the ramp on departure
    C. Yes. While the ADA doesn't even require that Heather rent to Mel. Because she chooses to do so, she can make him remove the ramp
    D. No. Since the building is now ADA complaint, the ramp must remain

80. **Ms. Millie's cookies has a lease in the local shopping mall. Her lease agreement states that she is to pay $13.00 per square foot for the space and a portion of her net sales to the landlord on a quarterly basis. This type of lease is:**
    A. Gross Lease
    B. Net Lease
    C. Ground Lease
    D. Percentage Lease

81. **The type of estate the landlord retains when property is leased to another:**
    A. Leasehold Estate
    B. Leased Fee Estate
    C. Fee Simple Estate
    D. Net Lease

82. **The most typical purpose of a deed restriction is to**
    A. ensure that the property will not become encumbered
    B. encourage varied uses of the property
    C. control future uses of the property
    D. limit costs of new houses in a subdivision

83. **A buyer wants to buy a larger house and open a beauty salon in her home. She tells the listing licensee her plans and looks at property with that licensee. They find a property she likes, and she makes an offer that is accepted. After closing and moving into the property, she finds out there are deed restrictions in the subdivision that prohibit a business operating out of one's home. Which of the following is true?**
    A. The buyer was solely responsible for researching the deed restrictions before buying the property
    B. The licensee was representing the seller and had no duty to the buyer to investigate the restrictions
    C. Since the licensee knew of the buyer's intended use, the licensee should have ascertained whether the property could be used for that purpose
    D. The seller was solely liable for telling the buyer she would be unable to open a beauty shop in the property

84. **Which would NOT be an example of private controls on a property contained in a deed?**
    A. A Fee Simple Determinable
    B. A Fee Simple Absolute
    C. Defeasible Fee
    D. Conditional Fee

85. **A husband and wife have owned a property for 6 years and they have occupied it for the last four. They bought the property for 320,000 and sold it for 650,000.On what amount would they pay in capital gains tax?**
    A. Zero
    B. $510,000
    C. $20,000
    D. $290,000

86. **A city condemns a 10-foot strip of a property owner's land for a public bicycle path. The owner will be able to use the house and most of the lot. Is she eligible for compensation?**
    A. Yes, because the city is exercising its zoning power to her disadvantage
    B. Yes, because the city is exercising its power of eminent domain, so she's entitled to compensation
    C. No, because the city is exercising its police power for the public good
    D. No, because she the city only took a 10-foot strip of land

87. **A prospective buyer should be able to rely on a statement made by a broker when:**
    I. The statement concerns the property's current income
    II. The prospective buyer does not have access to the property for a personal inspection
    III. The broker, while showing the house, tells the prospective buyer that the gazebo and flower garden make the backyard the prettiest in town
    A. I only
    B. II only
    C. I and II only
    D. I, II, and III

88. **In a private conversation, a principal agrees to sell her house to a buyer for a price lower than the listing price if the buyer will wait to buy until after the broker's exclusive right-to-sell listing agreement expires. If the principal and the buyer proceed as planned and the broker can prove collusion, the broker may receive:**
    A. Damages from both the principal and the buyer
    B. The full commission designated in the original listing contract
    C. Half the commission designated in the original listing contract
    D. None of the above

89. **A real estate broker authorized to find a buyer for a particular parcel of property is what type of agent?**
    A. Universal
    B. General
    C. Special
    D. None of the above

90. **A primary purpose of the Real Estate Settlement Procedures Act is to:**
    A. Inform the buyers and sellers of all settlement costs in real estate transactions
    B. Control the number of non-federally related mortgage loans in the country
    C. Standardize the amount of all settlement costs in real estate closings
    D. Standardize settlement procedures in all parts of the country

Chapter 12 Answers

1. B. Home warranties that are not already on the home will not become effective until the closing. What is covered is highly dependent upon the language of the warranty

2. B. The licensee will explain to the seller his obligations under fair housing. If the seller insists, the licensee will not be allowed to take the listing.

3. A. The only thing the licensee should tell the third-party buyer here is that he has an opportunity to inspect and let the buyer decide

4. B. Supply and Demand since it states that when Supply is up, prices are down and when supply is down, house prices are higher

5. C. This would not be a fair housing violation unless it is discrimination based on race. All other discrimination against fair housing categories would be allowed as long as there is no discrimination in the membership

6. B. Housing communities made up of people over the age of 62 can discriminate against children. Those communities do not have to show the 80% that is required by over 55 communities

7. B. Redlining and the bank's risk doesn't matter. The bank should only look at the client who is seeking the loan. If the property doesn't appraise at the set price, that is a different story. But a bank cannot have a blanket policy of not lending in certain areas

8. D. All licensees should check the ownership of record to ascertain that they are dealing with correct parties who can sign the listing and make a decision. Even though all children are there, a 4th child or another person could own the property

9. D. The license law is only concerned with funds that the broker is holding in trust for another. These are broker funds and while it may be poor record-keeping, it is not a license law violation

10. B. Puffing in advertising is totally permitted. It is a statement that a reasonable person would recognize as untrue, primarily an opinion

11. B. While you are always a fiduciary to your client, there are certain limitations. Any discussion relating to fair housing, whether to a principal or third party is inappropriate.

12. B. Waste occurs when one person in possession of another person's property engages in acts which diminish the value of the property. Constructive eviction is a claim made by a tenant. Laches is when a person fails to bring a claim and the breach of habitability is when a landlord fails to repair items in a lease arrangement

13. A. Contracts with minors are voidable at the minor's option. If there is no property description, it would be void

14. B. Laches is a doctrine that can prevent a person from suing when they waited too long, but there is no time period required by law

15. C. A contingency means that what we are talking about doesn't happen until something happens before it., i.e., finance contingency means that the buyer doesn't have to buy unless the bank agrees to give the buyer a loan

16. B. A party who used trust and confidence to influence another into entering into a contract is called undue influence and that contract is voidable

17. B. Constructive Fraud (aka Negligent misrepresentation) is when a person in the transaction who has a duty to give correct information mistakenly reveals incorrect information

18. B. Agency agreements between brokers and sellers are special agencies and terminate once the closing occurs

19. C. No fair housing violation has been committed because a licensee is not allowed to show properties based on race or any of the fair housing categories

20. A. Mary's best reply would be to direct her client to the local school district for them to find the information themselves as discussion of this topic would be a fair housing violation. All discussions are not violative of the law, only those discussions relating to the fair housing categories. For example, if the discussion was about how many married couples were in the neighborhood, Mary could answer

21. C. Tom would not have to disclose that the seller is moving out of state because it doesn't necessarily have bearing on the sale. The seller's financial status certainly does and issues relating to the house, whether patent or latent, should be disclosed to clients

22. D. Frank would be acting beyond the scope of his authority and could be liable (not definitely as in C) unless Alice ratifies Frank's action

23. D. The licensee is not the AGENT under the listing, the broker ABC Realty is. Therefore, the listing continues

24. B. Home warranties typically would cover the mechanical breakdown of items in the home. Title claims would be covered by the title insurance, the home catching fire and the slip and fall would be covered by the homeowner's insurance

25. A. Because building codes are an exercise of police power, there is no entitlement to compensation

26. B. A 1031 exchange is a way for investors to defer income taxes until a much later date. There are many rules such as on any sale, the investor must find a like kind property to buy, cannot touch the proceeds but must bring in a qualified intermediary, and the properties must be used in a trade or business

27. A. The law provides several exceptions as to when a person on the Do Not Call Registry can be contacted. Any prior client can be contacted for up to 18 months since the last transaction that you had with them. However, once the client asks that you do not contact them any longer, you must cease all calls

28. C. The home can be listed "as is" but it doesn't get rid of the duty to disclose all latent defects in the home that the agent is aware of

29. B. The Lead Based Paint disclosure is required for all houses built prior to 1978, but there is no requirement that the purchaser inspect for lead. This right can be waived

30. B. The leak is a material item that cannot be discovered and as such, must be disclosed

31. D. The question here asks what MUST be done: The law states that opting out is required

32. A. An option is a unilateral contract where the person could buy or not buy, but the price is set at the time of the signing of the option

33. B. An optionee never has an obligation to purchase or exercise the option. It is simply an option IF he chooses to exercise it

34. C. Parol evidence is a doctrine that states that the court will only view the document to determine the agreement. If items were orally discussed and then not put into writing, they won't be given effect. Once an agreement is put into writing, the court will only look to the writing

35. A. Because buyer and seller are both making intentional promises, it is an express bilateral contract. Because the promises are not yet completed, it is executory

36. B. Once the parties are in contract, the rights of the parties are determined by the language of the contract.

37. A. That the contract was not put in writing prevents the parties from seeking relief in court. It may be a valid contract, but it is unenforceable

38. B. All tenant in common owners can lease, sell, mortgage their portion of the unit without the others consent

39. D. A right to use the land of another that runs with the land. In every situation here, the statement holds true

40. A. If owner A purchases a view easement from the owner of the property being sold, it will run with the land. Then, any subsequent owners could not build in a matter that would impair the view of owner A

41. A. Execution of sale is a term used with the court orders a sheriff sale, could be after a foreclosure or tax sale

42. C. There is no indication that this owner abandoned his property. Also, keep in mind that abandonment issues would only come into play if he had a loan on the property

43. B. Grantees are allowed to take property in fictitious names as long as that property is reconveyed in that name

44. A. An interest in the life estate can always be sold, but the actual property cannot. Essentially, the life tenant is selling whatever interest he/she has in the property. But, once that person dies, the interest also dies

45. B. Always true is that the company would both be regulated by the state which it is incorporated in and the state in which it purchases the property

46. C. Mechanic's lien can only be maintained by the person who IMPROVES a property. A broker does not

47. B. A judgment lien ALWAYS affects the real and personal property of the debtor

48. B. A contractual covenants are promises between the parties. It is not normally considered an encumbrance on the property

49. C. Any conflict between public and private restrictions will always have the stricter one prevailing

50. B. The best course of action would be to apply for an injunction which would stop the neighbor's activity

51. A. Constructive eviction is where a tenant claims that property is unusable in the matter intended due to the landlord's actions

52. C. Statute of frauds goes to the fact that real estate contracts must be in writing to be enforceable

53. C. Once the optionor grants an option, it cannot be revoked by the optionor

54. C. Because the owner prepared a will, it doesn't matter that she doesn't have surviving family as long as there are people named in the will that can be found

55. A. Quiet title action clears clouds off of the title. In adverse possession cases and when a party is unavailable, we utilize a quiet title action

56. C. The original offer is terminated because the seller has now submitted a counteroffer

57. D. Color of title actions are only used with adverse possession claims. Color of title is a method of shortening the adverse possession timeline

58. D. Gift Deeds are the only ones that do not require consideration. We simply say that it is present

59. A. Zoning, Building Codes, Environment Protection Laws are the most likely police powers examples

60. D. Yes, the neighbor would be able to sue and get an injunction bringing forth the violation of zoning codes

61. B. Yes, the broker is liable for negligent misrepresentation because if the broker told her about the boundaries, he should've made it clear that the boundaries weren't exact or advised her to contact a surveyor

62. C. The state cannot rescind contracts. Rescission is a right given by the law only. Further, the agent's breach has nothing to do with broker contracts

63. A. Agency is the law that determines when a principal is responsible for an agent's actions

64. C. Any agency is formed in any situation where one person hires another to act on his behalf or in his stead

65. B. No, because while there is a duty of obedience, the law requires that all offers be presented to the principal for his or her rejection

66. D. All of the above are license law violations. Agents are not allowed to share commissions with unlicensed people and could lose their license if convicted of a felony. Further, undisclosed dual agency is illegal

67. D. Agents do not conduct title searches, attorneys or escrow agents do

68. A. Both brokers would be owed a commission in this situation. Because the owner did not cancel the first listing and signed with a second broker, they are both entitled to a commission. The second broker should always inquire before taking a listing but if the seller lies, he will owe a commission to both

69. A. The only responsibility of the agent in this instance is to find a ready willing and able buyer for the property

70. A. Earnest money is considered liquidated damages (an amount the seller can keep) if the buyer doesn't perform

71. D. If a principal revokes an agency, the agency is terminated. However, the principal may still owe the agent for the termination

72. D. Any can be used. The property management agreement is an agency agreement. Therefore, it is negotiated. So, the parties can agree to anything

73. C. Is an example of blockbusting - inducing others to sell based on the presence of minorities

74. A. RESPA disclosures are required on any federally insured or guaranteed first mortgage. While many banks disclose under RESPA, the key importance is that any loans that will be purchased in the conforming secondary market require RESPA disclosures

75. C. While there are many fair housing exemptions, no discrimination against racial minorities can be granted an exemption

76. A. Capitalization rates are the direct relationship of the property's income and value

77. B. A neighborhood analysis gives a true indication as to the estimation of value

78. D. All are considered depreciation and will be subtracted from replacement cost

79. D. All factors will affect the demand for housing. Increase in population will increase demand; Age will decrease demand; and migration can increase or decrease depending on which way the migration is occurring

80. D. Functional depreciation goes to how the home functions to contemporary standards. A floor plan change is incurable

81. B. The income approach is primarily used on investment properties. While it is not the only approach that can be used, if the Cap Rate and Income is available, it will be given the most weight

82. D. Equity is the amount that a person has in the house that is unencumbered (no loan). Thus, the largest down payment would give this buyer the highest equity

83. B. The Veteran can pay the difference in price if the house doesn't appraise for the VA's certified amount

84. B. In order for a mortgage to exist, there must be two things: A promissory note (Debt) and a security instrument which pledges the property in case of default (mortgage)

85. B. Absolutely, there are no restrictions. Once all loans are paid off, the Veteran is free to continue borrowing

86. D. Regulation Z refers to TILA and it requires cost of the loan, not the settlement costs (RESPA). Recording fees and title insurance premiums would go on the RESPA statement

87. B. Both the FHA and MGIC are mortgage insurers, but only MGIC issues PMI

88. D. FHA down payment is ALWAYS 3.5% at a minimum

89. A. Increasing or decreasing reserve requirements are not correlated to interest rates other than to say that if the Fed increases interest rates, lending will slow. If lending slows, the banks have more money in reserves, so there would be no need for the Fed to increase the reserve requirements

90. C. FHA and VA are insurers and guarantors only. All others are secondary market lenders

1. C. While the seller would be able to discriminate under certain circumstances, in this instance, because a broker is involved, he cannot. If the broker took this listing, it would amount to an improper listing since Muslims are a protected class

2. D. Fair Housing prohibits the use of certain categories in advertising, but does allow it when using for direction clarity, not preference

3. B. Appeals relating to property assessments are brought to The Board of Arbitration

4. B. All former clients can be called for up to 18 months since the last transaction, regardless of registry status. Same rule applies for former contacts, but only up to 3 months

5. C. Trust accounts, always considered client's funds, are not subject to attachment

6. B. John would be claiming under Mrs. Murphy's exemption which states that as long as John is living in the property, doesn't use discriminatory advertising or a broker, he can discriminate

7. C. Any attempt to limit competition or monopolize the market. Meeting with other brokers to set commission rates would be a violation because it limits choices of the consumer

8. D. An act done by a licensee that limits the choices of a buyer based on a protected category

9. C. Because interest payments are tax deductible and points are simply considered to be pre-paid interest, it is also tax deductible

10. A. Blockbusting is the act of inducing sellers to sell because any of the protected minorities are moving into the neighborhood. It is not just limited to race

11. C. Because a broker/agent was used, the owner cannot take advantage of an exemption

12. D. The agent/seller has the obligation to disclose lead potential in any home that was built prior to 1978. The obligations include providing a disclosure that the house may have lead, that the purchaser has a 10 day right to inspect, and there is no requirement to abate the lead

13. A. As Jenna is independent contractor, Cityscape cannot force her to work certain hours, although it can force her to agree to abide by certain rules and regulations of the brokerage

14. C. The reason why Janeesha can accept the second offer is because she wasn't notified yet of Harry's acceptance. The parties are not in contract unless there is acceptance and notification. An offer is open for a stated time, but any party can revoke an offer prior to acceptance. Here, Janeesha revoked the offer to Harry once she accepted the offer from the second party

15. B. Jalen's contract would be voidable due to innocent misrepresentation which only requires that a mistake of a material fact is made and that the party relied on the error

16. B. A digital signature contract is both valid and enforceable with respect to the digital signature. Digital signatures are treated the same as written ones

17. A. Once the parties are in contract, the contract will contemplate that things can happen prior to the closing. Here, the best thing for the parties to do is to read what they agreed to. Jill would not be able to automatically get her money back or cancel the contract. This is also not a supervening illegality because there was no law change

18. A. The above describes an option contract which is always unilateral since only one party, John, as seller is making a promise

19. B. Parol Evidence - If the parties make promises that do not make it into the contract, their oral promises will not be given effect and the court will only look at the document itself

20. B. There is no contract here at all. Peter's death will end all negotiations

21. C. Time is of the essence clauses mean that the time frame stated in the contract is strict. Whomever, in this case, doesn't close by December 14, 2022, is in breach of contract

22. D. All of the above. All three terms are used for this arrangement. Because Mary will pay Janice for a period of time and hold equitable title, we can assume that Janice will have legal title for the duration

23. D. Todd's only obligation was to bring a ready willing and able buyer. Although the amount was less than asking, once Mary signed the agreement, Todd fulfilled the obligation

24. C. An implied agency is created when an agent leads a buyer to believe he is representing the buyer. Derek's actions and promises here potentially caused an implied agency

25. A. Price changes are done by amendment to the contract. Amendments are meant to change the underlying contract where addenda are meant to clarify provisions of the underlying contract, but not change it

26. B. Fraud means that there is a lack of genuine assent which makes the contract voidable

27. C. The statute of frauds states the certain real estate contracts and leases over 1 year must be in writing to be enforceable

28. C. Punitive (punishment) damages are never available for contracts actions

29. B. Constructive Fraud (aka Negligent misrepresentation) is when a person in the transaction who has a duty to give correct information mistakenly reveals incorrect information

30. B. Regulation Z (Truth in Lending Act) covers all residential loans and personal family and household loans. It is intended to allow all borrowers compare the cost of credit before selecting a lender

31. B. The primary function of the secondary mortgage market is to re-infuse the primary market with cash. Because mortgage lenders will eventually run out of cash, it sells the notes to the secondary market in order to acquire more cash

32. C. Land contracts (aka contracts for deed and installment sale agreements) are a form of owner financing. Possession and control are transferred to the purchaser, who has equitable title throughout the purchase. The seller retains legal title so in the event of foreclosure, it is often a more expedited process

33. A. An exculpatory clause excuses a borrower from deficiency judgment. Upon foreclosure, the bank will only go after the home and any entitlement to deficiency is waived

34. C. A VA loan is guaranteed by the government up to a certain amount and has an 100% LTV ratio. Because the government is guaranteeing the payment on behalf of the veteran, no PMI insurance is involved

35. D. Partially amortized loans have a period of payment of principal and interest, but it doesn't amortize to a zero balance. The schedule is cut short and at maturity, the borrower will owe a balloon payment of the amount left. Fully amortized goes to zero, straight term is an interest only loan with a balloon, and a graduated payment loan is a period of a lesser than required payment

36. C. Secured: It is a loan based on the home's equity and as such, a lien will be placed on the property. Some of the other answers are true some of the time, but not ALWAYS

37. D. Conventional loans are typically 20% down. FHA is 3.5%; VA and USDA are both 0%

38. C. Owner Financing could only be a land contract or purchase money mortgage, but here, the title is transferred immediately. That only occurs in a purchase money mortgage

39. B. Partial release clause would allow the developer to develop each parcel that is secured by the loan and sell each off as he finished the build

40. A. Because the hot tub essentially became part of the gazebo, it will be considered a fixture. So, neither the gazebo nor the hot tub can be taken on sale

41. C. Because the property goes to the heirs of the deceased, it is tenant in common ownership

42. D. The shelves are trade fixtures and as long as the tenant removes them prior to expiration of the lease, he can take them. The key here is business tenant and installed by the tenant, not the landlord

43. A. Lake/Ocean rights are Littoral and because the parking spaces and boat ramp are titled to that property, it is appurtenant to it

44. B. Because the mirror was customized to fit into the built-in bookshelf, the two items were married to work together. Even though the mirror was still free standing, it will be classified as a fixture

45. D. In order to select abandonment, there must be some positive action to indicate it. Here, the fence without a gate provides that proof. The children had permission to use the easement so they could not have acquired it by prescription

46. D. A fee simple determinable is a private encumbrance (place on the property by a landowner not the government) that affects how the property is used by placing a restriction on the deed of the property

47. C. Because the freestanding bookshelf was built into the wall, it will be considered a fixture. As such, it cannot be taken. So, August will lose his lawsuit with the purchaser, but because the agent made an incorrect assumption, he will win his lawsuit against the agent

48. D. Termination of agencies are effective immediately, whether oral or written, unless the contract says otherwise

49. C. Because children are protected under the FAMILY category, a no kids advertisement is not permissible

50. C. There is no problem listing property that needs repairs, but all latent defects must still be disclosed. No agent can use the term "as is" to get around the disclosure requirement

51. D. In accordance with your contract with ACME. One requirement is that all affiliation agreements should address commission with the broker while in the employ and when the agent departs the brokerage

52. B. All agents must turn earnest money over to the brokers as soon as possible unless all parties have agreed to another time. The commission doesn't assume after hours deposits during the evening or weekends

53. B. The sales agent's (or any agent's) authority is given to him by the terms of the agency agreement. Here, the agency agreement is the affiliation agreement between agent and broker

54. C. Net Listings are those where the seller is stating that he wants to clear a certain amount at closing, but that the broker can take any amount left over as commission. These are illegal in most states

55. D. While Jane is working with the buyer, she doesn't represent the buyer. However, John Apple Realty represents the seller, thereby making Jane an agent of the seller. Jane represents whomever her broker represents in a transaction

56. C. There was no duty to disclose here since the agent wasn't representing the buyer and the defect was patent

57. C. Linda should continue to take offers to the seller until the deal closes. However, no other offer can be accepted while there is a contract on the house.

58. B. A warranty deed is the best one you can get. It is the one that contains all 5 warranties and guarantees good title to the property

59. A. A reservation would be where a seller sells the entire parcel of land but would like to continue to USE something on that property. An exception, on the other hand, is when a person only sells a portion of the land and excludes from the conveyance another part. An exception would often require a new survey

60. B. This is a typical "stay in your lane" question. Although you learn many concepts in pre-license, all you can do here is tell the seller's agent to contact and attorney and report back to you. You don't know if the closing can occur, and you will not give advice as to specific performance as that would be the unauthorized practice of law

61. D. A deed signed by an unauthorized representative is void and all successive documents are void, resulting in a title cloud

62. A. Deeds must be signed and delivered during the grantor's lifetime to be considered valid

63. D. Adverse Possession is a claim made when a person attempts to take title of property of another openly, continuously and without permission, for the statutory period of time. All elements must be present for a claim

64. A. Anytime a deed is transferred from one person to another, a tax must be paid when that new deed is recorded. It is based on the sales price of the home

65. A. Sale, Patent, Will, Gift. Operation of Law, Foreclosure, and Court Action are not voluntary transfers

66. B. Functional obsolescence is a type of depreciation that is tied to how the property functions in today's society. If the property doesn't function to contemporary standards (small bedrooms, 5 bedrooms/1 bath, oil rather than natural gas), it is said to be functionally obsolete. Whether it is curable, or incurable is dependent upon the item spoken about. Because appliances are easily changed, it would be considered curable functional obsolescence. Small bedrooms are functional but incurable

67. B. Because this movement is external to the property, it is economic obsolescence

68. C. Because there was an increase in value after putting the lots together, the builder also accomplished plottage

69. A. Narrative report is the most complete report and is used in most actions other than regular residential

70. B. When calculating NOI, Depreciation, Debt Service on the property, and Income Taxes are never a part of the calculation

71. D. As a result of the chicken factory, there are no home sales in the area, leading to lower prices. Because the house cannot be moved, it is incurable economic obsolescense

72. C. The appraiser would most likely use Gross Rent Multiplier to compare the sales prices with the rental rates of both properties and because the subject property has a higher rent, using this formula, it will have a higher value

73. D. A home warranty will not cover for items that are already known as defective. It is for items that unexpectedly break throughout the period of the policy

74. D. Agents must disclose latent (hidden) defects to third parties (customers). Here, the damaged septic tank is the only choice that could be hidden

75. A. All latent (hidden) defects must be disclosed. The leaky roof showing stains in the ceiling is a patent defect that doesn't have to be disclosed

76. C. As an agent, you are obligated to keep your principal informed of any matter that affects the business at hand. Even though part of that is to get the seller the highest price for his home, your information cannot guarantee that

77. D. The best time for you to make the disclosure is when the relationship between the parties becomes serious, but that the earliest possible opportunity

78. A. You must disclose this information regardless of what the seller is telling you to do. The law requires disclosure of material information to purchasers. You are aware of the information and aware that it will decrease the value of the property so it must be disclosed

79. B. The ADA requires that Heather allow the ramp to be installed, but also allows Heather to make Mel bear the cost of removal upon departure

80. D. Percentage leases are typically in shopping malls and the tenant pays a base rent plus a percentage of sales or profit, depending on landlord preference

81. B. The landlord continues to hold a fee estate that is leased to a tenant. So, we refer to it as a leased fee estate

82. C. Most deed restrictions are intended to place some limitation on the future use of the property

83. C. The licensee would be responsible in this case because the inability to use the property as intended is a material fact that needed to be disclosed. Material facts must be disclosed to both clients and third parties

84. B. A Fee Simple Absolute wouldn't have any private controls in the deed. All other answers will have conditions placed on the property

85. A. Married couples who have lived in and owned their home for 3 of the last 5 years get a $500,000 profit exemption from capital gains. Here, the total profit on the sale was $330,000, but since they have a $500,000 exemption, they won't pay capital gains

86. B. It doesn't matter whether it's a 10-foot strip on the entire property, the owner is entitled to compensation under eminent domain

87. C. The broker would not be responsible if he made the comment in III as that amounts to puffing

88. B. He would receive the full commission from his principal as that is who he has the agency with. The buyer, although part of it, has no obligation to the broker

89. C. A special agent is hired to perform a specific act. Here, the agent is hired for the act of finding a particular parcel. After it is found that agency ends

90. A. RESPA is so that all buyers have an indication of projected and final settlement costs for that institution and can compare the settlement costs to other institutions

The key to success is hard work, dedication, consistency, and determination. If you follow these practices, you will be successful.

Congratulations on becoming a real estate agent and I wish you all the best in your future endeavors!

Kalimah J. Jenkins Esq., MBA

We have attempted to take the greatest care to limit errors in this guide.
If you find an error, please feel free to email us at: INFO@KJMETHOD.COM